★ U.S. ★
FLEA MARKET
D I R E C T O R Y

U.S. FLEA MARKET

DIRECTORY

SECOND EDITION

ALBERT
LaFARGE

The CONFIDENT COLLECTOR™

AVON BOOKS ◆ NEW YORK

AVON BOOKS
A division of
The Hearst Corporation
1350 Avenue of the Americas
New York, New York 10019

Copyright © 1993, 1996 by Albert LaFarge
Cover photo by Gail Dubov
The Confident Collector and its logo are trademarked properties of Avon Books; interior design by Robin Arzt
Published by arrangement with the author
Visit our website at http://AvonBooks.com
Library of Congress Catalog Card Number: 96-96037
ISBN: 0-380-78494-7

First Avon Books Printing: August 1996

AVON TRADEMARK REG. U.S. PAT. OFF. AND IN OTHER COUNTRIES, MARCA REGISTRADO, HECHO EN U.S.A.

Printed in the U.S.A.

RA 10 9 8 7 6 5 4 3

*Elephants are always drawn smaller than life,
but a flea always larger.*

—Jonathan Swift

*Wherein could this flea guilty bee,
Except in that drop which it suckt from thee?*

—John Donne

ACKNOWLEDGMENTS

I wish to thank the following individuals and institutions for their help in the preparation of the first edition of *The Confident Collector: U.S. Flea Market Directory:*

Robert Allen; Claire Bocardo; Craig and Karol Ann Boyce; California State Library in Sacramento; Ricardo Chiong; Butler Library at Columbia University; Martha Gross; Dorothy Harris; Dan Herbert; N.B. Informatics, Inc. (especially Richard Holmes in Technical Support); Ann LaFarge; Antoinette LaFarge; John Pendaries LaFarge; Louisa LaFarge; Library of Congress; Louisiana State Library in Baton Rouge; Grace Macmillan; Allie Middleton; New Mexico State Library in Santa Fe; New York Public Library; Marian Oaks; Dean Pallozzi; Rusty Rhoades; John Ryan; Peter J. Tampas; Tennessee Flea Market Association; Texas State Library in Austin; Chuck, Sarah, and Shelley Von Berg.

In addition, the following people have been especially helpful in preparation of the second edition of this guide:

Christopher Artis; Bandicoot; Peter Becker; Amanda Beesley; Kathryn Brennan; Elizabeth Burns; Katharine Butler; Denise Chenoweth; John and Jean Cole; Lisa Considine; Andrea Dunlevy; John Farley; John Grant; Christopher Johnsen; Alan Kaplan; Tildy LaFarge; Jack Macrae; Doug Mendini; Ray Meyerson; Mushroom (Rock Island, Illinois); Nota Bene, Inc. (especially John Oldham in Technical Support); Jay Ottaway; Beverly Pallozzi; Peter Perez; Helen Robinson; Bruce Sherwin; Victoria Shoemaker; Mark Sweeney; Michael Taylor; Katrin Velder; and Craig West.

CONTENTS

INTRODUCTION

MAIN LISTINGS

CONTENTS

APPENDIX

INTRODUCTION

Welcome to the fascinating and profitable world of flea markets! With this guide in hand, you can select from a wide variety of the best flea markets across the country and gain valuable information on where to find them, when to visit, what you're likely to discover when you get there, and how to go about setting up your own stand if you want to be a vendor.

What Is a Flea Market?

When we hear the term "flea market," what normally comes to mind is a place to find bargains on antiques and collectibles (or maybe on some unidentified piece of "junque"). Generally, a flea market can be described as an open-air market for second-hand articles and antiques, no matter how many buyers or sellers may be in evidence. If flea markets tend to escape precise definition, nevertheless people generally know one when they see one. For the purposes of this book, I have defined a flea market as any regularly recurring event involving several independent vendors of used merchandise, antiques and collectibles, discounted new merchandise, etc.—but *not* exclusively new merchandise at *list* price, because then what you have is an ordinary shopping mall (a not too distant relative of the flea market). Given these criteria, I have made every effort to be inclusive in judging what is and isn't a true flea market.

In my view, the best flea markets offer diverse types of merchandise and accommodate a wide range of vendors, both long-term and transient, including those who might come only for a day or so, perhaps to sell the surplus of an attic or garage. Among the types of operations excluded from this directory are small, one-owner shops that nonetheless call themselves flea markets. In my travels and research I have come across a great number of antiques shops around the country, and though many of these are fine little stores, there is not room for them in this guide.

INTRODUCTION

A Brief History of the Flea Market

Today's American flea market is a modern version of a phenomenon that has endured throughout history in all civilized societies—wherever there is a high concentration of people, there will be market days when they assemble for the exchange of goods and services. The marketplace of the ancient Greeks (known as the *agora*) was a central place of assembly where peasants sold produce, and where fishmongers, bakers, and all manner of tradespeople had their stalls. Bankers and money changers set up tables where in our society one might find automatic teller machines. The agora also served as a general meeting place for citizens who frequented it for diverse purposes, including the meeting of friends and acquaintances and the hearing of news. In classical Rome, the *forum* was originally a marketplace located in the center of town, which eventually became the focus of political and social life as civic buildings grew up around it during the city's rise to greatness; throughout the Roman Empire, towns were established on a plan that incorporated a centrally located civic forum for a variety of functions. Such organized "forums" for buying, selling, and trading grow up naturally in all communities as an efficient way of satisfying basic commercial needs.

There is general agreement that the term "flea market" is a literal translation of the French *marché aux puces* (the Parisian Marché is justly famous), an outdoor bazaar named after those pesky little parasites of the order *Siphonaptera* (or "wingless bloodsucker") that infested the upholstery of old furniture brought out for sale. Indeed, at many American flea markets you will still find that old upholstered furniture is either strictly inspected or banned altogether from the sale floor in order to prevent a bug problem. While a flea market by any other name is still a flea market in my book, Americans refer to them variously as swap meets (a term prevalent on the West Coast), trade days, and by a host of other names such as Swap-O-Rama, Swap 'N' Shop, Peddlers' Fair, Trading Center, Flea Emporium, Flea Mall. Naturally, at any of these places you will find people coming from far and wide to find the best bargains on new and used merchandise, antiques, collectibles, and good old-fashioned "junque."

Flea markets operate just about anywhere there is available space—in vacant parking lots, drive-in movie theaters, speedways and racetracks, sporting facilities, fairgrounds, self-storage facilities, revamped supermarkets, and other converted retail spaces (including former shopping malls that have gone bust!). Most convene on weekends (and sometimes Friday), but many also conduct business on the odd weekday or even, in some high-traffic areas, on a daily basis. A new market may meet as infrequently as once or twice a year and over time grow to monthly, weekly, or even daily operation depending on demand. Often a flea market's hours of operation are determined by the primary user of the space: parking garages accommodating commuters' cars during weekdays, for instance, often yield to bargain hunters on weekends, or a drive-in theater may feature vendors' wares until dusk, then show a movie—or, as is common, a fairground may run a flea market regularly *except* when the fair comes to town.

First Monday Trade Days in Canton, Texas, one of the country's oldest and biggest flea markets, dates back to 1873 when the district judge set aside court days on which all stray horses in the district would be auctioned off (back then it was known as "Hoss Monday"). Before long, people were coming from all over Texas for these auctions, some bringing their own goods to trade or sell. As the tradition grew, the streets of downtown Canton were soon overflowing with animals, supplies, and produce. The event grew with each passing year until the townspeople began to look upon First Monday with disdain, dreading the horde that descended upon their city for one weekend each month. The city eventually passed an ordinance against trading in the street, but by then the crowds had grown too large to control, and First Monday continued to swell. With the rise of the mass-produced automobile in the 1930s, the importance of the horse as a means of transportation began to decline and it was presumed that "Hoss Monday" would slowly die out, but that prediction didn't come to pass. First Monday had developed a reputation for great bargains on all manner of things, and it continued to grow. In 1965 the city of Canton purchased six and one half acres of land and designated it as a trading area divided into spaces for traders to rent for a small fee; the trading area was soon overflowing, so the city bought more

INTRODUCTION

land. Since that time, First Monday Trade Days has grown to overtake the town. (See listing on page 400.)

Tips on Buying and Selling

The standard lore is that the best bargains are to be found by showing up early and staying late in the day. Keep that in mind, but the main objective is just to get there, whenever you can. Then the main order of business is for buyer and seller to agree on a fair price for an item of interest to the buyer. Prices listed are generally negotiable, but it does not necessarily follow that the buyer must always negotiate a price lower than marked. Sellers vary in their readiness to negotiate, but for the most part, you will find that if you tell the seller your true estimate of what an object is worth to you, you may persuade the seller to release the item for a price substantially lower than originally listed. By being honest and cautious, knowing what you want and relying on your own good judgment, you will have the best chance of succeeding in the marketplace.

Rules and Regulations

Overall, flea market operators strive to make available the widest variety of products possible within the parameters of safety, the law, and good taste. For varying reasons, many flea markets place restrictions on the sale of certain types of merchandise. Virtually all markets categorically forbid the sale of illegal items such as certain types of weapons (switchblades, throwing stars, unlicensed firearms, etc.), illicit drugs, stolen goods, and counterfeit or "gray market" products whose sale violates copyright or patent laws. The vast majority of flea markets ban pornography, liquor, or any distasteful or potentially harmful items. Many markets restrict the sale or even presence of potentially dangerous animals (such as vicious dogs or poisonous snakes); chemicals or gases (some ban propane indoors for safety reasons); and fireworks. (As mentioned earlier, some market operators submit old upholstered furniture to inspection for insects or even ban such merchandise from the sale area altogether in an effort to ward off the eponymous fleas and other pests.) Often, managers designate a separate section for food, pets, or other merchandise whose containment is seen to improve the general atmosphere of the market. A flea market operator may feel the need to restrict the sale of items that are perceived as being present in excess, especially cheap new merchandise such as costume jewelry, socks, sunglasses, or T-shirts. Vendors of such items may be confined to one end of the market or limited to selling their wares only on particular days.

Each market reserves the right to use its discretion in controlling what types of merchandise are offered for sale. Some will not tolerate "subversive" literature; others ban "racially denigrating" items; some specifically forbid palm readers, games of skill, gambling, and similar carnival-type operations. Managers undertake these measures in the name of protecting the consumer as well as themselves and other vendors.

Taxes and Licensing for Flea Market Vendors

In general, the vendor assumes full responsibility for obtaining all applicable licenses and for remitting sales taxes directly to the state. Flea market operators are generally cooperative in assisting prospective vendors with advice about any applicable state or local taxes and licenses. Market operators regularly demand proof of a state tax identification number and any required vending permits before allowing vendors to set up, since the state requires the operators to furnish such information in their tax returns. Prospective vendors are advised to contact the department of taxation and finance (or the board of equalization) for the state in which a particular market is located. Each state has a toll-free number to call for an application for registration as a sales tax vendor, which will include information on filing procedures and regulations. Once registered and approved by the state, a vendor is granted a certificate of authority to collect applicable taxes. Vendors who purchase items wholesale may present a state-issued resale certificate to suppliers to avoid paying taxes on those items until sales taxes have been collected from the consumer. In some cases, the state may allow onetime vendors of household items to bypass sales tax registration altogether, but prospective vendors should make the appropriate inquiries before proceeding, just to be sure. Systematic record keeping is important for tax reasons, since it will enable a vendor to prepare complete and accurate tax returns, which must show gross sales, taxable sales, and sales taxes due, among other things. Furthermore, an unexpected tax audit will be a much less stressful experience if transaction records have been kept up-to-date and neatly organized. Prospective flea market vendors should protect themselves by maintaining organized and detailed records from the outset.

State or local licensing may be required for the sale of certain items, notably some types of prepared foods. When in doubt, check with the flea market manager and/or with the state's department of business permits (again, there should be a toll-free number). Generally, a vendor who purchases prepackaged food items from a wholesaler will not need a separate license—the wholesaler or initial preparer bears that responsibility—but a vendor who prepares and packages food for resale will probably be subject to safety inspections and licensing through the state's department of agriculture and markets or the county department of health. (Certain items that are not subject to rapid microbial growth of bacteria—for instance, canned foods, bread, cookies and cakes—may not require such a license, but it is wise to check, since rules can vary by county.) Consequently, most flea market operators have strict rules governing the sale of food items prepared on the premises and will commonly grant exclusive concessions to responsible chefs. Vendors who plan to sell food items at a flea market are advised to check in advance with the manager and ask about any state or local regulations that may apply.

How to Use This Directory

This directory is the product of a nationwide survey conducted by phone and mail in 1995. The author has also personally visited many (though far from all) of the markets listed in this guide. The author and publisher have made every effort to verify and reproduce with the greatest possible accuracy all relevant information received from respondents as well as to ensure that the widest possible spectrum of quality flea markets has been given the chance to participate in our survey.

An appendix at the end of this book provides **brief listings** of markets whose operators were contacted by phone but did not furnish complete information by the publisher's deadline.

The following explanations are offered to help the reader understand the various elements comprising each full listing.

The term "weekend" has been used consistently throughout this book to mean Saturday and Sunday; Friday is not considered part of the weekend as used here, and is thus indicated separately where applicable. **Hours of operation** are often estimates, since many flea markets begin as soon as the first seller sets up and continue until the last one leaves. Also, open-air markets are naturally dependent upon good weather. It is always advisable to call ahead to make sure a market will be open when you plan to arrive—especially if you are going out of your way to visit.

While many flea markets operate year-round, virtually all have seasonal fluctuations in attendance. Information concerning the average **number of vendors** attending a given flea market is based primarily on estimates offered by the market operator. For most listings a range is given indicating the number of vendors in low and high season. For open-air markets there is generally a lower turnout of vendors (and, correspondingly, shoppers) during the colder months, but at many markets, especially those in southern resort communities, the busiest part of the year is the middle of winter when the tourist season is at its peak, and summer is off-season due to the heat. Indoor markets in colder climates also tend to be most active during the winter season, and some even suspend operation entirely for the summer months.

The description of **types of merchandise** available at a given market is based mainly on operators' recollections of what they have seen regularly over time and therefore represents merely *trends* rather than specific indications of what types of items will be available on any given visit. The reader should keep in mind that some items are seasonal (especially fresh produce), and some types of merchandise might be available in great quantity from a number of vendors one week and then altogether absent the next. Flea markets are by nature unpredictable as far as which vendors might show up with what merchandise on

INTRODUCTION

any given market day—but that is a big part of the excitement!

The **vendor space rental rates** printed in this guide are best used for comparison or merely to provide a rough sense of current rates. All rates were reported in 1995 and are subject to change without notice. Prospective vendors seeking to confirm current rates are advised to make inquiries directly to the managers of the targeted markets at the addresses or phone numbers shown. Fax numbers are also supplied where available.

The following symbols indicate:

 The market provides wheelchair access.

 The market provides public toilet facilities.

The author has made every effort to ensure that this book is the most up-to-date reference available, and the information has been thoroughly revised and expanded for this new edition. Readers' comments, corrections, additions, or other suggestions on how to improve this guide for future editions are always welcome. Please address all written communications to the author in care of The Confident Collector at Avon Books.

Happy hunting!

MAIN LISTINGS

ALABAMA

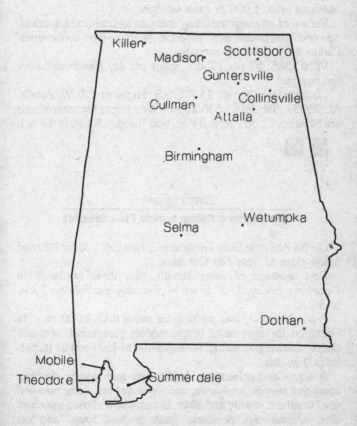

Killen

Madison Scottsboro

Guntersville

Cullman Collinsville

Attalla

Birmingham

Wetumpka

Selma

Dothan

Mobile

Theodore Summerdale

Attalla
Mountain Top Flea Market

At 11301 U.S. Highway 278 West.
Every Sunday, 5 A.M. to dark.
Free admission; plenty of free parking. In operation for over 25 years; indoors year-round, and outdoors, weather permitting. Averages up to 1,000 or more vendors.

Variety of offerings including antiques and collectibles, crafts, new and used goods, fresh produce, etc. Nine food concessions. Claims 40,000 visitors annually.

VENDORS: $7 per 10'x22' space per day. Reservations are not required.

Contact Janie Terrell, 11301 U.S. Highway 278 W, Attalla, AL 35954. Tel: (800) 535-2286 (office hours for reservations are Monday, 12:30 P.M. to 3 P.M., and Tuesday, 8 A.M. to 4 P.M.).

Birmingham
Birmingham Fairgrounds Flea Market

On the Alabama State Fairgrounds; take Exit 120 off I-20 and follow signs to State Fair Complex.

First weekend of every month, plus three weekends in December: Friday, 3 P.M. to 9 P.M.; Saturday and Sunday, 7 A.M. to 6 P.M.

Free admission; free parking for more than 2,000 cars. In operation for over seven years; indoors year-round, and outdoors, weather permitting. Averages 400 to 450 vendors (capacity 500 booths).

Antiques and collectibles, books, new and vintage clothing, coins and stamps, cookware, crafts and fine art, dolls, new and used furniture, jewelry and silver, lamps, new and used merchandise, oriental rugs, porcelain, fresh produce, toys, "and lots more." Snacks and hot meals are served on the premises.

VENDORS: From $45 per indoor space for three days, or $25

per outdoor space. Reservations are recommended two weeks in advance.

Contact Cindy, 621 Lorna Square, Birmingham, AL 35216. Tel: (205) 822-3348 or (800) 362-7538.

Birmingham
Farmer's Flea Market

At 414 Finley Avenue, at 4th Street. Take Finley Avenue exit off I-65 North (between Montgomery and Nashville).

Daily, 8 A.M. to 5 P.M.

Free admission; free parking for up to 35 cars. In operation for several years; indoors year-round, and outdoors, weather permitting. Averages close to 60 vendors year-round, (capacity 46 indoors and 25 outdoors).

Antiques and collectibles, books, new clothing, cookware, new and used furniture, jewelry, new and used merchandise, fresh produce, and toys. Snacks and hot meals are served on the premises.

VENDORS: $4 per space per day outdoors or $6 indoors. Reservations are on a first-come, first-served basis for outdoor spaces.

Contact Emory Turner, 414 Finley Avenue West, Birmingham, AL 35204. Tel: (205) 254-9852 or (205) 251-8737.

Collinsville
Collinsville Trade Day

On Highway 11 South. Take Route 68 from I-59, then turn right onto U.S. 11; or go left from Route 68 after leaving Route 411 at Leesburg, AL.

Every Saturday, all day.

Free admission; parking available at 50 cents per car. In

operation for close to 40 years; indoors and outdoors, rain or shine. Averages close to 1,000 or more vendors.

Antiques and collectibles, books, new clothing, coins and stamps, cookware, crafts and fine art, new and used furniture, jewelry and silver, livestock, new and used merchandise, poultry and fresh produce, seafood, and toys. Snacks and hot meals are served on the premises. "The old original" and "the big one in Collinsville," drawing more than 30,000 shoppers weekly.

VENDORS: $8 per 10'x12' space indoors per day or $5 per 15'x20' space outdoors. Reservations are not required.

Contact Ann Thomas, Manager, P.O. Box 298, Collinsville, AL 35961. Tel: (205) 524-2127.

Cullman
Cullman Flea Market

On Route 278 off I-65 (take Exit 308).

Every weekend, 8 A.M. to 5 P.M.

Free admission; over nine acres of free parking. In operation since 1989; indoors year-round, and outdoors, weather permitting. Averages 250 to a capacity of more than 500 vendors.

Antiques and collectibles, baked goods, books, new and vintage clothing, cookware, crafts and fine art, new and used furniture, jewelry and silver, new merchandise, pottery and porcelain, fresh produce, tools and hardware, and toys. Snacks and hot meals are served by two food concessions on the premises; 24-hour security. "Nicest and cleanest in the South."

VENDORS: From $20 to $30 per weekend depending on location; inquire for monthly rates. Reserve from two weeks to a month in advance.

Contact Del or Gene Bates, 415 Lincoln Avenue S.W., P.O. Box 921, Cullman, AL 35055. Tel: (205) 739-0910.

Dothan
Jed's Country Mall and Flea Market

Highway 231, 10 miles south of Dothan and 3 miles north of the Alabama-Florida state line.

Every Friday, Saturday, and Sunday, 8 A.M. to 5 P.M.

Free admission; acres of free parking. In operation since November 1989; indoors and outdoors, rain or shine. Averages 75 to 100 vendors (capacity 138 indoor booths plus 46 acres outdoors).

Antiques and collectibles, books, new and vintage clothing, cookware, crafts, new and used furniture, new and used merchandise, porcelain, fresh produce, and toys. Snacks and hot meals are served on the premises. RV hookups available for small fee; showers available for overnighters. Formerly J. Hooter's. Market is now developing several specialty shops.

VENDORS: From $6 per 10'x10' space per day. Reservations are recommended.

Contact Jim Easterly, 12657 South U.S. 231, Cottonwood, AL 36320. Tel: (334) 677-7234.

Dothan
Sadie's Flea Market

At 1990 U.S. 231 South, five miles south of Dothan, just past the Olympia Spa Country Club; eight miles north of the Florida line.

Every Friday, Saturday, and Sunday, 8 A.M. to 5 P.M.

Free admission; 60 acres of free parking. In operation for over six years; indoors year-round, and outdoors, weather permitting. Averages 250 to a capacity of 300 vendors.

Antiques and collectibles, books, new clothing, coins and stamps, cookware, crafts and fine art, new and used furniture, jewelry and silver, livestock, new and used merchandise, poultry and fresh produce, and toys. Two snack bars on the premises.

Shower and RV park on the premises. Average of 2,000 shoppers per weekend.

VENDORS: $3 per outdoor space or $6 indoors on Saturday or Sunday (free setup on Friday); electricity is available at $3 per day. Reservations are recommended a week in advance.

Contact Sarah or Kenneth West, 105 Olympia Drive, Dothan, AL 36301. Tel: (334) 677-5138.

Guntersville
All American Trade Day

At 11190 U.S. Highway 431, between Albertville and Guntersville.

Every weekend, 8 A.M. to 5 P.M.

Free admission; free parking. In operation for over six years; indoors, outdoors, and under cover, year-round. Averages 400 to 700 vendors (capacity over 800 vendor spaces).

Antiques and collectibles, books, new and vintage clothing, coins and stamps, cookware, crafts and fine art, fish, new and used furniture, jewelry and silver, livestock, new merchandise, pottery and porcelain, poultry and fresh produce, and toys. Restaurant on the premises; 24-hour security indoors. Seven miles from the Boaz Outlet Center. Well advertised with over 30,000 shoppers daily.

VENDORS: Indoors: $10 per 8'x10' space per day, $70 per month; outdoor tables under sheds: $5 per day. Reservations are not required.

Contact Jim or Gladys Cornelius, 11190 U.S. Highway 431, Guntersville, AL 35976. Tel: (205) 891-2790.

Killen
Uncle Charlie's Flea Market

On Highway 72 West, 30 miles west of Athens and 7 miles east of Florence, Alabama. Exit off I-65 Highway 72.

Every weekend (plus Labor Day and the Friday after Thanksgiving), 9 A.M. to 5 P.M.

Free admission; free parking for over 1,000 cars. In operation for over 14 years; indoors year-round, and outdoors, weather permitting. Averages 100 to 150 vendors (capacity 200).

Antiques and collectibles, books, new and vintage clothing, coins and stamps, cookware, crafts and fine art, new and used furniture, jewelry and silver, knives, leather, livestock, new and used merchandise, fresh produce, seafood, toys, "and many others." Snacks and hot meals are served on the premises.

VENDORS: $15 per space for one day, $25 for both days, $75 for four weekends. Reservations are required from week to week.

Contact Tom Mabry, P.O. Box 190, Killen, AL 35645. Tel: (205) 757-2256 or (800) 542-2848.

Madison
Limestone Flea Market

At the intersection of Highway 72 and Burgreen Road between Athens and Huntsville.

Every weekend, 9 A.M. to 5 P.M.

Free admission; free parking. In operation for over five years; indoors, rain or shine. Averages 300 to a capacity of 455 vendors on 40 acres.

Antiques and collectibles, books, new and vintage clothing, crafts, new and used furniture, household items, jewelry, new and used merchandise. Five food concessions on the premises. "North Alabama's largest indoor market."

VENDORS: $38 per 10'x10' space per weekend, including table and electricity. Reservations are required.

ALABAMA /Mobile

Contact Donald Conley, Manager, 30030 Highway 72 West, Madison, AL 35758. Tel: (205) 233-5183.

Mobile
Flea Market Mobile

At 401 Schillinger Road North. Take I-65 to Airport Blvd. West to Schillinger Road North, one and a half miles on the left.

Every weekend, 9 A.M. to 5 P.M.

Free admission; free parking for up to 800 cars. In operation for over four years; indoors and outdoors, rain or shine. Averages up to a capacity of 500 vendors.

Full spectrum of antiques, collectibles, new and used goods, new and vintage clothing, cookware, crafts, new and used furniture, jewelry, fish, poultry, livestock, pets, fresh produce, tools. Concessions serving a variety of foods and beverages (try the boiled and roasted peanuts and the roasted corn on the cob). Overnight security throughout weekend.

VENDORS: $20 per space for one day or $30 for both days. Reservations are recommended.

Contact Daryl Thompson, General Manager, 401 Schillinger Road North, Mobile, AL 36608. Tel: (334) 633-7533 (office is open daily).

Scottsboro
First Monday Trade Day

On the courthouse square; use Routes 72 and 79 to downtown Scottsboro.

First Monday of every month and the preceding Sunday, 7 A.M. to 5 P.M.

Free admission; street parking. In operation for over 53 years; outdoors, rain or shine. Averages 250 to 500 vendors.

Antiques and collectibles, books, cookware, crafts, new and

used furniture, jewelry and silver, and some new merchandise. Snacks and hot meals are served on the premises.

VENDORS: $15 per space per two-day event. Reserve a month in advance; all vendors must obtain a vending permit at the Scottsboro Police Department at the address shown below (Ask for Dispatch Office—enter on south side of building).

Contact Gayle Moore, 409 South Broad Street, Scottsboro, AL 35768. Tel: (205) 574-4468 (office hours are Monday through Friday, 8 A.M. to 4:30 P.M.).

Selma
Selma Flea Market

On Highway 80 Bypass at River Road.
Every weekend, 5 A.M. to whenever.
Free admission; free parking. In operation for over eight years; indoors, outdoors, and under cover, rain or shine. Averages 350 to 400 vendors.

Antiques and collectibles, books, new and vintage clothing, cookware, crafts, new and used furniture, jewelry, new merchandise, poultry and fresh produce, toys—and "bargains." Snacks and hot meals are served on the premises. RV parking is available.

VENDORS: $7 per space per day under cover, $5 outdoors. Reservations are not required.

Contact Gary Maluda, 606 River Road, Selma, AL 36703. Tel: (334) 875-0500 or (334) 874-9525.

Summerdale
Highway 59 Flea Market

On Highway 59 between Robertsdale and Foley.
Every weekend, 8 A.M. to 5 P.M.
Free admission; 27 acres of free parking. In operation since

1985; outdoors, rain or shine. Averages close to 300 vendors on 27 acres of selling space.

Full spectrum of antiques and collectibles, new and used goods, and fresh produce. Snack bar on the premises. Mobile home parking facilities; hot shower facilities. Well advertised through TV, radio, and newspaper announcements.

VENDORS: $5 per space per day; $5 overnight fee. Reservations are not required.

Contact Franklin "Red" Cotton, P.O. Box 160, Summerdale, AL 36580. Tel: (334) 989-6642.

Theodore
South Alabama Flea Market

At 6280 Theodore Dawes Road. Take Exit 13 off I-10 and go south one mile, and market will be on the left.

Daily, 8 A.M. to 6:30 P.M.

Free admission; free parking for up to 200 cars. In operation for over eight years; indoors year-round, and outdoors, weather permitting. Averages 35 to 75 vendors.

Antiques and collectibles, books, cookware, crafts, new and used furniture, jewelry, new and used merchandise, and toys. Snacks are served on the premises. Lots of shade trees.

VENDORS: $3 per table per day outdoors, $20 per week indoors. Reservations are not required.

Contact Marie Massengill, 6511 Highmount Drive, Theodore, AL 36582. Tel: (334) 653-4736 or (334) 653-5004.

Limited

Wetumpka
Hilltop Flea Market

On Highway 231 North (next to state rest stop), north of Montgomery.

Every weekend, 7 A.M. to 5 P.M.

Free admission; free parking for up to 300 cars. In operation for over 13 years; indoors year-round, and outdoors, weather permitting. Averages up to a capacity of 25 vendors.

Antiques and collectibles, books, vintage clothing, coins and stamps, cookware, crafts and fine art, new and used furniture, jewelry and silver, new merchandise, pottery and porcelain, fresh produce, and toys. Snacks and hot meals are served on the premises.

VENDORS: $10 per space for one day or $15 for the weekend. Reservations are not required.

Contact David E. Davis, 6527 Briarwood Lane, Montgomery, AL 36110. Tel: (235) 284-0288.

Wetumpka
Santuck Flea Market

At 662 Dexter Road, 25 miles north of Montgomery. Take Route 231 North to Highway, and turn at the 131 mile marker.

First Saturday of each month from March through December, from daybreak to 2 P.M.

Free admission; ample free parking. In operation for over 19 years; outdoors, rain or shine. Averages 300 to 400 vendors.

Antiques and collectibles, books, new clothing, cookware, crafts and fine art, new and used furniture, jewelry, new and used merchandise, fresh produce, and toys. Snacks and hot meals are served on the premises. Operated by volunteers from Santuck community, and proceeds go to the local fire department.

VENDORS: $20 per space per day. Reservations are required—check for a waiting list.

Contact Jack S. Johnson, President, Route 2, Box 134X, Wetumpka, AL 36092. Tel: (334) 567-7400.

ALASKA

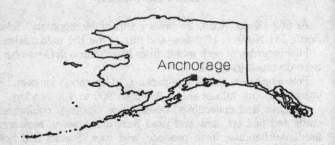

Anchorage

Anchorage
Saturday Market

In the parking lot at 3rd and E Streets, across from the Hilton Hotel.

Every Saturday from mid-May through mid-September, 10 A.M. to 6 P.M.

Free admission; free parking. In operation for over four years; outdoors, rain or shine. Averages close to a capacity of 400 vendors.

Antiques and collectibles, new merchandise, crafts, and produce in season. Food is available on the premises.

VENDORS: from $25 per 9'x15' space. Reservations are required.

Contact Dave Harbour, 700 West 6th Avenue, #206, Anchorage, AK 99501. Tel: (907) 276-7207.

ARIZONA

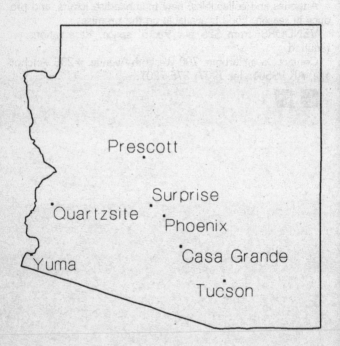

Prescott

Surprise

Quartzsite

Phoenix

Casa Grande

Yuma

Tucson

Casa Grande
The Shoppers Barn Swap Meet

At 13480 West Highway 84 at Selma Road, between Phoenix and Tucson. Take the C.G. Eloy exit off I-10, then south two miles.

Every Friday, Saturday, and Sunday, all day.

Free admission; free parking. In operation for over 10 years; outdoors, weather permitting. Average number of vendors not reported.

Antiques and collectibles, new clothing, cookware, crafts, new and used furniture, jewelry, new and used merchandise, fresh produce, toys—"anything goes." Grocery store nearby.

VENDORS: Inquire for rates; overnights OK. Reservations are not required.

Contact Bud Gray, P.O. Box 10250, Casa Grande, AZ 85230. Tel: (520) 836-1934.

Phoenix
American Park 'N' Swap

At 3801 East Washington Street.

Every Wednesday, 4 P.M. to 10 P.M.; every Friday, 6 A.M. to 10 P.M.; and every Saturday and Sunday, 6 A.M. to 4 P.M.

Admission $1 per person (50 cents on Wednesday); parking (for up to 6,000 cars) is free with admission. In operation for over 33 years; indoors and outdoors, rain or shine. Averages 1,800 to a capacity of 2,500 vendors.

Antiques and collectibles, books, new and vintage clothing, coins and stamps, cookware, crafts and fine art, new and used furniture, jewelry and silver, new merchandise, pottery and porcelain, fresh produce, and toys. Snacks and hot meals are served on the premises. Friendly staff running a "smooth operation" offering "everything you can think of from A to Z."

VENDORS: $15 per space per day on Saturday or Sunday

(corners $35); $7 on Wednesday or Friday. Reservations are not required.

Contact Richard K. Hogue or Mike Linskey, 3801 East Washington Street, Phoenix, AZ 85034. Tel: (602) 273-1258 or (602) 273-1259.

Phoenix
Fairgrounds Antique Market

On the Arizona State Fairgrounds, at 19th Avenue and McDowell Road. Take the McDowell exit off I-17 and drive east one mile, or take the 19th Avenue exit off westbound I-10 and go north one quarter mile.

Third weekend of every month (except October): Saturday, 9 A.M. to 5 P.M., and Sunday, 10 A.M. to 4 P.M.

Admission $1 per person; free admission for children 14 and under; parking for several thousand cars at $3 per car. In operation since 1986; indoors, rain or shine. Averages 100 to 150 vendors during summer months and 300 to 600 in winter.

Antiques and collectibles, books, vintage clothing, coins and stamps, crafts and fine art, dolls, used furniture, jewelry and silver, porcelain, toys, used merchandise, and a lot more. Snacks and hot meals are served on the premises. Arizona's largest monthly collector's market, with as many as 10,000 shoppers daily during the busy winter season.

VENDORS: $60 per 8'x10½' space per weekend, and $35 for each additional space. Prepaid reservations are required a week in advance.

Contact Jack Black Enterprises, P.O. Box 61172, Phoenix, AZ 85082-1172. Tel: (602) 943-1766 or (800) 678-9987.

Phoenix
Paradise Valley Swap Meet

At 2414 East Union Hills Drive; go north on Cave Creek Road to Union Hills Drive, and the market is on the northeast corner.

Every Friday, Saturday, and Sunday, 5 A.M. to 3 P.M.

Free admission; free parking for up to 150 cars. In operation for over 14 years; outdoors, weather permitting. Averages 50 to 125 vendors (capacity 150).

Antiques and collectibles, new and vintage clothing, new and used furniture, jewelry and silver, fresh produce, pets, and new merchandise; also real estate brokers and palm readers. Snack bar on premises.

VENDORS: $10 per space per day; $15 for a corner space. Reservations are recommended.

Contact Viola Cirio, 2414 East Union Hills Drive, Phoenix, AZ 85024. Tel: (602) 569-0052. Day of market, ask for Joe or Kelly.

Prescott
Peddler's Pass

At 2201 Clubhouse Drive, six miles east of Prescott on Highway 69.

Every Friday, Saturday, and Sunday, 8 A.M. to 4 P.M.

Free admission; free parking for up to 700 cars. In operation for over eight years; outdoors, weather permitting. Averages 100 to 275 vendors (capacity 300).

Antiques and collectibles, new and vintage clothing, coins and stamps, crafts and fine art, new merchandise, fresh produce, jewelry and silver items. Snacks and hot meals are served on the premises.

VENDORS: $5 per 10'x25' space per day; $8 per 20'x20' space; $10 per 20'x25' space; $20 per 20'x40' space; add $2 per day for corner spaces; electricity $4 per day, more for largest

19

spaces. Reservations are advised by the middle of the week preceding market days.

Contact Robert H. Scott, 2201 Clubhouse Drive, Prescott, AZ 86301. Tel: (602) 775-4117 (office) or (602) 778-5299 (home).

Quartzsite
The Main Event

On I-10, at Milepost 17 in La Paz County.

Shops open daily year-round, but the "Main Event" spans three weekends (sixteen days) every year—generally the last week of January and the first week of February, but call for dates (1997 dates: January 11–26, a bit earlier than usual); all day.

Free admission; over 100 acres of free parking. In operation for over 13 years; outdoors and under cover, rain or shine. Averages up to a capacity of 1,500 vendors during the "Main Event."

Antiques and collectibles, books, new and vintage clothing, coins and stamps, cookware, crafts and fine art, fish, new and used furniture, jewelry and silver, livestock, new merchandise, pottery and porcelain, poultry and fresh produce, toys, ROCKS, ROCKS AND MORE ROCKS (i.e., gems and minerals), and just about everything else. Snacks and hot meals are served on the premises. Camping, electrical hookups, barbershop, and mail service; hot-air balloons, classic car show, fireworks, camel and ostrich races, rodeo, horseshoe pits, country and polka music; 16-page brochure provides event schedule and maps of the site. Quartzsite's "Annual Gemboree," one of the largest flea markets in the country (and probably the largest gem show), attracts over a million visitors.

VENDORS: $426 per 18'x32' space per event with full hookup; more for corner spaces; $400 per 10'x15' indoor tent space. Reservations are not required.

Contact Howard Armstrong, P.O. Box 2801, Quartzsite, AZ 85346-2801. Tel: (520) 927-5213; fax: (520) 927-5355.

Surprise
Surprise Swap Meet

At 12910 Santa Fe Drive, across the railroad tracks from Grand Avenue (Highways 60 and 89), east of Dysart Road.

Every Thursday, 3 P.M. to 10 P.M., and Saturday and Sunday, 6:30 A.M. to 3 P.M.

Free admission; free parking for up to 350 cars. In operation for over 15 years; indoors and outdoors, rain or shine. Averages close to 300 or more vendors (capacity 350).

Antiques and collectibles, books, cookware, crafts, used furniture, jewelry and silver, new and used merchandise, fresh produce, and toys. Snacks and hot meals are served on the premises.

VENDORS: Thursday, $6 for a 10-foot-wide space or $9 for a 20-foot-wide space; Saturday or Sunday, $5 for a 10-foot-wide space or $8 for as big a space as needed. Reservations are not required.

Contact R. Vukanovich, P.O. Box 1425, Surprise, AZ 85374. Tel: (602) 583-1616.

Tucson
Tanque Verde Swap Meet

At 4100 South Palo Verde Road. Take Palo Verde exit north off I-10 and go about one half mile and market will be on the left.

Every Wednesday and Friday, 3 P.M. to 11 P.M., and every Saturday and Sunday, 7 A.M. to 11 P.M.

Free admission; 20 acres of free parking. In operation for over 20 years; outdoors, year-round. Averages up to a capacity of several hundred vendors on 30 acres of selling space.

Antiques and collectibles, books, new and vintage clothing, coins and stamps, cookware, crafts and fine art, new and used furniture, jewelry and silver, new and used merchandise, porcelain, fresh produce, and toys. Cafeteria and snack concessions on the premises. More than 50,000 shoppers every weekend.

VENDORS: From $11 to $15 per space depending on size and location (spaces start at 11'x26'). Reservations are not required.

Contact Ken Fiore, P.O. Box 19095, Tucson, AZ 85731-9095. Tel: (520) 294-4252.

Yuma

Arizona Avenue Swap Meet

At 1749 Arizona Avenue.

Daily from October through March, 8 A.M. to 5 P.M.

Free admission; free parking for up to 150 cars. In operation for over 20 years; outdoors, weather permitting. Averages 75 to a capacity of 130 vendors.

Antiques and collectibles, books, new and vintage clothing, cookware, crafts, used furniture, jewelry, new and used merchandise, fresh produce, and toys. Snacks and hot meals are served on the premises.

VENDORS: $6 per 18'x20' space per day or $25 per week; tables are available at 50 cents each. Reservations are not required.

Contact Bob Butcher, Manager, 1749 Arizona Avenue, Yuma, AZ 85365. Tel: (602) 343-1837.

ARKANSAS

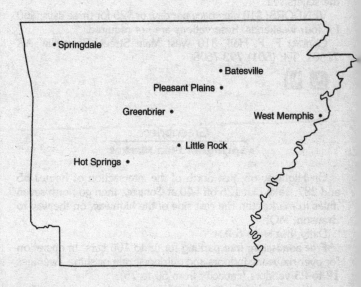

• Springdale

• Batesville

Pleasant Plains •

Greenbrier •

West Memphis •

• Little Rock

Hot Springs •

Batesville
America's Flea Market

At 310 West Main Street (lower Main) in downtown Batesville.

Every Friday, Saturday, and Sunday, all day.

Free admission; street parking. In operation since 1980; indoors, year-round. Averages up to 100 or so vendors.

Treasure of all kinds: antiques and collectibles, new and vintage clothing, coins and stamps, cookware, crafts, fresh produce, and jewelry. Snacks and hot meals are served on the premises. Air-conditioned comfort. "Where the buyers buy and the sellers sell."

VENDORS: $10 per space per day, or $25 for three days; $60 for four weekends. Reservations are not required.

Contact F. F. Hall, 310 West Main Street, Batesville, AR 72501. Tel: (501) 793-7508.

Greenbrier
Springhill Flea Market

On Highway 65, just north of the intersection of Routes 65 and 287. Take Exit 125 off I-40 at Conway, then go north seven miles to market (on the east side of the highway, on the way to Branson, MO).

Daily, 8 A.M. to 6 P.M.

Free admission; free parking for up to 100 cars. In operation for over six years; indoors and outdoors, rain or shine. Averages 12 to 25 vendors (capacity from 50 to 75).

Antiques and collectibles, books, new and vintage clothing, crafts, used furniture, jewelry, new and used merchandise, porcelain, and fresh produce. Food is not served on the premises.

VENDORS: $5 per 16'x20' indoor space per day, or $35 per week, or $90 per month; free setup outdoors. Reservations are not required.

Contact Bill R. Wisler, 660 Highway 65 North, Greenbrier, AR 72058. Tel: (501) 679-9106.

Hot Springs
Hot Springs Flea Market

At 2002 Higdon Ferry Road, less than one block off Highway 7, across from the Hot Springs Mall; follow billboards and directional signs.

Daily, 9 A.M. to 6 P.M.

Free admission; free parking for up to 200 cars. In operation for over seven years; indoors, outdoors, and under cover, rain or shine. Averages up to 100 vendors outdoors plus more indoors.

Antiques and collectibles, books, new and vintage clothing, cookware, crafts, pottery and porcelain, jewelry and silver, new and used furniture, coins and stamps, and fresh produce in season. Snacks and hot meals are served on the premises. A growing 11-acre market with plans for additional booth space and parking; there are also plans for a summer farmers' market.

VENDORS: About $7.50 per day for an outdoor stall or an 8-foot table indoors. Reservations are recommended.

Contact Betty Jackson, 2002 Higdon Ferry Road, Hot Springs, AR 71913. Tel: (501) 525-9927 or (501) 525-9304.

Hot Springs
Snow Springs Flea Market

At 3628 Park Avenue, at the intersection of Route 5 and Highway 7 North, five miles from downtown.

Every Friday, Saturday, and Sunday, plus any holidays that fall on Thursday or Monday, 8 A.M. to 5 P.M.

Free admission; free parking for up to 100 cars. In operation for over 25 years; outdoors, weather permitting. Averages 15 to 50 vendors (capacity more than 60).

Full spectrum of antiques, collectibles, new and used merchandise, and fresh produce. Snacks and hot meals are served on the premises. Live music.

VENDORS: $6.25 per day for a booth, or $15.25 for three days. Open tables are $6 per day, with three tables per space. $12 per space for setup with trailer. Reserve a week in advance.

Contact J. L. Long, 3628 Park Avenue, 7 North, Hot Springs, AR 71901. Tel: (501) 624-7469.

Little Rock
Memphis Flea Market

At 13000 I-30. From Memphis, take I-40 to I-30 to Exit 128, then continue west one mile, and market will be on the right. From Texarkana, take I-30 to Exit 126 crossover, then continue east, and market will be on the left.

Weekends of the second and fourth Saturdays of each month, 8 A.M. to 6 P.M.

Admission $1 per person; ample free parking. Duration of market not reported; indoors and outdoors, rain or shine. Averages 200 to 300 vendors (capacity 800).

Antiques and collectibles, baseball cards, books, new and vintage clothing, coins and stamps, cookware, crafts and fine art, new and used furniture, jewelry and silver, porcelain, toys, and a range of new and used merchandise. Snacks and hot meals are served on the premises.

VENDORS: $50–$60 per 10'x10' space indoors or 10'x12' space outdoors. Reservations are not required.

Contact Jim Hembree, General Manager, 13000 Interstate 30, Little Rock, AR 72209. Tel: (501) 455-1001.

Pleasant Plains
Pleasant Plains Flea Market

On Highway 167, 15 miles south of Batesville and 18 miles north of Bald Knob.

Every Friday, Saturday, and Sunday, 8 A.M. to 5 P.M.

Free admission; free parking for up to 200 cars. In operation for over 11 years; outdoors and under cover, rain or shine. Averages 40 to 65 vendors.

Antiques and collectibles, books, vintage clothing, cookware, crafts and fine art, used furniture, jewelry, new and used merchandise, porcelain, fresh produce, and toys. Snacks and hot meals are served on the premises. Electrical hookups (but no water or septic) for campers.

VENDORS: $12 per space per weekend. Reservations are not required.

Contact Manager, P.O. Box 201, Pleasant Plains, AR 72568. Tel: (501) 345-2720 or (501) 668-3434.

Springdale
Oak Grove Flea Market

At the corner of Elm Springs and Oak Grove Roads. From Springdale, turn to Huntsville, approximately four miles on left. From Route 71 Bypass, take Elm Springs exit and turn left, then go approximately one half mile, and market will be on the left.

Every weekend, 8 A.M. to 5 P.M.

Free admission; free parking. In operation for over 18 years; indoors and outdoors, rain or shine. Averages 50 to 75 vendors.

Antiques and collectibles, books, used furniture, porcelain, new and used merchandise, and toys. Snacks and hot meals are served on the premises.

VENDORS: $5 per outdoor space per day. Reservations are not required.

Contact Ramona or Bob Wallis, 3 South Ethel Avenue,

Fayetteville, AR 72701. Tel: (501) 756-0697 or (501) 521-5791.

West Memphis
West Memphis Flea Market

At 512 East Broadway. Easy access from I-55 or I-40. Take Seventh Street to Broadway, then right on Broadway about two blocks and market is on the right.

Every Thursday through Sunday, 10 A.M. to 6 P.M.

Free admission; free parking for up to 1,500 cars. In operation for over ten years; indoors and outdoors, rain or shine. Averages close to 60 vendors.

Antiques and collectibles, new and vintage clothing, cookware, crafts, new and used furniture, jewelry, household items, tools, silk flowers, and fresh produce. Snacks are served on the premises. Campground in the area. Easy access to Memphis, local convention centers, and the greyhound dog track.

VENDORS: Inquire for rates, which vary seasonally. Reservations are not required.

Contact Juanita or Butch Mosier, P.O. Box 2392, West Memphis, AR 72301. Tel: (501) 735-9332 or (501) 735-1644.

CALIFORNIA

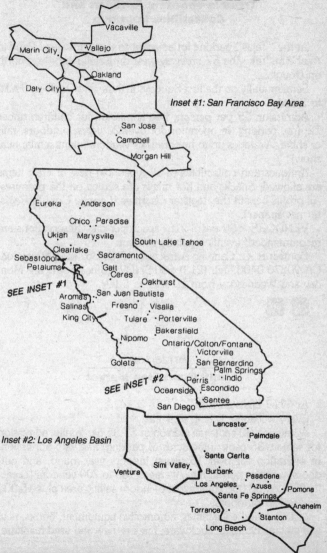

Inset #1: San Francisco Bay Area

Marin City

Vacaville

Vallejo

Oakland

Daly City

San Jose

Campbell

Morgan Hill

Eureka   Anderson

Chico Paradise

Ukiah Marysville

Clearlake

Sebastopol

Petaluma

South Lake Tahoe

Sacramento

Galt

Ceres

Oakhurst

SEE INSET #1

Aromas   San Juan Bautista

Salinas   Fresno   Visalia

King City   Tulare · Porterville

Nipomo

Bakersfield

Ontario/Colton/Fontana

Victorville

San Bernardino

Goleta   Palm Springs

SEE INSET #2   Perris   · Indio

Oceanside   Escondido

San Diego   Santee

Inset #2: Los Angeles Basin

Lancaster

Palmdale

Santa Clarita

Simi Valley   Burbank   Pasadena

Ventura   Azusa   Pomona

Los Angeles

Santa Fe Springs   Anaheim

Torrance   Stanton

Long Beach

Anaheim
Trouble-shooters Antiques and Collectibles Roundup

At the "Tejas" parking lot adjacent to the Arrowhead Pond in Anaheim. Take the 57 Freeway west on Katella and then north on Douglass.

Semiannually on the first Sundays in June and October, 9 A.M. to 3 P.M.

Admission $5 per person; free admission for children under 12; free parking. In operation for over 20 years; outdoors, rain or shine. Averages up to hundreds of vendors (giant semiannual show).

Antiques and collectibles of all types. No new or craft items are allowed. Snacks and hot meals are served on the premises. All profits benefit the Register Charities (*Orange County Register* newspaper).

VENDORS: $50 per 8'x18' space per day. Reservations are recommended; events regularly sell out.

Contact R. G. Canning Attractions, P.O. Box 400, Maywood, CA 90270-0400. Tel: (213) 560-SHOW (office hours are Monday and Wednesday from 10 A.M. to 5 P.M.

Anderson
Jolly Giant Flea Market

At 6719 Eastside Road.

Every weekend, 6 A.M. to 4 P.M.

Admission 50 cents per person or $1.35 per family; admission for seniors 35 cents; nine acres of parking, free with admission. In operation for over 16 years; indoors year-round, and outdoors, weather permitting. Averages 150 to 200 vendors (capacity 250) on 88,000 square feet of indoor selling area plus 15,000 square feet outdoors.

Antiques and collectibles, automotive equipment, books, new and vintage clothing, cookware, fine art, new and used furniture, jewelry and silver, new and used merchandise, porcelain, and tools. Snacks and hot meals are served on the premises. A clean and friendly market and one of the biggest between Sacramento and Portland, Oregon.

VENDORS: $6 per 10'x10' space on Saturday, $8 on Sunday. Reservations are not required.

Contact Patti or Jim Smith, 6719 Eastside Road, Anderson, CA 96007. Tel: (916) 365-6458.

Aromas
The Big Red Barn

At 1000 Highway 101, 17 miles north of Salinas and 17 miles south of Gilroy.

Every weekend, 7 A.M. to 5 P.M. (antiques shops are open every Wednesdy through Sunday).

Free admission; 20 acres of parking at $3 per car. In operation for over 25 years; indoors and outdoors, rain or shine. Average number of vendors not reported.

Antiques and collectibles (baseball cards, bottles, coins and stamps, Disneyana, etc.), new and vintage clothing, cookware, crafts, new and used furniture, glassware, jewelry and silver, new merchandise, tools, and fresh produce. Snacks and hot meals, including outdoor barbecue, are served on the premises. Friendly, family-style flea market with indoor antiques shops.

VENDORS: $10 on Saturday, or $25 on Sunday; $35 for Saturday and Sunday. Reservations are recommended a week in advance.

Contact Debra Hagan, Director of Operations, 1000 Highway 101, Aromas, CA 95004. Tel: (408) 422-1271 or (408) 726-3101.

Azusa
Azusa Swap Meet

At 675 East Foothill Boulevard, a mile north of the 210 Freeway (take the Azusa Avenue exit), then a half-mile east on Foothill Boulevard.

Every Sunday, 6 A.M. to 4 P.M.

Free admission; free parking for up to 1700 cars. In operation for over twenty-eight years; outdoors, rain or shine. Averages 400 to a capacity of 885 vendors.

Antiques and collectibles, books, new and vintage clothing, cookware, crafts and fine art, new and used furniture, jewelry and silver, fresh produce and seafood, new and used tools; lots of new merchandise. Snacks and hot meals are served on the premises.

VENDORS: $21 per space per Sunday or $70 per month. Reserve a week in advance.

Contact James Edwards, Proprietor, 675 East Foothill Boulevard, Azusa, CA 91702. Tel: (714) 640-4603. Day of market, call Mr. Cisneros, Manager, at (818) 334-8915.

Bakersfield
Fairgrounds Swap Meet

At the corner of Union and Ming Avenues. Take Fairgrounds exit off Highway 99, or take Union Avenue exit off Highway 58.

Every weekend, 6 A.M. to 3 P.M.

Admission 50 cents per person on Saturday and 75 cents on Sunday; ample parking at $1 per car. In operation for over eight years; outdoors, year-round. Averages 300 to 350 vendors (capacity 380).

Antiques and collectibles, books, new and vintage clothing, coins and stamps, cookware, crafts and fine art, new and used furniture, jewelry and silver, new and used merchandise, porcelain, fresh produce, tools, toys, Western tack. Snacks and hot meals are served on the premises. "Just a neat market that appeals to all!"

VENDORS: $9 per space on Saturday or $12 on Sunday (corner spaces $3 extra per day); electricity is available at $3 per day. Reservations are not required.

Contact Ed Murphy, 312 Stable Avenue, Bakersfield, CA 93307. Tel: (805) 833-1733 or (800) 881-9700.

Burbank
The Pickwick

At the Pickwick Banquet and Entertainment Center, 1001 Riverside Drive, at the corner of Main Street. Easy access from Freeways 101, 134, and 5.

Fourth Sunday of every month, 9 A.M. to 3 P.M.

Admission $3 per person; free parking for up to 300 cars. In operation for over 11 years; indoors, rain or shine. Averages close to 150 vendors year-round.

Antiques and collectibles, books, vintage clothing, fine art, used furniture, jewelry and silver, and toys. Snacks are served on the premises.

VENDORS: From $100 to $175 per space per day. Reserve three months in advance.

Contact Caskey Lees, P.O. Box 1637, Topanga, CA 90290. Tel: (310) 455-2886.

Campbell
Second Saturday Flea Market

At the Campbell Center. Take the Hamilton exit off Highway 880, then west approximately four blocks to Winchester Boulevard, then left, and go half a block on the right at the shopping center.

CALIFORNIA / Ceres

Second Saturday of every month, 7 A.M. to 5 P.M.

Free admission; free parking for 150 cars. In operation for over 19 years; outdoors, rain or shine. Averages 40 to 60 vendors (capacity 80).

Variety of offerings including antiques and collectibles, new and used goods, and fresh produce. Snacks and hot meals are served on the premises. Friendly and clean atmosphere.

VENDORS: $10 per 10'x17' space per day. Reservations are not required.

Contact Carl or Jack, 1769 South Winchester Boulevard, Campbell, CA 95008. Tel: (408) 866-5131.

Ceres
Ceres Flea Market

At 1651 East Whitmore Avenue, off Highway 99.

Every weekend, 6 A.M. to 3 P.M.

Admission $1 per carload on Sunday, free on Saturday; parking is free on Saturday and included with admission on Sunday. In operation for over 15 years; outdoors and under cover, rain or shine. Averages 400 to 450 vendors.

Baseball cards, books, new and vintage clothing, cookware, crafts and fine art, new and used furniture, jewelry and silver, new and used merchandise, fresh produce, seafood, and toys. Snacks and hot meals are served on the premises.

VENDORS: From $5 to $10 per space on Saturday, or from $22 to $30 on Sunday. Reserve a week in advance.

Contact Joann Fluharty, P.O. Box 35, Ceres, CA 95307. Tel: (209) 537-9827.

Chico
Cal's Flea Market

At the Silver Dollar Fairgrounds, at Fair Street and Park.

Every weekend (except when the fairgrounds are in use), 9 A.M. to 4 P.M.—call for dates.

Free admission; ample free parking. In operation for over 15 years; indoors, year-round. Averages up to 50 vendors.

Antiques and collectibles, books, garage-sale items, new and used merchandise. Snacks are served on the premises.

VENDORS: $6 per 12'x12' space per day. Reservations are not required.

Contact Cal Bieberdorf, Manager, 1809 Drendel Circle, Paradise, CA 95969. Tel: (916) 892-9205.

Clearlake
Clearlake Flea Market

At 16080 Davis Street, off Highway 53. Follow the County Landfill signs off Highway 53 to Davis Street.

Every Friday, Saturday, and Sunday, 9 A.M. to 4 P.M.

Free admission; free parking. In operation for over 14 years; indoors and outdoors, rain or shine. Averages 75 to 100 vendors (capacity 125).

Antiques and collectibles, cookware, crafts, used furniture, jewelry, new and used merchandise, and toys. Snacks and hot meals are served on the premises. Under new ownership. "Largest shopping village and flea market in Lake County."

VENDORS: $10 per space per day. Reservations are recommended.

Contact Beatrice or Leslie Wurzburger, P.O. Box 4297, Clearlake, CA 95422. Tel: (707) 995-2304.

Colton
Maclin's Open Air Market

At 1902 West Valley Boulevard, between the Riverside Avenue and Pepper Avenue exits off I-10, just north of the freeway.

Every Thursday, Saturday, and Sunday, 5:30 A.M. to 3 P.M.; furniture auction every Thursday at 10 A.M.

Free admission; ample free parking. In operation for over 59 years; outdoors, rain or shine. Averages 150 to 200 vendors (capacity 300).

Antiques and collectibles, new clothing, cookware, crafts and fine art, frozen fish, luggage, new and used furniture, jewelry and silver, new brand-name and discount merchandise, pottery and porcelain, fresh produce, toys, watches, and used merchandise. Pizza Hut, Taco Bell, the Market Grill, and the Outdoor Cactus Cantina on the premises. Kiddie rides and ponies; live music for the market; antiques and furniture auction every Thursday, rain or shine. A high-volume market with good amenities—targeted to bargain hunters.

VENDORS: From $7 to $20 per 10'x10' space per day or $20 to $35 per 10'x20' space depending on location, plus a $5 insurance fee. Reservations are not required but can be arranged by calling on the preceding Wednesday between 1 P.M. and 4 P.M.; day of market, spaces are rented on a first-come, first-served basis.

Contact Paula Stevens, 1902 West Valley Boulevard, Colton, CA 92324. Tel: (909) 877-3700 or (800) 222-SHOP; for reservations call (909) 431-5353.

Daly City
Century Geneva Swap Meet

At the Geneva Drive-In, 607 Carter, next door to the Cow Palace. Take the Cow Palace exit off Highway 101 or 280.

Every weekend, 7 A.M. to 4 P.M.

Admission 25 cents per person on Saturday, 75 cents on

Sunday; free parking. In operation for "many years"; outdoors, weather permitting. Averages 75 to 150 vendors (capacity of 250).

Antiques and collectibles, books, new and vintage clothing, jewelry, new merchandise, fresh produce, toys, and a large variety of used merchandise. Snacks and hot meals are served on the premises.

VENDORS: $10 per car-sized space on Saturday and $15 on Sunday. Reservations are not required.

Contact Lance Edwards, 607 Carter Street, Daly City, CA 94016. Tel: (415) 587-0515.

Escondido
Escondido Swap Meet

At 635 West Mission Avenue. Take I-15 to Valley Parkway East, then left on Quince, then left onto Mission.

Every Wednesday, Thursday, Saturday, and Sunday, 7 A.M. to 4 P.M.

Admission 50 cents on Wednesday, Thursday, or Saturday; 75 cents on Sunday; free parking. In operation for over 27 years; indoors and outdoors, rain or shine. Average number of vendors not reported.

Antiques and collectibles, books, new and vintage clothing, cookware, crafts, new and used furniture, jewelry and silver, new merchandise, and fresh produce. Snacks and hot meals are served on the premises.

VENDORS: $10 per space on Wednesday or Thursday, $14 on Saturday, $17 on Sunday. Reservations are not required.

Contact Lee Porter, 635 West Mission Avenue, Escondido, CA 92025. Tel: (619) 745-3100.

Eureka
Flea Mart by the Bay

At 1200 West Del Norte. Turn off Highway 101 onto Del Norte (at the Motel 6) and head west to the market.

Every Friday, Saturday, and Sunday, 8 A.M. to P.M.

Free admission; free parking for up to 500 cars. In operation for over 15 years; indoors, year-round. Averages 50 to a capacity of 125 vendors.

Antiques and collectibles, books, vintage clothing, cookware, crafts, fishing supplies, used furniture, jewelry and silver, new and used merchandise, records, and toys. Snacks and hot meals are served on the premises. Near a public fishing pier and picnic area.

VENDORS: $5 per table per day, or $10 for all three days; monthly rates are $56 per 8'x10' booth or $112 per 8'x20' booth. Reservations are not required.

Contact Leah Patton, Manager, 1200 West Del Norte Street, Eureka, CA 95503. Tel: (707) 443-3103.

Eureka
Redwood Flea Market

At 3750 Harris Street in the main Exhibit Building.

Approximately 15 weekends spread throughout each year—call for dates, 8 A.M. to 4 P.M.

Admission 25 cents; free admission for children age 12 and under; free parking. In operation for over 26 years; indoors, year-round. Averages 80 to 125 vendors (capacity 150).

Antiques and collectibles, books, new and vintage clothing, coins and stamps, cookware, crafts and fine art, used furniture, jewelry and silver, toys, and new merchandise. Snacks are available on the premises.

VENDORS: $9 per table per day. Reserve a few days in advance.

Contact Manager, 2363 First Street, McKinleyville, CA

95521. Tel: (707) 839-3049 or (707) 442-8770. Day of market, call the pay phone at (707) 442-9631.

Fresno
Cherry Avenue Auction

At 4640 South Cherry Avenue, between Central and American Avenues. From the south, take Highway 99 to American Avenue, then east to Cherry Avenue, then north to market; from the north, take Highway 99 to Jensen off-ramp, then west to Cherry Avenue, then south approximately three miles.

Every Tuesday and Saturday, 6 A.M. to 4 P.M.

Admission 50 cents per person; free admission for children under 11; parking for up to 800 cars at $2 per car. In operation since 1942; outdoors, year-round. Averages 700 to 1,000 vendors.

Antiques and collectibles, books, new and vintage clothing, cookware, crafts, new and used furniture, poultry and fresh produce, seafood, tools, and toys. American, Mexican, and Chinese food is served on the premises. Pony rides, carousel.

VENDORS: $8 for two spaces on Tuesday, from $10 to $20 for one space on Saturday. Reservations are recommended.

Contact W. D. Mitchell, Owner, or Neil Burson, Manager, 4640 South Cherry Avenue, Fresno, CA 93706. Tel: (209) 266-9856. Day of market, call Neil Burson or Richard Pilegard.

Galt
Galt Wholesale/Retail Flea Market

At 890 Caroline Avenue. Take the Central Galt exit off Highway 99, turn left on Fairway, and follow the green signs to the market, with entrances off Caroline and Chabolla.

Every Wednesday, 7 A.M. to 5 P.M.; wholesale market every

Tuesday, 6 A.M. to 5 P.M.; retail market every Tuesday, 10 A.M. to 5 P.M.

Free admission; free parking for up to 1,300 cars. In operation for over 33 years; outdoors, rain or shine. Averages close to its capacity of 860 vendors year-round.

Antiques and collectibles, books, new and vintage clothing, coins and stamps, cookware, crafts and fine art, jewelry, new and used merchandise, fresh produce, and toys. Snacks and hot meals are served on the premises.

VENDORS: $30 per space on Tuesday, and $17 per space on Wednesday. Reservations are required for daily and monthly rentals.

Contact City of Galt, 380 Civic Drive, Galt, CA 95632. Tel: (209) 745-2437 (enter 0 at the tape) or (209) 745-4695 (City Hall).

Goleta
Santa Barbara Swap Meet

At 907 South Kellogg Avenue.

Every Sunday, 7 A.M. to 3 P.M.

Admission $1 per person; parking for up to 600 cars at $1 per car. In operation for over 27 years; outdoors, weather permitting. Averages 230 to 270 vendors (capacity 320).

Antiques and collectibles, books, new and vintage clothing, coins and stamps, cookware, crafts and fine art, used furniture, jewelry and silver, new merchandise, pottery and porcelain, fresh produce, and toys—mostly garage-sale items and used merchandise. Snacks and hot meals are served on the premises. "If it's legal, you can find it here."

VENDORS: $17 per space per day; weekly and monthly reservation fees are $10 and $25 respectively. Reservations are not required.

Contact Robert Strojek, 907 South Kellogg Avenue, Goleta, CA 93117. Tel: (805) 967-4591.

Indio

Maclin's Indio Open Air Market

At 46-350 Arabia Street, directly behind the Riverside County Fairgrounds. Take Monroe Street off I-10 East, then go right onto Indio Boulevard (Highway 111) and then left to Arabia.

Every Wednesday evening, 4 P.M. to 10 P.M.

Free admission; ample free parking. Duration of market not reported; outdoors, year-round. Averages close to 100 vendors (capacity 120).

New and used items, furniture, fresh produce, crafts, jewelry, and much more. Snacks are served on the premises.

VENDORS: $15 per space per day. Reservations are not required.

Contact Maclin Markets, Inc., 7407 Riverside Drive, Ontario, CA 91761. Tel: (909) 984-5131 or (800) 222-SHOP.

Indio

Sun Air Swap Meet

At 84-245 Indio Springs Drive. Take I-10 to Auto Center Drive North, then right onto Indio Springs Drive.

Every Tuesday evening, 4 P.M. to 11 P.M.

Admission $1 per person over fourteen years old; free parking for up to 1,200 cars. In operation for over 25 years; outdoors, weather permitting. Averages 210 to 250 vendors (capacity 290).

Antiques and collectibles, books, new clothing, cookware, crafts and fine art, new and used furniture, jewelry and silver, new and used merchandise, porcelain, fresh produce, and toys. Snacks are served on the premises.

VENDORS: $18 per space per day. Reservations are not required.

Contact John Blazej, P.O. Box 10170, Indio, CA 92202-2510. Tel: (619) 347-9474 or (805) 526-3483.

King City
King City Rotary Annual Swap Meet

On the Salinas Valley Fairgrounds, at 626 Division.

Annually, the first Sunday in April or the last Sunday in March, 7 A.M. to 5 P.M.

Admission $2 per person; free parking for up to 500 cars. In operation for over 27 years; indoors and outdoors, rain or shine. Average number of vendors not reported.

Antiques and collectibles, books, used furniture, and new merchandise. Hot meals are served on the premises.

VENDORS: $20 per space. Reservations are not required.

Contact Judy Hostette, Manager, P.O. Box 611, King City, CA 93930. Tel: (408) 385-0414.

Lake Perris
Maclin's Lake Perris Open Air Market

At Lake Perris Fairgrounds, 18700 Lake Perris Drive. Take Ramona Expressway exit off 215 Freeway, then go about two miles and market will be on the left.

Every weekend, 5:30 A.M. to 3:00 P.M.

Free admission; ample free parking. In operation since 1993; indoors and outdoors, year-round. Averages 50 to 75 vendors.

Antiques and collectibles, books, new and vintage clothing, new and used furniture, cookware, crafts, jewelry, pets, fresh produce, tools, and brand-name new and used merchandise. Pizza Hut, Market Grill, and beer garden on the premises. Occasional horse and dog shows, motocross, music festivals, rodeos, and more. Convenient RV parking is available; call (909) 654-2546.

VENDORS: From $12 to $25 per 15'x20' space per day depending on location. Reservations are not required; day of market, spaces are rented on a first-come, first-served basis.

Contact Lynn Estes, 18700 Lake Perris Drive, Perris, CA 92571. Tel: (909) 940-5464 or (800) 222-SHOP.

Lancaster
Lancaster Chamber of Commerce Semi-Annual Flea Market

At 155 East Avenue I. Take Avenue I exit in Lancaster and go east approximately five miles, then go one block north from the intersection of Division Street and Avenue I.

Semiannually, on the third Sunday in May and the first Sunday in October, 9 A.M. to 5 P.M.

Admission $2 per person; free admission for children under six; ample free parking. In operation since 1966; indoors and outdoors, rain or shine. Averages 500 to 600 vendors (capacity 850).

Antiques and collectibles, books, new and vintage clothing, coins and stamps, cookware, crafts and fine art, new and used furniture, jewelry and silver, new and used merchandise, fresh produce, and toys. Food is available on the premises. Pony rides and petting zoo for the kids.

VENDORS: From $60 to $70 per 8'x10' space indoors, or from $40 to $60 per 10'x10' space outdoors. Reservations are required well in advance.

Contact Lancaster Chamber of Commerce, 44335 Lowtree Avenue, Lancaster, CA 93534-4167. Tel: (805) 948-4518.

Long Beach
Outdoor Antique and Collectible Market

At the Long Beach Veterans Stadium. Take Lakewood Boulevard North exit off Freeway 405, then turn right onto Lakewood Boulevard and continue to Conant Street.

CALIFORNIA /Los Angeles

Third Sunday of every month (plus an added event in early November), 8 A.M. to 3 P.M.

Admission $3.50 per person; free admission for children; free parking for up to 10,000 cars. In operation since 1982; outdoors, rain or shine. Averages close to 800 vendors.

Antiques and collectibles only—but a wide assortment. Snacks and hot meals are served on the premises.

VENDORS: From $45 to $65 per space per day. Reserve a year in advance.

Contact Donald or Lynn Moger, Americana Enterprises, Inc., P.O. Box 69219, Los Angeles, CA 90069. Tel: (213) 655-5703.

Los Angeles
Alameda Swap Meet

At 4501 South Alameda Street, between 45th Street and Slauson.

Daily (except Tuesday): weekdays, 10 A.M. to 7 P.M., and weekends, 8 A.M. to 7 P.M.

Free admission; free parking for up to 500 cars. In operation since 1985; indoors, year-round. Averages close to 300 vendors.

New merchandise only: clothing, cookware, crafts, electronics, furniture, jewelry, toys, and various merchandise, plus fresh produce. Snacks and hot meals are served on the premises. This one's not for used or antique merchandise.

VENDORS: Inquire for rates (waiting list). No transient vendors.

Contact George Constant, 4501 South Alameda Street, Los Angeles, CA 90058. Tel: (213) 233-2764.

Marin City
Marin City Flea Market

At 147 Donahue (at Drake), just off Highway 101 at the Marin City/Sausalito exit, 12 miles north of San Francisco.

Every weekend, 5 A.M. to 4 P.M.

Free admission; parking for approximately 2,000 cars at $2 per car. In operation since 1975; outdoors, weather permitting. Averages 100 to 150 vendors.

Antiques and collectibles, books, new and vintage clothing, coins and stamps, cookware, crafts and fine art, ethnic arts, new and used furniture, jewelry and silver, new and used merchandise, prints and posters, and toys. Snacks and hot meals are served on the premises. Draws from 1,700 to 2,000 customers per day on average.

VENDORS: From $20 per car-size space per day; half price on Saturday. Reservations are recommended a week to a month in advance (some space available on a first-come, first-served basis).

Contact Gene Clark, Manager, P.O. Box 2032, Sausalito, CA 94965. Tel: (415) 332-1441 (office hours are Monday through Thursday, 2 P.M. to 4 P.M., and Friday, 10 A.M. to noon). During market hours call (415) 331-6752.

Marysville
Marysville Flea Market

At 1468 Simpson Lane, off Highway 20.

Every weekend plus holidays, 6 A.M. to 2 P.M.

Free admission; acres of free parking. In operation for over 35 years; indoors year-round, and outdoors, weather permitting. Averages 200 to a capacity of 250 vendors.

Antiques and collectibles, books, new and vintage clothing, coins and stamps, cookware, crafts, used furniture, jewelry and silver, livestock, new and used merchandise, poultry and fresh produce, tools, and toys. Snacks and hot meals are served on the premises. Friendly atmosphere.

VENDORS: $5 for two tables on Saturday, $10 on Sunday ($15 for a covered space on Sunday). Reservations are not required.

Contact Betty Foster or Richard Sinnott, 1468 Simpson Lane, Marysville, CA 95901. Tel: (916) 743-8713.

Morgan Hill
Morgan Hill Flea Market

At 140 East Main Street. Take Dunne Avenue exit to downtown Morgan Hill, then right on Monterey Street to Main Street, then right on Main and one block from there to market.

Every weekend, 7:30 A.M. to 6 P.M.

Free admission; free parking. In operation since 1964; outdoors, rain or shine. Averages 100 to 125 vendors (capacity 125 dealers).

Full spectrum of antiques, collectibles, new and used goods, new and vintage clothing, cookware, crafts, and fresh produce. Snack bar.

VENDORS: $12 per space on Saturday, $13 per space on Sunday. Reservations are required a week in advance.

Contact Jim Ahlin, 140 East Main Street, Morgan Hill, CA 95037. Tel: (408) 779-3809.

Nipomo
Nipomo Swap Meet and Buyer's Mart

At 263 North Frontage Road (101 Freeway); off-ramp is Tefft Street.

Every Friday, Saturday, and Sunday, 6 A.M. to 6 P.M.

Admission $1 per person on Saturday or Sunday, free Friday; ample parking at $2 per car (free on Friday). In operation for over 15 years; indoors year-round, and outdoors, weather permitting. Averages 300 to a capacity of 400 vendors.

Antiques and collectibles, books, new clothing, coins and stamps, cookware, crafts, new and used furniture, jewelry, new and used merchandise, fresh produce, and toys. Snacks and hot meals are served on the premises.

VENDORS: Reserved spaces are $2 on Friday, $8 on Saturday, and $11 on Sunday; unreserved spaces are $9 on Saturday and $13 on Sunday. Reservations are recommended a week in advance.

Contact Robert Folkerts, 263 North Frontage Road, Nipomo, CA 93444. Tel: (805) 929-7000. Day of market, call John Anderson or Howard Bevery.

Oakhurst

Mountain Peddler's Fair

On Route 41 East. From Merced, take Route 140 to Maripose, then Route 49 South to Route 41E in Oakhurst.

Two weekends annually, in May and September, all day—call for dates.

Free admission; ample free parking. In operation for over 15 years; outdoors, rain or shine. Averages close to its capacity of 400 vendors.

Antiques and collectibles, books, vintage clothing, crafts and fine art, used furniture, jewelry and silver, porcelain, toys, and used merchandise (no new merchandise allowed). Snacks and hot meals are served on the premises. Sponsored by the Eastern Madera County Chamber of Commerce.

VENDORS: From $100 to $110 per space for the weekend. Reserve a month in advance.

Contact Lori Crow, Eastern Madera County Chamber of Commerce, 49074 Civic Circle, Oakhurst, CA 93644. Tel: (209) 642-4244.

Oakland
Coliseum Swap Meet

At 5401 Coliseum Way, one block north of the Coliseum Sports Complex. Take the High Street exit off Freeway 880.

Every Friday, Saturday, and Sunday, 6:30 A.M. to 4 P.M.

Free admission; free parking for more than 500 cars. In operation for over 15 years; outdoors, weather permitting. Averages up to a capacity of 410 vendors.

Antiques and collectibles, books, new clothing, new and used furniture, jewelry, new and used merchandise, fresh produce, and toys. Snacks and hot meals are served on the premises.

VENDORS: $10 per space on Wednesday, Thursday, or Friday, $15 on Saturday or Sunday. Reservations are not required.

Contact Byron Herbert, 5401 Coliseum Way, Oakland, CA 94601. Tel: (510) 533-1601.

Oakland
Nor Cal Swap Meet

At Seventh and Fallon Streets in the parking lot.

Every weekend, 7 A.M. to 4 P.M.

Admission 50 cents per person; free admission for children under 12; free parking for up to 500 cars. In operation for over six years; indoors, year-round. Averages 250 to 400 vendors (capacity 500).

Collectibles, clothing, miscellaneous "junk," new merchandise, and fresh produce. Food concession stand on the premises.

VENDORS: $15 per double space (minimum); $7 per additional space. Reservations are on a first-come, first-served basis.

Contact Manager, 1150 Ballena Blvd., Suite 211, Alameda, CA 94501. Tel: (510) 769-7266.

Oceanside

Oceanside Swap Meet

At 3480 Mission Avenue. Take I-5 to Mission Avenue, then go east two miles.

Every Friday, Saturday, and Sunday, plus holiday Mondays, 7 A.M. to 3 P.M.

Admission 35 cents on Friday, 50 cents on Saturday, 75 cents on Sunday; free parking. In operation for over 20 years; indoors and outdoors, rain or shine. Average number of vendors not reported.

Antiques and collectibles, books, new and vintage clothing, cookware and crafts, new and used furniture, jewelry and silver, new merchandise, and toys. Snacks and hot meals are served on the premises.

VENDORS: $6 per space on Friday, $13 on Saturday, $16 on Sunday, $8 on holiday Monday. Reservations are not required.

Contact Ernest Murray, 635 West Mission Avenue, Escondido, CA 92025. Tel: (619) 757-5286 or (619) 745-3100.

Ontario

Maclin's Ontario Open Air Market

At 7407 Riverside Drive at the corner of Campus Avenue, between Euclid and Grove. Go south off the Pomona Freeway (Route 60); freeway off-ramps are Euclid and Grove.

Every Tuesday, Saturday, and Sunday, 5:30 A.M. to 3 P.M. (vendors may show up as early as 5:30 A.M.).

Admission 50 cents per person; plenty of free parking. In operation for over 57 years; outdoors, rain or shine. Averages 200 to 300 vendors (capacity 452).

Baseball cards, books, new clothing, comics, cookware, crafts, fine art, fish, new furniture, jewelry, knives, fresh fish and seafood, fresh produce and baked goods. Snacks and hot meals are served at a restaurant on the premises; there is also a full bar with large-screen TV. Kiddie rides and ponies; live music for the market. Livestock auction every Tuesday, rain or shine. Experience shopping the old-fashioned way in laid-back, family-style surroundings targeted to bargain hunters. "We're rustic, not backward."

VENDORS: From $7 to $20 per 10'x10' space per day or $20 to $35 per 10'x20' space depending on location, plus a $5 insurance fee. Reservations are not required but can be arranged by calling on the preceding Friday, between 1 P.M. and 4 P.M.; day of market, spaces are rented on a first-come, first-served basis.

Contact Special Events Department, 7407 Riverside Drive, Ontario, CA 91761. Tel: (909) 984-5131 or (800) 222-SHOP; for reservations, call (909) 431-5353.

Palmdale

Antelope Valley Swap Meet at Four Points

At 5550 Pear Blossom Highway at the intersection of Highway 138, five miles east of Palmdale.

Every weekend, 6 A.M. to 3:30 P.M.

Admission 50 cents per person on Saturday and $1 on Sunday; free parking for up to 1,500 cars. In operation for over 20 years; outdoors, rain or shine. Averages close to 300 vendors year-round (capacity 400).

Antiques and collectibles, books, new and vintage clothing, coins and stamps, cookware, crafts, new and used furniture, jewelry and silver, new merchandise, pottery and porcelain, fresh produce, and toys. Hot and cold meals (including homemade corn dogs, authentic Mexican food, and biscuits and gravy) are served on the premises. Live Country and Western bands on Sundays; pony rides.

VENDORS: $7 on Saturday; $12 on Sunday; $15 for both days. Reservations are recommended.

Contact Joyce Bruce, P.O. Box 901807, Palmdale, CA 93590. Tel: (805) 273-0456.

Palm Springs
Palm Springs Market Fair

At 5955 East Ramon Road. Take I-10 to Gene Autrey Trail exit, then five miles on Gene Autrey Trail, then left onto Ramon.

Every Friday, Saturday, and Sunday, 5 P.M. to 10 P.M. (June through September), or 8 A.M. to 3 P.M. (October through May).

Free admission; ample free parking. A new market (in operation since October 1994); outdoors, year-round. Averages close to its capacity of 640 vendors.

Antiques and collectibles, books, new and vintage clothing, coins and stamps, cookware, crafts and fine art, new and used furniture, garage-sale items, jewelry and silver, fresh produce, new and used merchandise, and toys. Snacks and hot meals are served on the premises (there's a beer garden, too). "The outdoor shopping paradise."

VENDORS: $38 per 18'x20' space per day. Reserve a month in advance.

Contact Dave Chandler, 5955 East Ramon Road, Palm Springs, CA 92264. Tel: (619) 327-1109 or (800) 337-8121.

Paradise
Cal's Depot Flea Market

At the intersection of Black Olive and Pearson Roads.

Every Friday, Saturday, and Sunday, 9 A.M. to 4 P.M.

Free admission; free parking. In operation for over 15 years; indoors and outdoors, year-round. Averages 30 to a capacity of 50 vendors indoors plus many more outdoors.

Antiques and collectibles, garage-sale items, new and used merchandise. Food is available on the premises.

VENDORS: $5 per table outdoors. Reservations are not required.

Contact Cal Bieberdorf, 1809 Drendel Circle, Paradise, CA 95969. Tel: (916) 872-4943.

Pasadena
Pasadena City College Flea Market

1570 East Colorado Boulevard. Take Freeway 210 to Pasadena and exit on Hill Boulevard heading south; go six blocks, then left on Del Mar and park in the lot on the left.

First Sunday of every month, 8 A.M. to 3 P.M.

Free admission; free parking for more than 3,000 cars. In operation for over 18 years; outdoors, rain or shine. Averages close to its capacity of 500 vendors.

Antiques and collectibles, vintage clothing, crafts and fine art, new and used furniture, jewelry and silver, toys, and used merchandise. Snacks and hot meals are served on the premises. "Largest flea market this side of the Rose Bowl."

VENDORS: $45 for three parking spaces per day. Reserve three to six months in advance—long waiting list.

Contact Lana Fields, 1570 East Colorado Boulevard, Room CC214, Pasadena, CA 91006. Tel: (818) 585-7906.

Pasadena
Rose Bowl Flea Market

At the Rose Bowl, at Rosemont and Arroyo, near the junction of Foothill Freeway (210), Ventura Freeway (134), and Pasadena Freeway (110). Follow signs posted in town.

Second Sunday of every month, 9 A.M. to 3 P.M.

Admission $5 per adult; children under 12 admitted free. Early admission (from 6 A.M.) is available at $10. Special group rates; ample free parking. In operation for over 25 years; outdoors, rain or shine. Averages 1,500 to 1,600 vendors.

Full spectrum of antiques, collectibles, new and used merchandise (such as furniture, clothing, household items, and junque), cookware, crafts, and just about anything else you can imagine. Hot meals are available. Unquestionably California's largest flea market, and among the largest and most colorful in the world, with an average daily customer attendance of approximately 20,000. Good celebrity watching!

VENDORS: From $30 to $90 per space per day. Reservations are recommended 60 days in advance for better locations.

Contact R.G. Canning Attractions, P.O. Box 400, Maywood, CA 90270-0400. Tel: (213) 588-4411 or (213) 587-5100 on Monday or Wednesday for more information.

Petaluma
Petaluma Fairground Flea Market

On the Fairgrounds, at the intersection of East Washington and Payron Streets.

Every weekend (except from June through mid-July), 8 A.M. to 4:30 P.M.

Free admission; ample free parking. In operation since 1978; indoors year-round and outdoors, weather permitting. Averages up to 56 vendors under cover plus another 75 tables outdoors.

Antiques and collectibles, books, new and vintage clothing, coins and stamps, cookware, used furniture, jewelry and silver, new and used merchandise, porcelain, and toys. Food is not served on the premises.

VENDORS: $3 per table per day. Reservations are not required.

Contact John Letinich, Treasurer, 420 Western Avenue, Petaluma, CA 94952. Tel: (707) 763-1242.

Pomona
Valley Indoor Swap Meet

At 1600 East Holt Boulevard. Take the Indian Hill exit off Freeway 10 and go south to Holt.

Every Friday, Saturday, and Sunday, 10 A.M. to 6 P.M.; open daily for the two weeks preceding Christmas.

Admission $1 per person; free admission for senior citizens and children under 12; free parking for over 1,000 cars. In operation for over ten years; indoors. Averages close to a capacity of 350 vendors year-round.

Antiques and collectibles, books, new and vintage clothing, coins and stamps, cookware, crafts and fine art, new and used furniture, jewelry and silver, new merchandise, porcelain, poultry and fresh produce, seafood, and toys; very little used merchandise. Snacks and hot meals are served on the premises. Annual beauty pageant. There is also an outdoor street fair and farmers' market four times a year—call for dates.

VENDORS: $320 per 10'x10' space for a four-week block (all three days). Reserve a week in advance.

Contact Robyn Gordon, 1600 East Holt Boulevard, Pomona, CA 91766. Tel: (909) 620-4792 or (909) 620-5083 (office hours are Friday, Saturday, and Sunday, 10 A.M. to 6 P.M., and Thursday, 9 A.M. to noon).

Porterville
Porterville College Swap Meet

At 100 East College Avenue.

Every Saturday, 6 A.M. to 3 P.M.

Admission 50 cents per person; free parking for up to 450 cars. In operation since 1981; outdoors, year-round. Averages close to 275 vendors (capacity 400).

Antiques and collectibles, books, new and vintage clothing, cookware, crafts and fine art, new and used furniture, jewelry and silver, new and used merchandise, porcelain, fresh produce, seafood, and toys. Snacks and hot meals are served on the premises.

VENDORS: $10 per space per day. Reserve three days in advance.

Contact Bill Goucher, 100 East College Avenue, Porterville, CA 93257. Tel: (209) 781-3130, extension 254.

Sacramento
Auction City Flea Market

At 8521 Folsom Boulevard, about eight-tenths of a mile west of Watt Avenue, between Howe Avenue and Watt Avenue, directly off Highway 50.

Every weekend, 7 A.M. to 5 P.M.

Free admission; acres of free parking. In operation for over 27 years; indoors and outdoors, rain or shine. Averages up to several hundred vendors.

Antiques and collectibles, books, new and vintage clothing, coins and stamps, cookware, crafts and fine art, new and used furniture, new and used merchandise, porcelain, eggs and fresh produce, and toys. Snacks and hot meals are served on the premises.

VENDORS: $20 for one table, $30 for two (limit two tables per vendor); one car allowed per setup; dealers are required to obtain a city license. Reservations should be made during office hours (Wednesday and Friday, 9 A.M. to 5 P.M.).

Contact Manager, 8521 Folsom Boulevard, Sacramento, CA 95826. Tel: (916) 383-0880 or (916) 383-0950.

Salinas
Salinas Flea Market

At 925 North Sanborn Road, at the Skyview Drive-In Theater.

Every weekend, 7 A.M. to 3 P.M.

Free admission; free parking for up to 700 cars. In operation for over 18 years; outdoors, rain or shine. Averages 100 to a capacity of 200 vendors.

Antiques and collectibles, books, new and vintage clothing, coins and stamps, cookware, crafts and fine art, fish, new and used furniture, jewelry and silver, fresh produce, and toys. Snacks and hot meals are served on the premises.

VENDORS: Inquire for rates. Reserve a week in advance.

Contact Art Jackson, 925 North Sanborn Road, Salinas, CA 93905. Tel: (408) 758-6792 or (408) 424-1477 (snack bar at the drive-in).

San Bernardino
San Bernardino Swap Meet

At the National Orange Showgrounds in San Bernardino.

Every Sunday, 6 A.M. to 3 P.M.

Admission $1; free admission for children under 12; ample free parking. In operation for over 37 years; outdoors, rain or shine. Averages up to 800 vendors ("endless" capacity).

Garage-sale items, some antiques and collectibles, new merchandise, fresh produce, new and used furniture, new and vintage clothing. Hot meals are available on the premises. Promoters call it the largest weekly outdoor flea market in San Bernardino County and "a fantastic place for the average guy to clean out the garage and make a few bucks."

VENDORS: From $8 to $40 per space per day. Reservations are recommended.

Contact R.G. Canning Attractions, P.O. Box 400, Maywood, CA 90270-0400. Tel: (213) 560-SHOW.

San Diego

Kobey's Swap Meet at the Sports Arena

At 3500 Sports Arena Boulevard, between I-5 and I-8, in the Sports Arena parking lot. Take Rosencrans exit off I-5 and I-8, then turn right onto Sports Arena Boulevard, and market will be on the right.

Every Thursday through Sunday and most holidays, 7 A.M. to 3 P.M.

Admission $1 per person; 75 cents for senior citizens; free admission for children under 12 and handicapped persons; free parking for more than 2,500 cars. In operation since 1980; outdoors, rain or shine. Averages up to 800 or more vendors (capacity 1,000).

Antiques and collectibles, books, new and vintage clothing, cookware, crafts and fine art, coins and stamps, flowers, new and used furniture, jewelry and silver, new merchandise, records and tapes, toys, computer equipment, and fresh produce. Snacks and hot meals are served on the premises. San Diego County's largest open-air market, boasting 30,000 to 40,000 shoppers weekly.

VENDORS: $25 and up per day on Saturday or Sunday, $6 to $12 on Thursday, $8 to $16 on Friday for reserved spaces; $20 unreserved (day of market). Reservations are not required.

Contact Chris Haesloop, General Manager, P.O. Box 81492, San Diego, CA 92138. Tel: (619) 226-0650 or (619) 523-2700. Day of market, call (619) 692-1581.

San Jose

Capitol Flea Market (aka San Jose's Old Fashioned Capitol Flea Market)

On Capitol Expressway and Monterey Highway. Take Route 101 to Capitol Expressway exit west, and the market is four stoplights up on the right side.

Every Thursday, Saturday, and Sunday, 6 A.M. to 5:30 P.M.

Admission 50 cents per person on Thursday, $1 on Saturday or Sunday; free admission for children under 12; acres of free parking. In operation for over 15 years; outdoors, rain or shine. Averages close to 1,000 vendors year-round.

Antiques and collectibles, books, new and vintage clothing, coins and stamps, cookware, crafts and fine art, new and used furniture, jewelry and silver, livestock, new and used merchandise, porcelain, poultry and fresh produce, seafood, and toys. Snacks and hot meals are served on the premises. Live music every Saturday and Sunday. "World's largest garage sale" includes a huge farmer's market. Used car and truck sale every Saturday and Sunday.

VENDORS: $12 per 20'x20' space on Thursday, $15 on Saturday, $20 on Sunday. Reservations are not required.

Contact Jason Garner, 3630 Hillcap Avenue, San Jose, CA 95136. Tel: (408) 225-5800.

San Jose

The Flea Market

At 1590 Barryessa Road, between Highways 680 and 101. From Route 680, take west exit onto Berryessa Road; from Route 101, take 13th Street exit west to Hedding, then left onto Hedding (which becomes Berryessa after crossing over Route 101), and follow signs.

Every Wednesday through Sunday, 7 A.M. to 6 P.M.

Free admission; parking for more than 10,000 cars at $1 per car Wednesday through Fridays, and $3 on weekends. In operation since 1960; outdoors, rain or shine. Averages 2,000 to a capacity of 2,300 vendors on 120 paved acres of selling area.

Collectibles, books, new and vintage clothing (including discount fashions and children's apparel), cookware, crafts and fine art, flowers, new and used furniture, paintings, plants, pottery, quarter-mile-long "Produce Row," tools ("from bonsai pruning shears to power miters"), toys, T-shirts, and all manner of new and used merchandise. More than 25 snack bars and restaurants plus more than 60 roving snack and beverage carts. All sorts of visitor attractions including an old-fashioned carousel, two arcades, "California's largest" farmers' market, playground pony rides for kids, and more. Some call this the largest flea market in the United States; the promoter claims 80,000 visitors attend each weekend—more than four million visitors annually. Wednesday's the day for the best bargains; and compared with the weekend madness, Thursday and Friday offer the calmer pace of a neighborhood swap meet.

VENDORS: $15 per 17'x20' space on Wednesday, $5 per day on Thursday or Friday, $25 per day on Saturday or Sunday (first Saturday of each month is only $10); call for weekly and monthly rates. Reservations are not required.

Contact Patrick Detar, Manager, 1590 Berryessa Road, San Jose, CA 95133. Tel: (408) 453-1110.

San Juan Bautista

San Juan Bautista Antique Flea Market/Peddler's Fair

In the center of historic downtown San Juan Bautista, two miles off Highway 101 (30 miles south of San Jose).

Twice annually, on the first Sunday in June and the first Sunday in August, 8 A.M. to 5 P.M.

Admission $1 per person (donation); free parking. August event has been going since 1964, the June event since 1990; outdoors, weather permitting. Averages up to a capacity of 400 vendors on the August date, and approximately 250 vendors in June.

Antiques and collectibles, books, new and vintage clothing, crafts, used furniture, jewelry and silver, new and used merchandise, and toys. Snacks and hot meals are served on the premises. Managed by the local chamber of commerce. June event draws as many as 35,000 shoppers, and the August event draws about 10,000.

VENDORS: $30 per 10'x12' space for the June event and $150 per 10'x14' space for the August event. Reserve in February for the June event and in April for the August event.

Contact Lisa McShane, c/o Chamber of Commerce, P.O. Box 1037, San Juan Bautista, CA 95045-1037. Tel: (408) 623-2454 or (408) 623-0674.

Santa Clarita
Saugus Swap Meet

At 22500 Soledad Canyon Road. From Los Angeles, take I-5 northbound to Valencia Blvd., then go east on Valencia three miles, and market will be on right side.

Every Sunday, 7 A.M. to 3 P.M.

Admission $1 per person; free admission for children under 12; free parking for up to 7,000 cars. In operation since the 1960s; outdoors, rain or shine. Averages 700 to a capacity of more than 900 vendors.

Antiques and collectibles, cookware and crafts, new and vintage clothing, electronics, new and used furniture, household and decorative items, jewelry and silver, pottery and porcelain, fresh produce, auto accessories, lamps, and shoes. Snacks and hot meals are served on the premises. Average Sunday attendance is estimated at 18,000 customers. Among the largest weekly swap meets in Southern California.

VENDORS: From $20 to $45 per 16'x20' space per day, depending on location; one vehicle per space; vendors must bring their own display equipment. Reservations are not required.

Contact Mr. Ray Wilkings, 22500 Soledad Canyon Road,

Santa Clarita, CA 91350. Tel: (805) 259-3886 or (805) 716-6010; office hours are 8 A.M. to 3 P.M., Sunday through Friday.

Santa Fe Springs
Santa Fe Springs Swap Meet

At 13963 Alondra Blvd. Take Santa Ana Freeway (Route 5) south of Los Angeles approximately 25 miles; Valleyview Blvd. exit, north on Valleyview to Alondra Blvd., west on Alondra.

Every Wednesday, Thursday, Saturday, and Sunday, 7 A.M. to 3:30 P.M.; every Friday night from May through October, 5 P.M. to 10 P.M.

Admission 50 cents on Wednesday; 75 cents on Friday night; 75 cents on Saturday or Sunday; free parking for up to 2,500 cars. In operation for over 33 years; outdoors, rain or shine. Averages 150 to a capacity of 721 vendors (varies according to season and market day).

Baseball cards, books, new clothing, comics, cookware, crafts, fresh produce, silver, and toys. Jewelry, clothing, sports shoes, T-shirts, and sunglasses are sold in "excessive amounts" and thus the number of vendors of such items is restricted, and these items are sold in selected areas of the market. (Sales of socks are restricted on weekends.). Snacks and hot meals are served on the premises.

VENDORS: $10 per 15'x25' space on Wednesday, $25 on Friday night, and from $25 to $30 on Saturday or Sunday; free setup on Thursday. Reservations are not required, but reserved spaces can be substantially cheaper; monthly discount given; cash only.

Contact Rick Landis, 13963 East Alondra, Santa Fe Springs, CA 90670. Tel: (310) 921-4359; reservation office is closed Monday and Tuesday.

Santee
Santee Swap Meet

At 10990 Woodside Avenue North. Take the Riverford exit off Route 67 North, then go left to Woodside.

Every weekend, 6 A.M. to 2 P.M.

Admission 50 cents; free parking. In operation for over nine years; outdoors, rain or shine. Average number of vendors not reported.

Antiques and collectibles, books, new and vintage clothing, cookware, crafts, new and used furniture, jewelry and silver, new merchandise, and toys. Snacks and hot meals are served on the premises.

VENDORS: $8 on Saturday, $10 on Sunday. Reservations are not required.

Contact Mr. Greg Crowder, 635 West Mission Avenue, Escondido, CA 92025. Tel: (619) 449-7927 or (619) 745-3100.

Sebastopol
Midgley's Country Flea Market

At 2200 Gravenstein Highway South. Take I-101 to Route 116 west to Sebastopol, about eight or nine miles, and market will be on the left.

Every weekend, 6:30 A.M. to 4:30 P.M.

Free admission; free parking. In operation for over 21 years; outdoors and under cover, rain or shine. Averages up to several hundred vendors (but in the hundreds).

Household items, plants, antiques and collectibles, fresh produce, and new merchandise. Two snack bars.

VENDORS: From $15 per 4'x8' space including one table; some spaces are covered. Reservations are not required.

Contact Rosalie Midgley, 2200 Gravenstein Highway South, Sebastopol, CA 95472. Tel: (707) 823-7874.

Simi Valley
Simi Valley Swap Meet

At 361 Tierra Rejada Road.

Every Sunday, 7 A.M. to 3 P.M.

Admission $1 per person over 14 years old; free parking for up to 1,100 cars. In operation for over 30 years; outdoors, weather permitting. Averages 310 to 390 vendors (capacity 500).

Antiques and collectibles, books, new clothing, cookware, crafts and fine art, new and used furniture, jewelry and silver, new and used merchandise, porcelain, fresh produce, and toys. Snacks are served on the premises.

VENDORS: $18 per space per day. Reservations are not required.

Contact John Blazej, Manager, P.O. Box 180, Simi Valley, CA 93062-0180. Tel: (805) 526-3483.

South Lake Tahoe
Tahoe Flea Market

At the Elks Lodge, 2094 Highway 50 (at Elks Club Drive), one mile south of the South Lake Tahoe Airport.

Every Sunday from May through October (plus Saturday on Memorial Day, July Fourth, and Labor Day weekends), 8 A.M. to 5 P.M.

Admission 75 cents; free parking for up to 120 cars plus additional street parking. In operation for over 19 years; outdoors, weather permitting. Averages up to 100 vendors (capacity 116).

Antiques and collectibles, books, new and vintage clothing, coins and stamps, cookware, crafts and fine art, new and used furniture, jewelry and silver, new merchandise, pottery and porcelain, fresh produce, and toys. Snacks and hot meals are served on the premises. Indoor bar/lounge.

VENDORS: From $10 per 10'x15' space; tables and umbrellas (for shade) are available at $5 each. Spaces are assigned on a first-come, first-served basis.

Contact Randy Mundt, P.O. Box 10645, South Lake Tahoe, CA 96158. Tel: (916) 541-3967. Day of market, call Randy at the Elks Lodge, (916) 577-2094.

Stanton
Indoor Swap Meet of Stanton

At 10401 Beach Boulevard (at Cerritos), between Route 91 and 22 Freeway, two miles south of Knotts Berry Farm.

Daily except Tuesday: weekdays, 10 A.M. to 7 P.M., and every Saturday and Sunday, 10 A.M. to 6 P.M.

Free admission; free parking for up to 250 cars. In operation for over seven years; indoors, year-round. Averages 70 to 75 vendors (200 indoor spaces).

Antiques and collectibles, books, new clothing, cookware, crafts and fine art, new furniture, jewelry and silver, livestock, new merchandise, porcelain, poultry, and toys (mostly new merchandise). Snacks and hot meals are served on the premises. More than 200 stores and services.

VENDORS: Inquire for monthly rates. Reservations are not required.

Contact John Sakajian, Manager, P.O. Box 187, Stanton, CA 90680. Tel: (714) 527-1234. Day of market, call Avo Dakessian or Jila Ilami at (714) 527-1112.

Torrance
The Roadium Open Air Market

At 2500 Redondo Beach Blvd., between Freeway 405 and the Harbor Freeway; take the Redondo Beach exit off either freeway.

Daily except Thanksgiving Day, Christmas Day, and New

Year's Day: weekdays, 6 A.M. to 4 P.M.; weekends, 6 A.M. to 3 P.M.

Admission 50 cents on Monday, Tuesday, Thursday, and Friday; $1.25 on Wednesday; $1.50 on Saturday and Sunday; free parking for up to 12,000 cars in nearby lot, with shuttle service to market. In operation since 1955; outdoors, rain or shine. Averages close to 480 vendors year-round.

Antiques and collectibles, books, new and vintage clothing, coins and stamps, cookware, crafts and fine art, fish, fresh produce, new and used furniture, jewelry and silver. Snacks and hot meals are served on the premises. The market features new, used, and antique goods Monday through Friday; on weekends the market is devoted to new merchandise; billed as well advertised, and clean.

VENDORS: $16 per 10'x18' space on Monday, Tuesday, Thursday or Friday; $30 on Wednesday; from $22 to $42 on Saturday and from $14 to $42 on Sunday, depending on location; all vendors must have a California resale permit. Reserve a week in advance, in person with cash; no mail or phone reservations are accepted.

Contact General Manager, 2500 West Redondo Beach Blvd., Torrance, CA 90504. Tel: (213) 321-3709; fax: (213) 321-0114.

Tulare

Open Country Flea Mart

At 23090 Road 152. Take Tulare Central exit off Freeway 99, then three and a half miles east to Road 152; market is on the corner.

Every Sunday, 5 A.M. to 3 P.M.

Admission 50 cents; free admission for children; free parking for up to 3,000 cars. In operation for over 18 years; outdoors and under cover, rain or shine. Averages close to 400 vendors.

Antiques and collectibles, new clothing, cookware, jewelry, new merchandise, and fresh produce. Snacks and hot meals are served on the premises; "best Mexican food around."

VENDORS: From $10 per 15'x20' space. Reservations are not required.

Contact Rick Bateman, 23090 RD 152, Tulare, CA 93274. Tel: (209) 686-9588.

Tulare
Tulare County Fairgrounds Swap Meet

At 215 East Alpine Avenue. Take Bardsley exit off Route 99 west to "Ost. N." to gate to flea market.

Every Tuesday, Wednesday, and Friday, 5:30 A.M. to 3 P.M. (except during fair for several days a year in September and March—call for this year's fair dates).

Free admission; unlimited free parking. In operation for over nine years; outdoors, rain or shine. Averages close to 50 vendors year-round (more on Wednesdays, the big day).

Antiques and collectibles, books, new and vintage clothing, cookware, crafts and fine art, new and used furniture, jewelry and silver, livestock, new and used merchandise, pottery and porcelain, poultry and fresh produce, and toys. Snacks are available on the premises.

VENDORS: From $5 per 20'x20' space per day. Reservations are not required.

Contact Clifton Williams, 215 East Martin Luther King, Jr., Avenue, Tulare, CA 93274. Tel: (209) 686-4707.

Ukiah
Ukiah Flea Market

At 1055 North State Street, on the Redwood Empire Fairgrounds. Take Highway 101 north to North State Street exit and then south one half mile.

Every weekend, 7 A.M. to whenever.

Free admission; free parking for up to 2,000 cars. A new market (in operation just over two years); indoors, year-round. Averages 40 to 60 vendors (capacity 75).

Antiques and collectibles, books, vintage clothing, coins and stamps, cookware, crafts, farm equipment, used furniture, jewelry and silver, porcelain, tools, toys, and used merchandise. Hot meals are served on the premises. A country-style market serving the Redwood Empire.

VENDORS: $10 per space per day. Reservations are not required.

Contact Bob Bazzano, 190 Ford Road, Space #118, Ukiah, CA 95482. Tel: (704) 468-4626.

Vacaville
Flea-for-All

At Andrew's Park. Take I-80 to Monte Vista/Nut Tree exit, then left on Monte Vista Avenue, six blocks down, across from Albertson's.

Twice a year in April and October, 9 A.M. to 5 P.M.—call for dates.

Free admission; free parking for up to 200 cars. In operation for over 18 years; outdoors, weather permitting. Averages up to about 130 vendors.

Antiques and collectibles, books, bottles, new and vintage clothing, coins, cookware, crafts, used furniture, jewelry, knives, pottery and porcelain, and birds. Snacks and hot meals are served on the premises by concessions operated by the local chamber of commerce, which sponsors the event.

VENDORS: $35 per 10'x10' space per day; $50 per 20'x20' space. Oversize vehicles are permitted only in the 20'x20' spaces. No water, electricity, or tables are provided for merchants. No food or beverages may be sold at the market. Reservations accepted with advance payment; cancellation fees; spaces are available on a first-come, first-served basis.

Contact Vacaville Chamber of Commerce, 300 Main Street,

Vacaville, CA 95688. Tel: (707) 448-6424; fax: (707) 448-0424.

Vallejo
Napa-Vallejo Flea Market

On Highway 29, halfway between Napa and Vallejo.
Every Sunday, 6 A.M. to 5 P.M.
Free admission; parking for up to 5,000 cars at $2 per car. In operation for over 38 years; indoors and outdoors, rain or shine. Averages 700 to 1,000 vendors (capacity 1,200).

Antiques and collectibles, books, new and vintage clothing, cookware, crafts and fine art, new and used furniture, jewelry, new merchandise, porcelain, fresh produce, seafood, and toys. Snacks are available on the premises. Billed as one of the oldest and best flea markets in California.

VENDORS: $15 per table per day. Reservations are not required.

Contact Harry, Nelson, or Tom Harding, 303 Kelly Road, Vallejo, CA 94590. Tel: (707) 226-8862.

Ventura
101 Swap Meet

At 4826 East Telephone Road. Take 101 Freeway to Telephone Road, and market will be on the right side, at the drive-in.
Every weekend, 6 A.M. to 3 P.M.
Free admission; free parking. In operation for over 30 years; outdoors, weather permitting. Averages 450 to a capacity of 550 vendors.

Collectibles, books, new clothing, cookware, crafts, new and used furniture, jewelry and silver, new and used merchandise, porcelain, fresh produce, seafood, and toys. Snacks and hot meals are served on the premises.

VENDORS: From $15 to $30 per space on Sunday; Saturdays are free for vendor setup. Reservations are not required.

Contact Terry Leach, Manager, 4826 East Telephone Road, Ventura, CA 93003. Tel: (805) 644-5043 or (805) 644-5061.

Ventura
Ventura Flea Market and Swap Meet

At the Ventura County Fairgrounds.

Seven times a year, 9 A.M. to 3 P.M.—call for dates.

Admission $3 per person; ample free parking. In operation for over 17 years; outdoors, rain or shine. Averages up to 800 vendors (capacity 1,200).

A mix of antiques, garage-sale items, and new merchandise (but no fresh produce or knives). Hot meals are available on the premises. Some 10,000 customers pass through the turnstiles daily.

VENDORS: From $20 to $40 per space per day. Reserve three weeks in advance for spaces in better locations.

Contact R. G. Canning Attractions, P.O. Box 400, Maywood, CA 90270-0400. Tel: (213) 560-SHOW.

Victorville
Victorville Swap Meet

At 14800 Seventh Street.

Every weekend, 8 A.M. to 3 P.M.

Admission $1 per person; free parking. In operation for over 13 years; outdoors, weather permitting. Averages close to 350 vendors year-round (capacity 360).

Antiques and collectibles, books, new and vintage clothing, coins and stamps, cookware, crafts, fish, new and used furniture, jewelry and silver, new merchandise, pottery and porcelain, poultry and fresh produce, and toys—"everything." Snacks and hot meals are served on the premises. No food concessions.

VENDORS: From $13 per 18'x20' space on Saturday and $10 on Sunday. Reservations are not required.

Contact Mary Goude, 14800 Seventh Street, Victorville, CA 92392. Tel: (619) 245-0070.

Visalia
Visalia Sales Yard

At 29660 Road 152.

Every Thursday and Sunday, 5 A.M. to whenever.

Free admission; free parking. In operation for over 43 years; outdoors, rain or shine. Averages up to a capacity of 500 vendors.

Antiques and collectibles, books, new clothing, cookware, crafts, new and used furniture, new and used merchandise, poultry and fresh produce, seafood, and toys—"you name it." Snacks and hot meals are served on the premises.

VENDORS: $8 per 10'x10' space per day; $10 reservation fee (spaces generally booked up on Thursday). Reservations are recommended.

Contact Paul Furnas, 29660 Road 152, Visalia, CA 93291. Tel: (209) 734-9092. Day of market, contact Don Brumley.

COLORADO

Fort Collins

Lafayette · Henderson

Northglenn

Englewood

Colorado Springs ·

· Pueblo

Trinidad ·

Colorado Springs
The Flea Market

At 5225 East Platte Avenue (Highway 24), just west of Powers Boulevard. Take Highway 24 east approximately five miles from downtown Colorado Springs.

Every weekend, 7 A.M. to 4 P.M.; flea, farmers', and craft market open every Friday from June through September, 7 A.M. to 2 P.M.

Admission $1 per person; free parking for over 600 cars. In operation for approximately 25 years; outdoors, year-round. Averages 125 to a capacity of over 500 vendors.

Antiques and collectibles, books, new clothing, coins and stamps, cookware, crafts, new and used furniture, jewelry and silver, new and used merchandise, fresh produce, and toys. Snacks and hot meals are served on the premises. All-blacktop vending area where "you'll find everything under the sun."

VENDORS: $13 per 20'x20' space daily for regular spots, $23 for prime spots; electricity is available at $5 per day. Reservations are not required (reserved spaces incur an added $3 charge).

Contact Randy Cloud, Manager, P.O. Box 7229, Colorado Springs, CO 80933. Tel: (719) 380-8599.

Englewood
Arapahoe Flea Market

At 3400 South Platte Drive in the Denver suburb of Englewood, at the Cinderella City Drive-In Theatre.

Every weekend, 6 A.M. to 4 P.M.

Admission $1 per person; free parking for up to 5,000 cars. In operation for over 15 years; outdoors, rain or shine. Averages 100 to 500 vendors (capacity 600).

Antiques and collectibles, books, new and vintage clothing, coins and stamps, cookware, crafts and fine art, new and used furniture, jewelry and silver, new merchandise, pottery and porcelain, fresh produce, toys, and vehicles (including boats, campers, and trailers). Food is not served on the premises. Camping facilities available.

VENDORS: $10 per space per day (plus $1 for city vending license). Reservations are not required.

Contact R. L. Lunders, P.O. Box 41, Englewood, CO 80110. Tel: (303) 789-2710 (weekends only).

Fort Collins
Fort Collins Indoor Flea Market

At 6200 South College Avenue (Route 287), 1.8 miles south of Fort Collins.

Daily, 10 A.M. to 6 P.M.

Free admission; free parking for up to 50 cars. In operation for over 11 years; indoors, year-round. Averages close to 84 vendors year-round.

Antiques and collectibles, used furniture, new merchandise, and jewelry. Food is not available on the premises.

VENDORS: $140 per 10'x10' space per month plus 6 percent commission on sales. Market does not allow transient vendors; waiting list for long-term vendors.

Contact Bob Stephens or Vince Barnhart, 6200 South College Avenue, Fort Collins, CO 80525. Tel: (303) 223-6502.

Henderson
Mile High Flea Market

At 7007 East 88th Avenue, at the junction with I-76, just north of Denver.

Every Wednesday, Saturday, and Sunday, 7 A.M. to 5 P.M.

Admission $1 per person on Wednesday, $2 on Saturday or Sunday; free admission for children under 12; free parking for up to 5,000 cars; indoors year-round, and outdoors, weather permitting. Averages 1,000 to 1,800 vendors (capacity 2,000) on 80 paved acres of selling space.

Antiques and collectibles, books, new and vintage clothing, coins and stamps, cookware, crafts and fine art, new and used furniture, jewelry and silver, new and used merchandise, porcelain, fresh produce, seafood, and toys. Snacks and hot meals are served on the premises. Attracts over 40,000 buyers per weekend.

VENDORS: $10 per space on Wednesday, $17 per space on Saturday or Sunday. Reservations are not required.

Contact Andrew L. Hermes, Owner/General Manager, or Chris Jackson, Operations Director, 7007 East 88th Avenue, Henderson, CO 80640. Tel: (303) 289-4656; fax: (303) 286-1922.

Lafayette
Lafayette Indoor Flea Market

At 130 East Spaulding. From Highway 287, turn east onto Spaulding, and the market is on that corner just behind the Conoco gas station. Close to Denver and Boulder.

Daily, 10 A.M. to 6 P.M.

Free admission; free parking for up to 95 cars. In operation for over five years; indoors, rain or shine. Averages close to 115 vendors.

Full spectrum of antiques and collectibles, new and used goods, jewelry and silver, crafts, fine art, and "remote-control hobbies." Snacks are served on the premises. Formerly called the Boulder Valley Indoor Flea Market.

VENDORS: Monthly rentals only: $1.35 per square foot plus 10 percent commission on sales. Reservations are not required.

Contact Bill Hopkins, 130 East Spaulding, Lafayette, CO 80026. Tel: (303) 665-0433.

Northglenn
Collectors' Corner

At 10615 Melody Drive in Northglenn (in the greater Denver area).

Daily, 10 A.M. to 6 P.M. (Sunday, noon to 6 P.M.).

Free admission; ample free parking. In operation for over four years; indoors, year-round. Averages 70 to a capacity of 100 vendors.

Antiques and collectibles, new and used furniture, primitives, and breweriana. Food is not available on the premises.

VENDORS: $120 per 8'x10' space per month. Reservations are not required.

Contact Gene or Pat Corwin, 10615 Melody Drive, Northglenn, CO 80234. Tel: (303) 450-2875.

Pueblo
Sunset Swap Meet

On the Colorado State Fairgrounds, at 2641 I-25 North (use Exit 104).

Every Friday, Saturday, and Sunday, 7 A.M. to 5 P.M.

Free admission; free parking for up to 3,000 cars. In operation for over 14 years; indoors and outdoors, rain or shine. Averages 110 to 190 vendors (capacity 200 in summer).

Antiques and collectibles, books, new clothing, cookware, crafts, used furniture, jewelry and silver, new and used merchandise, fresh produce, and toys. Snacks and hot meals are served on the premises. Advertised statewide as southern Colorado's largest swap meet.

VENDORS: $12 per space per day (plus $2 if space is reserved). Reservations are not required.

Contact Mr. John Musso, 1400 Sante Fe Drive, Pueblo, CO 81006. Tel: (719) 584-2000 or (800) 647-8368; fax: (719) 546-2269.

Trinidad
Penny Lane Flea Market

I-25 at Exit 11, across the freeway from the Holiday Inn.

Every weekend, from Memorial Day through Labor Day, 8 A.M. to dark.

Free admission; free parking for up to 100 cars. In operation for over eight years; outdoors, weather permitting. Averages 15 to a capacity of 40 vendors.

Antiques and collectibles, books, used furniture, household items, jewelry, new and used merchandise, fresh produce in season, and toys. Food is not served on the premises.

VENDORS: From $8 to $10 per space per weekend (prices the same for Saturday only). Reservations are not required.

Contact Lisa or Lane Baker, 9850 Santa Fe Trail, Trinidad, CO 81082. Tel: (719) 846-3143.

CONNECTICUT

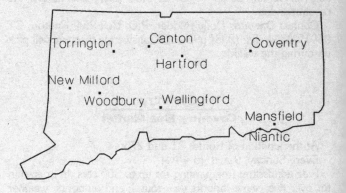

Torrington

Canton

Coventry

Hartford

New Milford

Woodbury

Wallingford

Mansfield

Niantic

Canton
The Cob-Web

At the junction of Routes 44 and 202, near Route 179.

Every Sunday from May through October, 9 A.M. to whenever.

Free admission; free parking. In operation for over 29 years; outdoors, weather permitting. Averages up to 60 vendors.

Antiques and collectibles, books, new clothing, crafts, new and used furniture, jewelry and silver, new merchandise, and toys. Lunch cart with burgers, hot dogs, chili, and nachos. Camping, motels, and restaurants nearby. "Clean and green." Indoor shop on the grounds.

VENDORS: $18 per 20'x20' space per day or $30 prepaid for two days; tables, chairs, umbrellas, and tents are also available for rental. Setup begins at 7:30 A.M. Reservations are recommended.

Contact Dawn or Dolly Rudder, P.O. Box 954, Canton, CT 06019-0354. Tel: (203) 693-2658 (answering machine will pick up during the week).

Coventry
Coventry Flea Market

At the junction of Routes 31 and 275.

Every Sunday, 9 A.M. to 4 P.M.

Free admission; free parking for up to 300 cars. In operation for over five years; indoors year-round, and outdoors, weather permitting. Averages close to its capacity of 70 vendors.

Antiques and collectibles, books, coins, vintage clothing, cookware, crafts, dolls, used furniture, glassware, jewelry and silver, toys, used merchandise. Full snack bar on the premises.

VENDORS: From $10 per day for a 5'x10' space. Reserve two days in advance.

Contact Joe Fowler, 110 Wall Street, Coventry, CT 06238. Tel: (203) 742-1993.

Hartford

Flea and Swap Market at Hartford Jai-Alai

At 89 Weston Street. Take Exit 33 (Jennings Road) off I-19.

Every weekend plus holiday Mondays, 9 A.M. to 4 P.M.

Free admission; free parking for up to 800 cars. In operation since May 1995; outdoors, weather permitting. Averages 125 to a capacity of 250 vendors.

Antiques and collectibles, new and vintage clothing, crafts, used furniture, jewelry and silver, new and used merchandise, fresh produce, tools, and toys. Food concessions and Italian deli.

VENDORS: $15 per space per day; ask about monthly rates. Reservations are recommended.

Contact Darlene O'Keeffe or Bill Sabra, 42 Ohio Avenue, Long Beach, NY 11561. Tel: (203) 727-4000.

Mansfield

Eastern Connecticut Flea Market

At 228 Stafford Road, at the Mansfield Drive-In Theatre, at the intersection of Routes 31 and 32.

Every Sunday from early spring through Thanksgiving, 9 A.M. to 3 P.M.

Free admission; parking for more than 1,000 cars at 50 cents per car. In operation for over 20 years; outdoors, weather permitting. Averages up to 200 vendors (capacity 225).

Antiques and collectibles, books, new and vintage clothing, coins and stamps, cookware, crafts, used furniture, jewelry and silver, new and used merchandise, porcelain, fresh produce, tools—"bargains galore!" Snacks and hot meals are served on the premises.

VENDORS: $20 per space per day. Reservations are not required.

Contact Michael R. Jungden, 228 Stafford Road, Mansfield, CT 06250. Tel: (203) 456-2578.

New Milford
Elephant Trunk Flea Market

At 490 Danbury Road (Route 7). Take Exit 7 (Route 7 North) off I-84, and turn right at the end of the long exit ramp onto Route 7 North and follow five miles; the market will be on the left.

Every Sunday from mid-March through the Sunday before Christmas, 6 A.M. to 3:30 P.M.

Free admission; free parking for up to 1,200 cars. In operation for over 18 years; outdoors, weather permitting. Averages 100 to 300 vendors (capacity 475).

Antiques and collectibles, books, new and vintage clothing, coins and stamps, cookware, crafts and fine art, electronics, new and used furniture, jewelry and silver, new and used merchandise, plants, porcelain, fresh produce, and toys. Eight food vendors on the premises.

VENDORS: $25 per 20'x20' space per day. Reservations are not required.

Contact Gregory H. Baecker, 23 Deerwood Lane, Woodbury, CT 06798. Tel: (203) 355-1448.

Niantic
Between the Bridges: A Flea Market

At 65 Pennsylvania Avenue. Take Exit 74 off I-95, then turn right and go three miles and market will be on the left, two blocks from the beach.

Daily except weekends, 10 A.M. to 5 P.M.

Free admission; ample free parking. In operation since 1992; indoors, year-round. Averages up to a capacity of 60 vendors.

Antiques and collectibles, and used furniture. Snacks and hot meals are served on the premises.

VENDORS: $45 per five-day week. Reservations are not required.

Contact Diane or John Deer, 65 Pennsylvania Avenue, Niantic, CT 06357. Tel: (203) 691-0170.

Torrington
Wright's Barn

Off Route 4 (on Wright Road), between Torrington and Goshen. Take Exit 44 off Route 8 to Route 4, look for easy-to-find large signs.

Every weekend, 10 A.M. to 4:30 P.M.

Free admission; ample free parking. In operation for over 15 years; indoors, year-round. Averages 25 to 35 vendors on two floors of selling space.

Antiques and collectibles, books, cookware, crafts and fine art, used and antique furniture, jewelry and silver, glassware, household items, porcelain, postcards, old prints and paintings, old tools, and toys. There's a snack bar on the first floor. A pleasant New England market with something for everyone—"all kinds of treasures from Grandma's attic and Grampa's out-back barn."

VENDORS: $20 per 10'x12' space per weekend. Reservations are recommended.

Contact Millie Wright, Manager, Wright Road, Torrington, CT 06790. Tel: (203) 482-0095.

Limited

Wallingford
Redwood Country Flea Market

At 170 Hartford Turnpike. Take exit 13 off I-91 or exit 64 off Wilbur Cross Parkway.

Every weekend plus Good Friday, Memorial Day, July Fourth, and Labor Day, 8 A.M. to 4 P.M.

Free admission; free parking for 300 cars. In operation for over 23 years; outdoors year-round, weather permitting. Averages 75 to 85 vendors.

Antiques and collectibles such as baseball cards, books, bottles, new clothing, coins, comics, new furniture, jewelry, knives, fresh produce, and toys. Restaurant on premises. This one's crowded on both days.

VENDORS: Inquire for daily rates. Reservations are not required.

Contact Ken Dubar, Steven Hugo, or Mark Hugo, 12 Docker Drive, Wallingford, CT 06492. Tel: (203) 269-5497 or (203) 269-3500.

Woodbury
Woodbury Antiques and Flea Market

On Main Street South (Route 6). Take Exit 15 off I-84 onto Route 6 and travel three and a half miles straight into Woodbury, and the market will be on the right.

Every Saturday, 7 A.M. to 3 P.M.

Free admission; free parking. In operation for over 28 years; outdoors year-round, weather permitting. Averages 100 to a capacity of 150 vendors.

A vast and ever-changing selection of antiques and collectibles, books, china, new and vintage clothing, coins and stamps, new and used furniture, glassware, jewelry and silver, memorabilia, a wide array of new merchandise. Food vendors on the field offer hot dogs and burgers, grinders, fried dough, and ice cream. Widely promoted, with a strong presence of buyers and sellers;

rated the state's best Saturday market by *Connecticut Magazine*.

VENDORS: $30 per 20'x20' space per day. Reservations are recommended (but not required).

Contact Diane or Don Heavens, P.O. Box 184, Woodbury, CT 06798. Tel: (203) 263-2841.

DELAWARE

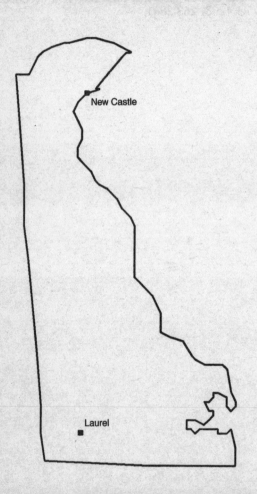

New Castle

Laurel

Laurel
Bargain Bill's Flea Market

At junction of Dual 13 and Route 9, in western Delaware, 14 miles north of Salisbury, Maryland, in the center of Delaware's eastern shore.

Every Friday, 8 A.M. to 4 P.M., and every Saturday and Sunday, 6 A.M. to 5 P.M.

Free admission; free parking. In operation since 1978; indoors year-round, and outdoors, weather permitting. Averages 200 to 400 vendors (capacity 600 tables outdoors).

Antiques and collectibles, books, new and vintage clothing, coins and stamps, crafts and fine art, new and used furniture, jewelry and silver, new and used merchandise, porcelain, fresh produce, seafood, and toys. Snacks and hot meals are served on the premises. Overnight camping, showers for indoor vendors. "Shore's Largest."

VENDORS: Indoors: $18.75 per 8'x10' space per day; outdoors: $10 for two tables per day. Reservations are not required.

Contact Leslie or Bill Brown, R.D. #4, Box 547, Laurel, DE 19956. Tel: (302) 875-9958 or (302) 875-2478.

New Castle
New Castle Farmers' Market

At the intersection of Routes 13 and 273, within 10 miles of the Maryland and Pennsylvania borders and 5 miles of the New Jersey border. Take Exit 5A off I-95 and follow signposts to Route 13 South.

Every Friday and Saturday, 10 A.M. to 10 P.M.; Sunday, 10 A.M. to 6 P.M.

Free admission; ample free parking. In operation for over 40 years; indoors and outdoors, rain or shine. Averages up to 150 outdoor vendors plus 60 indoor vendors.

Antiques and collectibles, fresh baked goods, vintage clothing, cookware, crafts and fine art, and jewelry (used items only in the flea market); fish, flowers, poultry, and fresh produce at the farmers' market; new merchandise in the indoor market. Food is available on premises. No sales tax. Pennsylvania Dutch merchants; an exceptionally clean market.

VENDORS: Outdoors: $12 per 20'x20' space on Friday, $16 on Saturday and Sunday (includes room for vehicle); indoors: monthly leases only—inquire for rates. Reservations are not required for outdoor spaces.

Contact Manager, Route 13 and Hares Corner, New Castle, DE 19720. Tel: (302) 328-4102.

DISTRICT OF COLUMBIA

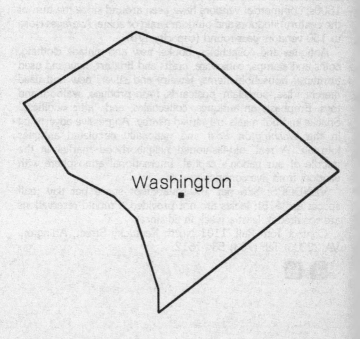

Washington

Washington, D.C.
Flea Market at Eastern Market

Along Seventh Street, S.E. (one block from Pennsylvania Avenue on Capitol Hill). Use the Eastern Market stop on the Orange or Blue subway line.

Every Sunday from March through Christmas (except the first Sunday in May), 10 A.M. to 5 P.M. (vendors may set up as early as 8:30 A.M.).

Free admission; street parking. In operation since 1984 under current management (Eastern Market was originally built in 1873, and the farmers' market has been going on since the early 1800s; commercial vendors have been around since the turn of the century); indoors and outdoors, rain or shine. Averages close to 150 vendors year-round (capacity 175).

Antiques and collectibles, books, new and vintage clothing, coins and stamps, cookware, crafts and fine art, new and used furniture, household items, jewelry and silver, new and used merchandise, porcelain, postcards, fresh produce, seafood, and toys. Emphasis on antiques, collectibles, and "attic oddities." Snacks and hot meals are served nearby. Aggressive advertising in the *Washington Post* and nationally circulated antiques journals. A real, old-fashioned neighborhood market in the middle of our nation's capital. International atmosphere with vendors from five continents.

VENDORS: $25 per 100-square-foot space per day (half spaces are $15); tables are not provided. Prepaid reservations are required at least a week in advance.

Contact Tom Rall, 1101 North Kentucky Street, Arlington, VA 22205. Tel: (703) 534-7612.

Washington, D.C.
Georgetown Flea Market

Located in the parking facility of Rosario Education Center, on Wisconsin Avenue between S and T Streets N.W. (school's official address is 1819 35th Street, N.W.), across from the Georgetown Safeway supermarket.

Every Sunday from March through mid-December, 9 A.M. to 5 P.M.; vendor setup begins at 6 A.M.

Free admission; parking nearby. In operation since 1973; outdoors, weather permitting. Averages close to 100 or more vendors.

Antiques and collectibles of all descriptions, baseball cards, knickknacks, used stuff ripe for recycling—just about anything goes. One food vendor on the premises.

VENDORS: $10 per 10'x4' space (small—no parking—drop off and load only); $20 per single space; $30 per double space or a single space on Furniture Row. Reservations are recommended—there's often a waiting list.

Contact Michael Sussman, 2109 M Street, N.W., Washington, D.C. 20037. Tel: (202) 223-0289 (recording) or (202) 296-4989 (office).

FLORIDA

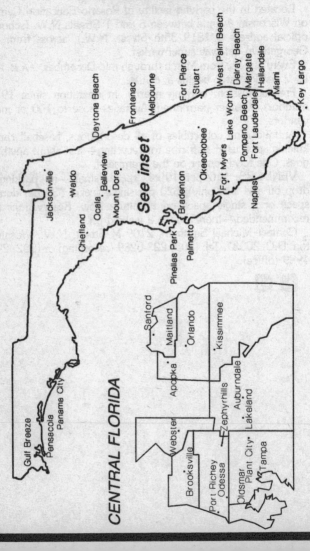

CENTRAL FLORIDA

See inset

Gulf Breeze
Pensacola
Panama City

Jacksonville
Chiefland
Waldo
Ocala
Belleview
Mount Dora
Pinellas Park
Palmetto
Bradenton

Daytona Beach
Frontenac
Melbourne
Fort Pierce
Stuart
West Palm Beach
Lake Worth
Delray Beach
Pompano Beach
Margate
Fort Lauderdale
Hallandale
Miami
Key Largo

Okeechobee
Fort Myers
Naples

Sanford
Maitland
Apopka
Orlando
Kissimmee

Webster
Brooksville
Port Richey
Odessa
Zephyrhills
Auburndale
Lakeland
Oldsmar
Plant City
Tampa

Apopka
Three Star Flea Market

At 2390 South Orange Blossom Trail (Highway 441).
Every weekend, dawn to dusk.

Free admission; ample free parking. In operation for over 22 years; outdoors, rain or shine. Averages up to a capacity of 60 vendors.

Antiques and collectibles, books, new and vintage clothing, coins and stamps, cookware, crafts and fine art, used furniture, jewelry and silver, new merchandise, porcelain, fresh produce, and other miscellaneous items. Snacks and hot meals are served on the premises. Features a lot of garage-sale items.

VENDORS: $10 per space per day includes tables (and clothes rack if needed). Reserve a week in advance.

Contact Mary C. Markson, Owner, 2390 South Orange Blossom Trail, Apopka, FL 32703-1870. Tel: (407) 293-2722.

Auburndale
International Market World

At 1052 Highway 92 West, east of Lakeland (approximately one hour from both Orlando and Tampa).
Every Friday, Saturday, and Sunday, 8 A.M. to 5 P.M.

Free admission; 30 acres of free parking. In operation for over thirteen years; indoors and outdoors, rain or shine. Averages 800 to a capacity of 1,000 vendors.

Antiques and collectibles, books, new clothing, coins and stamps, cookware, crafts and fine art, new and used furniture, jewelry and silver, livestock, new and used merchandise, porcelain, poultry and fresh produce, seafood, toys, and "virtually any kind of item." Snacks and hot meals are served on the premises. Karaoke on Saturday and Sunday; special events. One of Florida's largest markets. Near the world-famous Cypress Gardens.

VENDORS: $7 per space on Friday, $14 on Saturday or Sunday, or $35 per three-day weekend, or $140 per month. Reservations are not required.

Contact Manager, 1052 Highway 92 West, Auburndale, FL 33823. Tel: (813) 665-0062.

Belleview
The Market of Marion

At 12888 Southeast U.S. Highway 441, three miles south of Belleview and 13 miles south of Ocala, in Marion County.

Every weekend (plus every Friday from October through April), 8 A.M. to 4 P.M.

Free admission; free parking for more than 6,000 cars. In operation for over seven years; indoors year-round, and outdoors, weather permitting. Averages 275 to 450 vendors (capacity more than 500).

Antiques and collectibles, books, new clothing, cookware, crafts, new furniture, jewelry and silver, new and used merchandise, porcelain, fresh produce, and toys. Snacks and hot meals are served on the premises. Marion Nature Park is nearby, with exotic and domestic animals.

VENDORS: May through October: $13 per space per day under cover, $5 outdoors; November through April: $15 per space under cover or $7 outdoors, except $4 to $7 on Fridays depending on location. Reservations are recommended.

Contact Steven Shaddix, Owner, or Kathy Shaddix, Manager, 12888 Southeast U.S. Highway 441, Belleview, FL 34420. Tel: (904) 245-6766.

Bradenton
Red Barn Flea Market

At 1707 First Street East (U.S. Route 41). Take Exit 42 off I-75 onto State Route 64 to U.S. Route 41, then go left and market will be about a mile down the road on the left.

Every Wednesday, Saturday, and Sunday, 8 A.M. to 4 P.M. Plaza area is open daily except Monday.

Free admission; free parking for up to 1,475 cars. In operation for over 15 years; indoors, outdoors, and under cover, year-round. Averages 450 vendors in summer to a capacity of more than 650 in winter.

Antiques and collectibles, books, new clothing, coins and stamps, cookware, crafts and fine art, new and used furniture, jewelry and silver, new and used merchandise, porcelain, toys, fresh produce, and seafood. Snacks and hot meals are served on the premises. Other services include a bike shop, hair salon, stereo store, tackle shop, travel agency, tropical fish store, etc. This large and diverse market publishes its own 16-page "where to find it" guide; in addition to the flea market there is a retail plaza with about twenty stores.

VENDORS: $18 per space per day outdoors or under cover; $25 per day indoors. Reservations are not required.

Contact Lois Ploegstra, Manager, 1707 First Street East, Bradenton, FL 34208. Tel: (800) 274-FLEA or (813) 747-3794; fax (813) 747-5583.

Bradenton
Roma Flea Market

At 5715 15th Street East (old Highway 301). Take I-75 to State Road 70 and go west to Old 301 Blvd., then turn left and head south to 57th Avenue East, first traffic light.

Every weekend, 8 A.M. to 4:30 P.M.

Free admission; free parking. In operation for over 23 years;

indoors and outdoors, weather permitting. Averages 20 to 75 vendors (capacity about 100).

Books, vintage clothing, cookware, electronics, used furniture, jewelry, fresh produce, some new but mostly used merchandise such as TVs, radios, stereo equipment, and guns—a large variety of things. An old-fashioned flea market.

VENDORS: $6.42 per 10'x10' space. Reservations are recommended.

Contact Manager, 5715 15th Street East, Bradenton, FL 34203-6847. Tel: (813) 756-9036.

Brooksville
Airport Mart Flea Market

At 17375 Spring Hill Drive.

Every weekend, 8 A.M. to 3 P.M.

Free admission; ample free parking. In operation since May 1978; indoors and outdoors, rain or shine. Averages up to 300 vendors (capacity 450 including 300 outdoors under cover).

Antiques and collectibles, books, new and vintage clothing, coins and stamps, cookware, crafts and fine art, new and used furniture, jewelry and silver, new and used merchandise, porcelain, fresh produce, seafood, and toys. Hot meals are served on the premises.

VENDORS: From $5 to $10 per outdoor space on Saturday, $18.50 per weekend, or $60 per month; or $85 per 8'x12' space indoors including electricity. Reserve a week in advance.

Contact Scott or Jennifer Barker, 17375 Springhill Drive, Brooksville, FL 34609. Tel: (904) 796-0268.

Chiefland
McCormack Flea Market

On Highway 19 North (across from the Best Western motel). Every Friday, Saturday, and Sunday, 7:30 A.M. to 4 P.M.

Free admission; free parking for up to 350 cars. In operation for over ten years; indoors, year-round. Averages 250 to a capacity of 350 vendors.

Antiques and collectibles, books, new clothing, cookware, crafts, fish, used furniture, jewelry, new merchandise, pottery and porcelain, fresh produce, and toys. Restaurant and three snack bars on the premises. RV park next door. Full hookups available at $12 per day, $60 per week, $165 per month; tent sites are $7.50 per day.

VENDORS: $6 per space per day on Friday, $10 on Saturday, $8 on Sunday, or $22.50 for the three days (slighter higher rates apply October through December). RV hookups for vendors at booth sites available at $10 per night, $50 per week, or $150 per month. Reserve two weeks in advance in wintertime only.

Contact Jack McCormack or Lora Boice, P.O. Box 1970, Chiefland, FL 32626. Tel: (904) 493-1493.

Daytona Beach
Daytona Flea and Farmers' Market

On I-95 and U.S. Highway 92, one mile west of the Speedway.

Every Friday, Saturday, and Sunday, 8 A.M. to 5 P.M.

Free admission; plenty of free parking. In operation for over 14 years; indoors and outdoors, rain or shine. Averages 600 to 1,000 vendors in 1,000 covered booths plus over 150 outdoor spaces.

Antiques and collectibles, fresh produce (huge farmers' market), and much more. Food is served at snack bars and at the Hop-a-longs, Harley's, and Fleamingo Restaurants on the premises. Air-conditioned antiques mall. Over two million visitors annually, shopping on 40 acres of selling space.

VENDORS: From $8 per 8'x10' space on Friday, $15 on Saturday or Sunday, includes room for vehicle; inquire for monthly rates. Reservations are recommended.

Contact Robin Ruenheck, P.O. Drawer 2140, Daytona Beach, FL 32115. Tel: (904) 253-3330; fax: (904) 253-2347.

Delray Beach
Delray Indoor Flea Market

At 5283 West Atlantic Avenue. Take Exit 42 (Atlantic Avenue exit) off I-95 and go west three miles, or take the Delray Beach exit off the Florida Turnpike and go east two miles.

Every Thursday through Sunday (plus every Wednesday from November through April), 9 A.M. to 5 P.M.

Free admission; free parking for over 2,000 cars. In operation for over five years; indoors, year-round. Averages close to 180 vendors year-round.

New merchandise only: clothing, cookware, crafts and fine art, household items, jewelry and silver, toys; discount merchandise such as designer eyewear, handbags, perfume, and watches. Food is not served on the premises. Calls itself a flea market though there is no used, collectible, or antique merchandise, nor are accommodations made for transient vendors; specializes in name-brand merchandise at discount prices.

VENDORS: Year leases only. New products and services get priority. No transient vendors.

Contact Edina or David Frankel, 5283 West Atlantic Avenue, Delray Beach, FL 33484. Tel: (407) 499-9935.

Fort Lauderdale
Oakland Park Boulevard Flea Market

At 3161 West Oakland Park Boulevard, one and a half miles west of I-95 (West Oakland Park Boulevard exit).

Every Wednesday and Sunday, 10 A.M. to 7 P.M., and every Thursday, Friday, and Saturday, 10 A.M. to 9 P.M.

Free admission; free parking for up to 700 cars. In operation since 1971; indoors, year-round. Averages close to its capacity of 200 vendors.

A wide array of new merchandise including baseball cards, books, clothing, cookware, crafts and fine art, electronics, furniture, health and beauty aids, jewelry and silver, musical instruments, porcelain, and toys; fresh produce and seafood are also sold,. Snacks and hot meals are served on the premises. Services include chiropractor, insurance agency, auto repair shop, etc. Claims to be Fort Lauderdale's first flea market, with many long-term tenants (but don't look for antiques).

VENDORS: From $600 per month. No transient vendors.

Contact Leonard Bennis, Manager, 3161 West Oakland Park Boulevard, Fort Lauderdale, FL 33311. Tel: (305) 733-4617 or (305) 949-7959.

Fort Lauderdale
The Swap Shop of Fort Lauderdale

At 3501 West Sunrise Boulevard (at 31st Avenue), between I-95 and the Florida Turnpike (at the Thunderbird Drive-In).

Daily, 7 A.M. to 6 P.M.

Free admission; over 50 acres of parking at $1 per car on Saturday and Sunday (Monday through Friday free). In operation for over 25 years; indoors, outdoors, and under cover, rain or shine. Averages 1,500 to 2,000 vendors (capacity 2,500) on 80 acres with an air-conditioned 100,000-square-foot indoor pavilion.

Antiques and collectibles, books, new and vintage clothing,

coins and stamps, cookware, crafts and fine art, electronics, new and used furniture, jewelry and silver, new merchandise, pet supplies, pottery and porcelain, fresh produce, and toys. Snacks and hot meals are served at over 17 restaurants on the premises; 13-screen drive-in theater at night playing first-run movies; free circus every day; auctions daily. Also known as the Sunrise Swap Shop or the Thunderbird Swap Shop, it's one of the South's largest indoor/outdoor flea markets.

VENDORS: From $4 per 15′x20′ space on Tuesday, Wednesday, or Friday, from $10 on Saturday, or from $15 on Sunday; free setup on Monday and Thursday; inquire for monthly rates. Broward County vendor's license and Florida sales tax number are required. Reservations are required for multiday rentals only.

Contact Gerald Horner, 3121 West Sunrise Boulevard, Fort Lauderdale, FL 33311. Tel: (305) 791-7927; fax: (305) 792-1329.

Fort Myers
Fleamasters Flea Market

At 4135 Anderson Avenue (State Road 82). Take Exit 23 (State Road 82 exit) off I-75, then west for one and a quarter miles.

Every Friday, Saturday, and Sunday, 8 A.M. to 4 P.M.

Free admission; acres of free parking. In operation for over nine years; indoors and outdoors, rain or shine. Averages 700 to a capacity of 1,200 vendors.

Antiques and collectibles, books, new and vintage clothing, coins and stamps, cookware, crafts and fine art, fish, new and used furniture, jewelry and silver, new merchandise, fresh produce, and toys. Variety of restaurants and snack bars on the premises serving everything from burritos to funnel cakes. "Southwest Florida's Giant Flea market."

VENDORS: $20 per 10′x12′ space per day including two tables, or $53 per weekend; inquire for monthly rates. Reservations are not accepted.

Contact Donna Matthew, Market Manager, 4135 Dr. Martin Luther King, Jr., Boulevard, Fort Myers, FL 33916. Tel: (813) 334-7001.

Fort Myers
North Side Swap Shop

On Old Highway 41 North, a half mile south of the Shell factory, at the drive-in theater.

Every Wednesday, Saturday, and Sunday, 5:30 A.M. to 2 P.M.

Free admission; free parking. In operation for over 23 years; outdoors, rain or shine. Averages 100 to 250 vendors (capacity 365).

Antiques and collectibles, books, new clothing, cookware and crafts, new and used furniture, jewelry, new merchandise, and fresh produce. Hot meals are available on the premises.

VENDORS: $6 per space on Wednesday; $5 on Saturday and Sunday. Reservations are available for monthly rentals only.

Contact Mary Lou Palmer, P.O. Box 3476, Fort Myers, FL 33918. Tel: (813) 995-2254.

Fort Pierce
Biz-E-Flea Market

At 3252 North U.S. Route 1, between Vero Beach and Fort Pierce.

Every weekend, 7 A.M. to whenever.

Free admission; free parking for up to 1,000 cars. In operation for over 17 years; outdoors, rain or shine. Averages 60 to 100 vendors.

Antiques and collectibles, books, new and vintage clothing, cookware, crafts, new and used furniture, jewelry, new merchandise, fresh produce, and toys. Snacks and hot meals are served on the premises. Family-type market with "bargains galore."

VENDORS: From $15 per 12′x12′ space per day. Reservations are recommended.

Contact Tamra Corley-Dun, 3252 North U.S. Route 1, Fort Pierce, FL 34951. Tel: (407) 466-3063.

Frontenac/Cocoa
Frontenac Flea Market

At 5605 U.S. Highway 1, midway between Titusville and Cocoa; a half mile south of the Florida Power and Light plant, five miles from Spaceport U.S.A., and fifty miles from Orlando.

Every Friday, Saturday, and Sunday, 8 A.M. to 4 P.M., and daily the week before Christmas Day.

Free admission; free parking for up to 1,500 cars. In operation for over 16 years; indoors and outdoors, rain or shine. Averages 400 to 500 vendors (capacity over 1,000).

Antiques and collectibles, auto accessories, books, new and vintage clothing, coins and stamps, cookware, crafts and fine art, electronics, fish, new and used furniture, jewelry and silver, kitchen and household items, new merchandise, pets, plants, pottery and porcelain, fresh produce, sporting goods, and toys. Snacks and hot meals are served on the premises. Publishes its own little newspaper with map and vendor directory. On Brevard County's "space coast," near the Kennedy Space Center, local beaches, fishing areas, etc.

VENDORS: $11 daily for an uncovered 10′x20′ space; $15 for a covered 8′x10′ space with one table; monthly rates are $75 per uncovered space and $95 per covered space; roll-up garage door enclosures and shed spaces are available on a monthly basis; electricity is available at $3 per day. Reservations are recommended; call on the preceding Thursday.

Contact Mike Christian, Manager, P.O. Box 10, Sharpes, FL 32959. Tel: (407) 631-0241; office hours are Thursday, 9 A.M. to 5 P.M.; Friday, 7 A.M. to 5 P.M.; and weekends, 6:30 A.M. to 5 P.M.

Gulf Breeze
The Flea Market

At 5760 Gulf Breeze Parkway (Highway 98), fifteen miles east of Pensacola.

Every weekend, 9 A.M. to 5 P.M.

Free admission; ample free parking. In operation for over two years; outdoors, year-round. Averages close to 350 vendors (capacity 400).

Antiques and collectibles, books, new and vintage clothing, coins and stamps, crafts, new and used furniture, jewelry and silver, new and used merchandise, porcelain, fresh produce, and toys. Snacks and hot meals are served on the premises. Bus tours welcome.

VENDORS: $15 per space per day or $25 per weekend. Reservations are recommended.

Contact Audrey Thompson, 5760 Gulf Breeze Parkway, Gulf Breeze, FL 32561. Tel: (904) 934-1971 (office is open daily from 9 A.M. to 5 P.M.).

Hallandale
Hollywood Dog Track Flea Market

At 831 North Federal Highway. Take I-95 to Pembroke Road, then head east to the intersection of Pembroke Road and Route 1.

Every weekend, 8 A.M. to 3 P.M.

Admission 50 cents per person; parking at $1 per car includes admission for passengers. In operation since 1991; indoors and outdoors, weather permitting. Averages 200 to 600 vendors.

Antiques and collectibles, books, new and vintage clothing, cookware, crafts and fine art, new and used furniture, jewelry and silver, new and used merchandise, porcelain, fresh produce, and toys. Snacks and hot meals are served on the premises.

VENDORS: $11 per space per day for used merchandise, or

$27.50 per day for new merchandise; inquire for monthly rates. Reservations are not required for transient vendors.

Contact Daniel Adkins, 831 North Federal Highway, Hallandale, FL 33009. Tel: (305) 454-9400. Day of market call (305) 454-8666.

Jacksonville
The Bargain House of Fleas

At 6016 Blanding Boulevard, three miles north of I-295.

Every weekend, 7:30 A.M. to 5 P.M., and every Wednesday, 6 A.M. to 2 P.M.

Free admission; free parking for up to 300 cars. In operation for over 19 years; indoors and outdoors, rain or shine. Averages close to its capacity of 255 vendors (usually full on Wednesday).

Antiques and collectibles, books, new and vintage clothing, coins and stamps, cookware, crafts, used furniture, jewelry and silver, new and used merchandise, novelty items, plants, porcelain, fresh produce, records, tapes, and toys; airbrush artist. Snacks and hot meals are served on the premises. On a busy road in a residential district between two large naval bases.

VENDORS: $7 per yard space, $14 under shed, or $15 indoors on Saturday; $6 in yard or $8 under shed on Wednesday. Reservations are recommended a week in advance.

Contact Matthew Skenes, 6016 Blanding Boulevard, Jacksonville, FL 32244. Tel: (904) 772-8008; for vendor reservations, call Yvonne Sowell, Wednesday through Sunday.

Jacksonville
Beach Boulevard Flea Market

At 11041 Beach Boulevard.

Every weekend, 8 A.M. to 5 P.M.

Free admission; ample free parking. In operation for over four years; outdoors, year-round. Average number of vendors not reported.

Variety of offerings including antiques and collectibles, new and vintage clothing, crafts and fine art, new and used furniture, jewelry, new and used merchandise, fresh produce, and toys. Snacks and hot meals are served on the premises.

VENDORS: $12.78 per space per day. Reservations are recommended.

Contact Linda Olin, 11041 Beach Boulevard, Jacksonville, FL 32246. Tel: (904) 645-5961.

Jacksonville
The Market Place (Ramona Flea Market)

At 7059 Ramona Boulevard. Take the Lane Avenue exit off I-10 and then go south to Ramona Boulevard, then west three blocks and the market will be on the right.

Every weekend, 8 A.M. to 5 P.M. (vendors may arrive as early as 6:30 A.M.).

Admission 50 cents per person; free admission for children under 12; free parking for up to 3,000 cars. In operation since August 1971; indoors and outdoors, rain or shine. Averages close to its capacity of 900 vendors year-round.

Antiques and collectibles, books, new and vintage clothing, cookware, crafts, new and used furniture, jewelry and silver, new and used merchandise, porcelain, fresh produce, seafood, and toys. Snacks and hot meals are served on the premises.

VENDORS: Indoors—from $14.91 per 8'x8' space per day, or $116.45 per month, depending on location; outdoors—from $7.46 per 12'x30' space per day, or $58.22 per month. Reserve at least two weeks in advance.

Contact Rick Waller, Manager, 7059 Ramona Boulevard, Jacksonville, FL 32205. Tel: (904) 786-FLEA, (904) 786-1153, or (800) 583-FLEA.

Key Largo
Key Largo Flea Market

At 103530 Overseas Highway (Route 1, at mile marker 103.5), three-quarters mile north of Pennekamp State Park.

Every weekend, 8 A.M. to 4 P.M.

Free admission; free parking for up to 200 cars. In operation for over 13 years; indoors, year-round. Averages close to 50 vendors year-round.

Antiques and collectibles, books, new and vintage clothing, coins and stamps, cookware, crafts and fine art, fishing and marine supplies, new and used furniture, glassware, jewelry and silver, new and used merchandise, novelties, plants, porcelain, fresh produce, seafood, used tools, toys, wicker and baskets. Restaurant on the premises.

VENDORS: Monthly leases only: $123 per 10'x10' space or $203 per 10'x30' space or $300 per 10'x40' space, including electricity. Reservations are recommended.

Contact John Vincent, 103530 Overseas Highway, Key Largo, FL 33037. Tel: (305) 451-0677 or (305) 451-0922.

Kissimmee
192 Flea Market

At 4301 West Vine Street (Irlo Bronson Memorial Highway/Route 192), near the Disney World complex. Accessible from I-4 or the Florida Turnpike.

Daily, 9 A.M. to 6 P.M.

Free admission; free parking. In operation for over five years; indoors, year-round. Averages close to a capacity of 400 vendors year-round.

New merchandise including collectibles (baseball cards, coins and stamps, Disneyana, etc.), clothing, cosmetics, crafts and fine art, electronics, gift items, housewares, jewelry and silver, luggage, porcelain, fresh produce, and toys. Food court on the premises. Discount items and bargains galore, but no antiques or used merchandise is available here.

VENDORS: $18 per 10'x12' space per day including one table. Reservations are not required.

Contact Charlene Dean, 4301 West Vine Street, Kissimmee, FL 34746. Tel: (407) 396-4555.

Kissimmee

Osceola Flea and Farmers' Market

At 2801 East Irlo Bronson Memorial Highway (Route 192), southwest of Orlando. Take Exit 244 off the Florida Turnpike, then turn left onto Route 192 and proceed two and a half miles; market will be on the left. Or take the Route 192 exit off I-4 and go east about 15 miles on Route 192.

Every Friday, Saturday, and Sunday, 8 A.M. to 5 P.M.

Free admission; ten acres of free parking. In operation for over eight years; indoors and outdoors, rain or shine. Averages up to a capacity of 900 vendors.

Antiques and collectibles, books, new clothing, coins and stamps, cookware, crafts and fine art, dolls, fishing tackle, new and used furniture, jewelry and silver, new merchandise, pets, plants, pottery and porcelain, fresh produce, tools, hardware, and toys. Snacks and hot meals are served on the premises.

VENDORS: $17.50 per day; extra tables are $3.75 each per day; electricity is available at $2 per day. Reservations are recommended.

Contact Frank A. Buonauro, Jr., 2801 East Irlo Bronson Memorial Highway, Kissimmee, FL 34744. Tel: (407) 846-2811; in Orange County only, call (407) 238-1296.

Lakeland
King Flea

At 333 North Lake Parker Avenue. Take I-4 to Route 98 South.

Every Friday, Saturday, and Sunday, 8:30 A.M. to 5 P.M.

Free admission; free parking for up to 700 cars. In operation for over six years; indoors, year-round. Averages up to a capacity of 300 vendors.

Antiques and collectibles, books, new clothing, coins and stamps, cookware, crafts and fine art, used furniture, jewelry and silver, new and used merchandise, porcelain, fresh produce, and toys. Snacks and hot meals are served on the premises.

VENDORS: $12 per 10'x10' space per day; from $100 per space per month. Reservations are not required.

Contact Roman Cowan, 333 North Lake Parker Avenue, Lakeland, FL 33801. Tel: (941) (813) 688-9964.

Lakeland
Lakeland Farmers' Market

At 2701 Swindell Road, at Memorial Blvd. and Swindell Road. One mile east of I-4 on Memorial Blvd.

Every Thursday and Friday, 7 A.M. to 5 P.M.; every Saturday, and Sunday, 6 A.M. to 5 P.M.

Free admission; free parking for up to 2,000 cars. In operation for over 24 years; indoors and outdoors, rain or shine. Averages 200 to 240 vendors (capacity 300).

Full spectrum of antiques and collectibles, new and used goods, cookware, crafts, jewelry and silver, and fresh produce. Snacks and hot meals are served on the premises.

VENDORS: $10 per day on weekends, $4 on Friday for a covered booth, free on Thursday; lockup units available from $80 to $330 per month, but there is no overnight parking for vendors. Reservations are suggested at least a week in advance.

Contact Ann Edwards, Owner, or Bill Hudson, Manager, 2701 Swindell Road, Lakeland, FL 33805. Tel: (813) 682-4809 or (813) 665-3723.

Lake Worth
Lake Worth High School Flea Market

At 1701 Lake Worth Road, under the I-95 overpass (between 6th Avenue and 10th Avenue exits) next to the Tri-Rail Station, in the parking lot of the high school. Take Lake Worth exit off the Florida Turnpike, then go east five miles.

Every weekend, 3 A.M. to 3 P.M.

Free admission; free parking for up to 2,000 cars. In operation since 1987; outdoors (under cover) year-round, rain or shine. Averages 200 to a capacity of 300 vendors.

Antiques and collectibles, books, new and vintage clothing, coins and stamps, cookware, crafts and fine art, new and used furniture, garage-sale items, glassware, jewelry, new and used merchandise, porcelain, fresh produce, and toys. Several food trucks at the market. A not-for-profit market with a family atmosphere; proceeds go to Lake Worth High School scholarships. Crowds swell to more than 3,000 shoppers on busy days.

VENDORS: From $8 to $10 for a single parking space per day, depending on location; monthly rates are available. Reservations are on a first-come, first-served basis.

Contact Betty Brown, General Manager, P.O. Box 6592, Lake Worth, FL 33466-6592. Tel: (407) 439-1539; fax: (407) 533-6334; beeper: (407) 387-2740. Day of market, contact Manager by beeper.

Maitland
Ole Red Barn Flea Market

At 8750 South Highway 17/92.

Every weekend, 9 A.M. to 5 P.M. Produce market open seven days per week.

Free admission; free parking for up to 200 cars. In operation since 1968; outdoors and under cover, rain or shine. Averages 20 to 25 permanent vendors.

Antiques and collectibles, used furniture, glassware, china, and fresh produce. An old-fashioned small flea market.

VENDORS: $5 per 2'x8' table per day. Reservations are not required.

Contact Betty L. Smith, 2001 El Campo Avenue, Deltona, FL 32725. Tel: (904) 789-3945 or (904) 339-0667.

Margate
Margate Swap Shop

At 1000 North State Road 7. Take the Coconut Creek exit off the Florida Turnpike to Route 441, then south about one block, and market is on the east side.

Every Tuesday, Saturday, and Sunday, 5 A.M. to 2 P.M.

Free admission; preferred parking for up to 1,000 cars at 50 cents per car. In operation for over 18 years; indoors and outdoors, rain or shine. Averages 350 to a capacity of 600 vendors.

Antiques and collectibles, books, new clothing, coins and stamps, crafts, fish, new and used furniture, jewelry and silver, new merchandise, pottery and porcelain, fresh produce, and toys. Snacks and hot meals are served on the premises. Big on produce.

VENDORS: High season (from December through April): $8 per space on Saturday or Sunday, and $6 on Tuesday; low season $6 per space per day. Reservations are not required.

Contact Alex Gusman, 1000 North State Road 7, Margate, FL 33063. Tel: (305) 971-7927.

Melbourne
Super Flea and Farmers' Market

At 4835 West Eau Gallie Blvd., at the corner of I-95 and West Eau Gallie Blvd. Take Exit 72 west off I-95.

Every Friday, Saturday, and Sunday, 9 A.M. to 4 P.M.

Free admission; free parking for up to 1,500 cars. In operation for over 48 years; indoors, outdoors, and under cover, rain or shine. Averages 250 to 300 vendors (capacity 800).

Antiques and collectibles, new and vintage clothing, cookware, crafts, new and used furniture, jewelry and silver, fish, fresh produce, reptiles, plants, "gem mine" (where customers do the panning), dried fruits, nuts, and candies. Snacks and hot meals are served on the premises; bakery available. A family-style market that calls itself "America's great outdoor mall." Fridays were added "due to popular demand" in 1992.

VENDORS: From $16 to $20 per 8'x10' space per day, with one 4'x8' table included; monthly rates available for 10'x15' sheds; terms are cash only for daily vendors. Reservations are not required.

Contact Manager, 4835 West Eau Gallie Boulevard, Melbourne, FL 32934. Tel: (407) 242-9124.

Miami
Flagler Flea Market

At Northwest Seventh Street and 37th Avenue, at the Flagler Greyhound Track.

Every weekend, 9 A.M. to 4 P.M.

Admission 50 cents; free admission for children under 12; free parking for up to 1,820 cars. In operation since July 1984; indoors year-round, and outdoors, weather permitting. Averages 525 to 550 vendors (capacity 650).

Antiques and collectibles, new and vintage clothing, crafts and fine art, new and used furniture, jewelry and silver, fresh produce, and perfume. Snack bar on premises.

VENDORS: From $12 to $30 per space per day. Reserve in advance if possible.

Contact Armando R. Prats, P.O. Box 350940, Miami, FL 33135-0940. Tel: (305) 649-3022 or (305) 649-3000.

Miami
Flea Market U.S.A.

At 3013 Northwest 79th Street at 30th Avenue. Take 79th Street exit off I-95 and go west to 30th Avenue.

Every Wednesday through Sunday, 10 A.M. to 9 P.M.

Free admission; free parking. In operation for over 12 years; indoors and outdoors, year-round. Average number of vendors not reported.

Antiques and collectibles, books, new clothing, cookware, crafts and fine art, jewelry, new and used merchandise, and fresh produce. Snacks and hot meals are served on the premises.

VENDORS: $400 per space per month. Reservations are not required.

Contact Mrs. Ettie Studnik, 3015 Northwest 79th Street, Miami, FL 33147. Tel: (305) 836-3677. Habla español.

Miami
Liberty Flea Market

At 7900 Northwest 27th Avenue at 79th Street, in the Northside Shopping Center. Take the Northwest 79th Street exit west off I-95 to 27th Avenue.

Daily except Sunday: Monday, noon to 7 P.M.; Tuesday through Thursday, 10 A.M. to 7 P.M.; Friday and Saturday, 10 A.M. to 9 P.M.

Free admission; free parking for up to 1,000 cars. In operation for over seven years; indoors, year-round. Averages 60 to a capacity of 400 vendors.

New discount merchandise (no antiques, collectibles, or used items); fresh produce and seafood. Snacks and hot meals are served on the premises. In what used to be a Sears department store; expanding to a new floor that will bring its total selling area to 155,000 square feet. More of a "merchandise mart" than a true flea market, but a good place for bargains.

VENDORS: From $200 to $600 per 100-square-foot booth, depending on location. Annual leases only.

Contact Joseph Ha, 7900 Northwest 27th Avenue, Miami, FL 33147. Tel: (305) 836-9848.

Miami
Opa Locka/Hialeah Flea Market

At 12705 Northwest 42nd Avenue. Take I-95 South to Northwest 103rd Street exit, then go west four miles to 42nd Avenue.

Every Thursday through Sunday, 5 A.M. to 7 P.M.

Free admission; acres of free parking. In operation since 1985; indoors and outdoors, rain or shine. Averages 1,100 to 1,300 vendors (capacity 1,400).

Antiques and collectibles, books, new and vintage clothing, cookware, fine art, new and used furniture, jewelry and silver, new and used merchandise, porcelain, fresh produce, seafood, and toys. Snacks and hot meals are served on the premises.

VENDORS: From $15 per space per day. Reservations are not required.

Contact Scott Miller, 12705 Northwest 42nd Avenue, Miami, FL 33054. Tel: (305) 688-0500 or (305) 688-0525.

Mount Dora
Florida Twin Markets

On Highway 441, half a mile north of Route 46.

Every weekend, 8 A.M. to 4 P.M.

Free admission; 117 acres of free parking. In operation for over 11 years; indoors and outdoors, rain or shine. Averages 400 to 600 vendors; large outdoor vendor capacity.

Full spectrum of antiques and collectibles, new and used goods, and fresh produce, seafood, and meats. Snacks and hot meals are served on the premises. Florida Twin Markets consists of Renninger's Farmers and Flea Market and Renninger's Antique Center, open every weekend.

VENDORS: $13.50 per space per day in the open-air building; $7 per space per day outdoors. Reservations are not required.

Contact Bob Lynch, Manager, P.O. Box 1699, Mount Dora, FL 32757-1699. Tel: (904) 383-8393.

Naples
Naples Drive-in and Flea Market

At 7700 Davis Blvd. Take Exit 15 off I-75 and then go south, then right at the first stoplight; the market will be three miles down the road on the left.

Every weekend year-round, plus every Friday from October through April, 7 A.M. to 3 P.M.

Free admission; free parking for up to 500 cars. In operation for over 11 years; outdoors, rain or shine. Averages 100 to 200 vendors (capacity 220).

Antiques and collectibles, books, new and vintage clothing, coins and stamps, cookware, crafts, firearms, used furniture, jewelry and silver, new and used merchandise, porcelain, fresh produce, seafood, and toys. Snacks and hot meals are served on the premises.

VENDORS: $6 per space per day from June 1 through September 30, and $10 per day the rest of the year. Reservations are not required.

Contact Stephen Forbes, 7700 Davis Boulevard, Naples, FL 33942-5311. Tel: (941) 774-2900.

Ocala

Ocala Drive-In Flea Market

At 4850 South Pine Avenue, three and a half miles south of Ocala on Route 301/27/441.

Every weekend, 7 A.M. to 4 P.M.

Free admission; free parking for up to 1,000 cars. In operation for over 17 years; indoors and outdoors, rain or shine. Averages 300 to 400 vendors (capacity 450).

Antiques and collectibles, new and vintage clothing, cookware, crafts, jewelry and silver, livestock, poultry, fresh produce, carpet supplies, and auto tires. Snack bar on premises.

VENDORS: $9.50 per roofed space per day, plus tax; $7.50 per day for an exposed space. Reservations are not required.

Contact Lou or Sheri Williams, 4850 South Pine Avenue, Ocala, FL 34480. Tel: (904) 629-1325 or (904) 694-3706.

Odessa

Gunn Highway Flea Market

At the intersection of Gunn Highway and State Road 54.

Every weekend, 8 A.M. to 4 P.M.

Free admission; free parking for up to 1,500 cars. In operation since 1992; indoors, outdoors, and under cover, rain or shine. Averages up to several hundred vendors.

Antiques and collectibles, books, new and vintage clothing, coins and stamps, cookware, crafts and fine art, new and used

113

furniture, jewelry and silver, new merchandise, porcelain, fresh produce, and toys—"a million new items and thousands of antiques and collectibles." Snacks and hot meals are served on the premises. Storage sheds available. Formerly known as Bargaineer Flea Market, now a division of Wagonwheel Flea Market out of Pinellas Park, Florida.

VENDORS: Under cover: $7 per day for one space, $12 for two, $15 for three; outdoors: $6 for one space, $10 for two, $12 for three. Reservations are not required.

Contact David Huntley, 2317 Gunn Highway, Odessa, FL 33556. Tel: (813) 920-3181 (office open daily).

Okeechobee
Cypress Hut Flea Market

At 4701 Highway 441 South, seven miles south of downtown Okeechobee.

Every weekend, 6 A.M. to 5 P.M.

Free admission; free parking for up to 400 cars. In operation for over 18 years; indoors and outdoors, rain or shine. Averages 100 to 400 vendors.

Full spectrum of antiques, collectibles, new and used merchandise including clothing and furniture, meats, poultry, and fresh produce. Snacks and hot meals are served on the premises.

VENDORS: $5 per table per day. Reserve a week in advance.

Contact Joyce Ayers, 22 Timber Trail, Ormond Beach, FL 32074. Tel: (813) 763-5104.

Okeechobee
Trading Post Flea Market

At 3100 Highway 441 South, about two miles south of the center of Okeechobee. Look for the red and white roofs (next to K Mart).

Every weekend, 8 A.M. to 3 P.M.

Free admission; free parking for up to 500 cars. In operation for over eight years; indoors year-round, and outdoors, weather permitting. Averages 170 to a capacity of 270 vendors.

Antiques and collectibles, books, new and vintage clothing, coins and stamps, cookware, crafts, used furniture, jewelry and silver, new and used merchandise, pets and pet supplies, porcelain, fresh produce, and toys. A clean and friendly market.

VENDORS: Summer: $10.60 per 8'x10' space per day or $15.90 per weekend; winter: $14.84 per space per day or $21.20 per weekend; each space comes with one table. Reservations are recommended 10 days in advance during winter.

Contact Valerie Jordan, 3100 Highway 441 South, Okeechobee, FL 34974. Tel: (813) 763-4114.

Oldsmar

Oldsmar Flea Market

At 180 North Racetrack Road (at the intersection of Hillsborough Avenue).

Every Saturday and Sunday, 9 A.M. to 5 P.M.

Free admission; ample free parking. In operation since November 1980; indoors, year-round. Averages close to 800 vendors (capacity 1,200).

A variety of antiques and collectibles, household items, etc. Snacks and hot meals are served on the premises. Free Country and Western band from noon to 4 P.M. "The mightiest in the South."

VENDORS: $10 per 8'x10' space per day outdoors; inquire for monthly rates indoors. Reservations are not required.

Contact Babe Wright, Manager, P.O. Box 439, Oldsmar, FL 34677. Tel: (813) 855-1433. Day of market, call (813) 855-2587.

Orlando
Central Florida Farmer's Market

At 4603 West Colonial Drive.

Every weekend, 5 A.M. until dusk.

Free admission; free parking. In operation for over 16 years; outdoors, year-round. Averages 350 to 500 vendors (capacity 700).

Antiques and collectibles, books, new and vintage clothing, coins and stamps, cookware, crafts and fine art, new and used furniture, jewelry and silver, new and used merchandise, pets, plants, porcelain, fresh produce, seafood, and toys. Snacks and hot meals are served on the premises.

VENDORS: $9 per 16'x20' space per day. Reservations are not required.

Contact John Wild, 1552 Daly Street, Orlando, FL 32808. Tel: (407) 295-9448. Day of market, contact Mrs. Wild at (407) 296-3868.

Orlando
Colonial Flea Market

At 11500 East Colonial Drive (East Highway 50) at Alafaya Trail, near the University of Central Florida. Take East-West Expressway to Alafaya Trail, then go north to Highway 50, then left two blocks.

Every Friday, Saturday, and Sunday, 8 A.M. to 5 P.M.

Free admission; free parking. In operation for over nine years; indoors and outdoors, rain or shine. Averages 400 to a capacity of 550 vendors (winter is high season).

Antiques and collectibles, new clothing, cookware, crafts, fresh produce, new merchandise, used furniture, and other items. Snacks and hot meals are served on the premises. Offers 24-hour security. Claims to be East Orlando's only flea market; formerly known as the University Flea Market.

116

VENDORS: From $5 to $13 per day, electricity included; overnighters welcome at $4 per night. Reservations are not required.

Contact Norb Kolb, 11500 East Colonial Drive, Orlando, FL 32817. Tel: (407) 380-8888 or (407) 679-8705.

Palmetto
Midway Flea Market

At 10816 U.S. Highway 41 North. Take Route 75 to Exit 45 west to Highway 41, then north one half mile and market will be on the right.

Every Wednesday, Saturday, and Sunday, 8 A.M. to 4 P.M.; front row of booths is open seven days a week. Gates open at 6:30 A.M. for vendors.

Free admission; approximately 12 acres of free parking. In operation since 1987; indoors, outdoors, and under cover, rain or shine. Averages up to a capacity of 1,000 vendors.

Antiques and collectibles, books, new and vintage clothing, crafts and fine art, glassware, pottery and porcelain, jewelry and silver, new and used furniture, fish, poultry, fresh produce, plants, pets, household items, Western wear, fireworks, toys, videos, knives and firearms, auto parts, sports equipment, and boating and fishing supplies. Four restaurants and a wide variety of food vendors. Buses welcome. Billed as a clean and modern market with old-fashioned prices.

VENDORS: $6 per 10'x10' space per day outdoors; inquire for monthly indoor or outdoor rates. Reserve two to three weeks in advance.

Contact Joseph Kucej, 10816 U.S. Highway 41 North, Palmetto, FL 34221. Tel: (813) 723-6000.

Panama City
15th Street Flea Market

At 2233 East 15th Street. Take 15th Street exit off Highway 98 and market is across from the Bay Country Fairground.

Every Wednesday through Sunday: Wednesday, Thursday, and Friday, 9 A.M. to 4 P.M. and every Saturday and Sunday, 8 A.M. to 5 P.M.

Free admission; ample free parking. In operation for over 15 years; indoors year-round, and outdoors, weather permitting. Average number of vendors not reported.

Antiques and collectibles, books, new and vintage clothing, coins and stamps, cookware, crafts, new and used furniture, jewelry and silver, new and used merchandise, porcelain, fresh produce, and toys. Snacks are served on the premises.

VENDORS: $2 per table on Wednesday, Thursday, or Friday; $4 per outdoor table ($5 under shelter) on Saturday or Sunday. Reserve three to four days in advance.

Contact Leo Adkins, 2224 East 18th Street, Panama City, FL 32405. Tel: (904) 769-0137 or (904) 769-7401.

Pensacola
T and W Flea Market

At 1717 North T Street. Coming in on I-10, take Exit 3 for Highway 29 South to W Street, then turn right; it is approximately four miles on the left.

Daily, 6 A.M. to whenever.

Free admission; free parking. In operation since 1979; indoors and outdoors, rain or shine. Averages up to 400 vendors (capacity 500).

Variety of offerings including antiques and collectibles, new and used goods, produce, and poultry—"you name it, we have it." Snacks and hot meals are served on the premises. Showers for overnight campers. Well advertised on TV and radio, and in newspapers. Tables have been booked every weekend for the past three years, according to the manager.

VENDORS: From $8 per table per day; $5 per night over-night charge. Reservations are required a week in advance.

Contact Franklin "Red" Cotton, 1717 North T Street, Pensa-cola, FL 32505. Tel: (904) 433-4315 or (904) 433-7030.

Pinellas Park
Mustang Flea Market

At 7301 Park Boulevard. Take Exit 15 off I-275 and go west five miles and market will be on the right.

Every Wednesday through Sunday, 6 A.M. to 1 P.M.

Free admission; free parking for up to 2,000 cars. In operation for over 20 years; outdoors, year-round. Averages 200 to a capacity of 450 vendors.

Antiques and collectibles, books, new and vintage clothing, cookware, crafts, used furniture, jewelry and silver, new and used merchandise, porcelain, fresh produce, seafood, and toys. Snacks and hot meals are served on the premises. Calls itself the "world's largest yard sale."

VENDORS: $2.50 per space on Wednesday, Thursday, or Friday, and $6 per space on Saturday or Sunday. Reservations are not required.

Contact Betty Guinn, 7301 Park Boulevard, Pinellas Park, FL 34665. Tel: (813) 544-3066.

Pinellas Park
Wagonwheel Flea Market

At 7801 Park Blvd. (74th Avenue), between Belcher and Starkey Roads in Pinellas Park (midway between Saint Peters-burg and Clearwater). Take Exit 15 West off I-275.

Every weekend, 7:30 A.M. to 4 P.M.

Free admission; parking for up to 6,000 cars at $1 per car (free tram from parking lot to various areas of the market). In operation since 1967; indoors, outdoors, and under cover, rain or shine. Averages 1,200 to 1,800 vendors on 125 acres (capacity 2,000 booths including 1,300 under cover).

Antiques and collectibles, books, new and vintage clothing, coins and stamps, cookware, crafts and fine art, new and used furniture, jewelry and silver, new merchandise, porcelain, fresh produce, and toys. Food is available from 19 concessions including the Wagonwheel Food Court, with seating for 300. On the site of the annual Pinellas County Fair, which runs for five days and nights annually in late March. "20 million customers can't be wrong!"

VENDORS: $9.50 per day under cover, or $6 per day in open air. Reserve a week in advance.

Contact Misty Lynch, 7801 Park Boulevard, Pinellas Park, FL 34665. Tel: (813) 544-5319.

Plant City
Country Village Market Place

At 3301 Highway 39 North. Take Exit 13 off I-4, then turn north on State Road 39 and go a mile to first stoplight, and market will be on the left.

Every Wednesday, Saturday, and Sunday, 6 A.M. to 6 P.M.

Free admission; two acres of parking at 75 cents per car. In operation for over 15 years; outdoors and under cover, year-round. Averages 200 to a capacity of 400 vendors (filled in winter months).

Antiques and collectibles, books, new and vintage clothing, cookware, crafts, used furniture, jewelry and silver, new and used merchandise, fresh produce, and toys. Restaurant and food carts on the premises. Game room. During the week a wholesale produce market operates on part of the property.

VENDORS: $5 per 10'x24' space per day; free setup in field on weekends only for sellers of used merchandise; inquire for monthly rates. Reservations are on a first-come, first-served basis for outdoor spaces; waiting list for indoor spaces.

Contact Ferris Waller, 3301 North Highway 39, Plant City, FL 33565. Tel: (813) 752-4670 or (813) 752-7088.

Pompano Beach
Festival Flea Market Mall

At 2900 West Sample, between Powerline and Exit 69 off Florida's Turnpike, two miles west of I-95.

Every Tuesday through Friday, 9:30 A.M. to 5 P.M., and every weekend, 9:30 A.M. to 6 P.M. (closed Tuesdays from June through September, but open on Christmas Day and New Year's Day).

Free admission; free parking. In operation for over five years; indoors, year-round. Averages close to 600 vendors on 400,000 square feet of selling area.

Antiques and collectibles, books, new and vintage clothing, crafts and fine art, electronics, jewelry, toys, and used merchandise; all new merchandise is guaranteed. International Food Court with everything from McDonald's to cappuccino bar. Eight-screen theater, state-of-the-art arcade, hair salon. Combines flea-market prices and merchandise with mall-like amenities; don't expect a whole lot of antiques and collectibles, but there's a great variety of discount merchandise.

VENDORS: Inquire for rates. No transient vendors.

Contact Lauri Bomstein, 2900 West Sample Road, Pompano Beach, FL 33073-3026. Tel: (305) 979-4555 or (800) FLEA-MARKET; fax: (305) 968-3980.

Port Richey
U.S.A. Fleamarket

At 11721 U.S. Highway 19, between State Roads 52 and 54 (access from Route 41 and I-75).

Every Friday, Saturday, and Sunday, 8 A.M. to 4 P.M.

Free admission; free parking for more than 5,000 cars. In operation for over 10 years (formerly known as Fleamasters); outdoors and under cover, year-round, rain or shine. Averages 900 to a capacity of 1,100 vendors.

Antiques and collectibles, books, new and vintage clothing, coins and stamps, cookware, crafts and fine art, fish, new and used furniture, household items, jewelry and silver, livestock, new merchandise, pottery and porcelain, fresh produce, toys, Western wear, and much more. Snacks and hot meals are served on the premises. Massive local advertising. "An adventure in bargain shopping."

VENDORS: From $10 per 3'x8' aisle space to $13 per 10'x12' space on Friday; $16 on Saturday or Sunday; includes two tables; inquire for weekly or monthly rates; food concessions are three times monthly rate. Reservations are not required.

Contact Customer Service Office, 11721 U.S. Highway 19, Port Richey, FL 34668. Tel: (813) 862-3583.

Sanford
Flea World

On Highway 17/92 between Sanford and Orlando, next to Fun World. Take Exit 49 off Highway 4 and cross to 17/92 on Route 434, or take Exit 50 off Highway 4 and cross to 17/92 on Lake Mary Blvd.

Every Friday, Saturday, and Sunday, 8 A.M. to 5 P.M.

Free admission; free parking for up to 4,000 cars. In operation since May 1982; indoors and outdoors, rain or shine. Averages close to 800 vendors year-round (capacity over 1,000).

Antiques and collectibles, books, new and vintage clothing, coins and stamps, cookware, crafts and fine art, new and used furniture, jewelry and silver, new and used merchandise, porcelain, fresh produce, and toys—everything from apples to zirconia, including lawyer, dentist, and optometrist offices, barber and beauty shops. Snacks and hot meals are served on the premises. Free entertainment every Sunday; bingo twice daily on weekends; Fun World with go-cart tracks, miniature golf, bumper cars and boats, batting cages, nine midway rides, 350-game arcade, party facilities, and more. One of America's largest flea markets, on over 104 acres with an estimated three million shoppers annually.

VENDORS: Garage-sale items (used merchandise only): first space free (including one table), and each additional space $3 on Friday, and $5 on Saturday or Sunday; other merchandise: $7 on Friday for an 8'x10' space including a table and one electrical outlet, and from $14 to $15 per space on Saturday or Sunday, depending on location. Reservations are required except for "garage-sale" spaces, which are rented on a first-come, first-served basis.   Contact Manager, Highway 17/92, Sanford, FL 32773. Tel: (407) 330-1792.

Stuart
B and A Flea Market

On U.S. Highway 1 South, on Florida's "treasure coast." Take Palm City exit off the Florida Turnpike and follow signs for U.S. Highway 1, then right until Luckhardt Street, then left. Or take Exit 61 off I-95 and go east to Indian Street, then go to Route 1, then left to Luckhardt Street.

Every weekend, 8 A.M. to 3 P.M.

Free admission; ample parking at $1 per car. In operation since 1975; indoors year-round, and outdoors, weather permitting. Averages 400 to 600 vendors (capacity 700).

Antiques and collectibles, books, new and vintage clothing, coins and stamps, cookware, crafts and fine art, new and used

merchandise, jewelry and silver, nautical equipment, porcelain, poultry and fresh produce, toys, and much more. Snacks and hot meals are served on the premises. A big market with a family atmosphere.

VENDORS: From $14 per space per day under cover, or from $12 outdoors; inquire for monthly rates; tables are available at $2 per day. Reservations are required.

Contact Lynne Coastin, Operations Director, 2201 S.E. Indian Street, G-1, Stuart, FL 34997. Tel: (407) 288-4915.

Stuart
Lucky's Flea Market

At 1905 Southeast Luckhardt Street. Take Exit 61 off I-95, then go east on Route 76 for two and a half miles to Indian Street, turn right, then travel one mile and turn left onto Route 1, and the next traffic light will be Luckhardt Street; turn right and market will be on the left.

Every weekend, 8 A.M. to 3 P.M.

Free admission; free parking for up to 600 cars. In operation since 1970; outdoors, rain or shine. Averages 150 to 300 vendors (capacity 350) on 11 acres of selling area.

Antiques and collectibles, books, cameras, new and vintage clothing, coins and stamps, cookware, crafts, silk and dried flowers, used furniture, jewelry and silver, new and used merchandise, plants, porcelain, fresh produce, sporting goods (including golf equipment), tools, toys, and videotapes. Snacks and hot meals are served on the premises. Pony rides, locksmith, sewing machines. A family-owned and -operated flea market.

VENDORS: October through April: $12 per day per 12'x16' covered space with two tables, or $9 per day per 12'x36' space outdoors without tables. May through September: $10 per covered space per day, with two tables, or $7 per day outdoors without tables. Extra tables available at $1 each per day; electricity is available at between $1 and $3 per day in most selling areas; monthly storage of vendors' merchandise is available at additional charge of $20 per month. Reservations are recommended a week to two weeks in advance (but walk-ins are welcome).

Contact Greg or Alice Luckhardt, P.O. Box 1185, Stuart, FL 34995. Tel: (407) 288-4879 or (407) 286-2724; office hours are Monday, Wednesday, and Friday, 8:30 A.M. to 4:30 P.M.

Tampa
Big Top Flea Market

At State Road 582, 500 yards east of Exit 54 off I-75; market will be on the left. From I-4, take Exit 7 (I-75 exit) to I-75, then head north on I-75 to Exit 54.

Every weekend (and every Friday from October through April), 9 A.M. to 4:30 P.M.

Free admission; parking for up to 2,500 cars at $1 per car (free on Friday). In operation for over five years; indoors and outdoors, rain or shine. Averages close to 300 vendors year-round (capacity over 600 enclosed and covered spaces).

Antiques and collectibles, books, new and vintage clothing, coins and stamps, cookware, crafts and fine art, new and used furniture, household decor, jewelry (antique and costume), silver, new merchandise, porcelain, fresh produce, shoes, tools, and toys. Snacks and hot meals are served on the premises. Tour buses are welcome. Billed as Tampa's "cleanest, most modern flea market," with over 160,000 square feet of shopping area. Near Busch Gardens.

VENDORS: From $29 per 10'x12½' space per day indoors, or from $163 per month. Reservations are not required.

Contact Shaddix Management, 9250 East Fowler Avenue, Tampa, FL 33592. Tel: (813) 986-4004 or (813) 986-7160; fax: (813) 986-6296. Reservation office is open Wednesday through Friday, 8:30 A.M. to 5 P.M., and on market days from 7 A.M. to 5 P.M.

Tampa
Floriland Flea and Farmer's Market

At 9309 North Florida Avenue, between Linebaugh Avenue and Busch Boulevard, right off I-275 (Exit 33)—about two miles from Busch Gardens.

Every weekend, 9 A.M. to 5 P.M.

Free admission; free parking for up to 2,500 cars. In operation since 1992; indoors, year-round. Averages 300 to 350 vendors (capacity 800).

Antiques and collectibles, books, new and vintage clothing, coins and stamps, cookware, crafts, new and used furniture, jewelry and silver, new and used merchandise, exotic plants and pets, porcelain, fresh produce, seafood, and toys. Three full-service restaurants plus food concessions on the premises. Groups and tour buses are welcome. Tampa's biggest and most comfortable flea market, with an antiques center, live entertainment—a complete shopping extravaganza.

VENDORS: $27 per 10'x10' space per day, or $45 per weekend, or $173 per month. Reserve a week in advance.

Contact Harold H. Holden, General Manager, 9309 North Florida Avenue, Tampa, FL 33612. Tel: (813) 932-4319; fax: (813) 935-5558.

Waldo
Waldo Farmer's and Flea Market

On Highway 301, one mile north of Waldo (15 minutes from Gainesville)—look for the big horse.

Every Saturday, Sunday, and Monday, 7:30 A.M. to 4:30 P.M.; antiques mall open daily.

Free admission; 20 acres of free parking. In operation since 1975; indoors year-round, and outdoors, weather permitting. Averages 600 to 700 vendors on up to 40 acres of selling space.

Antiques and collectibles, books, new and vintage clothing,

coins and stamps, cookware, crafts, fish, new and used furniture, jewelry and silver, livestock, new merchandise, porcelain, poultry, fresh produce, and toys—everything from "bush hogs" (tractor-pulled grass cutters) to peanuts. Snacks and hot meals are served on the premises. Overnight parking allowed, and campers are welcome. Weekend attendance averages 30,000 shoppers.

VENDORS: From $6 per space per day. Reservations are recommended.

Contact Manager, 2373 Southwest Archer Road, Gainesville, FL 32608. Tel: (904) 468-2255.

Webster
Sumter County Farmer's Market

On Highway 471, north of Highway 50; 45 minutes south of Ocala, Florida; an hour north of Tampa, an hour west of Orlando, 45 minutes north of Lakeland.

Every Monday, 8 A.M. to 3 P.M. (except when Christmas Day falls on a Monday).

Free admission; free parking. In operation since 1937; indoors, outdoors, and under cover, rain or shine. Averages up to 1,700 vendors (capacity 2,000).

Antiques and collectibles, crafts, fresh produce, plants, citrus trees and ornamental plants, new and vintage clothing, jewelry and silver, new merchandise, new and used furniture. Snacks and hot meals are served on the premises. Large wholesale area; market covers over 40 acres.

VENDORS: Under cover: $9 per space per day including two tables (additional tables are available at $1 each); outdoor spaces: $7 per day. Every spot is permanently rented; line up at 7 A.M. Monday for cancellations.

Contact Larry Story, General Manager, P.O. Box 62, Webster, FL 33597. Tel: (904) 793-2021 or (904) 793-3551.

Webster
Webster Westside Flea Market

At Route 478 and Northwest Third Street.

Every Monday, 6 A.M. to whenever.

Free admission; acres of parking at $2 per car. In operation for several years; indoors and outdoors, year-round. Averages up to a capacity of 400 spaces under a shed plus an additional 600 outdoor vendors.

Antiques and collectibles, books, new and used merchandise, fresh produce. Two sit-down restaurants. Camping and showers. Classic car show and swap meet on the first Sunday of every month from September through June.

VENDORS: $12 per 10'x10' space under a shed per day. Reservations are recommended.

Contact Manager, 516 Northwest Third, Webster, FL 33597. Tel: (800) 832-7396. Day of market, call (904) 793-9877.

West Palm Beach
Farmers Market Mall

At 1200 South Congress Avenue, a mile south of Palm Beach International Airport.

Every Thursday through Saturday, 10 A.M. to 7 P.M., and every Sunday, 10 A.M. to 6 P.M.

Free admission; free parking for up to 500 cars. In operation since 1947; indoors, year-round. Averages 85 to 100 vendors (capacity 136).

Antiques and collectibles, books, new clothing, crafts and fine art, new and used furniture, jewelry and silver, new and used merchandise, porcelain, fresh produce, and toys. Snacks and hot meals are served on the premises.

VENDORS: Monthly rentals only; inquire for rates. Reservations are not required.

Contact Dwight Hanners, 1200 South Congress Avenue, West Palm Beach, FL 33406. Tel: (407) 965-1500.

Zephyrhills
Zephyrhills Flea Market

39336 Chancey Road, about a mile and a half east of route 301, on the south side of Zephyrhills.

Every Friday, Saturday, and Sunday from October through May, 8 A.M. to 3 P.M.

Free admission; free parking for up to 3,000 cars. In operation for over three years; indoors rain or shine, and outdoors, weather permitting. Averages close to 300 vendors (capacity 340).

Antiques and collectibles, books, new clothing, coins and stamps, cookware, crafts, new and used furniture, jewelry and silver, hardware, new and used merchandise, porcelain, fresh produce, tools, and toys. Snacks and hot meals are served on the premises.

VENDORS: $10 and up per space per day. Storage sheds are available. Reservations are not required.

Contact Grace Strope or Jerry Zuppa, 39336 Chancey Road, Zephyrhills, FL 33540. Tel: (813) 782-1483 or (800) 932-9674.

GEORGIA

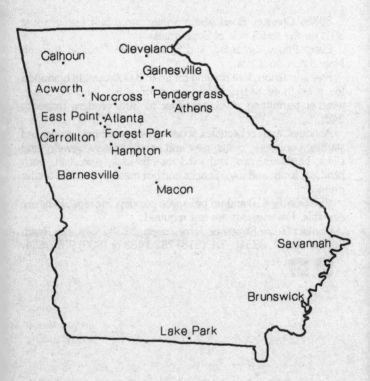

Calhoun
Cleveland
Gainesville
Acworth
Norcross
Pendergrass
East Point
Atlanta
Athens
Carrollton
Forest Park
Hampton
Barnesville
Macon
Savannah
Brunswick
Lake Park

Acworth
Great American Flea Market

At 3355 Cobb North Parkway.

Every weekend, 8 A.M. to 6 P.M.

Free admission; ample free parking. In operation for over 10 years; indoors year-round, and outdoors, weather permitting. Average number of vendors not reported.

Antiques and collectibles, books, cookware, new and used furniture, jewelry, livestock, new and used merchandise, porcelain, fresh produce, and toys. Snacks and hot meals are served on the premises.

VENDORS: $5 per space per day under cover; from $85 per space per month indoors. Reservations are not required.

Contact Rae Jean Wykoff, 3355 North Cobb Parkway, Acworth, GA 30101. Tel: (404) 974-9660.

Acworth
Lake Acworth Antiques and Flea Market

On Highway 41, at the intersection of Route 92. Take Exit 121 off I-75, then follow Highway 92 to Cobb Parkway (Old Route 41), then make a right on Route 41 until Route 92 turns off to Dallas, and the market will be on the left.

Every weekend, 7 A.M. to 5 P.M.

Free admission; parking available at $1 per car. In operation for over 21 years; indoors, outdoors, and under cover, rain or shine. Averages close to 400 vendors year-round (capacity 600).

Antiques and collectibles, books, new and vintage clothing, crafts, new and used furniture, jewelry and silver, new and used merchandise, porcelain, fresh produce, and toys. Snacks and hot meals are served on the premises.

VENDORS: $5 per 10′x10′ space per day. Reservations are not required.

131

Contact Wendell Tummlin, 4375 Cobb Parkway N.W., Acworth, GA 30101. Tel: (404) 974-5896.

Acworth
Yester-year Flea Market

At 4337 Highway 92, at the intersection with Route 41.

Every weekend, 8 A.M. to 5 P.M.

Free admission; parking for up to 750 cars at $1 per car. In operation for over 21 years; indoors year-round, and outdoors, weather permitting. Averages 275 to a capacity of 300 vendors.

Antiques and collectibles, books, new and vintage clothing, coins and stamps, cookware, crafts and fine art, new and used furniture, jewelry and silver, new and used merchandise, porcelain, fresh produce, and toys. Snacks and hot meals are served on the premises. Door prizes each week.

VENDORS: Indoors: $80 per space per month; covered: $10 per day; outdoors: $5 per day. Reserve a week in advance for covered spaces.

Contact Bill Abernathy, Owner, 105 Victory Drive, Woodstock, GA 30188. Tel: (404) 974-6259.

Athens
J and J Flea Market

At 3000 Commerce Road (Highway 441), four miles north of Athens.

Every Friday, Saturday, and Sunday, 8 A.M. to 5 P.M.

Free admission; free parking for up to 3,000 cars. In operation for over 11 years; indoors and outdoors, rain or shine. Averages close to its capacity of 800 vendors (500 indoors in three buildings plus another 300 outdoors).

Antiques and collectibles, books, new and vintage clothing,

cookware and crafts, used furniture, jewelry and silver, livestock, new and used merchandise, porcelain, poultry and fresh produce, and toys. "Great food at great prices." On 125 acres of wooded land on a major tourist route near the University of Georgia.

VENDORS: $8 per space per day indoors, $5 outdoors. Reservations are not required.

Contact Jerry Farmer, 3000 Commerce Road, Athens, GA 30607. Tel: (706) 613-2410. Day of market ask for Lee Black, Rental Manager.

Atlanta
Flea Market U.S.A.

At 1919 Stewart Avenue, S.W. (Highways 41 and 19), south of downtown Atlanta and north of the airport.

Every Thursday, 11 A.M. to 7 P.M.; Friday, 11 A.M. to 9 P.M.; Saturday, 10 A.M. to 9 P.M.; Sunday, noon to 7 P.M.; and Monday, 11 A.M. to 7 P.M.

Free admission; free parking for more than 1,000 cars. In operation for over seven years; indoors, year-round. Averages up to a capacity of 450 vendors on 100,000 square feet of selling area.

Antiques and collectibles, books, new clothing, cookware, new furniture, jewelry, new merchandise, fresh produce, and toys (no used merchandise). Snacks and hot meals are served on the premises. More like a discount mall than a flea market—but good for bargain hunters.

VENDORS: From $1 to $2 per square foot per week. Reserve a week in advance.

Contact Mr. Kim, 1919 Stewart Avenue, S.W., Atlanta, GA 30315. Tel: (404) 763-3078; beeper: (404) 901-2605.

Atlanta
Lakewood Antiques Market

At 2000 Lakewood Way. Take Exit 88 off I-75/85, to Highway 166 (south of the city) to Lakewood Freeway East.

Second full weekend of each month: Friday and Saturday, 9 A.M. to 6 P.M., and Sunday, 9 A.M. to 5 P.M.

Admission $3 per person; free admission for children under 12; free parking for up to 6,800 cars. In operation for over 18 years; indoors and outdoors, rain or shine. Averages 850 to 1,500 or more vendors.

Antiques and collectibles, architectural items, books, vintage clothing, fine art, garage-sale items, glassware, jewelry and silver, porcelain, and antique toys; no new merchandise. Restaurant on the premises. Camping is available on the grounds; showers are available for vendors; special motel rates available. Well publicized as the oldest flea market in Atlanta.

VENDORS: $75 per 8'x10' space per weekend indoors, or $65 per 10'x20' or 14'x15' space outdoors. Reservations are not required.

Contact Ed Spivey, P.O. Box 6826, Atlanta, GA 30315. Tel: (404) 622-4488.

Atlanta
Scott Antique Market

At the Atlanta Exposition Center, two miles east of Atlanta Airport. Take Exit 40 off I-285.

Second weekend of every month: Friday and Saturday, 9 A.M. to 6 P.M., and Sunday, 10 A.M. to 5 P.M.

Admission $3 per person; free parking for up to 3,000 cars. In operation for over nine years; indoors and outdoors, rain or shine. Averages close to a capacity of 1,200 vendors year-round.

Antiques and collectibles of all types. Snacks and hot meals are served on the premises.

VENDORS: $85 per 8'x10' space per weekend indoors, or

$65 outdoors. Reservations are not required for outdoor spaces.

Contact Don Scott, P.O. Box 60, Bremen, OH 43107. Tel: (614) 569-4112 or (614) 569-4912. Day of market, call (404) 361-2000.

Augusta
South Augusta Flea Market

At 1562 Doug Bernard Parkway (formerly New Savannah Road). From I-20, take Bobby Jones Expressway (520) toward airport to end of road, then left, and market is a mile ahead on the right.

Every weekend, 9 A.M. to 6 P.M.

Free admission; seven acres of free parking. In operation since 1978; indoors and outdoors, rain or shine. Averages close to 400 vendors.

Antiques and collectibles, books, electronics, new and used merchandise—"everything." Three restaurants and four concession stands on the premises. Biggest market in the area.

VENDORS: $5 per 12'x12' space; tables are available at $1 each. Spaces are assigned on a first-come, first-served basis.

Contact Ronald Rhodes, 1562 Doug Bernard Parkway, Augusta, GA 30906. Tel: (706) 798-5500.

Barnesville
M and M Flea Market

At 341 Industrial Drive (Highway 341), between Griffin and Barnesville.

Every weekend, dawn to dusk.

Free admission; free parking for up to 150 cars. In operation since 1991; indoors and outdoors, rain or shine. Averages 20 to 30 vendors (capacity 50).

Collectibles, cookware and crafts, used furniture, new and used merchandise, fresh produce, toys, and yard-sale items. Snacks and hot meals are served on the premises.

VENDORS: $3 per day for one table or $5 for two tables. Reserve a week in advance.

Contact J. B. Moss, 210 Old 41 Highway, Barnesville, GA 30204. Tel: (404) 358-1724.

Brunswick
Brunswick Flea and Farmers Market

At 204 Old Jesup Road, a mile and a half southeast of Exit 7A or 7B off I-95. Take route 341 South to Community Road east to Old Jesup Road.

Every Friday, Saturday, and Sunday, 8 A.M. to 4 P.M.

Free admission; 18 acres of free parking. In operation for over eight years; indoors year-round, and outdoors, weather permitting. Averages 25 to 40 vendors (capacity 150).

Antiques and collectibles, books, cookware, used furniture, secondhand household and business office equipment, and toys. Food is not served on the premises.

VENDORS: $10 per space per day. Reserve a week in advance.

Contact Richard Strickland, Manager, 204 Old Jesup Road, Brunswick, GA 31520. Tel: (912) 267-6787. Day of market, call Tom or Barbara Schuh.

Calhoun
New Town Flea Market

On New Town Road, right off I-75 (take Red Bud exit).
Every weekend, from sunrise to sunset.
Free admission; plenty of free parking. In operation for over

16 years; indoors, outdoors, and under cover, rain or shine. Averages 25 to 50 vendors (capacity 100).

Antiques and collectibles, books, vintage clothing, crafts, used furniture, jewelry and silver, new merchandise, fresh produce, and toys. Snacks and hot meals are served on the premises. Most vendors are the onetime yard-sale type.

VENDORS: $5 per space per day including tables; inquire for monthly rates. Reservations are not required.

Contact Earl Abernathy, 257 Iracille Lane N.E., Calhoun, GA 30701. Tel: (706) 625-9088.

Carrollton

West Georgia Flea Market

At 3947 Highway 27 North. Take Exit 3 (Bremen) off I-20 West and go south 2.4 miles and market will be on the left.

Every weekend, 8 A.M. to 4:30 P.M.

Free admission; free parking for up to 3,000 cars. In operation for over 15 years; indoors, year-round. Averages 250 to a capacity of 500 vendors.

Antiques and collectibles, books, new and vintage clothing, cookware, crafts and fine art, new and used furniture, jewelry, livestock, new and used merchandise, porcelain, poultry and fresh produce, and toys. Food concession on the premises serving full breakfast. RVs welcome; showers.

VENDORS: From $16 to $22 per space per weekend. Reserve a week in advance.

Contact Robert Emery, Owner, 746 Kierbow Road, Carrollton, GA 30117. Tel: (404) 832-6551.

137

Cleveland
Henry's Mountain Flea Market

On Highway 129, one mile south of Cleveland in the beautiful Blue Ridge Mountains of northeast Georgia (80 miles north of Atlanta and 23 miles north of Gainesville).

Every weekend, plus holidays, from April through November, 8 A.M. to 5 P.M.

Free admission; 10 acres of free parking. In operation for over nine years; indoors, regardless of weather. Average number of vendors not reported.

Antiques and collectibles, books, new and vintage clothing, coins and stamps, cookware, crafts and fine art, new and used furniture, jewelry and silver, new and used merchandise, porcelain, fresh produce, and toys. Snack bar serving breakfast and lunch. Camping on grounds with water, electricity, dump station, and showers. In high tourist area, with a friendly atmosphere.

VENDORS: $10 per space (with two 3'x8' tables) per day. Reservations are not required.

Contact Linda Macmillan, P.O. Box 1258, Cleveland, GA 30528. Tel: (706) 865-1716 or (706) 865-3216.

East Point
Greenbriar Flea Market

At 2925 Headland Drive. Take Route 166 exit off Route 285 (in southeast part of Atlanta) to Greenbriar Parkway, then turn at the second stoplight to Headland Drive; or take 75/85 South to 166 West to Campbellton Road to Greenbriar Parkway to Headland Drive.

Daily except Tuesday and Wednesday, 11 A.M. to 8 P.M., except noon to 6 P.M. on Sunday.

Free admission; ample free parking. In operation for over 11 years; indoors, year-round. Averages close to a capacity of 150 vendors.

Collectibles, books, new clothing, cookware, new furniture, general merchandise (but no used items), jewelry, and toys. Snacks and hot meals are served on the premises.

VENDORS: From $250 per 10'x10' space per month. Reservations are recommended.

Contact Jack Stewart, 2925 Headland Drive, East Point, GA 30344. Tel: (404) 349-3994.

Forest Park
South Atlanta Flea Market

At 4140 Jonesboro Road, a half mile south of Exit 40 off I-285.

Every Friday, noon to 9 P.M.; every Saturday, 10 A.M. to 9 P.M.; and every Sunday, noon to 6 P.M.

Free admission; acres of free parking. In operation since 1987; indoors, year-round. Averages close to 80 vendors year-round (capacity over 200 booths).

Collectibles, books, new and vintage clothing, coins and stamps, cookware, crafts, new and used furniture, gold and silver, new merchandise, tools, and toys. Snacks and hot meals are served on the premises. Air-conditioned.

VENDORS: $50 per 10'x12' space for three days (vendor has choice of best available location); monthly rentals from $150. Reservations are not required.

Contact Betty Ratledge, 4140 Jonesboro Road, Forest Park, GA 30050. Tel: (404) 363-6694.

Gainesville
Gainesville Flea Market

At 3600 Atlanta Highway (Highway 13 South). Take Exit 4 off I-985, then turn right and go past three traffic lights, then right onto Highway 13 South, and the market will be a quarter mile away on the right—look for signs at the building.

First weekend of every month, 9 A.M. to 5 P.M.

Free admission; free parking for up to 2,000 cars. In operation for over 17 years; indoors year-round, and outdoors, weather permitting. Averages close to a capacity of 70 vendors year-round.

Antiques and collectibles, books, coins, crafts, antique furniture, glassware, gold and costume jewelry, handmade quilts, silver, and toys. Snacks and hot meals are served on the premises.

VENDORS: $30 per weekend for one 10'x12' space or $50 for two spaces. Reservations are recommended.

Contact Johnny Benefield, P.O. Box 224, Oakwood, GA 30566. Tel: (404) 536-8068 or (404) 534-9157. Day of market, call (404) 534-9157.

Hampton
Sweeties Flea Market

At 2316 Highway 19-41, two miles south of the Atlanta Motor Speedway. Take Exit 77 off I-75, then straight out about 12-15 miles, and market will be on the right.

Every Friday, Saturday, and Sunday, 8 A.M. to 5:30 P.M.

Free admission; free parking for up to 500 cars. In operation for over 23 years; outdoors, year-round. Averages 75 to 220 vendors (capacity 250).

Antiques and collectibles, books, new clothing, coins and stamps, cookware, crafts, used furniture, jewelry and silver, new and used merchandise, fresh produce, and toys. Hot meals are served on the premises.

VENDORS: From $10 to $25 per space per day depending on size and location. Reserve a week in advance.

Contact Pat or Jim Martin, P.O. Box 181, Hampton, GA 30228. Tel: (404) 946-4721.

Lake Park
Bargainville Flea Market

Take Exit 2 off I-75 and go east, then right at the Hardee's, then one and a half miles farther on the left.

Every weekend, 9 A.M. to 5 P.M.

Free admission; 20 acres of free parking. In operation for over five years; outdoors and under cover, rain or shine. Averages 50 to 70 vendors (capacity 150).

Antiques and collectibles, new and vintage clothing, cookware and crafts, jewelry and silver, fish, livestock, poultry, fresh produce, and new merchandise. Snacks and hot meals are served on the premises.

VENDORS: $12 per covered, paved space per day. Reservations are not required.

Contact Terry Herndon, Route 3, Box 1050, Lake Park, GA 31636. Tel: (912) 559-0141 or (912) 559-5192.

Macon
Smiley's Flea Market and Antique Mall

At 6717 Hawkinsville Road (Highway 129 South), halfway between Macon and Warner. Take Exit 49 (northbound) or 49A (southbound) off I-75 in Macon, then go south four miles on Highway 247/129 and look for the big yellow sign on the right.

Every weekend, 7 A.M. to 6 P.M.; antiques mall is open daily, 9 A.M. to 6 P.M.

Free admission; free parking for up to 4,200 cars; buses and motor homes also accommodated. In operation since 1985;

indoors and outdoors, rain or shine. Averages 375 to 400 vendors (capacity 258 indoors plus 300 more under cover; antiques mall has over 80 dealers).

Antiques and collectibles, books, new and vintage clothing, coins and stamps, cookware, crafts, new and used furniture, jewelry and silver, new and used merchandise, porcelain, fresh produce, and toys. Snacks are available on the premises. Billed as Georgia's "largest and finest," with "hundred of dealers selling millions of items to thousands of buyers."

VENDORS: $11 per space per day (indoors or outdoors), $20 per weekend, or $65 for four weekends; electrical hookups available. Reservations are recommended five days in advance).

Contact Ben Compen, President, or Dick Hull, General Manager, 6717 Hawkinsville Road, Macon, GA 31206. Tel: (912) 788-3700.

Norcross

Georgia Antique Center and International Market

At 6624 I-85 North Access Road. Take Exit 36 (Pleasantdale exit) off I-85 northbound from Route 285, then go approximately one and a half miles on the access road, and market will be on the right.

Every Friday, noon to 7 P.M.; Saturday, 10 A.M. to 8 P.M.; and Sunday, noon to 7 P.M. (some shops are open daily).

Free admission; free parking for over 400 cars. In operation for over 11 years; indoors, year-round. Averages close to 200 vendors year-round, on 100,000 square feet of selling area.

Antiques and collectibles, books, vintage clothing, cookware, crafts and fine art, new and used furniture, glassware, jewelry and silver, new and used merchandise, porcelain, primitives, and toys. Snacks and hot meals are served on the premises. One of the most varied selections of antiques and collectibles in the greater Atlanta area.

VENDORS: $275 per 12'x14' space per month. Reserve 30 days in advance.

Contact Tony N. Sadri, Manager, 6624 I-85 North Access Road, Norcross, GA 30093. Tel: (404) 446-9292.

Norcross
The Gwinnett Flea Market and Antique Gallery

At 5675 Jimmy Carter Boulevard, at Exit 37 off I-85.

Every Wednesday and Thursday, noon to 7 P.M.; every Friday and Saturday, 11 A.M. to 8:00 P.M.; and every Sunday, noon to 7 P.M.

Free admission; free parking for approximately 730 cars. A new market (in operation since March 1989); indoors, rain or shine. Averages close to a capacity of 70 vendors.

Antiques and collectibles, books, new clothing, cookware, crafts and fine art, new and used furniture, jewelry and silver, new and used merchandise, porcelain, and toys. Snacks and hot meals are served on the premises.

VENDORS: Rentals generally on a monthly basis. Reserve a week in advance.

Contact Anne Osmerg, 5675 Jimmy Carter Blvd., Norcross, GA 30071. Tel: (770) 449-8189.

Pendergrass
Pendergrass Flea Market

Two hundred yards from Exit 50 off I-85.

Every weekend, 9 A.M. to 6 P.M.

Free admission; free parking for up to 1,200 cars. In operation for over three years; indoors year-round, and outdoors, weather permitting. Averages 350 to a capacity of 420 vendors on 130,000 square feet of selling area.

Antiques and collectibles, books, coins and stamps, cookware, crafts and fine art, new and used furniture, livestock, poultry and

143

fresh produce, new and used merchandise, oriental rugs, and toys. Snacks and hot meals are served on the premises.

VENDORS: $16 per 10'x10' space under cover per day, or $65 per 12'x20' lockable space per weekend. Reserve a week in advance.

Contact Dean Hogan, P.O. Box 384, Pendergrass, GA 30567. Tel: (706) 693-4466 or (404) 945-1900. Day of market, call Ms. Judy Wharton at (706) 693-4444.

Savannah
Keller's Flea Market

At 5901 Ogeechee Road. Take Exit 16 off I-95 southbound; market is at the corner of Routes 17 and 204.

Every weekend, 8 A.M. to 6 P.M. (Friday is vendor setup day, but buyers are welcome).

Free admission; free parking. In operation for over 10 years; indoors and outdoors, rain or shine. Averages up to a capacity of over 400 vendors.

Antiques and collectibles, new and vintage clothing, coins and stamps, cookware, crafts and fine art, new and used furniture, jewelry and silver, pottery and porcelain, new merchandise, and fresh produce. Janie Arkwright's Kitchen and Snack Bar serves "the world's best barbecue." Hot showers on premises.

VENDORS: From $10 to $18 per 10'x10' space per day; includes one eight-foot table; extra tables are $2 per day; electricity hookup for RVs is $2 per day; display electricity is $1.50 minimum per day. Rentals are on a first-come, first-served basis; telephone reservations are not accepted.

Contact Hubert or Cheri Keller, 5901 Ogeechee Road, Savannah, GA 31419. Tel: (912) 927-4848.

HAWAII

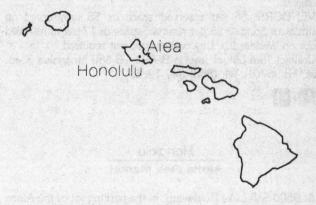

Aiea
Kam Super Swap Meet

At 98-850 Moanalua Road. Take Aiea exit off Moanalua/H-1 Freeway, and follow Moanalua Road to Kaonohi Street, then turn left, and market will be on the right as you're facing the ocean.

Every Wednesday, Saturday, and Sunday, plus some holidays, 5:30 A.M. to 1 P.M.

Free admission; free parking. In operation for over five years; outdoors, year-round. Average number of vendors not reported.

Antiques and collectibles, books, new and vintage clothing, cookware, crafts, new and used furniture, jewelry and silver, new and used merchandise, porcelain, poultry and fresh produce, seafood, and toys. Snacks and hot meals are served on the premises.

VENDORS: $6 per reserved space or $8 unreserved on Saturday or Sunday; $5 per reserved space or $7 per unreserved space on Wednesday. Reservations are not required.

Contact Tom Luk or Imelda Bayani, 98-850 Moanalua Road, Aiea, HI 96701. Tel: (808) 847-1985.

Honolulu
Aloha Flea Market

At 9500 Salt Lake Boulevard, in the parking lot of the Aloha Stadium in Honolulu on the island of Oahu. Take Halawa Stadium exit off H-1 Freeway.

Every Wednesday, Saturday, and Sunday, 6 A.M. to 3 P.M.

Admission 35 cents per person; free parking for up to several thousand cars. In operation since 1979; outdoors, rain or shine. Averages 500 to 1,000 vendors.

Antiques and collectibles, books, new and vintage clothing, coins and stamps, cookware, crafts and fine art, new and used furniture, jewelry and silver, new and used merchandise, porce-

lain, fresh produce, seafood, toys, and a variety of Hawaiian novelties. Snacks and hot meals are served on the premises.

VENDORS: From $10 to $42 per space per day depending on size and location. Reservations are not required.

Contact Edward Medeiros, 3478 Waialae Avenue, Honolulu, HI 96816. Tel: (808) 732-9611 or (808) 486-1529.

IDAHO

**See Appendix for
Brief Listings**

ILLINOIS

Pecatonica Woodstock Grayslake
Rockford Wheeling Mount Prospec
Rosemont
Sycamore Melrose Park
Saint Charles Chicago
Cicero
Sandwich Alsip

Kankakee

Peoria

Towanda

Springfield Urbana

Pana

Centralia
Belleville

Duquoin

Alsip
Tri-State Swap-O-Rama

At 4350 West 129th. Take I-294 (Tri-State Tollway) to Cicero Avenue (Route 50), then go south to 131st, then east to the market.

Every weekend, 7 A.M. to 4 P.M.

Admission 75 cents; free parking for up to 2,500 cars. In operation for over 15 years; indoors year-round, and outdoors, weather permitting. Averages 550 to a capacity of 750 vendors.

All types of new and used merchandise including baseball cards, books, bottles, new and vintage clothing, coins, comics, cookware, new and used furniture, fresh produce, silver, stamps, and toys. Hot meals are served on the premises.

VENDORS: $20 per space per day indoors; $18 outdoors. Reservations are not required.

Contact Jim Pierski, 4600 West Lake Street, Melrose Park, IL 60160. Tel: (708) 344-7300.

Belleville
Belleville Flea Market

At the Belle-Clair Exposition Center at the intersection of Routes 13 and 159 (fairgrounds).

Third full weekend of every month, 8 A.M. to 4 P.M.

Free admission; free parking for up to 1,000 cars. In operation for over 22 years; indoors year-round, and outdoors, weather permitting. Averages 400 to 600 vendors.

Antiques and collectibles, books, new and vintage clothing, coins and stamps, cookware, crafts and fine art, new and used furniture, jewelry and silver, porcelain, fresh produce, toys, and used merchandise. Snacks and hot meals are served on the premises. Biggest and best market in the area.

VENDORS: $13 per 10'x10' space per day outdoors; $15 per 8-foot table per day indoors. Reservations are required.

Contact Allen Wandling, 200 South Belt East, Belleville, IL 62220. Tel: (618) 235-0666.

Centralia
Don's Flea Market

At the intersection of Route 161 and I-57.

Every Friday through Monday, 9 A.M. to 4 P.M.

Free admission; free parking for up to 50 cars. In operation for over five years; indoors and outdoors, rain or shine. Averages 10 to 20 vendors (capacity 30) on more than 7,000 square feet of indoor selling area plus more outdoors in summer.

Antiques and collectibles, books, crafts, new and used furniture, jewelry and silver, new and used merchandise, porcelain, fresh produce, and toys—"thousands of items for a dollar or less." Food is not served on the premises. Largest dealers' auction in the area every Wednesday at 6:30 P.M. Over 7,000 square feet indoors plus outdoor space; two antiques shops next door.

VENDORS: $15 per 12'x12' indoor space per weekend. Reserve two weeks in advance.

Contact Don Mercer, 3846 State Route 161, Centralia, IL 62801. Tel: (618) 533-2949.

Chicago
Ashland Avenue Swap-O-Rama

At 4100 South Ashland. Take I-94 (Dan Ryan Expressway) to Pershing Road, then west to Ashland, then south two blocks.

Every Thursday, Saturday, and Sunday, 7 A.M. to 4 P.M.

Admission 50 cents; free parking for up to 2,000 cars. In operation for over five years; indoors year-round, and outdoors, weather permitting. Averages close to 725 vendors (capacity 850).

Baseball cards, books, bottles, new and vintage clothing, coins, comics, cookware, new and used furniture, jewelry, knives, and fresh produce. Hot and cold meals are served on the premises. Has absorbed many of the vendors from the historic Maxwell Street market.

VENDORS: Indoors: $15 per space on Saturday, $17 on Sunday; outdoors: $7 per space per day. Reservations are not required.

Contact Mr. Jim Pierski, 4600 West Lake Street, Melrose Park, IL 60160. Tel: (708) 344-7300.

Cicero

Casa Blanca Flea Market

At 3200 South Cicero Avenue (State Road 50), one mile north of I-55.

Every weekend, 8 A.M. to 5 P.M.

Admission 50 cents per person; 25 cents for senior citizens; free parking for up to 800 cars. In operation for over 11 years; indoors, outdoors, and under cover, rain or shine. Averages 220 to 300 vendors.

Antiques and collectibles, books, cameras, new and vintage clothing, cookware, electronics, new and used furniture, jewelry and silver, musical instruments, new merchandise, fresh produce, tools, and toys. Snacks and hot meals are served on the premises. A growing market.

VENDORS: $45 and up per indoor space per weekend, or $10 per outdoor space per day. Check in advance for availability of vendor spaces.

Contact Ron Keller, 3200 South Cicero Avenue, Cicero, IL 60650. Tel: (708) 652-0867.

Du Quoin
Giant Flea Market

On the State Fairgrounds, on Route 51 on the south side of Du Quoin.

Usually the first Sunday of every month—call for dates, 8:30 A.M. to 4:30 P.M.

Admission $1 per person; ample free parking. In operation for over nine years; indoors, year-round. Averages 60 to 100 vendors.

Antiques and collectibles, books, new and vintage clothing, jewelry and silver, new merchandise, and toys. Snacks and hot meals are served on the premises.

VENDORS: $12 per 8-foot table per day. Reserve two weeks in advance.

Contact John Crouch, P.O. Box 9500, Springfield, IL 62791. Tel: (217) 529-6939.

Grayslake
Lake County Antiques and Collectibles Show and Sale

At the Lake County Fairgrounds, at the intersection of State Route 120 and U.S. Route 45, five miles west of I-94 (halfway between Chicago and Milwaukee).

Second Sunday of every month, 8 A.M. to 4 P.M.

Admission $3 per person; early entry (6 A.M. to 8 A.M.) $10 per person; ample free parking. In operation for over 10 years; indoors year-round, and outdoors, weather permitting. Averages up to several hundred vendors on up to 90 acres of indoor and outdoor selling area.

Antiques and collectibles. Snacks and hot meals are served on the premises. A diverse selection, excellent for good-quality merchandise; four large indoor exhibit halls are restricted to antiques and collectibles; hundreds of vendors come from across the Midwest.

VENDORS: Indoors: $75 per 8′x13′ space or $60 per 10′x10′ space; outdoors: $65 per 12′x20′ space. Reservations are required for indoor spaces only.

Contact Manager, Lake County Promotions, P.O. Box 461, Grayslake, IL 60030. Tel: (708) 223-1433 or (708) 356-7499.

Kankakee
Giant Flea Market

On the County Fairgrounds. Take Exit 308 off I-57 and then go one mile south.

Second Sunday of every month except June, July, and August, 8:30 A.M. to 4:30 P.M.

Admission $1 per person; ample free parking. In operation for over nine years; indoors, year-round. Averages close to 50 vendors.

Antiques and collectibles, books, new and vintage clothing, jewelry and silver, new merchandise, and toys. Snacks and hot meals are served on the premises.

VENDORS: $12 per 8-foot table per day. Reserve two weeks in advance.

Contact John Crouch, P.O. Box 9500, Springfield, IL 62791. Tel: (217) 529-6939.

Melrose Park
Melrose Park Swap-O-Rama

At 4600 West Lake Street. Take any major expressway to Mannheim Road (Route 45) to where it intersects with Lake Street (Route 20).

Every Friday, Saturday, and Sunday, 7 A.M. to 4 P.M.

Admission 50 cents; free parking for up to 550 cars. In operation for over 10 years; indoors year-round, and outdoors, weather permitting. Averages 375 to 420 vendors.

Wide range of new and used merchandise, fresh produce, and collectibles. Snacks and hot meals are served on the premises.

VENDORS: Indoors: $17 per space on Saturday, $19 on Sunday; outdoors: $11 on Saturday, $13 on Sunday. Reservations are not required.

Contact Jim Pierski, 4600 West Lake Street, Melrose Park, IL 60160. Tel: (708) 344-7300.

Mount Prospect
Wolff's Marketplace

At 750 East Rand Road, one half mile east of Elmhurst Road (Route 83) and the Randhurst Shopping Center.

Every weekend, 9 A.M. to 5 P.M.

Admission 75 cents per person; free admission for seniors and children 12 and under; free parking for up to 700 cars. A new market (in operation since 1994); indoors, year-round. Averages 200 to 350 vendors (capacity 400).

Antiques and collectibles, books, new and vintage clothing, coins and stamps, cookware, crafts and fine art, new and used furniture, jewelry and silver, new and used merchandise, porcelain, and toys. Snacks and hot meals are served on the premises. Sports, comic, and magic collectibles shows twice monthly.

VENDORS: Summer: $16 per space on Saturday, $20 on Sunday; winter: $9 per space on Saturday, $23 on Sunday. Inquire for multispace discounts (summer only) and midweek storage rates. Reservations are not required.

Contact David or Donald Wolff, 970 Arkansas, Elk Grove Village, IL 60007. Tel: (708) 529-9590.

Pana

Dutch Mill Flea Market

At the intersection of Routes 51 and 16 East in Pana (pronounced PAY-na).

Every Friday, Saturday, and Sunday, 9 A.M. to 4:30 P.M.

Free admission; plenty of free parking. In operation for over five years; indoors and outdoors, rain or shine. Averages up to a capacity of 68 indoor and 28 outdoor vendors.

Antiques and collectibles, Avon products, books, new and vintage clothing, cookware, crafts, new and used furniture, jewelry and silver, new and used merchandise, porcelain, fresh produce, tools, and toys. Snack bar on premises; market is "known for its popcorn." Small, clean, family-run market.

VENDORS: Indoors: $10 per space per day includes three tables, or $25 for three days; outdoors: $2 per space per day. Reservations are not required.

Contact Mr. Carl Sparling, Route 2, Box 268, Pana, IL 62557. Tel: (217) 562-4825.

Pecatonica

The Pec Thing

At the Winnebago County Fairgrounds, on Route 20 between Freeport and Rockford. Turn north at the state police headquarters, to the sign on Seventh Street to the fairgrounds.

Two weekends a year, in May and September, 8 A.M. to 5 P.M.—call for dates.

Admission $2 per person; free parking. In operation for over 15 years; indoors, outdoors, and under cover, rain or shine. Averages up to a capacity of 400 vendors.

Antiques and collectibles, new and vintage clothing, crafts, garage-sale items, jewelry, and much more. Snacks and hot meals are served on the premises.

VENDORS: Inside: $50 per space per weekend; open shed: $35; outside space: $25; tables available at $7 each. Friday setup time is 2 P.M. to 9 P.M.; gates open for setup at 6 A.M. on market days. Reserve if possible; indoors booked from one show to the next; some outdoor space always available.

Contact Winnebago County Fair Office, P.O. Box K, Pecatonica, IL 61063. Tel: (815) 239-1641.

Peoria
Giant Flea Market

At the Expo Gardens. Take University Street exit off I-74 and go north to Northmoor Road, then go left a quarter mile.

Usually the fourth Sunday of every month from April through September, and the fourth weekend from October through March, 8:30 A.M. to 4:30 P.M.

Admission $1 per person; ample free parking. In operation for over 19 years; indoors, year-round. Averages 60 to 100 vendors.

Antiques and collectibles, books, new and vintage clothing, jewelry and silver, new merchandise, and toys. Snacks and hot meals are served on the premises.

VENDORS: $12 per 8-foot table for one day, or $18 for two days. Reserve two weeks in advance.

Contact John Crouch, P.O. Box 9500, Springfield, IL 62791. Tel: (217) 529-6939.

Rockford
Greater Rockford Indoor-Outdoor Flea Market

At Alpine and Sandy Hollow, one and a half blocks west of Alpine exit off Highway 20 on Sandy Hollow.

Every weekend, 9 A.M. to 4 P.M.

Free admission; free parking for up to 1,500 cars. In operation for over 20 years; indoors year-round, and outdoors, weather permitting. Averages 60 to over 100 vendors.

Variety of offerings including antiques and collectibles, new and used merchandise, cookware, crafts, glassware, jewelry, fresh produce, and "junque." Hot meals available on premises.

VENDORS: $25 per space per weekend, indoors or outdoors. Reservations are required one week in advance for indoor spaces only.

Contact Albert or Carol Fritsch, 6350 Canyon Woods Drive, Rockford, IL 61109. Tel: (815) 397-6683 or (815) 874-3362.

Rosemont
Wolff's Flea Market

At 6920 North Mannheim (between Higgins and Touhy, near O'Hare Airport), at the Rosemont Horizon. Take Lee Street exit off I-90 West (market is visible from exit), or take O'Hare Airport exit off I-90 East, then onto Mannheim North one mile to market.

Every Sunday from April through October, 7 A.M. to 3 P.M.

Admission 75 cents per person (50 cents for seniors and children under 12); free parking for up to 3,000 cars. In operation for over five years; outdoors, weather permitting. Averages up to 250 vendors in summer (capacity 700).

Antiques and collectibles, books, new and vintage clothing, coins and stamps, computers, cookware, crafts and fine art, used furniture, porcelain, fresh produce, toys, and used merchandise. Snacks and hot meals are served on the premises.

VENDORS: $20 per space per day; inquire for monthly rates. Reservations are not required.

Contact David and Donald Wolff, 970 Arkansas, Elk Grove Village, IL 60007. Tel: (708) 529-9590.

Saint Charles
Kane County Flea Market

On the Kane County Fairgrounds, at Route 64 and Randall Road, on the west side of Saint Charles (40 miles west of Chicago).

First Sunday of each month, 7 A.M. to 4 P.M., and the preceding Saturday, 1 P.M. to 5 P.M.

Admission $4 per person; free admission for children under 12; 100 acres of free parking. In operation for over 28 years; indoors, outdoors, and under cover, rain or shine. Averages 600 to 1,200 vendors.

Antiques and collectibles, books, vintage (and some new) clothing, crafts and fine art, "fancy junque," used furniture, jewelry and silver, new and used merchandise, primitives, and toys. Snacks, sandwiches, and hot meals are served on the premises (including a country breakfast on Sunday). One of the country's largest and most diverse markets, drawing vendors from many states; billed as "best in the Midwest or anywhere." This market has never canceled in nearly thirty years.

VENDORS: Indoors: $110 per booth per weekend; Open-sided shed: $90 per weekend; outdoors: $100 per 10'x20' space per weekend. Reservations required for indoor spaces when available; outdoor spaces are rented on a first-come, first-served basis.

Contact Helen B. Robinson, P.O. Box 549, Saint Charles, IL 60174. Tel: (708) 377-2252 (office hours are Monday through Friday, 9 A.M. to 5 P.M.).

Sandwich
Sandwich Antiques Market

On the fairgrounds on Route 34, 60 miles west of Chicago.

On six Sundays from May through October, 8 A.M. to 4 P.M.—call for dates.

Admission $4 per person; acres of free parking. In operation for over five years; indoors and outdoors, rain or shine. Averages up to a capacity of 550 vendors.

Antiques and collectibles. Snacks and hot meals are served on the premises. Furniture delivery service available. Billed as one of the best markets in the state; all merchandise guaranteed.

VENDORS: Inquire for rates. Reservations are required a month in advance.

Contact Manager, 1510 North Hoyne, Chicago, IL 60622-1804. Tel: (312) 227-4464.

Limited

Springfield
Giant Flea Market

At the State Fairgrounds. Take the Sangamon Avenue exit off I-55 and go one mile west.

Generally the third Sunday of every month except June through August (but dates can vary), 8:30 A.M. to 4:30 P.M.

Admission $1 per person; ample free parking. In operation for over 19 years; indoors, regardless of weather. Averages up to 100 vendors.

Antiques and collectibles, books, new clothing, coins and stamps, jewelry and silver, new merchandise, and toys. Snacks and hot meals are served on the premises.

VENDORS: $12 per 8-foot table per day. Reserve two weeks in advance.

Contact John Crouch, P.O. Box 9500, Springfield, IL 62791. Tel: (217) 529-6939.

Sycamore

Sycamore Music Boosters' Antique, Craft, and Flea Market

At the Sycamore High School, 60 miles west of Chicago Route 64. Take Route 23 south to Spartan Trail Drive to the high school.

Annually, the last full weekend before Halloween, 9 A.M. to 5 P.M.

Admission $1.50 per person; $1 for senior citizens, 50 cents for children; ample free parking. In operation for over 20 years; indoors, rain or shine. Averages up to 155 vendors (large vendor capacity).

Antiques and collectibles, handmade clothing, crafts and fine art, jewelry and silver, pumpkins, and holiday items. Food is available at a cafeteria serving homemade pies and barbecue. Average attendance is 15,000 customers; held in conjunction with the annual Sycamore Pumpkin Festival, said to be one of the largest events in Illinois, attracting approximately 180,000 people over the weekend.

VENDORS: $65 per 10'x12' space for the weekend. Reserve six months in advance.

Contact Beverly A. Smith, Sycamore Music Boosters, P.O. Box 432, Sycamore, IL 60178. Tel: (815) 895-6750.

Towanda

Towanda Antique Flea Market

In the town of Towanda, seven miles northeast of Bloomington. Take Exit 171 off I-55.

Every July Fourth, 9 A.M. to 5 P.M.

Free admission; free parking all over town. In operation for over 27 years; outdoors, rain or shine. Averages up to 200 vendors (capacity 225).

Antiques and collectibles, vintage clothing, coins and stamps, crafts, antique furniture, jewelry and silver, primitives, and

ILLINOIS / Urbana

Indian artifacts. Snacks and hot meals are available in town. Billed as the biggest flea market in central Illinois on July Fourth, with accompanying festivities in town.

VENDORS: $25 for a 12'x12' reserved space. Reserve three months in advance.

Contact Mary Merritt, P.O. Box 97, Towanda, IL 61776. Tel: (309) 728-2810 or (309) 728-2384.

Urbana
Urbana Antiques and Flea Market

On the fairgrounds in Urbana. From downtown Urbana at Monument Square, go toward Springfield, Ohio, on Route 68; go south several blocks to Park Avenue and turn left on Park Avenue to fairgrounds.

First full weekend of each month except August; Saturdays, 9 A.M. to 5 P.M.; Sundays, 9 A.M. to 4 P.M.

Admission 50 cents per person; free admission for children under 12; ample free parking. In operation for over 23 years; indoors and outdoors, rain or shine. Averages 150 to 350 vendors (large vendor capacity).

A wide range of new and used merchandise, collectibles, garage-sale items, etc.; fresh produce in season. Snacks and hot meals are served on the premises. This has been a busy market for antiques and collectibles for over two decades.

VENDORS: Indoors: $22 for three tables for the weekend; outdoors: $9 per day or $16 per weekend for 30-foot frontage. Reservations are required for indoor spaces.

Contact Elizabeth or Steve, Managers, 934 Amherst Drive, Urbana, IL 43078. Tel: (513) 653-6013 or (513) 788-2058.

162

Wheeling
Twin Flea Market

At 1010 South Milwaukee Avenue, between Willow and Dundee Roads, a five-minute drive from the 294 Tollway, at Loews Twin Drive-In. Next to the Pal-Waukee Airport.

Every weekend from April through November, 7 A.M. to 4 P.M.

Free admission; free parking for up to 2,000 cars. In operation for over 25 years; outdoors, rain or shine. Averages up to 500 vendors (capacity 850).

Antiques and collectibles, books, new and vintage clothing, coins and stamps, cookware, crafts and fine art, new and used furniture, jewelry and silver, new and used merchandise, porcelain, fresh produce, and toys. Snacks and hot meals are served on the premises. Security on the premises. One of the older flea markets in the Chicagoland area. Sunday is the big day, with more than 3,000 shoppers on busy days.

VENDORS: $12 per space on Saturday, $20 on Sunday. Reservations are not required.

Contact Ron Swislow, 1010 South Milwaukee Avenue, Wheeling, IL 60089. Tel: (708) 459-0078 or (708) 537-8223.

Woodstock
Summer Collectors Fairs and Markets

At the McHenry County Fairgrounds.

On three Sundays, usually on Memorial Day weekend, a weekend in July, and on Labor Day weekend—call for dates, 8 A.M. to 4 P.M.

Admission $2 per person; acres of free parking; indoors and outdoors, rain or shine. Averages up to several hundred vendors.

Antiques and collectibles, furniture, old toys—"thousands of treasures!" Food available on premises. Old car show on the August date.

ILLINOIS/Woodstock

VENDORS: Inside: $55 per 20'x10' space per day; pavilion: $45 per space; outside: $35 per space. Setup times are Saturday, noon to 9 P.M.; and Sunday, 6 A.M. to 8 A.M. Reservations are not required, but day-of-show bookings are $5 extra.

Contact Bob Zurko, Zurko's Midwest Promotions, 211 West Green Bay Street, Shawano, WI 54166. Tel: (715) 526-9769.

INDIANA

Gary — South Bend •   Shipshewana •

    • Cedar Lake

           Fort Wayne •

                Muncie •

   Indianapolis •

              Metamora •

              Brookville •

              Friendship •

            Canaan •

Evansville

Brookville
White's Farm Flea Market

On Highway 52, three miles southeast of Brookville.

Every Wednesday, daybreak to noon.

Free admission; free parking. In operation for over 14 years; indoors and outdoors, rain or shine. Averages 50 to 250 vendors.

Good variety of new and used merchandise including collectibles, new and vintage clothing, cookware, crafts, jewelry, knives, and fresh produce. Food available on premises. Livestock auction at 1:00 P.M.

VENDORS: $10 per 20'x24' space per day outdoors, or $15 per 10'x13' space indoors.

Contact Dave White, P.O. Box 53, Brookville, IN 47012. Tel: (317) 647-3574—Brookville Medical.

Canaan
Canaan Fall Festival Flea Market

On the village square in Canaan. Pick up Chief White Eye Trail (Route 62) on the hilltop at Madison, and go 10 miles from there on Route 62.

At the annual Fall Festival, Friday, Saturday, and Sunday of the second weekend in September: Friday, 9 A.M. to 10 P.M.; Saturday, 9 A.M. to 5 P.M.; and Sunday, 9 A.M. to 10 P.M.

Free admission; free parking. In operation for over 31 years; outdoors, rain or shine. Averages up to a capacity of 125 vendors.

Antiques and collectibles, cookware and crafts, new furniture, jewelry, fresh produce, and much more. Snacks are served on the premises; baked goods (including Mennonite baked products), homemade ice cream, and fish are sold by the Canaan Fire Department. Many other events are associated with the festival, including Little Indian Papoose Contest, old-fashioned parade, balloon toss, egg toss, horseshoe pitching, frog jumping and other contests, live entertainment, Chief White Eye Painting Contest, horse-drawn vehicle rides, and farm produce display. Old-fashioned parade on Saturday at 10:30 A.M.

VENDORS: $30 per 20'x20' space for the three-day weekend; electricity is $5 extra. Reservations are required by mid-August.

Contact Gale Ferris, R.R. #4, Box 155, Madison, IN 47250. Tel: (812) 839-4770, or call Helyn Bishop, Business Manager, at (812) 839-3741.

Cedar Lake

Barn and Field Flea Market

At 9600 West 151st Avenue at the corner of Parrish Avenue, one mile east of Route 41.

Every weekend, 9 A.M. to 5 P.M. during wintertime, otherwise dawn to 5 P.M.

Free admission; ample free parking. In operation for over 18 years; indoors year-round, and outdoors, weather permitting. Averages 30 to 250 vendors.

Antiques and collectibles, baseball cards, bottles, new and vintage clothing, coins, used furniture, jewelry, knives, dolls, antique firearms, clocks, and fresh produce; "70 percent antiques and collectibles, 30 percent new," according to the manager. Snack bar on premises. Farm atmosphere.

VENDORS: $3 per space on Saturday and $4 on Sunday; electricity is available at nominal charge; tables are available at $1 each. Reservations are required a week in advance if electricity is needed.

Contact Dolores or Carl Corey, P.O. Box 411, Cedar Lake, IN 46303-0411. Tel: (219) 696-7368.

Cedar Lake
Uncle John's Flea Market

At 15205 Wicker Avenue (State Route 41), nine miles south of Route 30.

Every weekend, early morning to 4 P.M.

Free admission; free parking for up to 1,000 cars. In operation for over 15 years; indoors year-round, and outdoors, weather permitting. Averages 200 to 300 vendors (capacity 500).

Antiques and collectibles, books, new and vintage clothing, coins and stamps, cookware, crafts and fine art, new and used furniture, jewelry and silver, new and used merchandise, porcelain, fresh produce, toys—about three quarters used merchandise. Snacks and hot meals are served on the premises.

VENDORS: $8 to $10 per outdoor space depending on size and location. Reservations are not required.

Contact John A. Lail, 15205 Wicker Avenue, Cedar Lake, IN 46303. Tel: (219) 696-7911.

Evansville
Diamond Flea Market

At 1250 Diamond Avenue (Highway 66 West) at the corner of Business Highway 41.

Every weekend, 9 A.M. to 5 P.M.

Free admission; free parking for approximately 200 cars. In operation for over nine years; indoors and outdoors, rain or shine. Averages 80 to 90 vendors.

Antiques and collectibles, books, new clothing, crafts, new and used furniture, jewelry and silver, new merchandise, pottery and porcelain, and toys (including dollhouses and miniatures). Snacks and hot meals are served on the premises. Credit cards accepted.

VENDORS: $25 per space per weekend indoors, $6 per day outdoors; tables are available at $2.50 each per day. Reservations are required for indoor spaces only—from about a week in advance during summer to up to two months in advance in fall and winter.

Contact Barbara Staub, 1250 East Diamond Avenue, Evansville, IN 47711. Tel: (812) 464-2675.

Fort Wayne
Speedway Mall Flea Market

At 217 Marciel Drive (at the intersection with Speedway Drive). Take Coliseum Boulevard to Speedway Drive, then go north two blocks, and market will be on the right.

Every Friday, 9 A.M. to 9 P.M., and every Saturday and Sunday, 9 A.M. to 5 P.M.

Free admission; free parking for up to 500 cars. In operation for over 21 years; indoors and outdoors, rain or shine. Averages 150 to a capacity of 160 or more vendors.

Antiques and collectibles, books, clocks and watches, vintage clothing, coins and stamps, cookware, crafts and fine art, used furniture, furs, jewelry and silver, new and used merchandise, porcelain, fresh produce, and toys. Snacks and hot meals are served on the premises.

VENDORS: $100 per 8'x13' space per month. Reservations are not required.

Contact Marciel H. Mills, Owner, 217 Marciel Drive, Fort Wayne, IN 46825. Tel: (219) 484-1239. Day of market, contact Martha Tom, Manager.

Friendship
Friendship Flea Market

On Route 62, six miles west of Dillsboro (50 miles west of Cincinnati). Take I-275 west to Exit 16, then west on Highway 50 to Dillsboro, then west on Route 62, six miles to market.

Two nine-day runs in June and September, in the middle of the month—call for dates, around the clock.

Free admission; parking at $1 per car for up to 2,000 cars. In operation since 1967; indoors year-round, and outdoors, weather permitting. Averages up to a capacity of 500 vendors.

Full spectrum of antiques and collectibles, coins and stamps, new and used goods, and fresh produce. Snacks and hot meals are served on the premises. The market is located next door to the National Muzzle-loading Rifle Association, whose members live in tepees and shoot the cap-and-ball rifle. Market draws over 100,000 shoppers per run.

VENDORS: $20 per day or $130 for nine days, including electricity; outdoor spaces are 20'x20'; indoor spaces are 10'x10'. Reservations are required.

Contact Tom Kerr or Jan Hopkins, 654 Wayskin Drive, Covington, KY 41015. Tel: (606) 341-1400 or (606) 356-7114. Day of market, call Tom Kerr at (812) 667-5645

Gary
Market City

At 4121 Cleveland Street, at 41st Street.

Every Friday, Saturday, and Sunday, 9 A.M. to 5 P.M.

Free admission; free parking for up to 650 cars. In operation for over five years; indoors and outdoors, rain or shine. Averages 200 to 275 vendors (capacity 350 vendors, on 30,000 square feet of indoor selling space plus more space outdoors).

Antiques and collectibles, books, new and vintage clothing, coins and stamps, cookware, crafts and fine art, new and used furniture, glassware, jewelry and silver, new and used merchandise, porcelain, fresh produce, tools, and toys. Hot meals are served on the premises. Claims to be about 80 percent new merchandise (including closeout name-brand items).

VENDORS: From $5 per outdoor space per day. Reservations are recommended.

Contact Bill House, 4121 Cleveland Street, Gary, IN 46408. Tel: (219) 887-3522.

Gary
Village Flea Market

At 1845 West Ridge Road. Take Grant Street South exit off I-94, then south on Grant about a mile and a half to Ridge Road, then right on Ridge Road and go one block.

Every Friday, Saturday, and Sunday, 9 A.M. to 5 P.M.

Free admission; free parking. In operation for over eight years; indoors, year-round. Averages 70 to 80 vendors (capacity 90).

Antiques and collectibles, books, new and vintage clothing, cookware, crafts, new and used furniture, hardware, jewelry and silver, new and used merchandise, porcelain, and toys. Free coffee and doughnuts all day.

VENDORS: $25 per 8'x10' space ($30 for a corner space) for three days, or $40 per 10'x13' wall space for three days. Reserve a week in advance.

Contact Joseph D. Harkin, 5719 Hohman Avenue, Hammond, IN 46320. Tel: (219) 933-6622 or (219) 980-1111.

Indianapolis
Liberty Bell Flea Market

At 8949 East Washington Street. Take Post Road exit off I-70 on the east side of Indianapolis, then go south two miles on Post Road to the corner of Washington Street.

Every Friday, noon to 8 P.M.; Saturday, 10 A.M. to 7 P.M.; and Sunday, 10 A.M. to 6 P.M.

Free admission; free parking for up to 350 cars. In operation since 1975; indoors year-round, and outdoors from mid-April through late November, weather permitting. Averages 150 to a capacity of 200 vendors.

171

Antiques and collectibles, books, new and vintage clothing, coins and stamps, cookware and crafts, electronics, fish, new and used furniture, jewelry and silver, leather goods, new merchandise, pottery and porcelain, fresh produce, tools, toys, video games, and decorating items (such as wallpaper, carpeting, and draperies). Snacks and hot meals are served on the premises.

VENDORS: $45 per 12'x14' space indoors per weekend (lockable—renters may leave merchandise from week to week). Rentals are on a first-come, first-served basis.

Contact Noble Hall, 8949 East Washington Street, Indianapolis, IN 46219. Tel: (317) 898-3180 or (317) 898-3181.

Indianapolis
West Washington Flea Market

At 6445 West Washington Street. Take Plainfield exit off I-465 and go a block and a half west on Washington Street, and market will be on the left (look for a big Liberty Bell on building).

Every Friday, 1 P.M. to 8 P.M., and every Saturday and Sunday, 11 A.M. to 6 P.M.

Free admission; free parking for up to 500 cars. In operation for over 13 years; indoors, year-round. Averages close to its capacity of 100 vendors.

Antiques and collectibles, books, new clothing, cookware, crafts and fine art, jewelry and silver, new and used merchandise, porcelain, fresh produce, and toys. Snacks and hot meals are served on the premises.

VENDORS: $45 per 12'x12' space per weekend, or $88 per 12'x24' space. Reserve a week in advance; sometimes there is a waiting list.

Contact Mirza Beg, 6445 West Washington Street, Indianapolis, IN 46241. Tel: (317) 244-0941.

Metamora
Canal Days Flea Market

On Route 52, eight miles west of Brookville, Indiana, and about 35 miles west of Cincinnati, Ohio.

First full weekend in October, 8 A.M. to 5 P.M.

Free admission; ample parking in pay lots nearby. In operation for over 28 years; outdoors, rain or shine. Averages close to 800 vendors (capacity 1,000).

Antiques and collectibles, books, new and vintage clothing, coins and stamps, crafts, new and used furniture, holiday items, jewelry, new and used merchandise, porcelain, quilts, and toys. Snacks and hot meals are served on the premises.

VENDORS: $75 and up per space. Reserve up to a year in advance.

Contact Historic Metamora, Inc., P.O. Box 76, Metamora, IN 47030. Tel: (317) 647-2194.

Muncie
Greenwalt's Flea Market

At the Delaware County Fairgrounds. Take I-69 to the Muncie/Franklin exit, then go approximately seven miles (road becomes McGalliard Avenue and Route 332) to Wheeling Avenue, then turn south and go seven blocks to the fairgrounds.

First or second weekend of every month except June through August; Saturday, 9 A.M. to 5 P.M., and Sunday, 9 A.M. to 4 P.M.—call for dates.

Free admission; ample free parking. In operation since 1976; indoors, year-round. Averages up to 75 vendors.

Antiques and collectibles, coins, crafts, new and used furniture, jewelry, knives, new merchandise, primitives, and toys. Hot meals are available on the premises. Smoking permitted. No alcoholic beverages allowed on the grounds.

VENDORS: $35 per 10′x10′ space per weekend; tables are

available at $6 each. Reservations are required—check with manager.

Contact Mary Greenwalt, 604 North Kettner Drive, Muncie, IN 47304. Tel: (317) 289-0194.

Shipshewana
Shipshewana Auction and Flea Market

On Route 5 south of town.

Every Tuesday and Wednesday from May through October: Tuesday, 7 A.M. to 5 P.M., and Wednesday, 7 A.M. to 3 P.M.

Free admission; ample parking at $2 per car. In operation for over 50 years; indoors and outdoors, rain or shine. Averages up to several hundred vendors.

Antiques and collectibles, books, new and vintage clothing, cookware, crafts and fine art, new and used merchandise, fresh produce, and more. Snacks and hot meals are served on the premises.

VENDORS: $30 per 20'x25' space for two days. Reservations are not required.

Contact Manager, P.O. Box 185, Shipshewana, IN 46565. Tel: (219) 233-9820.

South Bend
Thieves' Market

At the corner of Edison and Ironwood, near the Notre Dame campus.

Every weekend, 10 A.M. to 6 P.M.

Free admission; free parking for up to 400 cars. In operation for over 29 years; indoors and outdoors, rain or shine. Averages 30 to 35 vendors (capacity 45).

Antiques and collectibles, books, new and vintage clothing, fine art, used furniture, jewelry and silver, new merchandise, porcelain, oriental rugs, and toys. Food is not served on the premises. Specialty is estate and distinctive jewelry.

VENDORS: $5 per outdoor space per day. Reservations are not required.

Contact David Ciesiolka, P.O. Box 6114, South Bend, IN 46615. Tel: (219) 233-9820.

IOWA

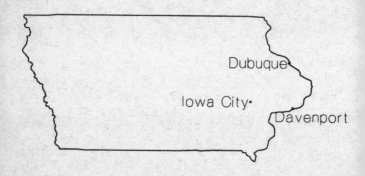

Dubuque

Iowa City·

Davenport

Davenport
Mississippi Valley Flea Market

At 2815 West Locust, on the Mississippi Valley Fairgrounds. Take I-80 to I-280 and look for Locust Street exit in Davenport.

Last Sunday of every month (except in July—inquire for July date), 7 A.M. to 3 P.M.

Admission $1.50 per person; ample free parking. In operation since 1969; indoors year-round, and outdoors, weather permitting. Averages close to 60 vendors year-round (large outdoor vendor capacity).

Antiques and collectibles, books, vintage clothing, coins and stamps, used furniture, household items, jewelry and silver, toys, and used merchandise. Snacks are served on the premises.

VENDORS: Inquire for rates. Reservations are recommended. Contact Robert H. Balzer, 2120 East 11th Street, Davenport, IA 52803. Tel: (319) 323-2319.

Dubuque
Dubuque Flea Market/Antique Show

At the Dubuque County Fairgrounds, five miles west on Highway 20.

Three Sundays a year in February, April, and October (last weekend of the month), 8 A.M. to 4 P.M. Setup time 6:30 A.M.

Admission $1 per person; free admission for children under 12; free parking. In operation for over 35 years; indoors and outdoors, rain or shine. Averages up to 150 vendors.

Antiques and collectibles, coins, new and vintage clothing, stamps, fine art, cookware, and crafts. Food on premises, including hot dogs, fries, doughnuts, and rolls. In addition to the flea market, there are two arts and crafts shows at the fairgrounds twice a year on Sundays in April and November (in the middle of each month). "One man's junque is another man's treasure."

VENDORS: Indoors: $11 per 8-foot space per day (wall space

$12); 8-foot tables and chairs furnished free with space; outdoors: $10 per 10'x20' space, no tables furnished. Reservations accepted for inside spaces only, with advance payment.

Contact Jerome F. Koppen, 260 Copper Kettle Lane, East Dubuque, IL 61025. Tel: (815) 747-7745. Day of market, call the fairgrounds at (815) 588-1406.

Iowa City
Sharpless Flea Market

At 5049 Hoover Highway NE, on I-80 at Exit 249, the easternmost Iowa City exit.

Second Sunday of every month except July and August, 8 A.M. to 4 P.M.

Admission $1.50 per person ($5 before 8 A.M.); free parking for more than 500 cars. In operation for over 20 years; indoors and outdoors, rain or shine. Averages close to 75 vendors (capacity of 200 tables).

Antiques and collectibles, new and vintage clothing, coins and stamps, used furniture, jewelry and silver, porcelain, and toys. Hot meals are served on the premises.

VENDORS: $12 per 8-foot table indoors (tables and chairs are provided) or $20 outdoors (no tables or chairs). Reserve a week to a month in advance for indoor spaces; outdoors on a first-come, first-served basis.

Contact Lisa or Julia Sharpless, 5049 Hoover Highway NE, Iowa City, IA 52240-8387. Tel: (319) 351-8888; fax: (319) 643-7372.

KANSAS

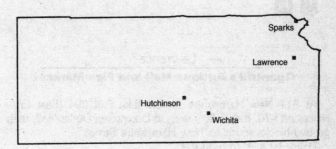

Hutchinson
Mid-America Flea Market

At the Kansas State Fairgrounds at 20th and Main, in the Industrial Building.

One Sunday every month (usually the first Sunday) except July through September—call for dates, 9 A.M. to 4 P.M.

Admission 50 cents; free parking. In operation for over 20 years; indoors, rain or shine. Averages up to 200 vendors.

This is an antiques and collectibles flea market. Snacks and hot meals are served on the premises.

VENDORS: $15 per 10'x12' space. Reservations are required two to three weeks in advance.

Contact Terry Masterson, P.O. Box 1585, Hutchinson, KS 67504-1585. Tel: (316) 663-5626. Day of market, call (316) 665-9000.

Lawrence
Quantrill's Antique Mall and Flea Market

At 811 New Hampshire Street. Take Exit 204 (East Lawrence) off I-70, then follow signs to Downtown Outlet Mall, then go two blocks south on New Hampshire Street.

Daily, 10 A.M. to 5:30 P.M.

Free admission; free parking for up to 2,000 cars. In operation for over 25 years; indoors, year-round. Averages close to 80 vendors on 20,000 square feet of selling area.

Antiques and collectibles (including military, fifties, and Coca Cola collectibles), books, vintage clothing, coins and stamps, cookware, fine art, used furniture, jewelry and silver, primitives, toys, and used merchandise. Snacks are served on the premises. Picture framing service is available. One of the oldest flea markets in Kansas.

VENDORS: From 90 cents to $1.10 per square foot per month; minimum lease period is two months (no transient vendors). Reservations are recommended.

Contact Randolph S. Davis, P.O. Box 971, Lawrence, KS 66044. Tel: (913) 842-6616 or (913) 842-1720.

Sparks

Sparks Flea Market

On old U.S. Highway 36 (Mission Road) at the K-7 highway, 23 miles west of St. Joseph, Missouri, and 24 miles north of Atchison, Kansas.

First Sunday in May and three preceding days; three days in mid-July (Friday, Saturday, and Sunday—call for dates); and Labor Day and the four preceding days, 8:30 A.M. to 6:30 P.M.

Free admission; parking for up to 700 cars at $1 (donation) per car. In operation for over 14 years; indoors and outdoors, weather permitting. Averages up to 200 vendors (capacity 300).

Antiques and collectibles, books, new and vintage clothing, coins and stamps, cookware, crafts, used and antique furniture, jewelry and silver, porcelain, fresh produce in season, toys, and used merchandise. Food concessions offer many tasty foods.

VENDORS: $40 per 20'x30' space outdoors or $50 per 10'x15' space indoors for entire show; electricity is available at $20 per show for outdoor spaces (provided free for indoor spaces); tables are available at $5 each for the entire show. Reserve at least two weeks in advance.

Contact Raymond Tackett, P.O. Box 223, Troy, KS 66087. Tel: (913) 985-2411. Day of market, call (913) 442-3311.

Limited

Wichita

Mid-America Flea Market

At the Kansas Coliseum, at I-135 and 85th Street North.

One Sunday each month except July and August—call for dates, which vary from month to month (usually toward the end of the month), 9 A.M. to 4 P.M.

Admission 50 cents; ample free parking. In operation for over 15 years; indoors, year-round. Averages up to 700 vendors.

Full spectrum of antiques and collectibles such as baseball cards, books, vintage clothing, and toys. Snacks and hot meals are served on the premises.

VENDORS: $15 per 8'x10' space. Reservations are required two to three weeks in advance.

Contact Terry Masterson, P.O. Box 1585, Hutchinson, KS 67504-1585. Tel: (316) 663-5626. Day of market, call (316) 755-2560.

Wichita
Village Flea Market

At 2301 South Meridian, at the corner of Pawnee in the southwest part of Wichita, a mile and a half north of I-235 Bypass, and a mile and a half south of Route 54.

Every Friday, Saturday, and Sunday, 9 A.M. to 5:30 P.M.

Free admission; free parking for up to 1,000 cars. In operation for over 20 years; indoors year-round, and outdoors, weather permitting. Averages 100 to 150 vendors (capacity 175).

Antiques and collectibles, books, new clothing, cookware, crafts, new and used furniture, jewelry and silver, new and used merchandise, and toys. Snacks and hot meals are served on the premises.

VENDORS: From $30 to $42 per space for all three days; tables are available at $4 for three days. Reservations are not required.

Contact Dale Cooper, 2301 South Meridian, Wichita, KS 67213. Tel: (316) 942-8263.

KENTUCKY

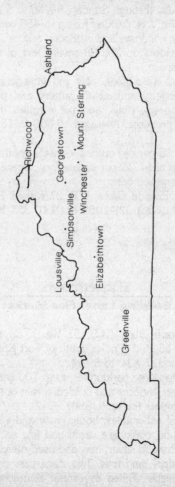

Ashland

Richwood

Georgetown

Mount Sterling

Simpsonville

Winchester

Louisville

Elizabethtown

Greenville

Ashland
Hillbilly Flea Market

Located on Russell Road (Route 23) north of Ashland—in front of Armco Steel.

Every Thursday through Sunday, 8 A.M. to 5 P.M.

Free admission; free parking for up to 450 cars. In operation for over 10 years; indoors and outdoors, rain or shine. Averages 100 to 150 vendors on 30,000 square feet of air-conditioned indoor selling space.

Antiques and collectibles, new and vintage clothing, cookware, crafts, jewelry and silver, pottery and porcelain, fresh produce, electronics, dolls, and pet supplies. Hot meals are served on the premises. Averages 10,000 to 15,000 shoppers per weekend.

VENDORS: $5 per day outdoors; inside booths are rented on a monthly basis at $1.25 per square foot. Space is rented on a first-come, first-served basis.

Contact Mr. Elwood Gibbs, U.S. 23/Russell Road, Ashland, KY 41101. Tel: (606) 329-1058 or (800) 357-1058.

Elizabethtown
Bowling Lanes Flea Market

At 4547 North Dixie (U.S. 31 West), 35 miles south of Louisville on I-65, and 8 miles south of Fort Knox.

Every weekend, 7 A.M. to 5 P.M.

Free admission; free parking for up to 700 cars. In operation for over 12 years; indoors and outdoors, rain or shine. Averages 125 to 300 vendors (capacity 350).

Antiques and collectibles, books, new and vintage clothing, coins and stamps, cookware, crafts and fine art, new and used furniture, jewelry and silver, new and used merchandise, porcelain, fresh produce, and toys. Two snack bars on the premises; hot meals available. Billed as central Kentucky's largest flea market, attracting regular vendors and customers from across Kentucky and neighboring states—with a good variety of merchandise.

VENDORS: Indoors: $8 per space per day; outdoors: $7 per 15'x27' space for a corner or shed spot. Reservations are on a first-come, first-served basis.

Contact Dean Taylor, 4547 North Dixie, Elizabethtown, KY 42701. Tel: (502) 737-7171 or (502) 737-5755.

Georgetown
Country World Flea Market

On Route 460 East, within sight of I-75; southbound take Exit 126 off I-75 to Route 62, then go right toward Route 460, then left to market entrance about one third of a mile down the road; northbound take Exit 125 off I-75 to Route 460, and market entrance will be about 200 feet across the road and to the right of exit ramp.

Every Friday, Saturday, and Sunday from the first weekend in April through the last weekend of November, from 7 A.M. Friday continuously until Sunday evening.

Free admission; ample free parking. In operation for over 27 years at various locations at current site since 1993; outdoors, rain or shine. Averages up to 200 vendors (capacity 450).

Antiques and collectibles, books, new and vintage clothing, coins and stamps, cookware, crafts, new and used furniture, jewelry and silver, new and used merchandise, porcelain, fresh produce, and toys. Snacks are available on the premises. Motels and RV parks nearby. One of Kentucky's largest weekly outdoor flea markets.

VENDORS: $8 per 14'x30' space on Saturday, $10 on Sunday; Friday is free with weekend booking or $3 without; electricity is available at $2 per day; tables are not provided; overnights OK. Reservations are on a first-come, first-served basis.

Contact Glenn Juett or Jack Mitchell, 111 Montgomery

Avenue, Georgetown, KY 40324. Tel: (502) 863-0474 or (502) 863-0289.

Greenville
Luke's Town and Country Flea Market

On Highway 62 West.

Every Monday, 8 A.M. to dark, and every Tuesday, from daylight until noon.

Free admission; limited free parking plus lots nearby at $1 per car. In operation for over 16 years; indoors year-round, and outdoors, weather permitting. Averages 100 to 400 vendors (capacity 600 vendors on 13 acres).

Antiques and collectibles, books, new and vintage clothing, coins and stamps, cookware, crafts, cosmetics and perfumes, pets, firearms, new and used furniture, jewelry and silver, livestock, new merchandise, poultry and fresh produce, shrubbery, and toys. Snacks and hot meals, including homemade biscuits and cornbread, are served on the premises. Mostly outdoors, with friendly, family atmosphere. Tuesday is the big market day.

VENDORS: $2 per space on Monday (except holidays); $3 and up per space on Tuesday. Electrical hookups are available, and overnight parking is welcome. Reservations are recommended.

Contact Wayne or Judy Rice, 2006 U.S. Highway 62 West, Greenville, KY 42345. Tel: (502) 338-4920 or (502) 338-6284.

Louisville
Derby Park Traders' Circle Flea Market

At 2900 South Seventh Street Road. Take 264 West to Taylor Boulevard, then right on Taylor, then at fifth light make a left onto Arcade; at the end of Arcade, take a left onto Seventh

Street Road and look for entrance about an eighth of a mile on the right.

Every Friday, Saturday, and Sunday, 9 A.M. to 6 P.M.

Free admission; six acres of free parking. In operation for over nine years; indoors and outdoors, rain or shine. Average number of vendors not reported.

Antiques and collectibles, new and vintage clothing, cookware and crafts, new merchandise, and fresh produce. Snacks and hot meals are served on the premises. Camping and electric hookups available; hot shower facilities. Run by Parker Commercial Storage and Distribution, Inc.

VENDORS: Indoors: $21 per day, $31 for three days; outdoors: $5 per day. Reservations are not required.

Contact Terry Marzian, 2900 Seventh Street Road, Louisville, KY 40216. Tel: (502) 636-FLEA or (502) 636-5817.

Mount Sterling
Mount Sterling October Court Days

On and around Main Street in the center of Mount Sterling, in Montgomery County 30 miles east of Lexington and 30 miles west of Morehead. Take Exit 110 off I-64.

The third Monday of every October and the weekend preceding, 8 A.M. to dark.

Free admission; ample street parking. In operation since the end of the 18th century; indoors and outdoors, rain or shine. Averages 900 to 1,000 vendors (capacity 3,000).

Antiques and collectibles, new and vintage clothing, cookware, crafts and fine art, new and used furniture, jewelry and silver, new merchandise, fresh produce, and more. Many food vendors. The "granddaddy of all flea markets," begun in 1792 and currently attended by over 70,000 people annually.

VENDORS: From $125 per 20'x20' space outdoors for three days; rates for food vendors are higher; plus city license at $20. Reserve as far ahead as possible; spaces are booked up months in advance.

Contact Ernest R. Begley, Jr., 40 Broadway, Mount Sterling, KY 40353. Tel: (606) 498-8725.

Richwood
Richwood Flea Market

At 10915 Dixie Highway (Route 25), 15 minutes south of Cincinnati, Ohio. Take Exit 175 off I-75.

Every weekend, 9 A.M. to 5 P.M.; every Tuesday, daybreak to whenever.

Admission $1 per car; parking for over 4,000 cars. In operation for over 11 years; indoors and outdoors (Tuesday is outdoors only), rain or shine. Averages close to 280 vendors.

Wide range of new and used merchandise including antiques and collectibles, jewelry, knives, fresh produce, and antique and modern firearms. Snacks and hot meals are served on the premises. Tuesday farmers' market starts at daybreak with over 200 vendors each week.

VENDORS: $50 per weekend outdoors, or from $35 to $80 indoors; Tuesdays: $10 per day outdoors. Reservations are required for indoor setups only.

Contact Mark Stallings, P.O. Box 153, Florence, KY 41022. Tel: (606) 371-5800.

Simpsonville
Shelby County Flea Market

At the northeast corner of Exit 28 off I-64, west of Lexington, Kentucky.

Every weekend, 9 A.M. to 5 P.M.

Free admission; 10 acres of free parking. In operation for over 10 years; indoors year-round, and outdoors, weather permitting. Averages 350 to 500 vendors on over 80,000 square feet of selling area.

Antiques and collectibles, books, new and vintage clothing, cookware, crafts and fine art, new and used furniture, jewelry and silver, new and used merchandise, porcelain, fresh produce, and toys. Snacks and hot meals are served on the premises.

VENDORS: $35 per indoor space per weekend, $12 per outdoor space per day. Reservations are required for indoor spaces only.

Contact Mr. Dana Smith, P.O. Box 8, Simpsonville, KY 40067. Tel: (502) 722-8883.

Winchester
Winchester Flea Market

At 4400 Oliver Road. Take Exit 94 off I-64.

Every weekend, 8 A.M. to 5 P.M.

Free admission; free parking for up to 500 cars. In operation for over five years; indoors and outdoors, rain or shine. Averages close to 50 vendors year-round (capacity 200).

Antiques and collectibles, books, new and vintage clothing, coins and stamps, cookware, crafts and fine art, antique firearms, new and used furniture, jewelry and silver, new and used merchandise, porcelain, fresh produce, records, tools, and toys. Snacks are available on the premises.

VENDORS: Indoors: $24 per 12'x12' space per weekend; outdoors: $5 per day. Reservations are not required.

Contact Raymond C. Huls, 202 Boone, Winchester, KY 40391. Tel: (606) 744-1179 or (606) 745-4332.

LOUISIANA

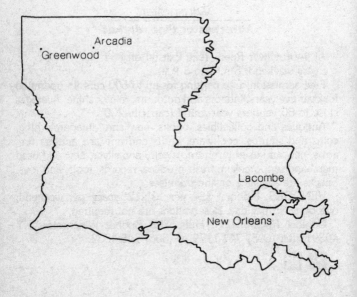

Arcadia
Bonnie and Clyde Trade Days

On Highway 9 South. Take Exit 69 off I-20, then go south for about three and a half miles (follow signs).

The Friday, Saturday, and Sunday before the third Monday of every month, from daybreak to dark.

Free admission; parking for several thousand cars at $3 per car. In operation since 1990; outdoors, year-round. Averages 200 to 325 vendors (capacity approximately 375).

Antiques and collectibles, books, new clothing, cookware, crafts and fine art, new and used furniture, pets, porcelain, poultry, fresh produce, and toys. Snacks and hot meals are served on the premises. "Washateria" (Laundromat) on the premises; overnight RV parking for $10 per night including water and electric hookups ($2 extra for sewage hookups).

VENDORS: $30 per regular lot per day, $70 per carport lot, $90 per pavilion lot. Reservations are not required but may be made up to two weeks in advance.

Contact Ed Jones, Manager, P.O. Box 243, Arcadia, LA 71001. Tel: (318) 263-2437.

Greenwood
Greenwood Flea Market

At 9249 Jefferson-Paige Road. Take Exit 5 off I-20. Near Shreveport, Louisiana.

Every weekend, 10 A.M. to 6 P.M.

Free admission and parking. In operation for over 10 years; indoors and outdoors, rain or shine. Averages 130 to a capacity of 150 vendors.

Antiques and collectibles, books, new clothing, coins and stamps, cookware and crafts, new and used furniture, jewelry and silver, new merchandise, pottery and porcelain, and toys. Snacks and hot meals are served on the premises.

LOUISIANA / Lacombe

VENDORS: $30 per 10'x15' booth per weekend, or $110 per month. Reservations are not required for outdoor spaces.

Contact Larry Millican, 9249 Jefferson-Paige Road, Greenwood, LA 71033. Tel: (318) 938-7201.

Lacombe
190 Trading Post Flea Market

At 31184 Highway 190 West, six miles west of Slidell. Take Lacombe exit off I-12 to Highway 190.

Every weekend, 9 A.M. to 5 P.M.

Free admission; free parking. In operation since the mid-1960s; indoors and outdoors, rain or shine. Averages 20 to a capacity of 30 vendors.

Antiques and collectibles, books, cookware, crafts and fine art, used furniture, jewelry, toys, and used merchandise. Snacks and hot meals are served on the premises.

VENDORS: $6 per table per day. Reservations are not required.

Contact Harold Fayard or Mary Fayard, 470 Pine Street, Slidell, LA 70460. Tel: (504) 882-6442 or (504) 641-3476. Day of market, call (504) 882-6442.

New Orleans
French Market Community Flea Market

At 1200 North Peters Street, where Elysian Fields meets the Mississippi River.

Daily, 7 A.M. to 7 P.M.

Free admission; parking available nearby in the lot behind the flood wall or the lot on Decatur Street. In operation since the 18th century in its current location; outdoors, weather permitting. Averages close to 250 vendors (capacity 350).

Antiques and collectibles, books, new and vintage clothing,

crafts, jewelry, new and used merchandise, fresh produce, seafood, and toys. Snacks and hot meals are served on the premises. Justly famous.

VENDORS: From $7 to $20 per space per weekday, or from $12 to $36 on Saturday or Sunday; city and state permits must be purchased prior to reservation. Reservations are not required.

Contact Sonny Davidson, c/o French Market Corporation, 1200 North Peters Street, New Orleans, LA 70117. Tel: (504) 596-3420 or (504) 596-3421.

New Orleans
Jefferson Flea Market

At 5501 Jefferson Highway, at the intersection of Clearview Park, off I-10.

Every Friday, Saturday, and Sunday, 10 A.M. to 6 P.M.

Free admission; free parking for up to 210 cars. In operation for over 18 years; indoors and under cover, year-round. Averages close to 100 vendors year-round.

Antiques and collectibles, books, cookware, fine art, new and used furniture, jewelry and silver, new merchandise. Hot and cold meals are available on the premises.

VENDORS: $15 per space (under cover) per day, table provided. Reserve a week in advance.

Contact Jim Russell, P.O. Box 23223, Harahan, LA 70183. Tel: (504) 734-0087.

MAINE

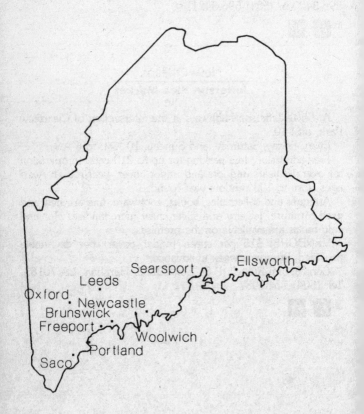

Brunswick
Fort Andross Indoor Flea Market

At 14 Main Street. Take Exit 24A off I-95 to get to Main Street.

Every weekend and holidays, 8 A.M. to 4 P.M.

Free admission; free parking. In operation for over four years; indoors, year-round. Averages up to 70 vendors (capacity 130).

Everything from brand-new to antiques—good mix of collectibles, gadgets, etc. Snacks are served on the premises. "No heat, no bugs, no rain."

VENDORS: From $10 per 8'x10' space per day. Reservations are recommended.

Contact Karen, Manager, 14 Main Street, Brunswick, ME 04011. Tel: (207) 729-0378 or (207) 865-4034.

Ellsworth
This 'n That Flea Market

On Route 1 (Hancock Road).

Every weekend, 8 A.M. to 9 P.M. (gift shop open daily).

Free admission; free parking. In operation for over five years; indoors year-round, and outdoors, weather permitting. Averages close to 25 vendors.

Antiques and collectibles, crafts, etc.—"this and that." Food is not served on the premises.

VENDORS: From $5 per space per day. Reservations are not required.

Contact Peggy Dorr, Route 1, Hancock Road, Ellsworth, ME 04605. Tel: (207) 667-2192.

Freeport
Red Wheel Flea Market

At 275 U.S. Route 1 South. Take Exit 17 off I-95 and go right onto Route 1, and market will be on the right.

Every weekend from May through October, 8 A.M. to 6 P.M.

Free admission; free parking for up to 200 cars. In operation for over 10 years; indoors and outdoors, rain or shine. Averages up to 60 vendors (capacity 120).

Antiques and collectibles, books, cookware, crafts, used furniture, tools, toys, and old stuff. Food is not served on the premises. There's a nice antiques shop on the premises also. While in Freeport, visit L.L. Bean store (open 24 hours) and many factory outlets.

VENDORS: Indoors: $25 per space per weekend; outdoors: $7 per space on Saturday and $10 on Sunday. Reservations are not required.

Contact Ed Collett, 275 U.S. #1 South, Freeport, ME 04032. Tel: (207) 865-6492.

Leeds
Red Roof Flea Market

On Route 202.

Every weekend in warm months, 9 A.M. to 3 P.M.

Free admission; free parking. In operation for over five years; outdoors, weather permitting. Averages up to about a dozen vendors.

Antiques and collectibles, books, used furniture, glassware, household items, new and used merchandise, and toys. Food is available on the premises. Small but nice market behind the Red Roof Store.

VENDORS: From $6 for two tables per day. Reservations are recommended.

Contact Ed Frost, P.O. Box 2000, Leeds, ME 04263. Tel: (207) 933-4533 or (207) 375-6291 or (207) 375-6246.

Newcastle

Foster's Flea Market and Antique Hall

On Route 1—watch for the big sign.

Every weekend from May through October, 8 A.M. to 4 P.M.

Free admission; ample free parking. In operation since 1953; indoors year-round, and outdoors, weather permitting. Averages up to 30 vendors.

Antiques and collectibles, books, household items, marine collectibles, tools, and used merchandise. Food is not served on the premises. Appraisals, estate sales and auctions, antiques bought and sold. This one's good for old-fashioned stuff.

VENDORS: Inquire for rates. Reservations are recommended.

Contact Robert L. Foster, P.O. Box 203, Newcastle, ME 04553. Tel: (207) 563-8150.

Oxford

Undercover Antique Mall and Flea Market

On Route 26, one half mile north of the Oxford Plains Speedway.

Daily from Memorial Day through Labor Day, every Friday through Monday during remainder of year, 8 A.M. to 5 P.M.

Free admission; free parking for over 100 cars. In operation for over eight years; indoors year-round, and also outdoors from May through September, weather permitting. Averages 60 to 75 vendors.

Antiques and collectibles, books, coins and stamps, crafts, jewelry and silver, porcelain, primitive reproductions, and toys. Snacks and hot meals are served on the premises. Primarily an indoor antiques and collectibles market with 60 to 70 vendors, but during summer season there are usually 20 to 30 outdoor vendors.

VENDORS: $5 per day for three tables in horseshoe shape. Reservations are recommended.

Contact Paul Chretien or Dale Farrar, Route 1, Box 1550, Oxford, ME 04270. Tel: (207) 539-4149 or (207) 897-4018.

Portland

Portland Expo Flea Market

At the Portland Exposition Building, 239 Park Avenue. Take Exit 6A or Exit 7 off the Maine Turnpike, and follow I-295 to Exit 5A (Congress Street), then turn left at the first set of lights to St. John Street, then go right ·at the next set of lights to Park Avenue. Parking is available 200 yards ahead on the left.

Every Sunday, 9 A.M. to 4 P.M.

Free admission; free parking for up to 350 cars. In operation since 1981; indoors, regardless of weather. Averages close to a capacity of 152 vendors.

Antiques and collectibles, books, new and vintage clothing, coins and stamps, cookware, crafts and fine art, new and used furniture, jewelry and silver, new and used merchandise, porcelain, and toys. Snacks and hot meals are served on the premises.

VENDORS: From $20 per space per day; discounts available for multispace blocks. Reserve a week in advance.

Contact Annette Crozier, 239 Park Avenue, Portland, ME 04102. Tel: (207) 874-8200.

Saco
Cascade Flea Market

On U.S. Route 1 at the corner of Cascade Road (Route 98). Take Exit 5 (Saco/Scarborough) off the Maine Turnpike, then after toll take Exit 2B (Scarborough) to Route 1 and then go north about two miles and market will be on the right.

Daily from April through October (but weekends are busiest), 6 A.M. to 5 P.M.

Free admission; free parking for up to 300 cars. In operation since 1972; outdoors, rain or shine. Averages close to its capacity of 200 vendors on weekends (about 75 during the week).

Antiques and collectibles, books, new and vintage clothing, cookware, crafts, new and used furniture, household items, jewelry and silver, new and used merchandise, fresh produce, toys—a pleasant mix of discount items and good old-fashioned flea-market stuff. Snacks and hot meals are served on the premises. Many tourist attractions nearby. One of northern New England's busiest outdoor family markets right on busy Coastal Route 1.

VENDORS: $8 per space day weekdays, $18 on Saturday, and $20 on Sunday or holidays; tables are available at $4 each on weekdays, $9 on Saturday, $10 on Sunday or holidays. Reserve a week in advance.

Contact Betty O'Donnell, 885 Portland Road, Saco, ME 04072. Tel: (207) 282-1800. Day of market, contact Betty, Wayne, or Ian.

Searsport
Hobby Horse Flea Market

On Bangor Road (Route 1), three miles north of central Searsport (30 miles south of Bangor and 10 miles north of Belfast).

Every Friday, Saturday, and Sunday from May through mid-

October (antiques mall open daily), 8 A.M. to 5 P.M.; there is some selling during the week.

Free admission; plenty of free parking. In operation for over 13 years; indoors and outdoors, weather permitting. Averages up to 30 vendors (capacity 36) plus 20 shops.

Antiques and collectibles, books, new and vintage clothing, cookware and crafts, new and used furniture, jewelry, new and used merchandise, military items, porcelain, and toys. Lunch wagon on the premises.

VENDORS: $6 per table per day. Reservations are not required.

Contact Mary E. Harriman, P.O. Box 215, Stockton Springs, ME 04981. Tel: (207) 548-2981.

Woolwich
Montsweag Flea Market

On Route 1 at the corner of Mountain Road in Woolwich, between Bath and Wiscasset.

Every weekend from early May through mid-October plus every Wednesday and Friday from June through August, 6:30 A.M. to 4 P.M. (Wednesday is strictly antiques and collectibles).

Free admission; three acres of free parking. In operation over 19 years; outdoors, weather permitting. Averages up to a capacity of 110 vendors.

Antiques and collectibles, crafts, used furniture, fresh produce, garage-sale items, glassware, jewelry, memorabilia, new and used merchandise, primitives, toys, and tools—a nice mix. Snack bar on the premises serves breakfast and lunch and those wonderful ice cream treats made by the famous Round Top Dairy of Damariscotta, Maine. (If you go to Wiscasset down the road, incidentally, don't miss the Sea Basket, on your left on Route 1, which has some of the best Maine clam cakes and chowder known to man). This is a fine example of a New England country flea market, with lots of old things for the "junktiquer" and a friendly atmosphere that is conducive to browsing.

VENDORS: From $7 to $10 per table per day ($7 for two tables on Friday). Reserve as far in advance as possible; regulars have first refusal.

Contact Norma Scopino, P.O. Box 252, Woolwich, ME 04579. Tel: (207) 443-2809.

MARYLAND

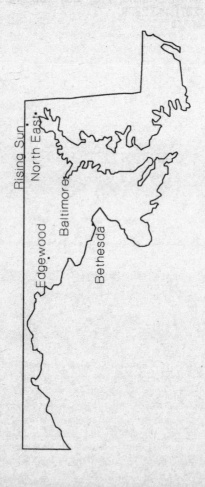

Baltimore
Patapsco Flea Market

At 1400 West Patapsco Avenue. Take I-95 to Route 295 West to Annapolis Road, then turn left onto Annapolis Road.

Every weekend, 7 A.M. to 4 P.M.

Admission 25 cents per person; ample free parking. In operation for over eight years; indoors year-round, and outdoors, weather permitting. Averages up to a capacity of 1,500 vendors.

Antiques and collectibles, books, new and vintage clothing, coins and stamps, cookware, crafts and fine art, new and used merchandise, porcelain, fresh produce, and toys. Snacks and hot meals are served on the premises. Billed as Maryland's largest indoor-outdoor flea market. "When you want the best we'll make you forget the rest."

VENDORS: From $10 to $20 per table per day. Reserve a week in advance.

Contact Bob Lomonico, 1400 West Patapsco Avenue, Baltimore, MD 21230. Tel: (410) 354-3041 or (410) 354-5262.

Bethesda
Farmer's Flea Market

At 7155 Wisconsin Avenue.

Every Sunday, from the first Sunday in March through the Sunday before Christmas, 8 A.M. to 5 P.M.

Free admission; ample free parking. In operation since 1973; outdoors, weather permitting. Averages up to 50 vendors.

Antiques and collectibles such as books, bottles, vintage clothing, coins, cookware, jewelry, knives, silver, and stamps. Snacks and hot meals are served on the premises. Located in an affluent suburb of Washington, D.C. The members of the Montgomery County Farm Women's Coop purchased the land and building back in 1930 to sell their produce directly to the public during the Great Depression.

VENDORS: $20 for a 20'x20' space per day. Reservations are not required—just show up at 8 A.M.

Contact James R. Bonfils, P.O. Box 39034, Washington, D.C. 20016 (telephone number not reported).

Edgewood
Bonnie Brae Flea Market

At 1301 Pulaski Highway (Route 40), between Routes 152 and 24 (20 miles out of Baltimore on the way to New York).

Every weekend, 7 A.M. to whenever.

Free admission; free parking. In operation since 1974; mainly outdoors, weather permitting. Averages 10 to 50 vendors (capacity 60 to 70).

Antiques and collectibles, baseball cards, books, clocks, crafts, fine art, used furniture, glassware (large selection of Depression glass), primitives, fresh produce, new merchandise, and toys. Snacks are available on the premises. Indoor shop specializes in glassware.

VENDORS: $15 per 10'x12' space per day. Reservations are not required.

Contact Angil Reynolds or Juanita A. Merritt, 1003 Magnolia Road, Joppa, MD 21085. Tel: (410) 679-6895 (shop) or (410) 679-2210 (residence).

North East
North East Auction Galleries Flea Market

At the junction of Route 40 and Mechanics Valley Road. Take Exit 100 off I-95 to Route 40, then east to Mechanics Valley Road, and the market will be on the left at the traffic light.

Every weekend, 7 A.M. to 5 P.M.

Free admission; free parking. In operation over 15 years;

indoors and outdoors, rain or shine. Averages 45 to 100 vendors.

Antiques and collectibles, books, new and vintage clothing, coins and stamps, cookware, crafts and fine art, new and used furniture, jewelry and silver, livestock, new merchandise, pottery and porcelain, and poultry and fresh produce. Snacks and hot meals are served on the premises. An 8,000-square-foot Amish market.

VENDORS: Indoors: $15 per 4'x8' table per day or $25 per weekend; outdoors: $10 per table per day. Reservations are recommended.

Contact Robert C. Burkheimer, 1995-99 Pulaski Highway, North East, MD 21901. Tel: (410) 287-5588.

Rising Sun
Hunter's Auction Service

On Route 276. Take Exit 93 off I-95 (northbound or southbound), then take Route 225 to dead end, then right onto Route 276 and go two and a half miles; market will be on the right.

Every Monday, 3 P.M. to 9 P.M.

Free admission; free parking for up to 1,500 cars. In operation for over 28 years; indoors year-round, and outdoors, weather permitting. Averages 100 to 150 vendors (capacity 250).

Antiques and collectibles, new clothing, crafts, new and used furniture, jewelry, new merchandise, fresh produce, and toys. Restaurant with home cooking, seating 40 people. Auction (same time as market). Family-owned.

VENDORS: $20 per space per day. Reservations are recommended.

Contact Norman E. or Carol A. Hunter, Route 276, Box 427, Rising Sun, MD 21911. Tel: (410) 658-6400.

MASSACHUSETTS

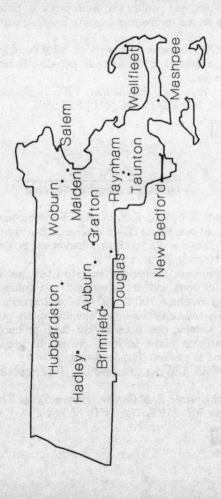

Salem

Wellfleet

Mashpee

Woburn

Malden

Raynham

Taunton

Grafton

Auburn

Hubbardston

Brimfield

Douglas

New Bedford

Hadley

Auburn
Auburn Antique and Flea Market

At 733 Southbridge Street (Route 12). Take Exit 10 off the Massachusetts Turnpike (I-90), or Exit 8 off I-290, or Exit 7 off I-395; then follow Route 12 south approximately one half mile.

Every Sunday year-round; every Saturday, April to November, 9 A.M. to 4 P.M.

Admission 50 cents for indoor market; free admission for children under 12; free parking for up to 500 cars. In operation for over 18 years; indoors every Sunday, year-round; outdoors (only) every Saturday, weather permitting. Averages 100 to a capacity of 200 vendors.

Antiques and collectibles, books, new and vintage clothing, coins and stamps, new and used furniture, jewelry and silver, fresh produce, rocks and minerals, tools, videotapes, and new merchandise. Hot meals are available on the premises. Only a 20-minute drive from Old Sturbridge Village, a major tourist attraction.

VENDORS: Indoors: $30 per 9'x9' space (Sunday only); outdoors: $10 on Saturdays, $15 on Sundays for a car-length space; 8-foot tables are available for rent at $3 each. Reservations are required for indoor spaces only.

Contact Manager, P.O. Box 33, Auburn, MA 01501. Tel: (508) 832-2763.

Brimfield
J and J Promotions Antiques and Collectibles Shows

On Route 20, a quarter mile west of the stoplight at Brimfield Common, and six miles west of Old Sturbridge Village. From New York, take I-95 north to Hartford, then I-84 east to Sturbridge and Route 20, then west on 20 for approximately six miles. From Boston or eastern New England, take Massachusetts Turnpike to Exit 9 (Sturbridge), then follow Route 20 west approximately six miles. Look for the tan colonial house with red shutters and the large red Auction Acresbarn.

Three two-day shows a year, in May, July, and September: Friday, 6 A.M. to 5 P.M. and Saturday, 8 A.M. to 5 P.M.

Admission $4 per person on Friday, $3 on Saturday; several acres of parking at $4 per car. In operation since 1959; outdoors, rain or shine. Averages 600 to 800 vendors.

Antiques and collectibles. Snacks and hot meals are served on the premises. The whole town explodes with antiques and collectibles on three summer weekends, and this market, one of several in the town, is its largest and the original "Brimfield."

VENDORS: Call for rates. Reservations are required.

Contact Jill Reid Lukesh or Judith Reid Mathieu, P.O. Box 385—Route 20, Brimfield, MA 01010-0385. Tel: (413) 245-3436 or (508) 597-8155.

Douglas
Douglas Flea Market

Off Route 16 and 146 at the Uxbridge/Douglas town line. Take 20E to 146 South to East Douglas exit or Lacky Dam; travel on Lacky Dam to four corners, then left; then first left over a bridge to the top of the hill and you're there.

Every weekend: Saturday, 10 A.M. to 2 P.M., and Sunday, 8 A.M. to 4 P.M.

Free admission; ample free parking. In operation for over eight years; indoors and outdoors, year-round. Averages up to a capacity of 25 vendors on 50 acres of selling area.

Antiques and collectibles, books, vintage clothing, cookware, new and used furniture, glassware, porcelain, primitives, and toys. Snacks and hot meals are served on the premises; try the homemade yogurt and ice cream. Located on the historic Bosma Farm, with hayrides on Sunday afternoons in summer.

VENDORS: $10 per space per day indoors, $2 per car-length space outdoors. Reservations are required for indoor spaces only.

Contact Marlene Alsop Bosma, P.O. Box 634, East Douglas, MA 01516. Tel: (508) 278-6027. Day of market, call (508) 476-3298.

Grafton
Grafton Flea Market

Located on Route 140 by the Grafton-Upton town line. Take Exit 21B (Upton) off Route 495, then go five miles to Route 140, then make a right turn and go one mile.

Every Sunday (and Monday holiday) from March through December, 7 A.M. to 5 P.M.

Admission 50 cents; free admission for children; free parking for up to 1,000 cars. In operation since 1970; indoors and outdoors, rain or shine. Averages up to a capacity of 300 vendors.

Everything from antiques and collectibles to new and used merchandise, new and vintage clothing, cookware, crafts, jewelry and silver, and fresh produce. Snack food (hamburgers and hot dogs, grinders) served on the premises. Unique pine grove atmosphere; attended by an average of 6,000 shoppers on good-weather days. "Come where the crowds are."

VENDORS: $25 per space indoors per day; $20 outdoors; shaded and exposed spaces are available. Reserve a week in advance.

Contact Harry Peters, P.O. Box 206, Grafton, MA 01519. Tel: (508) 839-2217.

Hadley
Olde Hadley Flea Market

At 45 Lawrence Plain Road (Route 47 South). Take Exit 19 off Route 91 North, then go eastbound on Route 9 for one mile, then south on Route 47 for two miles. Off Route 91 South, take

209

Exit 20, then go one mile to Route 9, then eastbound one mile to Route 47, then south two miles.

Every Sunday from late April through the end of October, 7 A.M. to 5 P.M.

Free admission; free parking for up to 500 cars. In operation for over 15 years; outdoors, weather permitting. Averages up to 200 vendors (capacity 250).

Antiques and collectibles, books, new and vintage clothing, coins and stamps, cookware, crafts, used furniture, jewelry and silver, pottery and porcelain, fresh produce, quilts, tools, and toys. Snacks and hot meals are served on the premises.

VENDORS: $17 per 25'x25' space per day. Reservations are not required.

Contact Raymond or Marion Szala, 45 Lawrence Plain Road, Hadley, MA 01035. Tel: (413) 586-0352.

Hubbardston
Rietta Ranch Flea Market

At 183 Gardner Road (Route 68).

Every Sunday from April through October, 6 A.M. to whenever.

Free admission; free parking for more than 1,000 cars. In operation for over 28 years; indoors year-round, and outdoors, weather permitting. Averages up to 500 vendors (capacity 600).

Antiques and collectibles, books, new and vintage clothing, coins and stamps, cookware, crafts, new and used furniture, jewelry and silver, new and used merchandise, porcelain, fresh produce, and toys. Snacks are served on the premises. Carnival atmosphere.

VENDORS: $10 per space per day including one table. Reservations are not required.

Contact Joyce or Ronnie Levesque, P.O. Box 35, Hubbardston, MA 01452. Tel: (508) 632-0559.

Malden
Malden Flea Market

At the corner of Route 60 and Ferry Street.

Every weekend, 9 A.M. to 5 P.M.

Admission 50 cents per person; free parking nearby. In operation for over four years; indoors, year-round. Average number of vendors not reported.

Antiques and collectibles, coins and stamps, cookware, crafts, used furniture, jewelry, new merchandise, and fresh produce. Snacks and hot meals are served on the premises.

VENDORS: $40 per space per weekend from October through April, $35 from May through September. Reserve a week in advance if possible.

Contact Stanley Krigman, 51 Lanard Road, Malden, MA 02148. Tel: (617) 321-9374 or (617) 324-9113.

Mashpee
Dick and Ellie's Flea Market

At 650 Falmouth Road (Route 28), a quarter mile from the Mashpee Rotary on Cape Cod.

Every Tuesday, Friday, Saturday, and Sunday from mid-April through mid-October, 6 A.M. to 5 P.M.

Free admission; free parking for up to 1,100 cars. In operation for over 21 years; outdoors, weather permitting. Averages up to a capacity of 250 vendors on 22 acres of selling space.

Antiques and collectibles, books, new and vintage clothing, coins and stamps, cookware, crafts and fine art, new and used furniture, garage-sale items, jewelry and silver, new and used merchandise, porcelain, fresh produce, and toys—"you name it!" Snacks and hot meals are served on the premises.

VENDORS: $15 per 20'x20' space on Tuesday or Friday, $20 per space on Saturday or Sunday; inquire for monthly rates. Reservations are on a first-come, first-served basis.

Contact Al or Mike Wiseman, 121 Smith Avenue, Mashpee, MA 02072. Tel: (508) 477-3550 or (617) 341-1572.

Methuen
Jolly Jim's Extravaganza

At the Valley Expo Center at the Methuen Mall. Easy access off Routes 93 and 495.

About two dozen three-day events (usually Friday through Sunday) from October through Christmas, 10 A.M. to 6 P.M.— call for dates and newsletter.

Admission $4 per person; free parking for up to 3,000 cars. In operation since 1979 (moved from Woburn in 1995); indoors, year-round. Averages up to a capacity of 700 vendors.

Mainly new merchandise: books, clothing, cookware, crafts, furniture, jewelry, porcelain, silver, and toys. Snacks and hot meals are served on the premises. Good variety.

VENDORS: From $10 per table per day, or from $195 per 10'x12' booth per weekend; electricity is available at $45. Reserve a month in advance.

Contact Marvin Getman, Show Promotion, Inc., 405 Waltham Street, #333, Lexington, MA 02173-7998. Tel: (617) 863-1516 or (800) 321-EXPO.

New Bedford
Whaling City Festival

In the Veterans Memorial Button Wood Park. From the north take Route 24 south to Route 140, then south to junction with Kempton Street (Route 6), and park is beyond intersection on the left. From the west (Providence) or east (Cape Cod), take I-195 to Route 140 South.

Annually, the Friday, Saturday, and Sunday of the second weekend in July, 9 A.M. to 9 P.M.

Free admission; ample free parking. In operation for over 26 years; outdoors, rain or shine. Averages up to 300 vendors (capacity 320).

Antiques and collectibles, books, new and vintage clothing, cookware, crafts and fine art, jewelry, silver, and new merchandise. Snacks and hot meals are served on the premises. Live entertainment, amusement park, car and bike show.

VENDORS: Inquire for rates. Reserve two months in advance.

Contact Louis Oliveira, 220 Union Street, New Bedford, MA 02740-5943. Tel: (508) 996-3348; fax: (508) 990-2367.

Raynham
Raynham Flea Market

At the intersection of Route 24 South, Route 44 West, and Route 495 South.

Every Sunday and holiday Monday, and Saturdays from Thanksgiving to Christmas, 8 A.M. to 6 P.M.

Admission 75 cents for adults, 50 cents for seniors, children free; ten acres of free parking. In operation for over 21 years; indoors and outdoors, rain or shine. Averages 500 to 800 vendors on 60,000 square feet of selling area.

Antiques and collectibles, books, new clothing, coins, comics, cookware, new and used furniture, jewelry, knives, new merchandise, novelties, fresh produce, silver, sporting goods, stamps, and toys. Variety of food concessions.

VENDORS: $30 inside, $20 outside. Reservations are suggested in busy season.

Contact Delsa Enterprises, Inc., Judson and South Streets, Raynham, MA 02767. Tel: (508) 823-8923; fax: (508) 824-2339.

Salem
Canal Street Antiques Flea Market

At 266 Canal Street. Take Route 95 or Route 1 or Route 128 to Route 114 through Downtown Salem to Canal Street (Route 1A).

Every Sunday, 8:30 A.M. to 4 P.M.

Admission 50 cents per person; free parking for up to 200 cars. In operation for over 12 years; indoors, year-round. Averages 120 to 160 vendors (capacity 180) on 24,000 feet of selling space.

Antiques and collectibles, coins and stamps, folk art and primitives, dolls, used furniture, glassware, jewelry and silver, paintings, prints, tools, toys—"if your grandma had it—we've got it." Snack bar on the premises.

VENDORS: $25 per 10'x10' space per week. Reservations are required—no transient vendors.

Contact Rick Boisvert, 266 Canal Street, Salem, MA 01970. Tel: (508) 744-7229.

Taunton
Taunton Expo Flea Market

At the Taunton Expo Center on Route 44.

Every weekend plus holiday Mondays, 8 A.M. to 5 P.M.

Admission $1 per person; free admission for children under 12; free parking for up to 8,000. In operation for over 10 years; indoors year-round, and outdoors, weather permitting. Averages up to 1,000 vendors on two floors indoors plus room for 500 vendors in outdoor paved lot.

Antiques and collectibles, new and vintage clothing, coins and stamps, cookware, crafts and fine art, new and used furniture, jewelry and silver, new merchandise, porcelain, fresh produce, seafood, and toys. Several food concession stands on the premises. Average attendance is 12,000 shoppers per weekend.

VENDORS: Indoors: $250 per 10'x10' space per month;

214

outdoors: $25 per 20'x20' space per weekend. Reservations are not required.

Contact David Horton, Route 44, Taunton, MA 02780. Tel: (508) 880-3800.

Wellfleet
Wellfleet Flea Market

On Route 6, on the Eastham/Wellfleet town line. After the Sagamore Bridge, stay on the Mid-Cape Highway and then go around the rotary in Orleans; take the second right off the rotary toward Provincetown, then go through four sets of lights and look for a big "Wellfleet Drive-In" sign on the left.

Every weekend and holiday Mondays from mid-April through October, plus every Wednesday and Thursday in July and August, 8 A.M. to 4 P.M.

Admission $1 per carload except $2 per carload on Sunday from the last Sunday in June through Labor Day Sunday; parking for up to 1,700 cars (free with admission). In operation for over 25 years; outdoors, rain or shine. Averages 75 to 230 vendors (capacity 350).

Antiques and collectibles, books, new and vintage clothing, coins and stamps, cookware, crafts and fine art, new and used furniture, jewelry and silver, new and used merchandise, porcelain, fresh produce, seafood (clams and oysters), toys, and other odds and ends—"bargains galore." Full snack bar on the premises. Playground. Cape Cod's biggest and best flea market.

VENDORS: $15 per space on Saturday or Thursday, $20 on Sunday or Wednesday. Reservations are not required.

Contact Eleanor Hazen, Wellfleet Drive-In, P.O. Box 811, Wellfleet, MA 02667. Tel: (508) 349-2520 or (508) 255-9619. Day of market, contact Eleanor Hazen.

MICHIGAN

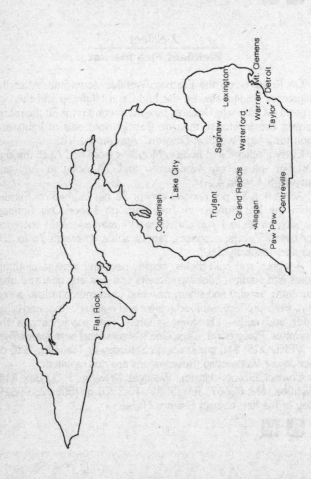

Allegan
Allegan Antique Market

At the Allegan County Fairgrounds. Take Allegan Exit off 131 Expressway or Route 196 (Exit 34) or Exit 60 off Route 94.

Last Sunday of every month from April through September, 7:30 A.M. to 4:30 P.M.

Admission $3 per person (group discounts are available); ample free parking. In operation for over 17 years; indoors and outdoors, rain or shine. Averages close to 300 vendors (capacity 352) in seven large buildings.

Antiques and collectibles, books, vintage clothing, country crafts, fine art, new and used furniture, glassware, jewelry, porcelain, toys, and wicker. Hot meals are served by seven food concessions on the premises. Shady picnic areas with tables; camping on the fairgrounds on Saturday evenings prior to market days. Billed as western Michigan's finest antiques market, located on the banks of the Kalamazoo River.

VENDORS: $55 per 12'x16' space indoors; $50 per 25'x25' space outdoors. Reserve two weeks in advance.

Contact Larry Wood, 2030 Blueberry Drive, N.W., Grand Rapids, MI 49504. Tel: (616) 453-8780 or (616) 887-7677.

Centreville
Caravan Antiques Market

On the Saint Joseph County Grange Fairgrounds, at 1510 North Hoyne. Use M-86 to Centreville, near Three Rivers and Kalamazoo.

Five Sundays a year, May through October, 7 A.M. to 4 P.M.—call for dates.

Admission $3 per person; free parking. In operation for over 23 years; indoors and outdoors, rain or shine. Averages up to 650 vendors.

Antiques and collectibles. Snacks and hot meals are served on the premises. Billed as one of the best antiques markets in the state.

VENDORS: Inquire for daily rates. Reserve a month in advance.

Contact Manager, 1510 North Hoyne, Chicago, IL 60622-1804. Tel: (312) 227-4464.

Limited

Copemish
Copemish Flea Market and Auction

At the intersection of Yates Road and M-115.

Every Friday, Saturday, and Sunday from May through October, 7 A.M. to dusk.

Free admission; three acres of free parking. In operation since the 1940s; under current management since 1994; outdoors, rain or shine. Averages up to 100 vendors (capacity 143).

Antiques and collectibles, books, new and vintage clothing, coins and stamps, cookware, crafts, fine art, new and used furniture, jewelry and silver, new and used merchandise, porcelain, poultry and fresh produce, and toys. Restaurant on the premises open Wednesday through Sunday; food booths outdoors during market hours.

VENDORS: $10 for one space per day, $19 for two spaces, $27 for three spaces, $34 for four; electricity is available at $3 per day. Reservations are recommended, especially for holidays.

Contact Jerry or Jason Dillingham or Jack Lardie, P.O. Box 116, Copemish, MI 49625. Tel: (616) 378-2430 or (616) 929-4317 or (616) 223-4359.

Detroit
Metro Flea Market

At 6665 West Vernor. Take I-75 to Livernois, then go one mile to Vernor.

Every Friday, Saturday, and Sunday, 9 A.M. to 5 P.M.

Free admission; free parking for up to 200 cars. In operation for over eight years; indoors year-round, and outdoors, weather permitting. Averages close to 70 vendors year-round.

Antiques and collectibles, books, new and vintage clothing, coins and stamps, cookware, crafts and fine art, new and used furniture, jewelry and silver, new and used merchandise, new and used tools, porcelain, poultry, fresh produce, seafood, and toys. Snacks and hot meals are served on the premises.

VENDORS: Inquire for rates. Reservations are recommended.

Contact Ralph Najor, 6665 West Vernor, Detroit, MI 48165. Tel: (313) 841-4890; fax: (313) 841-1405.

Flat Rock
Flat Rock Historical Society Antique and Flea Market

At the Flat Rock Speedway, one mile south of town on Telegraph Road. Telegraph Road is three miles west of I-75.

Twice a year, on the first Sundays in May and October, 8 A.M. to 4 P.M.

Free admission; free parking for up to 1,000 cars. In operation for over 20 years; outdoors, rain or shine. Averages up to 200 or more vendors.

Antiques and collectibles, vintage clothing (but no used clothing), cookware, crafts, jewelry and silver, new and used furniture, and toys. Snacks and sandwiches are served on the premises.

VENDORS: $25 per 20'x20' space per day. Reservations are not required.

Contact Flat Rock Historical Society, P.O. Box 337, Flat Rock, MI 48134. Tel: (313) 782-5220.

Grand Rapids
Jack Loeks' Flea Market

At 1400 28th Street S.W., about three miles west of Route 131 (use 28th Street/Wyoming exit), in the parking lot behind Studio 28 movie theater.

Every weekend from April through October, 5 A.M. to 4 P.M.

Admission 50 cents per person; free admission for children; ample free parking. In operation for over 30 years; outdoors, rain or shine. Averages up to 400 vendors (capacity 475).

Antiques and collectibles, books, new clothing, cookware, crafts, new and used furniture, garage-sale items, jewelry and silver, new and used merchandise, fresh produce, plants, toys. Snacks and hot meals are served on the premises.

VENDORS: $10 per 10'x20' space per day. Reservations are not required (must be made in person during market hours).

Contact Bruce Johns, 1400 28th Street S.W., Grand Rapids, MI 49509. Tel: (616) 532-8218. Day of market, call (616) 532-6301.

Lake City
Lake City Flea Market

At 518 Union Street, four blocks from town (and Lake Missaukee).

Daily from April through mid-December, 9 A.M. to 5 P.M.

Free admission; free parking for up to 200 cars. In operation for over 13 years; indoors and outdoors, rain or shine. Averages up to 30 vendors (capacity 50).

Antiques and collectibles, books, vintage clothing, cookware, new and used furniture, jewelry and silver, new merchandise, and sporting goods. Food is not available on the premises. Campground next door.

VENDORS: $4 per 10′x16′ space per day; electricity is available at $3 per day. Reserve three days in advance.

Contact R-Jay Bradley, 518 Union Street, Lake City, MI 49651. Tel: (616) 839-3206.

Lexington
Harbor Bazaar

At 5590 Main Street (Route 25), two blocks south of the stoplight.

Every weekend, 10 A.M. to 6 P.M.

Free admission; free parking for up to 150 cars. In operation for over eight years; indoors, year-round. Averages close to its capacity of 200 vendors.

Antiques and collectibles, books, new and vintage clothing, coins and stamps, cookware, crafts and fine art, new and used furniture, jewelry and silver, new and used merchandise, porcelain, and toys. Snacks and hot meals are served on the premises.

VENDORS: $27 per space per weekend. Reservations are recommended.

Contact E. R. Kinsley II, 5590 Main Street, Lexington, MI 48450. Tel: (810) 359-5333.

Mount Clemens
Gibraltar Trade Center North

At 237 North River Road. Take Exit 237 (North River Road/Mount Clemens) off I-84 and market will be a half mile down the road on the right.

Every Friday, noon to 9 P.M.; every Saturday, 9 A.M. to 9 P.M.; and every Sunday, 9 A.M. to 6 P.M.

Admission $1.50 per carload; free parking for more than

4,000 cars. In operation for over 4 years; indoors and outdoors, rain or shine. Averages up to a capacity of 1,200 vendors.

Antiques and collectibles, books, new and vintage clothing, cookware, crafts and fine art, new and used furniture, jewelry and silver, new and used merchandise, marine supplies, pottery and porcelain, sports equipment, toys, wallpaper, and wholesale closeouts. Snacks and hot meals are served on the premises. Specialty shows for sports cards, antiques, arts and crafts, guns, and knives are held weekly in a 50,000-square-foot Show Area. This large and well-advertised market boasts an average of 40,000 customers per weekend.

VENDORS: From $75 per 6'x12' space per weekend. Reserve a week in advance.

Contact George Phanawong, General Manager, or Robert Koester, President, 237 North River Road, Mount Clemens, MI 48043. Tel: (810) 465-6440.

Paw Paw
Reits Flea Market

At 45146 Red Arrow Highway, five miles west of Paw Paw. Take Exit 56 off I-94 (25 miles west of Kalamazoo) and go north to blinking light, then left on Red Arrow and go one mile.

Every Saturday, Sunday, and holiday Monday, 8 A.M. to 4 P.M.

Free admission; 20 acres of free parking. In operation for over 30 years; indoors year-round, and outdoors from mid-April through October, rain or shine. Averages up to 500 vendors (capacity 600).

Wide range of new and used merchandise including antiques and collectibles, fresh produce, plants—"something for everyone." Be sure to have a meal at Cathy's Kitchen on the premises; there's also a snack bar. A clean market located in Michigan's "fruit belt."

VENDORS: $10 per 22'x20' space per day. Reservations are not required.

Contact Robert Hixenbaugh, 54570 Elm Road, Mishawaka, IN 46545. Tel: (616) 657-3428.

Saginaw
Giant Public Market

At 3435 Sheridan Avenue. Take Exit 144/3 off I-75, then right to State, then left to Williamson, then right to market (about three miles down).

Every Friday and Saturday, 10 A.M. to 7 P.M., and Sunday, 10 A.M. to 6 P.M.

Free admission; free parking for over 500 cars. In operation for over eight years; indoors, year-round. Averages 80 to 100 vendors.

Antiques and collectibles, books, new and vintage clothing, coins and stamps, cookware, crafts and fine art, used furniture, jewelry and silver, new merchandise, pottery and porcelain, fresh produce, and toys. Snacks and hot meals are served on the premises. Market is well stocked, and there are many larger vendors who use 10 or more selling spaces (1,000 square feet or more) each.

VENDORS: $15 per 100-square-foot space per day; $36 per three-day weekend. Reservations are not required.

Contact Robert Reiss, 3435 Sheridan Avenue, Bridgeport, MI 48601. Tel: (517) 754-9090.

Taylor
Gibraltar Trade Center

At 15525 Racho Road. Take Exit 36 (Eureka Road) off I-75.

Every Friday, Saturday, and Sunday (daily from the Friday after Thanksgiving until Christmas): Friday, 10 A.M. to 9 P.M.; Saturday, 9 A.M. to 9 P.M.; and Sunday, 9 A.M. to 6 P.M.

Admission $1.50 per carload; free parking for more than

4,500 cars on 40 acres. In operation since 1980; indoors, outdoors, and under cover, rain or shine. Averages up to a capacity of 1,200 vendors (but this is said to be a large market).

Antiques and collectibles, books, new and vintage clothing, coins and stamps, cookware, crafts and fine art (including Native American artifacts), new and used furniture, glassware, jewelry and silver, marine supplies, new and used merchandise, pottery and porcelain, fresh produce, seafood, sporting goods, tools, and toys. Snacks and hot meals are served on the premises. Specialty shows for sports cards, antiques, arts and crafts, guns, and knives are held weekly in a 50,000-square-foot Show Area. A large and well-advertised market; see also its "sister" market in Mount Clemens, Michigan.

VENDORS: From $75 per 6'x12' space per weekend; various larger sizes are available. Reserve a week in advance.

Contact Jeff Turner, General Manager, or Susan Lenz, President, 15525 Racho Road, Taylor, MI 48180. Tel: (313) 287-2000; fax: (313) 287-8330.

Trufant

Trufant Auction and Flea Market

At 303 North C Street—in Montcalm County, approximately 35 miles northeast of Grand Rapids.

Every Thursday from April through October, dawn to 4 P.M. Auction starts at noon.

Free admission; ample free parking. In operation for over 40 years; outdoors, rain or shine. Averages 250 to 300 vendors (capacity 350).

Antiques and collectibles, books, new clothing, coins and stamps, cookware, crafts, new and used furniture, jewelry and silver, new and used merchandise, porcelain, fresh produce, and toys. Lunch-wagon-type food (burger, fries, etc.) is served on the premises.

VENDORS: $7 per 15 feet of frontage per day. Reservations are not required.

Contact Maurice Petersen, 13670 Dickerson Lake Road, Trufant, MI 49347. Tel: (616) 984-2160 or (616) 984-5155.

Warren
Country Fair Antique Flea Market

At 20900 Dequindre Boulevard. Take I-75 to 8 Mile Road Exit, then go eight miles to Dequindre Boulevard.

Every Friday, 4 P.M. to 9 P.M., and every Saturday and Sunday, 10 A.M. to 6 P.M.

Free admission; free parking. In operation for over 17 years; indoors, rain or shine. Averages up to 250 vendors year-round.

Variety of offerings including antiques and collectibles, and new and used goods. Snacks and hot meals are served on the premises.

VENDORS: $50 per week for a 10'x5' space. Reservations are recommended.

Contact Joe Sherman, 20900 Dequindre Boulevard, Warren, MI 48091. Tel: (810) 757-3740 or (810) 757-3741.

Waterford
Dixieland Flea Market

At 2045 Dixie Highway (Highway 10), at the corner of Telegraph Road (Highway 24), a few miles northwest of Detroit (south of Pontiac).

Every Friday, 4 P.M. to 9 P.M., and every Saturday and Sunday, 10 A.M. to 6 P.M.

Free admission; free parking for up to 800 cars. In operation since 1976; indoors year-round, and outdoors, weather permitting. Averages close to its capacity of 250 vendors year-round.

Antiques and collectibles, books, new and vintage clothing, cookware, crafts, new and used furniture, jewelry and silver, new

MICHIGAN / Waterford

and used merchandise, porcelain, and toys. Snacks and hot meals are served on the premises. "We wear a smile."

VENDORS: Indoors: $45 per 5'x10½' space per weekend, or $80 per 10½'x12' space; outdoors: $28 per space per weekend. Reservations are not required.

Contact G. Brown or Jill Gurwin, 2045 Dixie Highway, Waterford, MI 48328. Tel: (810) 338-3220.

MINNESOTA

Hinckley

Monticello

Wabasha

Hinckley
Hinckley Flea Market

On Highway 48 and I-35, between Famous Tobie's Restaurant and the Grand Casino. Take Exit 183 off I-35 (midway between Minneapolis and Duluth), then go four blocks east on Highway 48, and market will be on the left—look for five large red and white buildings.

Every Thursday through Sunday from the last weekend in April through the first full weekend in October, 8:30 A.M. to 5:30 P.M.

Free admission; free parking for up to 500 cars. In operation for over five years; indoors, outdoors, and under cover, rain or shine. Averages up to 180 vendors (capacity 200).

Antiques and collectibles, books, new and vintage clothing, coins and stamps, cookware, crafts and fine art, new and used furniture, jewelry and silver, new and used merchandise, porcelain, fresh produce, and toys—"everything from A to Z." Full-service restaurant on the premises. RV park, many campgrounds, and several motels nearby; hot showers on premises; shuttle bus to casino. "Minnesota's most modern flea market," a well-promoted market with approximately 30,000 to 50,000 shoppers passing through each day.

VENDORS: Indoors: $13 per space per day; under canopies: $10 per day; outdoors: $6 per day; stay all four days and get one free; multiple-space discounts. Reserve a week in advance.

Contact Walter "Micky" Nilsen, 2413 Hughitt Avenue, Superior, WI 54880. Tel: (715) 394-3526. Day of market, call (612) 384-9911.

Monticello
Osowski's Flea Market
(aka Orchard Fun Market)

On Orchard Road.

Every weekend, 9 A.M. to 5 P.M.

Free admission; ample free parking. In operation for over 20 years; indoors year-round, and outdoors, weather permitting. Averages 250 to 500 vendors.

Variety of offerings including antiques and collectibles, fresh produce, garage-sale items, new and used merchandise. Snacks are served on the premises.

VENDORS: $10 per space per day. Reservations are on a first-come, first-served basis.

Contact Alice Osowski, Owner, 1479 127th Street N.E., Monticello, MN 55362. Tel: (612) 295-2121.

Wabasha

Wabasha Indoor Flea Market

At Industrial Court and Highway 61.

Every weekend, 8 A.M. to 5 P.M.

Free admission; free parking for up to 75 cars. In operation since 1988; indoors year-round, and outdoors, weather permitting. Averages 40 to 60 vendors (capacity 65).

Antiques and collectibles, books, new clothing, crafts, new and used furniture, jewelry, new and used merchandise, porcelain, fresh produce, and toys. Snacks and hot meals are served on the premises.

VENDORS: Indoors: $8 per space per day; outdoors: $6 per space on Saturday, $10 for both days. Reserve a week in advance for indoor spaces.

Contact Arthur Carlson, 406 Grant Street, Wabasha, MN 55981. Tel: (612) 565-4767.

MISSISSIPPI

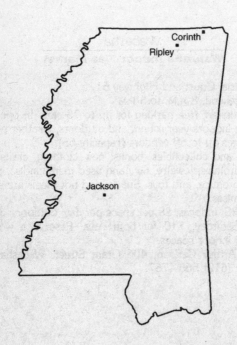

Corinth
Corinth Flea Market

At 1224 Highway 72 East (next to the Pizza Hut).

Every Wednesday and Thursday, 10 A.M. to 6 P.M.; every Friday and Saturday, 10 A.M. to 7 P.M.; and every Sunday, 1 P.M. to 6 P.M. (closed Monday and Tuesday).

Free admission; free parking for up to 300 cars. In operation since November 1987; indoors and outdoors, rain or shine. Averages 65 to 75 vendors (capacity 85 vendors on over 50,000 square feet of indoor shopping area plus outdoor space).

Antiques and collectibles, books, new clothing, coins and stamps, crafts, new and used furniture, jewelry and silver, new merchandise, and pottery and porcelain. Snacks and hot meals are served on the premises.

VENDORS: Indoors: $10 per 12'x12' space per day, or $25 per weekend (from Friday through Sunday), or $75 per month; outdoors: $5 per space per day; up to two 8'x2' tables furnished free of charge; camper hookups with water and electricity at $5 per day. Reservations are not required.

Contact Ray or Betty King, 1224 Highway 72 East, Corinth, MS 38834. Tel: (601) 287-1387 or (601) 287-9110.

Jackson
Fairgrounds Antique Flea Market

On the Mississippi State Fairgrounds complex. Take High Street exit off I-55.

Every weekend: Saturday, 8 A.M. to 5 P.M., and Sunday, 10 A.M. to 5 P.M.

Admission 75 cents per person; free parking for up to 500 cars. In operation for over 10 years; indoors, year-round. Averages 180 to 200 vendors (capacity 210).

Antiques and collectibles, books, new and vintage clothing, coins and stamps, cookware, crafts and fine art, new and used furniture, jewelry and silver, new merchandise, pottery and

231

porcelain, fresh produce, and toys. Snacks and hot meals are served on the premises.

VENDORS: $30 per booth along a wall per weekend; $40 per booth on an aisle. Reservations are not required; call on Mondays for information.

Contact Frank Barnett, P.O. Box 23579, Jackson, MS 39225-3579. Tel: (601) 353-5327.

Ripley
First Monday Trade Days

On Highway 15, south of Ripley, between New Albany and Walnut (approximately 75 miles southeast of Memphis).

First Monday of every month and the weekend preceding, from daybreak to dark.

Free admission; ample parking. In operation since 1893; outdoors, rain or shine. Averages close to 500 vendors (capacity 1,100) on 30 acres of selling space.

Antiques and collectibles, books, new and vintage clothing, coins and stamps, crafts, new furniture, household items, jewelry and silver, all kinds of new and used merchandise, livestock, poultry and fresh produce, toys, and pets. Full restaurant on the premises. Free electrical hookups, RV dump station, laundry room, shower facilities, church services every Sunday at 6 A.M. The "original" Ripley trade day claims to be Mississippi's largest, and among the oldest markets in the United States.

VENDORS: $25 for first 18'x18' space, $22.50 each additional space for the three-day event. Reserve two to four weeks in advance.

Contact Manager, 10590 Highway 15 South, Ripley, MS 38663. Tel: (601) 837-7442 or (601) 837-4051; for vendor reservations call (800) 4-RIPLEY weekdays.

MISSOURI

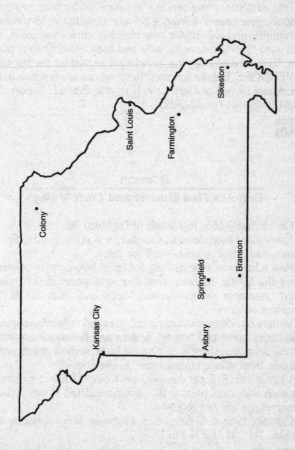

Asbury
Stateline Trade Center

On Highway 171, 20 miles north of Joplin on the Kansas/ Missouri state line.

Every Friday, Saturday, and Sunday, 9 A.M. to 6 P.M.

Free admission; free parking. In operation for over two years; indoors, year-round. Averages 30 to a capacity of 35 vendors.

Antiques and collectibles, new clothing, cookware, crafts, new and used furniture, jewelry, new and used merchandise, porcelain, tools, and old wagons. Snacks are served on the premises.

VENDORS: Inquire for rates. Reservations are recommended.

Contact Donna or Gary Lair, R.R. #1, Box 62, Asbury, MO 64832. Tel: (417) 642-5850.

Branson
Coffelt's Flea Market and Craft Village

On Highway 165, just south of Highway 76.

Every day, May through October, 9 A.M. to 6 P.M. Special shows three times a year—call for dates.

Free admission; free parking for up to 300 cars. In operation since the 1940s; indoors, outdoors, and under cover, rain or shine. Averages 40 permanent shops and from 40 to 100 transient vendors.

Variety of offerings including antiques and collectibles, garage-sale items, crafts and fine art. Snacks and hot meals are served on the premises; there is also an old-fashioned ice cream parlor. "Rustic farm village atmosphere" in the Ozarks.

VENDORS: $12 per day; $60 per week; $200 per month; $2 for each additional person; RVs accommodated at extra charge. Reservations are not required.

Contact Gerald Coffelt, 673 Highway 165, Branson, MO 65616. Tel: (417) 334-7611.

Colony
Colony #1 Flea Market

On Route V off Route K, a mile and a half northwest of town.

First weekend of every month from March through November, all day.

Free admission; free parking for up to 800 cars. In operation for over 15 years; outdoors, rain or shine. Averages close to 200 vendors (capacity 300).

Antiques and collectibles, books, new clothing, coins and stamps, cookware, crafts, new and used furniture, new and used merchandise, porcelain, poultry and fresh produce, and toys. Snacks and hot meals are served on the premises. Auctions every Friday at 7 P.M. and every Saturday at noon and 7 P.M.; shower house on grounds.

VENDORS: $9 per 20'x30' space per weekend; electricity is available at $6 per day. Reservations are not required.

Contact Danny or Dawnetta White, P.O. Box 71, Rutledge, MO 63563. Tel: (816) 434-5504.

Farmington
Fairgrounds Flea Market

On the Saint Francois County Fairgrounds, on Highway 67, a mile north of Farmington (60 miles south of Saint Louis).

Every weekend (except the first three weeks in August while fair is in progress), 9 A.M. to 4 P.M.

Free admission; free parking for up to 500 cars. In operation for over 12 years; indoors, outdoors, and under cover, rain or shine. Averages 80 to 120 vendors (capacity virtually unlimited).

Antiques and collectibles, books, new and vintage clothing, cookware, crafts, antique firearms, new and used furniture, jewelry, livestock, new merchandise, pets and supplies, pottery and porcelain, poultry and fresh produce, and toys. Snacks and hot meals are served on the premises. Draws a large crowd from as far away as Saint Louis.

VENDORS: $5 per space per day outdoors, $7 under cover; indoor rentals on a monthly basis only (inquire for details). Reservations are not required for outdoor rentals.

Contact David or Joyce Tripp, 1780 Highway AA, Farmington, MO 63640. Tel: (314) 756-1691 or (314) 756-7584.

Kansas City
Kansas City Flea Market

At 1800 Gennessee Street.

Three Sundays in July, August, and September (call for dates), 8 A.M. to 4 P.M. There is also a special two-day holiday market in North Kansas City in November—call for dates.

Admission $1 per person; free admission for children under 12; free parking for up to 3,500 cars. In operation since 1972; indoors, regardless of weather. Averages 300 to 450 vendors (capacity 485).

Antiques and collectibles, books, new clothing, coins and stamps, cookware, crafts, used furniture, jewelry and silver, "junque," toys, and used merchandise. Snacks are available on the premises. Claims to be the largest market in a 300-mile radius.

VENDORS: $35 per 10'x10' space per day; tables are available at $7 per day. Reservations are not required.

Contact Peak Promotions, 1153 Evergreen Parkway, Suite M-250, Evergreen, CO 80439. Tel: (800) 333-FLEA. Day of market, call switchboard at (800) 634-3942.

Saint Louis
Frison Flea Market

At 7025 Saint Charles Rock Road.

Every Friday, Saturday, and Sunday, 9 A.M. to 5 P.M.

Free admission; two and a half acres of free parking. In

operation since 1982; indoors and outdoors, weather permitting. Averages up to a capacity of 350 vendors indoors plus 50 more outdoors.

Variety of offerings including antiques and collectibles, new and used goods, coins and stamps, cookware, crafts, jewelry and silver, fish, poultry and livestock, and fresh produce. Snacks and hot meals are served on the premises.

VENDORS: $12 per 10'x10' space on Friday; $15 on Saturday; $12 on Sunday, inside or outside. Winter rates are $5 cheaper per day; storage and table included for long-term vendors (out-of-town vendors have first preference). Reservations are recommended; out-of-town vendors have priority.

Contact Jack Frison, 11440 South 40 Drive, Frontenac, MO 63131. Tel: (314) 727-0460, or use paging service at (314) 988-3222.

Sikeston

Tradewinds Trading Post and Auction

At 875 West Malone Avenue, on Old Highway 60 (known as West Malone in west part of town).

Every Thursday through Sunday, from dawn to dusk.

Free admission; free parking. In operation for over 16 years; indoors and outdoors, rain or shine. Averages up to 250 vendors (capacity 500).

"Anything that is legal to sell," including antiques, baseball cards and other collectibles, crafts, fish, furniture, poultry, and fresh produce. Hot meals are available on the premises.

VENDORS: $7 per space per day, $5 on Sunday. Reservations are not required.

Contact Manager, 875 West Malone, Sikeston, MO 63801-2558. Tel: (314) 471-3965 or (314) 471-8419 (leave message on machine).

Springfield
I-44 Swap Meet

At 1724 West Kearney, right off I-44 and Neergard. Take I-44 to Bypass 65, then Bypass 65 to Kearney exit, 2600 East Kearney, right on Neergard to swap meet.

Every weekend from mid-March through mid-December, from daybreak to dark.

Free admission; parking at $1 per car. In operation for over nine years; outdoors, rain or shine. Averages 200 to 400 vendors (capacity 600).

Variety of offerings including antiques and collectibles, new and used goods, native crafts, fresh produce, new and used furniture. Food available on premises.

VENDORS: $6 per space on Saturday, $8 on Sunday. Reservations are recommended.

Contact Manager, 2743 West Kearney, Springfield, MO 65803. Tel: (417) 864-4340.

MONTANA

See Appendix for Brief Listings

NEBRASKA

South Sioux City

Grand Island.

Omaha

Lincoln.

Grand Island
Great Exchange Flea Market

At 3235 South Locust Street at the intersection of Highway 34. Take Exit 312 off I-80 onto Route 281 and go north five miles to Highway 34, then two miles east to South Locust Street; or go four miles north from Exit 318 to Highway 34 and then four miles west to South Locust Street.

Daily except major holidays, 10 A.M. to 5 P.M., except Sunday, noon to 5 P.M.

Free admission; free parking for up to 150 cars. In operation for over four years; indoors, year-round. Averages close to a capacity of 60 vendors year-round.

Antiques and collectibles (including old advertising signs, bottles, comics, dollhouse furniture, and miniatures), books, cookware, crafts, new, used, and antique furniture, jewelry, new and used merchandise, and toys. Food is not served on the premises. Offers 8,000 square feet of mall-style shopping with permanent vendors.

VENDORS: Inquire for rates. No transients; permanent vendors only.

Contact Andrea or Pat Lee, 3235 South Locust, Grand Island, NE 68801. Tel: (308) 381-4075.

Lincoln
Pershing Auditorium Monthly Indoor Flea Market

At 226 Centennial Mall South, four blocks north of the State Capitol Building in downtown Lincoln.

One weekend a month, generally in the middle of the month—call for dates; hours, 10 A.M. to 5 P.M.

Admission 75 cents; street parking. In operation for over 17 years; indoors. Averages 50 to 70 vendors (capacity 70).

Full spectrum of antiques, collectibles, new and used goods. Snacks and hot meals are served on the premises.

VENDORS: $45 per weekend for three tables (8'x13'); $62 for five tables (8'x21'); $70 for seven tables (8'x29'). Reservations are required.

Contact Derek Andersen, P.O. Box 81126, Lincoln, NE 68501. Tel: (402) 471-7500.

Omaha

Treasure Trove Flea Mall

At 6606 Grover Street. Take 72nd Street exit off I-80 and go one block north to Grover Street, then go right six blocks.

Daily except Christmas and Thanksgiving, 9 A.M. to 6 P.M.

Free admission; ample free parking. A new market (in operation just over two years); indoors, year-round. Averages close to its capacity of 160 vendors on more than 16,000 square feet of selling area.

Antiques and collectibles, books, vintage clothing, cookware, crafts and fine art, new and used furniture, jewelry and silver, new and used merchandise, porcelain, and toys. Snacks are served on the premises.

VENDORS: Monthly rentals only: $37 per 5'x5' space or $70 per 5'x10' space. Reservations are not required.

Contact Rick or Karen Van Tuyl, 6606 Grover Street, Omaha, NE 68106. Tel: (402) 397-6811.

South Sioux City

Siouxland Flea Market

At 2111 Dakota Avenue.

Daily: Monday through Saturday, 9 A.M. to 6 P.M., and Sunday, noon to 6 P.M.

Free admission; free parking. A new market; indoors, year-round. Averages close to a capacity of 200 vendors year-round.

Antiques and collectibles, books, coins and stamps, cookware, crafts and fine art, new and used furniture, household items, jewelry and silver, new merchandise, plants, and pottery and porcelain. Snacks are available on the premises.

VENDORS: Monthly rentals only, from $30 to $100 per month, plus 10 percent commission on sales. Reserve three to four months in advance.

Contact Jim or Bobbie Gallup, 2111 Dakota Avenue, South Sioux City, NE 68776. Tel: (402) 494-3221 or (712) 259-0174.

NEVADA

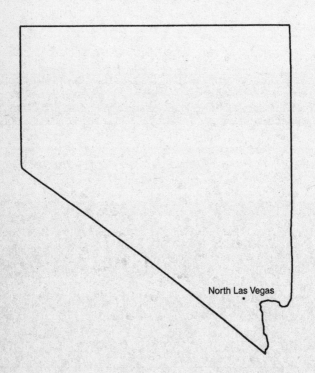

North Las Vegas

North Las Vegas
Broad Acres Swap Meet

At 2960 Las Vegas Boulevard North (at Pecos Street). Take Lake Mead Boulevard East exit and turn left onto Las Vegas Boulevard and go north one mile.

Every Friday, Saturday, and Sunday, 6:30 A.M. to 3 P.M.

Admission $1 per person; free admission for children under 12; 15 acres of free parking. In operation since 1977; outdoors, rain or shine. Averages 700 vendors in summer to a capacity of 1,000 vendors in winter.

Antiques and collectibles, books, new and vintage clothing, cookware, crafts, new and used furniture, porcelain, fresh produce, and toys—about 55 percent new merchandise and 45 percent used. Snacks and hot meals are served on the premises. A true outdoor swap meet, the oldest and largest in Nevada. Vendors come from all over, and crowds of shoppers can swell to 20,000 weekly (summer is low season and attracts 10,000 to 14,000 shoppers weekly).

VENDORS: $7 per space on Friday, $14 on Saturday or Sunday. Reservations are not required.

Contact Jake Bowman, P.O. Box 3059, North Las Vegas, NV 89030. Tel: (702) 642-3777.

NEW HAMPSHIRE

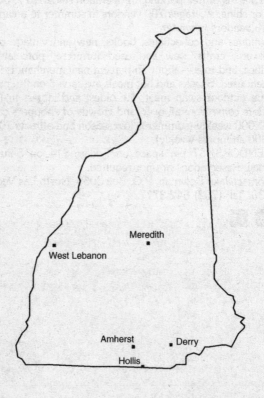

Meredith

West Lebanon

Amherst   Derry

Hollis

Amherst
Amherst Outdoor Antique Market

At 157 Hollis Road (Route 122 South). Take Exit 7W off Route 3 (Everett Turnpike, Nashua Bypass), then take Route 101A to Route 122, then left at 122, and market will be on your right about midway between 101-A and Route 130.

The last Sunday of every month from April through October, 6 A.M. to 3 P.M.

Free admission; ample parking at $5 per car. In operation since 1960; outdoors, weather permitting. Averages up to 460 vendors.

Variety of offerings including antiques and collectibles, and new and used goods. Good food available. This is part of the Amherst Outdoor Antique Auto Show—for dealers, collectors, and browsers.

VENDORS: Inquire for rates. Reservations are recommended—expect a waiting list.

Contact Werner or Elna Carlson, 51R Dudley Street, Arlington, MA 02174. Tel: (603) 673-2093 or (617) 641-0600.

Derry
Grandview Flea Market

At the junction of Route 28 and 28 Bypass. Take Exit 4 off Route 93 to Route 102, Derry Circle (Rotary). Take Route 28 Bypass half a mile; market is on left across from Clam Haven, at the lights.

Every weekend, 7 A.M. to 4 P.M.

Admission 50 cents per adult on Sunday, free on Saturday; free admission for children under 12; free parking for over 1,000 cars. In operation for over 28 years; indoors and outdoors, rain or shine. Averages 100 to 400 vendors (capacity 450); large grounds for outside vendor setups.

Antiques and collectibles, electronics, furniture, jewelry, knives, record albums and tapes, Western boots, belts, etc., new and used merchandise, household items, groceries and fresh produce. Snacks and hot meals are served on the premises. Live bands on every Sunday and some Saturdays; driving range nearby. As many as 7,000 shoppers on summer Sundays. Statues (one is a life-size representation of a pink, polka-dotted elephant) are placed throughout the grounds.

VENDORS: Outdoors: $20 per space per day; $1.50 table rental; indoor transient: $20 per space with three tables; indoor permanent: 20 cents per square foot when available. Reservations are required up to a week in advance (depending on weather).

Contact Martin or Kathi Taylor, 34 South Main Street, Derry, NH 03038. Tel: (603) 432-2326.

Hollis

Hollis Flea Market

At 436 Silver Lake Road.

Every Sunday from the first Sunday in April through the second Sunday in November, 7 A.M. to 4 P.M.

Free admission; parking is available at $1 per car. In operation for over 28 years; outdoors, weather permitting. Averages up to 200 vendors.

Antiques and collectibles, books, new and vintage clothing, coins and stamps, cookware, crafts, new and used furniture, jewelry and silver, new and used merchandise, porcelain, fresh produce, and toys. Snacks and hot meals are served on the premises. A well-known and well-attended market.

VENDORS: $14 per space per day. Reserve a week in advance.

Contact Gil or Alice Prieto, 436 Silver Lake Road, Hollis, NH 03049. Tel: (603) 882-6134 or (603) 465-7813.

Meredith
Burlwood Antique Center

At the intersection of Routes 104 and 3. Take Exit 23 off Route 93, then nine miles east on Route 104.

Daily, May through October, 10 A.M. to 5 P.M.

Free admission; free parking for over 100 cars. In operation for over 12 years; indoors. Averages up to 170 vendors.

Antiques and collectibles only; one floor of the building is devoted to antique furniture. Food is not available on the premises. In the heart of the lakes region of New Hampshire; good for upscale antiquers.

VENDORS: $18 per day per linear foot for built-in booths; no transients. Reserve a year in advance.

Contact Nancy J. Lindsey, HCR 68, Bunker Hill Road, South Tamworth, NH 03883. Tel: (603) 279-6387.

West Lebanon
Colonial Antique Market

On Airport Road (Route 12-A). Take Exit 20 off I-89 and look for the back of the building on Airport Road, then drive around to front, and office is the second door.

Daily (except Thanksgiving, Christmas, New Year's Day, and Easter): Monday through Saturday, 9 A.M. to 5 P.M., and Sunday, 6 A.M. to 4 P.M.

Free admission; free parking for up to 70 cars. In operation for over 21 years; indoors year-round, and outdoors seasonally on Sundays, weather permitting. Averages 50 to 90 vendors outdoors.

Antiques and collectibles, books, bottles, vintage clothing, coins and stamps, crafts and fine art, dolls, used furniture, estate jewelry and silver, postcards, tools, and toys. Hot meals are served on Sundays; snacks are available all week. Billed as "a real flea market" with good variety and turnover.

NEW HAMPSHIRE /West Lebanon

VENDORS: Indoors: $27.50 per space per week; outdoors: $12 per day (Sundays only). Reservations are not required.

Contact the Andersons, 5 Airport Road, Suite 23, Colonial Plaza, West Lebanon, NH 03784. Tel: (603) 298-8132.

NEW JERSEY

- Edison
- Belvidere
- East Rutherford
- Meyersville
- Union
- Warren
- Neshanic Station
- New Brunswick
- Flemington
- East Brunswick
- Lambertville
- Englishtown
- Howell
- Lakewood
- Palmyra
- Columbus
- New Egypt
- Berlin
- Manahawkin
- Absecon
- Dorchester

Absecon
L'Erario's Flea Market

At the intersection of Jim Leeds and Pitney Roads in Absecon Highlands. Call for further directions.

Every weekend, 7 A.M. until whenever.

Free admission; free parking. In operation for over 25 years; outdoors, weather permitting. Average number of vendors not reported (estimated up to 75).

Antiques and collectibles, new and vintage clothing, new and used furniture. A restaurant, a deli, and an ice cream parlor are on the premises, as well as a video shop and baseball card shop.

VENDORS: $15 per space on Saturday, $18 on Sunday. Reservations are not required.

Contact Joseph L'Erario, P.O. Box 572, Absecon, NJ 08201. Tel: (609) 652-0540.

Belvidere
Five Acres Flea Market

On Route 46. Take Exit 12 on Route 80, then south for seven miles to traffic light, then left, and market will be 1,500 feet ahead on the right.

Every weekend, plus holidays, 7 A.M. to 4 P.M.

Free admission; free parking. In operation for over 28 years; outdoors year-round, weather permitting. Averages 50 to 100 vendors (capacity 135).

Antiques and collectibles, books, new clothing, cookware, crafts, new and used furniture, jewelry, new merchandise, fresh produce. Snacks are available on the premises. Bar and game room on the premises.

VENDORS: $10 per space on Saturday, $15 on Sunday. Reservations are not required.

Contact Larry Werkheiser, P.O. Box 295, Belvidere, NJ 07823. Tel: (908) 475-2572.

Berlin
Berlin Farmer's Market

At 41 Clementon Road. Take Walt Whitman Bridge to Route 42 southbound to the Blackwood/Clementon exit, then onto Route 534 East for 6.2 miles. Or take the Tacony-Palmyra Bridge to Route 73 southbound, to Berlin Circle, then take second right onto Milford Road, then straight over Route 30 (at stoplight), then three fourths of a mile, and the market will be on the right.

Every weekend, 8 A.M. to 4 P.M.

Free admission; free parking for up to 1,500 cars. In operation for over 53 years (three generations); indoors year-round, and outdoors, weather permitting. Averages 100 to 600 vendors (capacity 700).

Antiques and collectibles, books, new and vintage clothing, coins and stamps, cookware, crafts, fish, poultry and fresh produce, new and used furniture, jewelry and silver, and toys. Also, butcher shop, barbershop, Western wear, household items, electronics, TV repair, records and tapes, and sporting goods. Snacks and hot meals are served on the premises, including a clam bar. Candy and health foods also available. One of the oldest and largest markets on the East Coast. Indoors there are over 80 stores with "mall merchandise at flea-market prices"; outdoors, flea and farmers' market stuff.

VENDORS: For sale of strictly used merchandise: $15 for one day or $20 for two days; for new merchandise: $25 for one day or $35 for two days. Reserve a week in advance if possible.

Contact Stan Giberson, Jr., 41 Clementon Road, Berlin, NJ 08009. Tel: (609) 767-1284 or (609) 767-1246.

Collingwood Park/Farmingdale
Collingwood Auction and Flea Market

On State Highways 33 and 34, one half mile west of the Collingwood traffic circle, four miles south of Colts Neck on Highway 34, and seven miles east of Freehold on Highway 33.

Every Friday, Saturday, and Sunday, 9 A.M. to 9 P.M.

Free admission; free parking for up to 2,500 cars. In operation for over 50 years; indoors and outdoors, rain or shine. Averages 300 to a capacity of 600 vendors.

Antiques and collectibles, books, new and vintage clothing, coins and stamps, cookware, crafts and fine art, new and used furniture, jewelry and silver, new and used merchandise, porcelain, fresh produce, seafood, and toys. Snacks and hot meals are served on the premises. Antique and shrub auctions, slot car racing track, craft shows.

VENDORS: From $6 per space per day. Reservations are recommended on Fridays.

Contact Roland Schneider, 1350 State Highway 33, Farmingdale, NJ 07727. Tel: (908) 938-7941.

Columbus
Columbus Farmer's Market

At 2919 Route 206 South, close to Route 295.

Every Thursday, Saturday, and Sunday, from dawn to whenever. Indoor shops are open Thursday and Saturday, 8 A.M. to 8 P.M.; Friday, 10 A.M. to 8 P.M.; and Sunday, 8 A.M. to 5 P.M.

Free admission; ample free parking. Duration of market not reported; indoors and outdoors, rain or shine. Averages 500 to a capacity of 1,500 vendors plus 70 indoor shops.

Antiques and collectibles, books, new and vintage clothing, coins and stamps, cookware, crafts and fine art, fish, new and used furniture, jewelry and silver, musical instruments, new merchandise, pottery and porcelain, fresh produce, tools, and toys. Also includes a bakery, restaurants. Shoe repair and locksmith also available.

VENDORS: $30 per space on Thursday; $10 on Saturday; $11 for the sale of used items and $30 for the sale of new items on Sunday. Reservations are recommended.

Contact Columbus Shopping Center, Inc., 2919 Route 206 South, Columbus, NJ 08054. Tel: (609) 267-0400.

Dorchester
Campbell's Flea Market

On Route 47 at Morristown Causeway, three miles south of the end of Route 55 in Cumberland County, at first traffic light.

Every weekend from March through December, 7 A.M. to 4 P.M.

Free admission; ample free parking. In operation for over 25 years; indoors year-round, and outdoors, weather permitting. Averages up to 100 vendors.

Antiques and collectibles, books, vintage clothing, cookware and crafts, jewelry, fresh produce, and toys. Deli sandwiches and an ice cream parlor on the premises. Country store—rural setting with shaded outdoor tables, located by the historic Maurice River.

VENDORS: $10 per table per day. Reservations are not required.

Contact Stewart or Terrie Campbell, Route 47, Dorchester, NJ 08316. Tel: (609) 785-2222.

East Brunswick
Route 18 Market

At 290 Route 18. Take Exit 9 off the New Jersey Turnpike, follow signs to East Brunswick; take Route 18 south to Prospect Street, then make a U-turn and go back north one block.

Every Friday, 11 A.M. to 9 P.M.; Saturday, 10 A.M. to 9 P.M.; and Sunday, 11 A.M. to 6 P.M.

Free admission; ample free parking. In operation since 1978; indoors, year-round. Averages close to 80 vendors year-round.

Antiques and collectibles, books, clothing, cookware, crafts, jewelry, new merchandise, flowers, shoes and socks, sports collectibles, lighting accessories, videotapes, records, T-shirts, leather and furs, carpets and rugs, wallpaper, and stereo equipment. Snacks and hot meals are served on the premises. Not for transient vendors; big attendance at what is dubbed a "multimerchandise market."

VENDORS: Six-month leases only (no transients); $500 per 10'x10' space. Reserve a day in advance.

Contact Barbara Passwaters, 290 Route 18, East Brunswick, NJ 08816. Tel: (908) 254-5080.

East Rutherford
Meadowlands Marketplace

At Giants Stadium parking lot 17, on Route 3 west. From I-80, take Route 46 east to Route 3 east to the Sports Complex. From New York City, use the George Washington Bridge to the New Jersey Turnpike south to Exit 16W to the Sports Complex; or from the Lincoln Tunnel, take Route 3 west to the Sports Complex. From the north, take the Garden State Parkway or Route 17 south to Paterson Plank Road to the Sports Complex.

Every Thursday and Saturday, plus Memorial Day, July Fourth, and Labor Day (Saturdays only, January through March), 9 A.M. to 5 P.M.

Free admission; ample parking for up to 20,000 cars. In operation for over five years; outdoors, rain or shine. Averages 400 to 700 vendors (capacity 1,000).

Antiques and collectibles, automotive accessories, books, CDs and tapes, new clothing, coins and stamps, cookware, crafts and fine art, new furniture, jewelry and silver, new merchandise, plants, porcelain, fresh produce, seafood, sporting goods, and toys and games. Snacks and hot meals, including American and ethnic fast food, are served on the premises. Special bus trip packages with money-saving coupons for groups and organizations. One of the largest outdoor flea markets in northern New Jersey, with a very diverse assortment of vendors.

VENDORS: $40 per space (equal to four parking spaces) on Thursday and $65 on Saturday; monthly rates available; tables not supplied. Reservations are not required.

Contact Larry Fishman, Meadowlands Sports Complex, East Rutherford, NJ 07073. Tel: (201) 935-5474; fax: (201) 935-5495.

Edison

New Dover United Methodist Church Flea Market

At 690 New Dover Road. Take Exit 131 (Iselin exit) off the Garden State Parkway and turn right onto Route 28 South, then one block to Wood Avenue, then right (north) on Wood Avenue two miles to New Dover Road (at second stoplight), then turn left (west) onto New Dover Road and go a block and a half to the church on your left.

Every Tuesday from the third Tuesday in March through the second Tuesday in December, 7 A.M. to 1 P.M.

Free admission; free parking for more than 75 cars. In operation for over 22 years; indoors and outdoors, rain or shine. Averages 20 to a capacity of 55 vendors.

New clothing, cookware, cosmetics, crafts, household items, jewelry, new and used merchandise, plants, and porcelain. Sandwiches are served on the premises.

VENDORS: From $20 to $30 per space per day. Reservations are on a first-come, first-served basis.

Contact Beverly Curtis or Ruth Hunt, c/o New Dover United Methodist Church, 690 New Dover Road, Edison, NJ 08820. Tel: (908) 381-7904 (market) or (908) 381-9478 (church office). Day of market, contact Joe Jorik at (908) 873-3098.

Englishtown
Englishtown Auction

At 90 Wilson Avenue. Take Exit 9 off New Jersey Turnpike onto Route 18 South for six miles, then turn right at Englishtown sign and travel six more miles.

Every weekend: Saturday, 7 A.M. to 4 P.M., and Sunday, 9 A.M. to 4 P.M.

Free admission; free parking. In operation since 1929; indoors and outdoors, rain or shine. Averages up to a capacity of 1,500 vendors in five buildings plus 40 acres outdoors.

Antiques and collectibles, books, new clothing, cookware, crafts and fine art, electronics, new and used furniture, jewelry and silver, leather goods, new and used merchandise, porcelain, fresh produce (plus bakery and butcher's shop), school and office supplies, seafood, and toys. Three food courts available.

VENDORS: From $5 per table per day. Reservations are not required.

Contact Carla, Manager, 90 Wilson Avenue, Englishtown, NJ 07726. Tel: (908) 446-9644; fax: (908) 446-1220.

Flemington
Flemington Fair Flea Market

At the Flemington Fairgrounds on Highway 31, one and a quarter miles north of the Flemington Circle; can be reached off Route 78 or Route 202.

Every Wednesday and Friday from April through November, 7 A.M. to 3 P.M.; annual Easter and Halloween festivals—call for dates.

Free admission; ample free parking. In operation for over 16 years; indoors and outdoors, rain or shine (unless the rain is superhard). Averages up to 150 vendors on 48 acres of selling space.

Antiques and collectibles, books, new and vintage clothing,

coins and stamps, cookware, crafts and fine art, dolls, new and used furniture, jewelry and silver, new merchandise, pottery and porcelain, fresh produce, and flowers and plants. Grocery items are available. In a beautiful country setting "filled with trees and perfect for a picnic." The fairgrounds have been in operation for over 136 years.

VENDORS: $6 per 8'x20' space per day; tables are available at $2 each; indoor rentals are $600 per season. Reservations are not required.

Contact Melissa L. Yerkes, 25 Kuhl Road, Flemington, NJ 08822. Tel: (908) 782-7326.

Howell
Basics Flea Market

At 2301 Highway 9 North, a mile north of I-195 and seven miles south of the Freehold Raceway on Route 9. Take Exit 98 off the Garden State Parkway, to I-195 West, Exit 28B (Route 9N exit), then one mile; or take Exit 7A off the New Jersey Turnpike to I-195 East, Exit 28B (Route 9), then one mile.

Every Friday and Saturday, 10 A.M. to 9 P.M., and every Sunday, 10 A.M. to 6 P.M.; mini-mall also open Wednesday and Thursday, 10 A.M. to 6 P.M.

Free admission; free parking for up to 1,000 cars. A new market; indoors, year-round. Averages up to a capacity of over 150 vendors on 100,000 square feet of selling area.

Antiques and collectibles, books, new clothing, cosmetics, crafts and fine art, electronics, fish, fishing tackle, flowers, new furniture, jewelry and silver, luggage, new merchandise, and wicker. Snacks and hot meals are served at a deli on the premises. Formerly called the Howell Flea Market and Great American Flea Market. Monthly activities such as baseball card shows, car shows, and bingo are scheduled—call for more information.

VENDORS: From $5 per space per day; inquire for weekly or monthly rates. Reservations are recommended.

Contact Don Vaughn, 2301 Highway 9N, Howell, NJ 07731. Tel: (201) 308-1105; fax: (908) 308-1145.

Lakewood
Route 70 Flea Market

At 117 Route 70, between the Garden State Parkway and Route 9.

Every weekend, 7 A.M. to 4 P.M., plus "yard sale" every Friday, 8 A.M. to 2 P.M.

Free admission; free parking for up to 1,000 cars. In operation for over 17 years; indoors and outdoors, rain or shine. Averages 400 to 1,000 vendors (capacity 1,200).

Antiques and collectibles, books, new and vintage clothing, coins and stamps, cookware, crafts and fine art, new and used furniture, jewelry and silver, livestock, new and used merchandise, porcelain, poultry and fresh produce, seafood, and toys— "we have it all." Snacks and hot meals are served on the premises. A true open-air flea market.

VENDORS: $7 per day for one 24-square-foot space, includes table; $12 for two spaces; $16 for three spaces; Friday $2 per table. Reservations are required.

Contact Yvonne Weintraub or Mike Gingrich, 117 Route 70, Lakewood, NJ 08701. Tel: (908) 370-1837.

Limited

Lambertville
Lambertville Antique Market

On Route 29, a mile and a half south of Lambertville. From Philadelphia, take I-95 North to Lambertville exit onto Route 29 approximately 10 miles, and market will be on the right. From New York, take Route 287 to Route 202 South to Lambertville exit and follow signs for Route 29.

Indoor antiques shops open year-round Wednesday through

Friday, 10 A.M. to 4 P.M., and Saturday and Sunday, 8 A.M. to 4 P.M.; outdoor antiques market is open year-round every Wednesday, Friday, Saturday, and Sunday.

Free admission; free parking for up to 350 cars. In operation since 1971; indoors, outdoors, and under cover, rain or shine. Averages 60 to 120 vendors.

Antiques and collectibles only (no new merchandise): books, vintage clothing and furniture, glassware, antique jewelry, toys, and much more. Restaurant serving "home-style" cooking on the premises. Three buildings contain six antiques shops plus over 60 showcases for quality merchandise. Upscale market for antiquers more than "junktiquers."

VENDORS: Indoor pavilion: $5 per space on Wednesday or Friday, $30 on Saturday ($25 if prepaid), $42 on Sunday; outdoors: $20 per space on Saturday, $34 on Sunday (covered booths are $36 on Sunday), prepaid. Reserve two to three weeks in advance (outdoor spaces do not require reservations on Saturdays).

Contact Tom or Heidi Cekoric or Robert Errhalt, 1864 River Road, Lambertville, NJ 08530. Tel: (609) 397-0456.

Limited

Manahawkin
Manahawkin Flea Market

At 629 East Bay Avenue. Take Exit 63 off the Garden State Parkway and follow signs to Manahawkin Business District until Bay Avenue.

Every Friday and Saturday, 8 A.M. to 6 P.M., and every Sunday, 8 A.M. to 5 P.M.

Free admission; free parking for up to 150 cars. In operation for over 18 years; indoors and outdoors, rain or shine. Averages 50 to 100 vendors.

Antiques and collectibles, new and vintage clothing, coins and stamps, cookware, crafts and fine art, jewelry and silver, pottery and porcelain, new merchandise, new and used furniture, and fresh produce. Snacks and hot meals are served on the premises.

VENDORS: $16 per space per day on Saturday and Sunday;

$6 on Friday. Tables are not supplied. Reservations are not required.

Contact Manager, P.O. Box 885, Manahawkin, NJ 08050. Tel: (609) 597-1017.

Meyersville
Meyersville Grange Antique Mart

On Meyersville Road.

Every Sunday, from the first Sunday in October through the last Sunday in April, 8 A.M. to 2 P.M.

Free admission; free parking for up to 100 cars. In operation for over 23 years; indoors, year-round. Averages up to a capacity of 37 vendors.

Antiques and collectibles, vintage clothing, fine art, used and antique furniture, porcelain, silver, and toys. Snacks are available on the premises.

VENDORS: From $20 to $25 per space per Sunday. Reservations are on a monthly or seasonal basis.

Contact Larry Lindbergh or Walter O'Neill, 149 Kline Boulevard, Berkeley Heights, NJ 07922. Tel: (908) 689-5188 or (908) 464-1598.

Neshanic Station
Neshanic Flea Market

At 160 Elm Street.

Every Sunday from March through Christmas, 7 A.M. to 2 P.M.

Free admission; two acres of parking at 50 cents per car. In operation for over 25 years; outdoors, weather permitting. Average number of vendors not reported.

Antiques and collectibles, books, new clothing, cookware,

crafts, used furniture, jewelry, fresh produce, toys, and used merchandise. Snacks (including but not limited to hot dogs, pork roll sandwiches, eggs and bacon) are served on the premises. Beautiful setting, friendly people, good selection of merchandise.

VENDORS: $12 per space per day; tables are not supplied. Reservations are not required.

Contact Mary Weiss, 100 Elm Street, Neshanic Station, NJ 08853. Tel: (908) 369-3660.

New Brunswick
U.S. #1 Flea Market and Antiques

On Route 1. Plans are underway to relocate in 1996—call ahead for new address.

Every Friday, noon to 9:30 P.M.; every Saturday, 10 A.M. to 9 P.M.; and every Sunday, 10 A.M. to 7:30 P.M.

Free admission; free parking (except Sunday, $1 per car) for up to 2,000 cars. In operation for over 20 years; indoors, year-round. Averages close to 500 vendors year-round (always with room for more).

Antiques and collectibles, books, new and vintage clothing, coins and stamps, cookware, crafts and fine art, electronics, fish, new and used furniture, jewelry and silver, military memorabilia, new merchandise, pets, pottery and porcelain, toys, and videos. Over 20 separate restaurants, delis, and food stands serving a variety of international foods. Shoe repair, portrait artist; live music every Sunday. Billed as the largest air-conditioned indoor flea market on the East Coast, with over 30,000 customers every week. New vendors are always welcome.

VENDORS: Inquire for daily, weekend, and monthly rates. Reservations are not required.

Contact Manager, Route 1, New Brunswick, NJ 08901. Tel: (908) 846-0902.

New Egypt

New Egypt Auction and Farmer's Market

On Route 537, a mile east of Route 528 (between Routes 528 and 539, six miles west of the Six Flags Great Adventure theme park and about seven miles from Fort Dix/Maguire AFB).

Every Wednesday and Sunday, 7 A.M. through the early afternoon.

Free admission; plenty of free parking. In operation for over 35 years; indoors year-round, and outdoors, weather permitting. Averages 30 to 100 vendors (capacity 200).

Antiques and collectibles, books, clothing, coins and stamps, cookware, crafts, electronics, new and used furniture, household items, jewelry and silver, pottery and porcelain, fresh produce, sporting goods and exercise equipment, automotive supplies, and toys. Snacks and hot meals are served on the premises. Machine shop, plumbing, recycling and salvage depot, etc. "Not just another shopping mall." Unpaved and low-key and friendly. Call for auction dates.

VENDORS: $6 per space on Wednesday, $7 on Sunday. Reservations are not required.

Contact Les Heller, 150 Evergreen Road, New Egypt, NJ 08533. Tel: (609) 758-2082; in New Jersey, call (800) 660-2582.

Palmyra

Tacony-Palmyra Flea Market

On Route 73 South.

Every weekend, 4 A.M. to 3 P.M.

Free admission; free parking for up to 850 cars. In operation for over 23 years; outdoors, rain or shine, year-round. Averages 275 to 425 vendors (capacity 450).

Antiques and collectibles, books, new clothing, coins and stamps, cookware, crafts and fine art, new and used furniture, jewelry and silver, new merchandise, pottery and porcelain, and fresh produce. Snacks and hot meals are served on the premises.

VENDORS: $15 per space on Saturday, $25 on Sunday. Reservations are not required.

Contact Manager, P.O. Box 64, Palmyra, NJ 08065. Tel: (609) 829-3000 or (609) 829-3001.

Union
The Union Market

At 2445 Springfield Avenue. Take Exit 142 off the Garden State Parkway—78 West to Exit 50B—then right at light, and make a left at the second light, and the market will be on the left.

Every Friday and Saturday, 11 A.M. to 9 P.M., and every Sunday, 11 A.M. to 6 P.M.

Free admission; free parking for up to 1,200 cars. In operation for over 17 years; indoors, year-round. Averages 200 to a capacity of 350 vendors.

All new merchandise: automotive supplies, books, collectibles (such as baseball cards, comics, toys), clothing, cookware, crafts, electronics, furniture, health and beauty aids, jewelry and silver, plants, and fresh produce. International food court on premises. Not for transient vendors or antiquers, but worth a peek for bargain hunters.

VENDORS: Long-term leases only. Inquire for rates.

Contact Ken Douglas, 2445 Springfield Avenue, Vauxhall, NJ 07088. Tel: (908) 688-6161.

Warren
Warren Market

Take Exit 36 off Route 78, then go south two miles to Big Flags, then right, and market will be a third of a mile on the left; or take Route 22 west to Warrenville Road, then go one mile north to Big Flags, then left, and market will be a third of a mile on the left.

Every Sunday from Easter through Christmas, 8 A.M. to 4 P.M.

Free admission; parking for up to 300 cars at $1 per car (suggested donation). In operation since 1971; outdoors, weather permitting. Averages close to its capacity of 150 vendors.

Antiques and collectibles, books, new and vintage clothing, coins and stamps, cookware, crafts, new and used furniture, jewelry and silver, new and used merchandise, porcelain, fresh produce, and toys. Snacks and hot meals are served on the premises. Supports the Washington Valley Volunteer Fire Company.

VENDORS: $15 for one table per day, $25 for two tables, $30 for three tables. Reservations are not required.

Contact Jerry Boschen, 12 Washington Valley Road, Warren, NJ 07059. Tel: (908) 469-2443.

NEW MEXICO

Farmington

Taos

Santa Fe

Albuquerque

Bosque Farms

Roswell

Carlsbad

Albuquerque
Fairgrounds Flea Market

At the New Mexico State Fairgrounds, at the intersection of Louisiana Boulevard and Central. Take South Louisiana Boulevard exit off I-40.

Every weekend (except in September), 6 A.M. to 4 P.M.

Free admission; parking for up to 1,000 cars at $2 per car. In operation for many years; outdoors, year-round. Averages 600 to 800 vendors.

Antiques and collectibles, books, new and vintage clothing, coins and stamps, cookware, crafts and fine art, new and used furniture, jewelry and silver, new and used merchandise, porcelain, fresh produce, tools, and toys. Snacks and hot meals are served on the premises.

VENDORS: $10 per 10'x10' space per day. Reservations are not required.

Contact Hugh Perry, P.O. Box 8546, Albuquerque, NM 87198. Tel: (505) 265-1791.

Albuquerque
Indoor Mercado

Off I-40 at 12th Street.

Every Friday, noon to 6 P.M., and every Saturday and Sunday, 10 A.M. to 6 P.M.

Admission 50 cents per person; free admission for seniors and children under 12; free parking. In operation for over five years; indoors, year-round. Averages up to 100 or more vendors.

Antiques and collectibles, Southwest arts and crafts, new and vintage clothing, new merchandise, jewelry and silver, and fresh produce. Food is available on the premises. This is a general indoor market close to Albuquerque's historic Old Town.

VENDORS: $220 per 10'x10' space per month. Reservations are required.

268

Contact Manager, 2035 12th Street, Albuquerque, NM 87104. Tel: (505) 243-8111.

Bosque Farms
BJ's Flea Market

At 1775-A Bosque Farms Boulevard.

Every Friday, Saturday, and Sunday during summer, 6:30 A.M. to 4 P.M.

Free admission; free parking for up to 200 cars. In operation for over 15 years; outdoors, rain or shine. Averages 20 to 40 vendors (capacity 75).

Antiques and collectibles, books, new clothing, cookware, crafts, new and used furniture, jewelry and silver, toys, and used merchandise. Snacks and hot meals are served on the premises. Good country flea market.

VENDORS: $7 per space per day. Reserve a week in advance.

Contact Bennie J. Garcia, 17-A Saxon Road, Los Lunas, NM 87031. Tel: (505) 869-6995.

Carlsbad
Sixth Street Flea Market

At 218 North 6th Street, a mile and a half west of the county courthouse.

Every Friday, Saturday, and Sunday, 7 A.M. to 4 P.M.

Free admission; free parking for up to 200 cars. In operation for over 22 years; indoors year-round, and outdoors, weather permitting. Averages 15 to 50 vendors (capacity 60).

Antiques and collectibles, books, new and vintage clothing, cookware, crafts, used furniture, jewelry, fresh produce, toys, and used merchandise. Snacks are served on the premises.

VENDORS: $5 per space on Saturday, $3 on Sunday; free setup on Friday. Reserve a week in advance.

Contact Manager, 200 North 6th Street, Carlsbad, NM 88220. Tel: (505) 885-3907.

Farmington
Farmington Flea Market

On Highway 550 between Farmington and Aztec.

Every Friday, Saturday, and Sunday, from dawn to dusk.

Free admission; acres of free parking. In operation for over 27 years; outdoors, rain or shine. Averages 65 to 160 vendors (capacity 300).

All types of new and used merchandise, furniture, household items—"everything." Snacks and hot meals are served on the premises. No charge for overnight parking.

VENDORS: $3 per space on Friday or Sunday, and $6.50 on Saturday. Reserve a week in advance if possible.

Contact Cathey Wright, 7701 East Main Street, Farmington, NM 87401. Tel: (505) 325-3129.

Roswell
Dalton's Flea Market

At 2200 South Sunset. From Main and Second in downtown Roswell, go north about a mile and a half, then turn west on Poe and go straight to the corner of Poe and Sunset.

Every weekend, 7 A.M. to 4 P.M.

Free admission; free parking for up to 150 cars. In operation for over 14 years; outdoors, rain or shine. Averages 25 to 40 vendors (capacity 60).

Antiques and collectibles, books, new clothing, cookware, crafts, used furniture, jewelry, new merchandise, and toys. Snacks and hot meals are served on the premises.

VENDORS: From $3 to $7 per space per day. Reserve a week in advance.

Contact Nell Ross, 2200 South Sunset, Roswell, NM 88201. Tel: (505) 622-7410.

Santa Fe
Trader Jack's Flea Market

On Taos Highway north of Santa Fe, by the opera grounds. Every Friday, Saturday, and Sunday, 7 A.M. to 7 P.M.

Free admission; free parking. In operation several years in its present location; outdoors, weather permitting. Averages 12 to 100 vendors (summer is the high season).

Antiques and collectibles, Native American and Mexican crafts and fine art, new and vintage clothing, new and used furniture, jewelry and silver, new and used merchandise, fresh produce. Food is not served on the premises. This is a funky but interesting market in a lovely part of New Mexico amid the Sangre de Cristo Mountains.

VENDORS: $5 per space on Friday, $10 per day on Saturday or Sunday. Advance reservations are not accepted—registration is in person on market days only.

Contact Jack or Caggie Daniels at the market. They won't give out a phone number or address—you just have to go up there, but it's still going strong.

Limited

Taos
Taos Rendezvous

On Paseo del Pueblo Sur (Highway 522), about four miles south of downtown Taos, on the left as you head into town— look for sign. (Rising rents in Taos forced the market to relocate in 1995.)

Every Friday, Saturday, and Sunday from May through October, 10 A.M. to 5 P.M.

Free admission; limited free parking. In operation for over

eight years; outdoors, weather permitting. Averages 50 to 100 vendors.

Antiques and collectibles, books, new and vintage clothing, Native American crafts, jewelry, new and used furniture, new and used merchandise. Snack bar on the premises. An authentic Southwestern flea market with a bustling crowd during peak summer season. Look for Rusty Rhoades and his handmade silver jewelry—tell him Albert sent you.

VENDORS: $10 per space per day. Reserve a week or two in advance.

Contact Bob Gherardi, P.O. Box 804, Angel Fire, NM 87701. Tel: (505) 377-3623.

NEW YORK

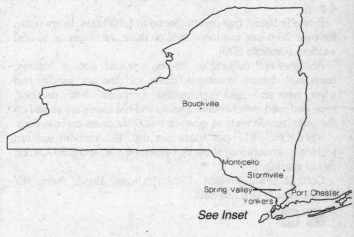

Bouckville

Monticello
Stormville
Spring Valley — Port Chester
Yonkers

See Inset

NEW YORK METRO AREA

New York City

Queens*

Westbury

Brooklyn

Elmont

Levittown
Massapequa Park

Staten Island

*Includes Flushing, Jamaica, and South Ozone Park

Avon
East Avon Flea Market

At 1520 Rochester Road (Route 15), south of Rochester, just
north of Routes 5 and 20.

Every Sunday from mid-May through mid-October, 6 A.M. to
4 P.M.

Free admission; free parking for up to 1,700 cars. In operation
for over 25 years; outdoors, rain or shine. Averages up to 350
vendors (capacity 500).

Antiques and collectibles, books, new and vintage clothing,
coins and stamps, cookware, crafts and fine art, jewelry and
silver, new and used merchandise, porcelain, fresh produce,
toys, and used merchandise. Snacks and hot meals are served on
the premises. Attracts as many as 6,000 shoppers on busy days.

VENDORS: $17 per space per day. Reservations are not
required; vendors may show up between 6 A.M. and 8:30 A.M. on
day of market.

Contact David Phillips, 1520 Rochester Road, Avon, NY
14414. Tel: (716) 226-8320.

Bouckville
Bouckville Antique Pavilion

In the center of Bouckville, on Route 20 (25 miles west of
Utica, 35 miles east of Syracuse, and 98 miles west of Albany).

Every Sunday, May through October—plus special shows on
the fourth Saturday and Sunday in June and the third weekend
in August (Wednesday through Sunday), 6 A.M. to 4 P.M.

Free admission; acres of free parking (except $2 parking at
the August show). In operation since 1984; indoors and outdoors, rain or shine. Averages 60 to 80 vendors, with as many as
110 at special shows.

Antiques and collectibles such as baseball cards, books, coins,
comics, used furniture, antique jewelry, porcelain, stamps, and

toys. No new merchandise. Snacks and hot meals are served on the premises. The August show is among the largest in the Northeast.

VENDORS: Sunday rates $10 and $15. Call for rates for the June and August events. Reservations are not required.

Contact Steve or Lynda Bono, R.D. #1, Box 111, Bouckville, NY 13310. Tel: (315) 893-7483.

Brooklyn
Cadman Plaza/Columbus Park

On Court Street between Montague and Johnson Streets, at the Brooklyn Civic Center.

Every Friday from April through Christmas, 8 A.M. to 6 P.M.

Free admission; street parking (public transportation recommended). In operation for over four years; outdoors, weather permitting. Average number of vendors not reported.

Antiques and collectibles, books, new and vintage clothing, crafts, jewelry and silver, and new merchandise. Snacks are served at the market. Sponsored by the New York City Department of Parks and Recreation.

VENDORS: $100 to $125 per space per day. Reserve a month in advance.

Contact Gio-Art Productions, Inc., 84 William Street, New York, NY 10038. Tel: (212) 809-5000 or (212) 809-7345.

Brooklyn
Seventh Avenue Flea Market
(aka P.S. 321 Recycling Center)

At 180 Seventh Avenue, in front of the school between First and Second Streets in Brooklyn's Park Slope.

Every weekend, 8 A.M. to 6 P.M.

NEW YORK / Claverack

Free admission; street parking (suggest using public transportation). In operation for over 10 years; outdoors, weather permitting. Averages 35 to a capacity of 60 vendors.

Antiques and collectibles, books, vintage clothing, electronics, used furniture, jewelry, kitchenware, toys, and used merchandise. Food is not served on the premises.

VENDORS: $25 per space per day. Reserve a week in advance.

Contact Fred Stern, 7112 Ridge Court, Brooklyn, NY 11209-1406. Tel: (718) 833-9864.

Claverack

Bryant Farms Antique and Flea Market

On Routes 9H and 23, 6 miles east of Hudson, New York, and 10 miles east of the New York State Thruway (I-87).

Every weekend, 9 A.M. to 5 P.M.

Free admission; free parking for more than 100 cars. In operation for over six years; indoors year-round, and outdoors, weather permitting. Averages 25 to 30 vendors (capacity 50).

Antiques and collectibles, books, new and vintage clothing, coins and stamps, cookware, crafts and fine art, used furniture, jewelry and silver, new and used merchandise, porcelain, fresh produce, sporting goods, tools, and toys. Snacks and hot meals are served on the premises. Auctions held monthly; buses are welcome.

VENDORS: $25 per 8'x10' space indoors per weekend, or $10 per 20'x20' space outdoors. Reserve up to a week in advance.

Contact Giulio DeLaurentis, P.O. Box 188, Claverack, NY 12513. Tel: (518) 851-9061 or (518) 851-3817.

Corinth
Corinth Flea Market

At 635 Main Street (Route 9N).

Every weekend plus holiday Mondays between Memorial Day and Labor Day, 10 A.M. to 5 P.M.

Free admission; free parking for hundreds of cars. In operation for over four years; outdoors, rain or shine. Averages a dozen or so to a capacity of thousands of vendors on 25 acres of selling area.

Antiques and collectibles, books, cookware, crafts and fine art, used furniture, garage-sale items, jewelry, new and used merchandise, and toys. Snacks and hot meals are served on the premises. Widely promoted. Several events including a Bluegrass Festival in mid-August.

VENDORS: $15 per space for one day, $20 for two days, $30 for three days; tables are available at $10 each. Weekend vendors may stay overnight free. Reserve two weeks in advance.

Contact Winona Sitts, 635 Main Street, Corinth, NY 12822. Tel: (518) 654-9424.

Elmont
Belmont (Racetrack) Flea Market

At the Belmont Raceway. Take Exit 266 off the Cross Island Parkway.

Every weekend from April through May and from late October through December (except on race days; call for further information), 7:30 A.M. to 4:00 P.M.

Admission $1.50 per carload or 50 cents per person on foot; free parking for up to 10,000 cars. In operation for over 21 years; outdoors, weather permitting. Average number of vendors not reported (capacity 2,000).

Antiques and collectibles, books, new and vintage clothing, coins and stamps, cookware, crafts and fine art, new and used furniture, jewelry and silver, new merchandise, pottery and porcelain, fresh produce, toys. Snacks and hot meals are served at an "international food court" on the premises. Mostly new merchandise at this "original outdoor racetrack flea market."

VENDORS: From $35 per space per day; call for monthly rates. Reservations are available by the month; some daily reservations are available.

Contact Joe Berchielli, Barterama Corporation, 257 Hempstead Turnpike, Elmont, NY 11003. Tel: (516) 775-8774.

Flushing
Busytown Mall

At 37-11 Main Street in Flushing, Queens.

Every Wednesday through Sunday: Wednesday and Thursday, 11 A.M. to 7 P.M.; Friday, 11 A.M. to 8 P.M.; Saturday, 10 A.M. to 7 P.M.; and Sunday, 11 A.M. to 6 P.M.

Free admission; municipal parking. In operation for over nine years; indoors, year-round. Averages up to a capacity of 150 vendors.

Discounted new merchandise only, including clothing, electronics, jewelry, leather goods, novelties, stationery, and toys. Food court on the premises. For bargain hunters looking for cheap new stuff.

VENDORS: Various long-term lease options available; rates vary from $500 up to $2,000 per month depending on size and location. Transient vendors not accommodated.

Contact Alex Mehran, 37-11 Main Street, Flushing, NY 11354. Tel: (718) 961-4111.

Jamaica
Saint Nicholas of Tolentine Flea Market

At 150-75 Goethals Avenue. Take Grand Central Parkway to 168th Street, then to Parsons Boulevard and Union Turnpike;

or take Long Island Expressway to 164th Street to Union Turnpike.

Call for dates (November through March), 9 A.M. to 5 P.M.

Free admission; free parking for up to 300 cars. In operation for over 17 years; indoors, rain or shine. Averages 75 to a capacity of 85 vendors.

Antiques and collectibles, books, new clothing, crafts, jewelry and silver, new merchandise, and toys—"anything that is not junk." Snacks are served on the premises.

VENDORS: $30 per space per day ($35 for a wall space). Reserve two weeks in advance.

Contact Jeanne Loehr, 80-09 161st Street, Jamaica, NY 11432. Tel: (718) 380-0536.

Levittown
Tri-County Flea Market

At 3041 Hempstead Turnpike.

Every Thursday and Friday, noon to 9 P.M., and every Saturday and Sunday, 10 A.M. to 6 P.M. (closed Christmas Day).

Free admission; free parking for up to 15,000 cars. In operation for over 12 years; indoors, rain or shine. Averages up to 400 vendors year-round.

Wide range of new and used merchandise including new clothing, jewelry (over 40 vendors, one of America's largest jewelry exchanges), furniture, meats (Polish deli), and fresh produce. Snacks and hot meals are served on the premises. Seven-day refund policy. Tour buses welcome. Four levels of air-conditioned indoor shopping.

VENDORS: Inquire for rates; various rental options are available. Reservations are not required.

Contact Barbara Eve, 3041 Hempstead Turnpike, Levittown, NY 11756. Tel: (516) 579-4500.

Massapequa Park
Busy Bee Compartment Store

At 5300 Sunrise Highway.

Daily except Tuesday and Wednesday: Monday and Saturday, 10 A.M. to 6 P.M.; Thursday and Friday, 10 A.M. to 9 P.M.; and Sunday, 11 A.M. to 6 P.M.

Free admission; free parking. In operation for over 13 years; indoors, rain or shine. Averages up to a capacity of 300 vendors.

New, discounted merchandise only, including books, clothing, cookware, crafts, electronics, furniture, leather goods, novelties, stationery, shoes, and toys; look for a new jewelry emporium on the second floor. Snacks and hot meals are served on the premises. For bargain hunters looking for cheap new stuff.

VENDORS: Various long-term or month-to-month rental options available; call for rates, which vary according to size and location. Reservations are recommended.

Contact Nancy Krokowski, 5300 Sunrise Highway, Massapequa Park, NY 11762. Tel: (516) 799-9090.

Montgomery
Flea Market at Orange County Airport

On Route 211.

Every Sunday from April through November, 8 A.M. to 5 P.M.

Admission 25 cents per person or 50 cents per carload; free parking with admission. A new market; outdoors, weather permitting. Up to several dozen vendors on 50 acres of grassy selling area.

Variety of new and used merchandise (sold in separate areas). Food is not served on the premises.

VENDORS: $20 per 20'x20' space per day for new merchandise, $10 per day for used merchandise. Reservations are recommended.

Contact Alan Finchley, 515 Boston Post Road, Port Chester, NY 10573. Tel: (914) 796-1000. Day of market, call Bill Sabia at (914) 344-2000.

Monticello
The Flea Market at Monticello Raceway

At the Monticello Raceway, on Route 17B in Sullivan County. Take Exit 104 off Route 17.

Every weekend plus holidays from Memorial Day through Labor Day, 9 A.M. to 5 P.M.

Free admission; free parking for up to 1,000 cars. In operation since 1976; outdoors, weather permitting. Averages up to 100 vendors (capacity 200).

"Upscale" new merchandise, mainly at discount prices. Not the place for antiques and collectibles but a great place for bargains on new goods. Snacks and hot meals are served on the premises. Live harness racing at the Raceway adjacent on Sundays and holidays. Located in the heart of the Catskill Mountain region of upstate New York.

VENDORS: From $25 to $40 per space per day. Reservations are not required; space is always available—management on site from 8 A.M. every market day.

Contact Alan Finchley, Manager, 42 Ohio Avenue, Long Beach, NY 11561. Tel: (914) 796-1000.

New York City
Annex Antiques Fair and Flea Market ("The Annex")

On Avenue of the Americas (Sixth Avenue) between 24th and 27th Streets, in four different parking lots.

Every weekend, 9 A.M. to 5 P.M.

Admission $1 per person on lot between 25th and 26th

NEW YORK/New York City

Streets; all others are free; limited street and garage parking; public transportation is recommended. In operation for over 27 years; outdoors, weather permitting. Averages 200 to a capacity of 600 vendors on peak days.

Saturday's market has everything imaginable in antiques, collectibles, and interesting secondhand stuff; on Sunday there is also new merchandise. Visit the new Annex Farmers' Market every Saturday on 24th Street across 6th Avenue from the flea market. Under the same management as The Garage down the street on 25th Street (see separate listing). Manhattan's largest and most comprehensive weekly collectibles market, located in a bustling commercial district of Manhattan.

VENDORS: From $50 to $100 per 9'x12' space on Saturdays, and from $60 to $135 on Sundays; all vendors must have and prominently display a New York State certificate of authority to collect sales tax. All space rental fees are payable one week in advance. Reserve as far in advance as possible.

Contact Michael Santulli, P.O. Box 7010, New York, NY 10116-4627. Tel: (212) 243-5343; fax: (212) 463-7099. Day of market, call Dan at (212) 243-7922.

New York City
Battery Park Market

In Battery Park, on State Street between the water and Battery Place.

Every Thursday from April through Christmas, 8 A.M. to 6 P.M.

Free admission; street parking (public transportation recommended). In operation for over four years; outdoors, weather permitting. Average number of vendors not reported.

Antiques and collectibles, books, new and vintage clothing, crafts, jewelry and silver, and new merchandise. Snacks are served at the market. Focus on multicultural crafts. Sponsored by the New York City Department of Parks and Recreation.

VENDORS: $100 to $125 per space per day. Reserve a month in advance.

Contact Gio-Art Productions, Inc., 84 William Street, New York, NY 10038. Tel: (212) 809-5000 or (212) 809-7345.

New York City
Bowling Green Plaza

At the corner of Broadway and State Streets in lower Manhattan.

Every Tuesday and Friday from April through Christmas, 8 A.M. to 6 P.M.

Free admission; street parking (public transportation recommended). In operation for over four years; outdoors, weather permitting. Average number of vendors not reported.

Antiques and collectibles, books, new and vintage clothing, crafts, jewelry and silver, and new merchandise. Snacks are served at the market. Focus on multicultural crafts. Sponsored by the New York City Department of Parks and Recreation.

VENDORS: $100 to $125 per space per day. Reserve a month in advance.

Contact Gio-Art Productions, Inc., 84 William Street, New York, NY 10038. Tel: (212) 809-5000 or (212) 809-7345.

New York City
The Columbus Circle Market

At 10 Columbus Circle on the Coliseum Plaza, on the west side of Columbus Circle by the Southwest corner of Central Park.

Daily from April through Christmas, 11 A.M. to 7 P.M.

Free admission; street parking only (public transportation is recommended). A new market (in operation since May 1995); outdoors and under cover, rain or shine. Averages 35 to 50 vendors.

Antiques and collectibles, books, new and vintage clothing,

crafts and fine art, jewelry and silver, new and used merchandise. Food kiosks serve snacks at the market; many restaurants are nearby.

VENDORS: $50 per 6-foot table per day; monthly rates are available for food and merchandise kiosks. Reserve two to three weeks in advance.

Contact Michael Santulli, Manager, P.O. Box 7010, New York, NY 10116-4627. Tel: (212) 243-5343; fax: (212) 463-7099.

New York City

Eastside Antique, Flea and Farmer's Market at P.S. 183

At Public School 183-M, 419 East 66th Street, between First and York Avenues (alternate entrance through schoolyard on 67th Street), a block away from Cornell Medical Center on the upper East Side of Manhattan.

Every Saturday, 6 A.M. to 6 P.M.

Free admission; metered street parking; public transportation is recommended. In operation for over 16 years; indoors, rain or shine, and outdoors, weather permitting. Averages 150 to 200 vendors.

Antiques and collectibles, books, new and vintage clothing, electronics (CDs, etc.), coins and stamps, cosmetics, costume jewelry, fine art, new and used merchandise, plants, porcelain, prints, fresh produce, baked goods, meats and seafood, free-range chickens, and toys. Snacks are served on the premises.

VENDORS: $45 per space per day indoors or $40 outdoors; tables are provided. Reserve a week in advance.

Contact Bobby, Manager, 447 East 65th Street, Apt. 4CC, New York, NY 10021. Tel: (212) 650-1429 or (718) 897-5992. Day of market, call the school at (212) 650-1429.

New York City
Fulton Street Plaza

On Cliff Street between Fulton and Beekman Streets, near lower Manhattan's South Street Seaport.

Every Wednesday from April through Christmas, 8 A.M. to 6 P.M.

Free admission; street parking (public transportation recommended). In operation for over four years; outdoors, weather permitting. Average number of vendors not reported.

Antiques and collectibles, books, new and vintage clothing, crafts, jewelry and silver, and new merchandise. Snacks are served at the market. Focus on multicultural crafts. Sponsored by the Pearl Street Park Association.

VENDORS: $100 to $125 per space per day. Reserve a month in advance.

Contact Gio-Art Productions, Inc., 84 William Street, New York, NY 10038. Tel: (212) 809-5000 or (212) 809-7345.

New York City
The Garage

112 West 25th Street, between Avenue of the Americas (Sixth Avenue) and Seventh Avenue—just 200 feet from the world-famous outdoor Annex Antique Fair and Flea Market.

Every weekend, 9 A.M. to 5 P.M.

Free admission; parking is available on third floor of garage (about $5 per car) or nearby. (Public transportation is recommended.) In operation since January 1994; indoors, year-round. Averages close to a capacity of 125 vendors year-round.

Antiques and collectibles, books and ephemera, vintage clothing, fine art, used furniture, jewelry and silver, oriental rugs, porcelain, and toys. Snacks are served on the premises. The Garage has quickly swelled to its indoor capacity and makes for a good complement to the outdoor Annex market around the corner on Sixth Avenue.

NEW YORK / New York City

VENDORS: $50 per 11'x12' space on Saturday; $75 on Sunday; $100 for both days. Vendors must have New York State sales tax license. Reserve two weeks in advance.

Contact Michael Santulli, P.O. Box 7010, New York, NY 10116-4627. Tel: (212) 647-0707; fax: (212) 463-7099. Day of market, call (212) 243-7922.

New York City
The Grand Bazaar

In a lot on 25th Street between Broadway and Avenue of the Americas (Sixth Avenue).

Every weekend, 6 A.M. to 5 P.M.

Free admission; street parking only. A new market; outdoors, rain or shine. Averages a few dozen to a capacity of 125 vendors.

Antiques and collectibles, crafts and fine art, used furniture, garage-sale items, and toys. Food is not served on the premises (but there are many restaurants nearby).

VENDORS: $55 per space on Saturday, $70 on Sunday. Reserve at least a week in advance.

Contact Ed Bloom or Kenny Parker, 384 Main Street, Armonk, NY 10504. Tel: (914) 273-1578. Day of market, call (212) 243-9124.

New York City
I.S. 44 Flea Market/Greenflea

At the schoolyard on 77th Street and Columbus Avenue, across the street from the American Museum of Natural History on Manhattan's upper west side, a block from Central Park.

Every Sunday except Easter, 10 A.M. to 5 P.M.

Free admission; street parking (public transportation recommended). In operation for over 15 years; indoors year-round,

286

and outdoors, weather permitting. Averages 225 to a capacity of 350 vendors.

Antiques and collectibles, baskets, books, new and vintage clothing, international crafts and fine art, new and used furniture, jewelry and silver, new and used merchandise, plants, porcelain, fresh produce, and toys (balance is about 40 percent old, 60 percent new merchandise, but antiques and crafts are well represented). Snacks are served on the premises, and there are many restaurants and food shops nearby. Proceeds from market benefit the students of I.S. 44, P.S. 87, and the district.

VENDORS: From $22 to $125 per space per day depending on size and location. Reservations are required—call for information.

Contact Judith Gehrke, Greenflea, Inc., 162 West 72nd Street, #4RR, New York, NY 10023. Tel: (212) 721-0900 (office hours are Monday through Wednesday, 11 A.M. to 2 P.M.). Sundays only, call (212) 877-7371.

New York City

SoHo Antiques and Flea Market

At 465 Broadway (corner of Grand Street, one block north of Canal Street). Use IRT local subway (#6 train) to the Spring Street or the Canal Street stop.

Every weekend, 9 A.M. to 5 P.M.

Free admission; metered street parking and garages nearby; public transportation is recommended. In operation since 1991; outdoors year-round, weather permitting. Averages 65 to 90 vendors (capacity 100).

Antiques and collectibles, architectural objects, books, vintage clothing, coins and stamps, cookware, crafts, fine and decorative arts, folk art, new and used furniture, glassware, jewelry and silver, memorabilia, textiles, and toys. Snacks and hot meals are available in the neighboorhood. Located in Manhattan's artsy SoHo district, with many interesting galleries, shops, restaurants, and museums nearby. A premier opportunity for unusual treasures—justly described as a must-stop on New York's weekend flea market trail.

VENDORS: From $60 to $100 per space per day depending on size and location. Reservations are recommended.

Contact Ted Brachfeld, Manager, SoHo, Inc., P.O. Box 337, Garden City, NY 11530. Tel: (212) 682-2000.

New York City
Spring Street Market

On the lot at 43 Spring Street, at the corner of Wooster Street. Daily, 11 A.M. to 7 P.M.

Free admission; street parking (public transportation recommended). In operation for over eight years; outdoors, weather permitting. Averages close to 15 vendors year-round.

New and vintage clothing and accessories, cosmetics, crafts, jewelry and silver, and leather goods. Food is not served on the premises (but there are a lot of options nearby). This is for budget fashion hounds, not antiquers.

VENDORS: Inquire for monthly rates. No transient vendors.

Contact Irwin Yesselman, 89 Silver Lake Road, Staten Island, NY 10301. Tel: (718) 273-8702. Day of market, call (917) 837-5941.

New York City
Thomas Payne Park

At Worth and Centre Streets, at the Civic Center in lower Manhattan.

Every Wednesday from April through Christmas, 8 A.M. to 6 P.M.

Free admission; street parking (public transportation recommended). In operation for over four years; outdoors, weather permitting. Average number of vendors not reported.

Antiques and collectibles, books, new and vintage clothing, crafts, jewelry and silver, and new merchandise. Snacks are served at the market. Focus on multicultural crafts. Sponsored by the New York City Department of Parks and Recreation.

VENDORS: $100 to $125 per space per day. Reserve a month in advance.

Contact Gio-Art Productions, Inc., 84 William Street, New York, NY 10038. Tel: (212) 809-5000 or (212) 809-7345.

New York City
Tower Records Flea Market

At 688 Broadway, in the lot next to the Tower Records at Fourth Street.

Every weekend, 10 A.M. to 8 P.M.

Free admission; street parking—public transportation recommended. In operation for over seven years; outdoors, rain or shine. Averages 50 to a capacity of 75 vendors.

Mostly new clothing, crafts, and jewelry, but there's a wide range of fashion statements for NYU students and others. Food is not served on the premises, but there are plenty of good restaurants nearby.

VENDORS: $10 per foot of frontage on aisle (space is 4½ feet deep). Reservations are not required.

Contact Irwin Yesselman, 89 Silver Lake Road, Staten Island, NY 10301. Tel: (718) 273-8702 or (917) 860-1217.

Port Chester
Empire State Flea Market and Jewelry Exchange

At the Caldor's Shopping Center, 515 Boston Post Road (Route 1). Take Exit 21 off I-95; or take Exit 12 off I-287. The market is located 15 miles from the Tappan Zee Bridge, 25 miles from the George Washington Bridge, on the New York–Connecticut border.

Every Friday, noon to 8:30 P.M.; Saturday and Sunday, 10 A.M. to 6 P.M.; daily operation with extended hours from Thanksgiving through Christmas.

Free admission; free parking for up to 1,900 cars. In operation since 1976; indoors, year-round. Averages up to a capacity of 300 vendors.

All vendors specialize in new merchandise substantially discounted from manufacturers' list prices. Not the place for antiquers, but shoppers can find many bargains on new goods. Snacks and hot meals are served on the premises. Billed as New York State's first indoor new merchandise market, with some 5,000 shoppers each market day.

VENDORS: Monthly rentals only, average $500 per space per month. Reserve at least a week in advance.

Contact Alan Finchley, 515 Boston Post Road, Port Chester, NY 10573. Tel: (914) 939-1800.

Preston Hollow

Preston Hollow Antique and Flea Market

At the intersection of Routes 145 and 81, where Albany, Greene, and Schoharie Counties meet; call for further directions.

Every Sunday, plus holiday Mondays, from May through October, 9 A.M. to 4 P.M.

Free admission; free parking for up to 300 cars. In operation for over three years; outdoors, rain or shine. Averages close to 50 vendors (capacity 150).

Antiques and collectibles, books, new clothing, crafts, new and used furniture, jewelry and silver, new merchandise, and porcelain. Snacks and hot meals are served on the premises.

VENDORS: $20 per space per day (New York State resale number required for all vendors). Reservations are recommended a week in advance, but vendors are welcome on day of market.

Contact Dorothy Como, R.D. #1, Box 88, Preston Hollow, NY 12469. Tel: (518) 239-4251.

Saratoga Springs
Stan's Flea Market

On Route 9, three miles north of town.

Every weekend from April through October, 9 A.M. to 4 P.M.

Free admission; free parking for up to 300 cars. In operation for over 17 years; outdoors, year-round. Averages 45 to 60 vendors (capacity 80).

A variety of new and used merchandise including antiques and collectibles, books, coins, used furniture, glassware, jewelry, fresh produce, and toys. Snacks and hot meals are served on the premises. Camping nearby.

VENDORS: $15 per space per day. Reservations are not required.

Contact Stanley Akers, 23 Meditation Way, Saratoga Springs, NY 12866. Tel: (518) 584-6938. Day of market, call (518) 584-4339.

South Ozone Park
Aqueduct Flea Market

At the Aqueduct Raceway. Take the Lefferts Boulevard exit off the Belt Parkway.

Every weekend from May through October and every Tuesday from April through Christmas, 7:30 A.M. to 4 P.M.

Admission $1.50 per carload or 50 cents per person on foot; free parking for up to 10,000 cars. In operation for approximately 23 years; outdoors, weather permitting. Average number of vendors not reported (capacity 2,000).

Antiques and collectibles, books, new and vintage clothing, coins and stamps, cookware, crafts and fine art, new and used

furniture, jewelry and silver, new merchandise, pottery and porcelain, fresh produce, and toys. Snacks and hot meals are served at the "international food court" on the premises. Mostly new merchandise at this "original outdoor racetrack flea market."

VENDORS: From $35 per space per day. Reservations accepted for monthly and sometimes for daily rentals.

Contact Joe Berchielli, Barterama Corporation, 257 Hempstead Turnpike, Elmont, NY 11003. Tel: (516) 775-8774.

Spring Valley
Spring Valley Flea Market

At 122 East Central Avenue. Take Exit 14 off I-87 and make a right turn at the traffic light, and go straight down nine blocks, and the market will be on the left side.

Every Friday, 5 P.M. to 10 P.M.; Saturday, 10 A.M. to 9 P.M.; and Sunday, 10 A.M. to 7 P.M.

Free admission; free parking for up to 600 cars. In operation for over 15 years; indoors, year-round. Averages up to 700 vendors year-round.

New merchandise only: baseball cards, books, clothing, comics, cookware, crafts, fine art, furniture, jewelry, and toys. Snacks and hot meals are served on the premises. Billed as "one-stop shopping for all your needs" in a mall-like atmosphere—but not for "junktiquers."

VENDORS: Inquire for weekly or monthly rates. Reservations are a week in advance.

Contact Al Bonnadonna or Robert Levi, 122 East Central Avenue, Spring Valley, NY 10977. Tel: (914) 356-1171.

Staten Island
Antiques, Crafts, and Collectibles Flea Market

At 441 Clarke Avenue.
First Sunday in May, June, and October, and the second Sunday in September, 10 A.M. to 5 P.M.

Admission $1 per person; 50 cents for children under 17; parking nearby. In operation for over 25 years; outdoors, weather permitting (check for rain dates). Averages close to 145 vendors (capacity 155).

Antiques and collectibles, books, vintage clothing, cookware, crafts and fine art, flowers, used furniture, jewelry and silver, porcelain, toys, and used merchandise. Snacks and hot meals are served on the premises.

VENDORS: $30 per 10'x19' space per day. Reserve as far as possible in advance.

Contact Julie Nolan, Staten Island Historical Society, 441 Clarke Avenue, Staten Island, NY 10308. Tel: (718) 351-1611 or (718) 351-9414.

Staten Island
Yankee Peddler Day

At Historic Richmond Town. Take the Staten Island Ferry to the S74 bus to Richmondtown; by car from the ferry terminal, turn left onto Bay Street and go about two miles, then turn right onto Vanderbilt Avenue, then at the fourth light bear left onto Richmond Road, then about five miles ahead turn left onto Saint Patrick's Place. Follow signs to Restoration parking. Call for other directions.

Annually, the first Sunday in May, 10 A.M. to 5 P.M.; there are also arts, crafts, and antiques fairs on the first Sunday in June and October and the second Sunday of September with the same types of items.

Admission $1 per person; children 50 cents; free parking. In operation for over 15 years; outdoors, with rain date. Averages up to a capacity of 150 vendors.

Antiques and collectibles, books, coins and stamps, handmade items, vintage clothing, used furniture, pottery and porcelain, jewelry, and more. Snacks and hot meals are served on the premises.

VENDORS: $35 per 10'x19' space (one parking space). Reservations are required a month in advance.

Contact Education Department, Staten Island Historical Society, 441 Clarke Avenue, Staten Island, NY 10306. Tel: (718) 351-1611 or (718) 351-9414; fax: (718) 351-6057.

Stormville

Stormville Airport Antique Show and Flea Market

At the Stormville Airport on Route 216 (between Routes 52 and 55) in Dutchess County.

Five Sundays per year in May, July, August, September, and October, dawn to dusk; call for dates.

Free admission; free parking for approximately 3,000 cars. In operation for over 25 years; outdoors, rain or shine. Averages up to 600 vendors (capacity 800).

Antiques and collectibles, books, new and vintage clothing, coins and stamps, cookware and crafts, new and used furniture, jewelry and silver, new merchandise, pottery and porcelain, and toys. Snacks and hot meals are served on the premises. Lodging nearby. "Fun for the whole family."

VENDORS: $55 per day with advance payment; $60 on weekend of market; vendors may set up on the preceding Saturday. Reservations are recommended.

Contact Pat Carnahan, P.O. Box 125, Stormville, NY 12582. Tel: (914) 221-6561.

Westbury
Roosevelt Raceway Flea Market

At the Roosevelt Raceway on Old Country Road, accessible from the Long Island Railroad or by car from the Long Island Expressway.

Every Sunday year-round, every Saturday in November and December, and every Wednesday from April through December, 8 A.M. to 5 P.M.

Free admission; ample parking at $2 per car. In operation for over 17 years; indoors and outdoors, rain or shine. Averages 1,500 to over 2,000 vendors.

Antiques and collectibles, books, new and vintage clothing, cookware, crafts and fine art, fish, new and used furniture, jewelry and silver, new merchandise, pottery and porcelain, fresh produce, and toys. Snacks and hot meals are served on the premises.

VENDORS: $65 per 10'x28' space per day; $45 per day if paid on a monthly basis. Reservations are not required.

Contact Jeff Lake, P.O. Box 978, Westbury, NY 11590. Tel: (516) 222-1530.

Whitehall
Whitehall Flea Market

At 259 Broadway (Route 4) in Whitehall, 25 miles west of Rutland, Vermont, and 65 miles north of Albany, New York.

Every Sunday, 7:30 A.M. to 3:30 P.M.

Free admission; free parking for up to 100. In operation for over 12 years; indoors year-round, and outdoors, weather permitting. Averages up to 80 vendors.

Antiques and collectibles, books, vintage clothing, coins and stamps, cookware, crafts, used furniture, garage-sale items, jewelry, fresh produce, rabbits, and toys. Snacks and hot meals are served on the premises. Run by the local chamber of commerce.

NEW YORK/Yonkers

VENDORS: $6 per 8-foot table per day, indoors or outdoors. Reserve a week in advance.

Contact Nicholas Deutsch, c/o Whitehall Chamber of Commerce, R.D. #2, Box 2924, Whitehall, NY 12887. Tel: (518) 499-2292; fax: (518) 499-2437.

Yonkers
Yonkers Raceway Market

At the Yonkers Raceway. Take Exit 2 (northbound) or Exit 4 (southbound) off the New York State Throughway (I-87).

From the last Sunday in March through the last Sunday before Christmas, 9 A.M. to 4 P.M.

Admission $1 per person or $2 per carload; parking for up to 8,500 cars at $2 per car. In operation for over 10 years; indoors, rain or shine. Averages 350 to 450 vendors.

A variety of new and used merchandise including books, clothing, collectibles (baseball cards, comics, etc.), furniture, jewelry, fresh produce, and toys. Snacks and hot meals are served on the premises. Access to racetrack for simulcast betting.

VENDORS: $40 per Sunday per space reserved, or $50 unreserved. Reservations are not required.

Contact Marty McGrath, Yonkers Raceway, Yonkers, NY 10704. Tel: (914) 963-3898 or (914) 968-4200, ext. 216.

NORTH CAROLINA

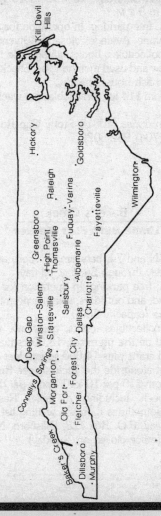

Kill Devil
Hills

Hickory

Greensboro
High Point
Thomasville
Raleigh
Fuquay-Varina
Salisbury
Albemarle
Charlotte
Fayetteville
Wilmington
Goldsboro

Deep Gap
Winston-Salem
Statesville
Dallas

Connelly's Springs
Morganton
Old Fort
Forest City
Fletcher
Baker's Creek
Dillsboro
Murphy

Albemarle
Albemarle Flea Market

At 40818 Stony Gap Road.

Every Friday and Saturday, 10 A.M. to 10 P.M., and every Sunday, 11 A.M. to 9 P.M.

Free admission; free parking. In operation for over five years; indoors, rain or shine. Averages close to 40 vendors.

Antiques and collectibles, books, garage-sale items, new and used furniture, new and used merchandise. Snacks are served on the premises; two fish houses nearby.

VENDORS: From $14 for three tables per week. Reservations are required.

Contact Lyman Jones, 40818 Stony Gap Road, Albemarle, NC 28001. Tel: (704) 982-5022.

Baker's Creek
Uncle Bill's Flea Market

On Route 441-N and 74, between Dillsboro and Cherokee.

Every Wednesday through Sunday, all day.

Free admission; free parking. In operation for over 10 years; indoors year-round, and outdoors, weather permitting. Averages up to 150 vendors (capacity 200).

Antiques and collectibles, crafts, glassware, fresh produce. Snacks are served on the premises; 18,000 square feet permanent antiques and crafts plus 14,000 square feet of covered flea market area, right alongside the Tuckaseegee River.

VENDORS: From $10 per 10'x10' space per day under cover or $30 per week including a table. Reservations are recommended—sometimes there's a waiting list.

Contact Ben Seay, P.O. Box 728, Dillsboro, NC 28725. Tel: (704) 586-9613 (office closed on Tuesday).

Charlotte
Metrolina Expo

At 7100 North Statesville Road. Take Exit 16-A (Sunset Road) off I-77 and follow signs to fairgrounds.

First Saturday of every month, and the Thursday and Friday preceding, 8 A.M. to 5 P.M., and Sunday, 9 A.M. to 5 P.M.; there is also an antiques and variety market on the third Saturday of the month and Sunday the next day.

Free admission; several acres of free parking. In operation for over 27 years; indoors year-round, and outdoors, weather permitting. Averages 1,500 to 5,000 vendors.

Antiques and collectibles, books, vintage clothing, crafts, used and antique furniture, and toys. Snacks and hot meals are served on the premises.

VENDORS: Inquire for rates. Reserve at least three weeks in advance.

Contact Aileen Lisk, P.O. Box 26652, Charlotte, NC 28221. Tel: (800) 824-3770 or (704) 596-4643.

Connellys Springs
I-40 Trade Lot

At Connelly Springs Road, beside I-40 at Exit 113 (Rutherford College exit) between Hickory and Morganton; coming off exit, turn right if coming eastbound, or left if westbound.

Every weekend, 6 A.M. to 5 P.M.

Free admission; ample free parking. In operation for over 18 years; outdoors, weather permitting. Average number of vendors not reported.

Antiques and collectibles, books, new and vintage clothing, coins and stamps, cookware, crafts and fine art, new and used furniture, jewelry and silver, livestock, new and used merchandise, porcelain, poultry and fresh produce, tools, and toys. Snacks and hot meals are served on the premises. "Just a plain, old-fashioned flea market."

VENDORS: $8 per shed per day or $5 per space in the field; $50 per reserved space per month. Reservations are not required.

Contact Jean Hildebran or Dale Willis, Route 3, Box 620, Connellys Springs, NC 28612. Tel: (704) 879-9970.

Dallas
I-85/321 Flea Market

At 3867 Dallas–High Shoals Highway. From I-85 in Gastonia (approximately 25 miles south of Charlotte and 60 miles north of Spartanburg, South Carolina), head north on Route 321 for three miles to Cherryville exit, then turn right at traffic light, and market is two miles ahead on the right.

Every weekend, 8 A.M. to 4 P.M.

Free admission; free parking. In operation for over 10 years; indoors and outdoors, rain or shine. Averages 400 to a capacity of 600 vendors.

Antiques and collectibles, cosmetics, new clothing, coins and stamps, crafts, electronics, new and used furniture, fine and costume jewelry, silver, livestock, new and used merchandise, oriental rugs, pets, fresh produce, tools, toys, and wicker. Snacks and hot sandwiches are served on the premises.

VENDORS: Indoors: $20 per 12'x12' space per day or $125 per month; includes two tables with own door and parking space. Outdoors: $12 per day or $80 per month for covered shed with two tables; $8 per day or $40 per month for open space with two tables. Reserve two weeks in advance for indoor spaces.

Contact David Stewart, 3867 High Shoals Highway, Dallas, NC 28034. Tel: (704) 922-1416; digital pager: (704) 834-8093.

Deep Gap
Wildcat Flea Market

At 8156 Highway 421 South, one half mile from the Blue Ridge Parkway entrance, eight miles east of Boone.

Every Friday, Saturday, Sunday and, holidays from May through October, 10 A.M. to 5 P.M., except Saturday, 9 A.M. to 9 P.M.

Free admission; four acres of free parking. In operation since 1973; indoors rain or shine, and outdoors, weather permitting. Averages up to 60 vendors (but room for many more).

Antiques and collectibles, books, cookware, mountain crafts, new and used furniture, gift items, glassware, jewelry and silver, musical instruments and recordings, new merchandise, novelties, porcelain, fresh produce, and toys. Restaurant on the premises. Tour buses welcome. Auction every Saturday at 7 P.M., year-round.

VENDORS: Indoors: $100 per 10'x10' space per month inside main building or $35 in warehouse area; outdoors: $5 per 8'x10' space under cover on Saturday or Sunday, free on Friday. Reservations are recommended.

Contact Elaine, Jack, or Kevin Richardson, 8156 U.S. Highway 421 South, Deep Gap, NC 28618. Tel: (704) 264-7757.

Dillsboro
441 Flea Market

On Highway 441, one mile south of Dillsboro.

Every Friday, Saturday, and Sunday, from daylight to dark.

Free admission; free parking for 200 cars. In operation for over 20 years; outdoors and under sheds, rain or shine. Averages 15 to a capacity of 60 vendors.

An eclectic market with new merchandise, antiques and collectibles, tools, fresh produce, cookware, crafts, books, and jewelry. Snacks and hot meals are served on the premises. A rustic affair known for the best chili dogs in the South.

VENDORS: $5 per space per day under shed, $3 in open air. Reservations are required two weeks in advance.

Contact Padgett McCoy, P.O. Box 414, Sylva, NC 28779. Tel: (704) 586-6768.

Fayetteville
Raeford Road Flea Market

At 5207 Raeford Road (Route 401), off I-95 and across from the Lafayette Ford dealership.

Every Friday, Saturday, and Sunday, 7:30 A.M. to 5 P.M.

Free admission; free parking for up to 500 cars. In operation for over 16 years; outdoors, rain or shine. Averages 100 to 150 vendors (capacity 200).

Antiques and collectibles, books, new and vintage clothing, coins and stamps, cookware, crafts, new and used furniture, jewelry and silver, new and used merchandise, porcelain, poultry and fresh produce, and toys. Snacks and hot meals are served on the premises. Near Fort Bragg and Pope Air Force Bases.

VENDORS: $4 per space on Friday, $5 on Saturday, $5 on Sunday; spaces range in size from 15'x20' to 20'x25'. Reservations are recommended.

Contact Camille Leonardo, 912 Hemlock Drive, Fayetteville, NC 28304. Tel: (910) 425-8053.

Fletcher
Smiley's Flea Market and Antique Mall

On Route 25, halfway between Asheville and Hendersonville. Take Exit 13 off I-26, then go north on Highway 25 (back toward Asheville) for about a half mile, and the market will be on the right.

Friday, Saturday, and Sunday, 8 A.M. to 5 P.M.; there is also an antiques mall (with over 60 dealers) open daily, 10 A.M. to 5

P.M., and a craft mall (with 200 vendor spaces) open every Wednesday through Sunday, 10 A.M. to 5 P.M.

Free admission; free parking for up to 3,000 cars; buses and motor homes also accommodated. In operation since 1984; indoors, outdoors, and under cover, rain or shine. Averages 350 to 450 vendors (capacity 500 spaces including 300 under cover).

Antiques and collectibles, books, new and vintage clothing, coins and stamps, clocks, cookware and crafts, electronics, new and used furniture, jewelry and silver, new and used merchandise, musical equipment, porcelain, fresh produce, records, tapes, CDs, and toys. Snacks (including good funnel cakes) and hot meals are served on the premises. Formerly the Fletcher Marketplace Antique Mall and Flea Market; this is a sprawling market with good action year-round.

VENDORS: Indoors: from $5 to $10 per space per day depending on size, plus some "shoppes" with monthly rentals (average about $200 per month); outdoors: $3 per table/space. Reservations are not required.

Contact Manager, P.O. Box 458, Fletcher, NC 28732. Tel: (704) 684-FLEA or (704) 684-3515.

Forest City
74 Bypass Flea Market

At 180 Frontage Road. Market is visible from Exit 180 (Forest City) off 74 Connector.

Every Friday, Saturday, and Sunday except Christmas (produce market every Wednesday and Thursday), 7 A.M. to 4 P.M.

Free admission; free parking for up to 250 cars. In operation for over 10 years; indoors year-round, outdoors and under cover, weather permitting. Averages 60 to a capacity of 150 vendors.

Antiques and collectibles, books, new and vintage clothing, crafts and fine art, new and used furniture, jewelry, new and used merchandise, fresh produce, tools, and toys. Snacks and hot meals are served on the premises.

VENDORS: $1 per outdoor space on Friday, $2 on Saturday or Sunday; $5 per space under shed on Friday, $6 on Saturday or Sunday. Reservations are not required except for indoor spaces.

Contact Gary Hardin, 180 Frontage Road, Forest City, NC 28043. Tel: (704) 245-7863.

Fuquay-Varina
Fuquay Flea Market

On Highway 55 East. From Raleigh, take Route 401 south to Highway 55E, then left on 55E a quarter mile and market will be on the left.

Every weekend, 8 A.M. to 5 P.M.

Free admission; free parking for up to 350 cars. In operation for over 14 years; indoors, year-round. Averages 130 to a capacity of 150 vendors on 130,000 square feet indoors.

Antiques and collectibles, books, new and vintage clothing, cookware and crafts, new and used furniture, jewelry, fresh produce, and toys. Snacks are available on the premises.

VENDORS: From $14 per 12½'x15' space per day. Reserve a week in advance.

Contact Jimmy Tilley, Manager, P.O. Box 607, Fuquay-Varina, NC 27526. Tel: (919) 552-4143.

Goldsboro
Goldsboro Flea Market

At 2102 Wayne Memorial Drive (right behind the Days Inn). Take the Wayne Memorial Drive exit off I-70 Bypass.

Every weekend: Saturday, 8 A.M. to 5 P.M., and Sunday, 10 A.M. to 5 P.M.

Free admission; free parking for up to 350 cars. In operation for over five years; indoors and outdoors, rain or shine. Averages 275 to 300 vendors (capacity 350).

Antiques and collectibles, books, new clothing, cookware and crafts, new and vintage clothing, new furniture, jewelry and silver, new and used merchandise, porcelain, fresh produce, and toys. Snacks and hot meals are served on the premises. "Where the customers send their friends." On the route to North Carolina's Crystal Coast; draws as many as 10,000 shoppers every weekend.

VENDORS: Indoors: $20 per 10'x12' space per day or $32 for two days; outdoors: $10 per space; some spaces include Peg-Board and shelf; electricity and tables are $1 each per day when available. Reservations are not required.

Contact Keith Hartzog, 3927-A Highway 177 South ALT, Dudley, NC 28333. Tel: (919) 734-6656 or (919) 736-4422 or (800) 282-FLEA.

Greensboro
Greensboro Flea Market

At 4000 McConnell Road. Take Exit 130 off I-85, two miles north of Greensboro and ten miles south of Burlington.

Every weekend, 8 A.M. to 5 P.M.

Free admission; free parking for up to 750 cars. In operation since September 1991; indoors and outdoors, rain or shine. Averages up to 70 vendors.

Antiques and collectibles, books, new and vintage clothing, cookware, crafts and fine art, new and used furniture, grocery items, jewelry and silver, new and used merchandise, porcelain, fresh produce, tools, and toys. Snack bar on the premises. "Well-landscaped, exceptionally pretty" environment.

VENDORS: Indoors: $25 per weekend on a monthly basis; outdoors: $5 per 4'x8' table per day. Reservations are not required.

NORTH CAROLINA/Greensboro

Contact Calvin White, 4000 McConnell Road, Greensboro, NC 27406. Tel: (910) 697-2707.

Greensboro
Super Flea Flea Market

At the Greensboro Coliseum; follow signs posted on all roads into Greensboro.

Weekend of the second Sunday of every month from June through December: Saturday, 8 A.M. to 5 P.M., and Sunday, 10 A.M. to 5 P.M.

Admission $1.50 per person; parking for up to 5,200 cars at $1 per car. In operation for over 19 years; indoors, year-round. Averages close to its capacity of 300 vendors year-round.

Antiques and collectibles, books, new and vintage clothing, coins and stamps, cookware, crafts and fine art, new and used furniture, jewelry and silver, new and used merchandise, porcelain, and toys. Snacks are served on the premises.

VENDORS: $60 per 8'x10' space per weekend, includes a table and two chairs; extra tables are available at $6 each; electricity is available at $25 per weekend. Reserve two weeks in advance.

Contact William D. Smith, 703 Simpson Street, Greensboro, NC 27401. Tel: (910) 373-8515.

Hickory
Springs Road Flea Market

At 3451 Springs Road, near the St. Stephen's High School. Every weekend, 8 A.M. to 4 P.M.

Free admission; ample free parking. In operation for over five years; indoors, outdoors, and under cover, year-round. Averages up to a couple hundred vendors.

Antiques and collectibles, books, new clothing, coins and

306

stamps, cookware, crafts, new and used furniture, jewelry and silver, new and used merchandise, porcelain, fresh produce, and toys. Hot meals are served on the premises.

VENDORS: $5 per space per day outdoors, $6 under cover; inquire for indoor rates. Reservations are recommended; waiting list for indoor spaces.

Contact Manager, Springs Road, Route 2, Hickory, NC 28601. Tel: (704) 256-7669.

High Point
Westchester Flea Market

At 2200 Westchester Drive (Highway 68). Easy access from I-40 and Business Routes 29 and 70.

Every Saturday, 8 A.M. to 5 P.M., and every Sunday, 9 A.M. to 5 P.M.

Free admission; free parking for up to 600 cars. In operation since 1992; indoors, year-round. Averages up to a capacity of 325 vendors.

Antiques and collectibles, books, new clothing, coins and stamps, cookware, crafts and fine art, fishing tackle, flowers, new and used furniture, jewelry and silver, new and used merchandise, oriental rugs, pets, porcelain, fresh produce, and toys. Snack bar on the premises. Supervised arcade with over 50 games; picture framing. The only flea market in High Point, near all the furniture outlet stores.

VENDORS: $15 per 10'x12' space per day, includes one 2'x8' table; additional tables available at $1 per day; electricity is available at $2 per day. Reservations are required.

Contact Manager, P.O. Box 7524, High Point, NC 27264. Tel: (910) 884-5063.

Kill Devil Hills
Indoor Flea Market

At 306 West Lake Drive, across from Kentucky Fried Chicken. Turn west off U.S. Route 158.

Every Saturday, 9 A.M. to 4 P.M., and every Sunday, noon to 4 P.M.

Free admission; free parking for up to 100 cars. In operation for over five years; indoors, year-round. Averages 15 to 50 vendors (capacity 80 or more).

Antiques and collectibles, books, new and vintage clothing, coins and stamps, cookware, crafts, used furniture, jewelry and silver, new and used merchandise, porcelain, and toys. Snacks are served on the premises.

VENDORS: $10 per 5'x10' space on Saturday and $5 on Sunday; $15 per 8'x8' space on Saturday and $7.50 on Sunday; inquire for monthly rates. Reservations are not required.

Contact Fred Bear, P.O. Box 718, Kill Devil Hills, NC 27948. Tel: (919) 441-8830.

Morganton
Jamestown Flea Market

On Jamestown Road. Take Exit 100 off I-40 and travel one mile toward town.

Every weekend, 7 A.M. to 5 P.M.

Free admission; free parking. In operation for over 13 years; indoors, outdoors, and under cover, rain or shine. Averages 300 to a capacity of 400 vendors.

Antiques and collectibles, automotive supplies, books, new and vintage clothing, coins and stamps, cookware, crafts, new and used furniture, hardware, jewelry and silver, new and used merchandise, porcelain, fresh produce, and toys. Snacks and hot meals are served on the premises. Vendors overnight OK.

VENDORS: Indoors: $10 per space per day; outdoors: $5

exposed or $6 under shed; tables are provided; electricity is provided for most spaces. Reservations are recommended.

Contact Pierre Winkler, P.O. Drawer 764, Morganton, NC 28655. Tel: (704) 584-4038 (office hours are Thursday afternoon and all day Friday).

Murphy
Decker's Flea Market

At the junction of Routes 19 and 129 (Blairsville Highway), two hours north of Atlanta (take I-75), or two hours west of Asheville, North Carolina (take Highway 74).

Every weekend, 7 A.M. to 3 P.M.

Free admission; free parking for up to 250 cars. In operation since 1981; indoors year-round, and outdoors, weather permitting. Averages 50 to 75 vendors (capacity 90).

Antiques and collectibles, books, new and vintage clothing, cookware, crafts and fine art, used furniture, jewelry and silver, livestock and farm supplies, new and used merchandise, porcelain, poultry and fresh produce, and toys. Snacks and hot meals are served on the premises.

VENDORS: $5 and up per space per day; tables are provided. Reserve a week in advance.

Contact Jerry or Chad Decker, P.O. Box 453, Murphy, NC 28906. Tel: (704) 837-5753.

Old Fort
Catawba Trading Lot

At I-40 and Catawba River Road. Take Exit 73 off I-40.

Every Friday, Saturday, and Sunday, 7:30 A.M. to whenever.

Free admission; free parking for up to 200 cars. In operation for over four years; outdoors and under sheds, rain or shine. Averages up to 80 vendors (50 outdoors and 30 under sheds).

Antiques and collectibles, books, new and vintage clothing, cookware, crafts, used furniture, jewelry, porcelain, poultry and fresh produce, and toys; no new merchandise. Snacks and hot meals are served on the premises. Prime location in western North Carolina. "Come out and catch the frontier spirit with us."

VENDORS: Free setup outdoors; inquire for monthly rates for shed spaces. Reservations are not required.

Contact Phillip Lowery, P.O. Box 269, Old Fort, NC 28762. Tel: (704) 668-4737 or (704) 668-4511.

Raleigh
Fairgrounds Flea Market

On the North Carolina State Fairgrounds, located at the intersection of Blueridge Road and Hillsborough Street.

Every weekend (except October), 9 A.M. to 5 P.M.

Free admission; ample free parking. In operation for over 23 years; indoors and outdoors, rain or shine. Averages 250 to 500 vendors on 200,000 square feet of selling area.

Large selection of antiques and collectibles, crafts, furniture, new and used merchandise—a good mix. Food is available on the premises. "The oldest, the biggest, and the best" in town.

VENDORS: $13 per 10'x20' space per day. Reservations are recommended.

Contact Joan Long, P.O. Box 33517, Raleigh, NC 27636. Tel: (919) 829-3533.

Raleigh
Raleigh Flea Market Mall

At 1924 Capital Boulevard. Take the Capital Boulevard exit off the Raleigh Beltline (I-440), going toward downtown Raleigh, then go left at the third stoplight.

Every weekend, 9 A.M. to 5 P.M.

Free admission; 11 acres of free parking. In operation since 1987; indoors year-round, and outdoors, weather permitting. Averages up to several hundred vendors.

Antiques and collectibles, books, new and vintage clothing, coins and stamps, cookware, crafts and fine art, new and used furniture, jewelry and silver, new and used merchandise, porcelain, fresh produce, seafood, and toys—"everything from A to Z." Snacks and hot meals are served on the premises. Includes 100,000 square feet of indoor space plus a large outdoor vending area with shaded spaces.

VENDORS: $10 per outdoor space per day. Waiting list on indoor spaces; outdoor spaces are on a first-come, first-served basis.

Contact Doug Brown, 1924 Capital Boulevard, Raleigh, NC 27604. Tel: (919) 839-0038.

Salisbury
Webb Road Flea Market

At 905 Webb Road, four miles south of Salibury. Take Exit 70 off I-85.

Every weekend, 8 A.M. to 5 P.M.

Free admission; free parking for over 1,000 cars. In operation for over 10 years; indoors, outdoors, and under cover, rain or shine. Averages up to a capacity of more than 800 vendors.

Antiques and collectibles, new and vintage clothing, cookware, crafts and fine art, new and used furniture, jewelry and silver, new merchandise, pottery and porcelain, and fresh produce. Snack bar and other concessions on the premises. Security on premises. Video game room; rest rooms have baby-changing area. Large regional market with daily attendance of 10,000 or more customers.

VENDORS: Indoors: $60 per 10'x10' space for four weeks, includes one table; when available, indoor spaces are $10 per day. Outdoors: from $5 to $9 per space under cover. Electricity is available at a small fee; showers available for vendors. Reservations are recommended.

Contact John Nash, Jr., 905 Webb Road, Salisbury, NC 28146-8536. Tel: (704) 857-6660.

Statesville
Sharon's Discount Flea Market

On Highway 21. Take Exit 151 off I-40, then go north a mile and a half on Highway 21; or take Exit 54 off I-77 and go a mile south on Highway 21.

Daily, 9 A.M. to 6 P.M. (Fridays, 9 A.M. to 8 P.M.).

Free admission; free parking for up to 250 cars. In operation for over three years; indoors year-round, and outdoors, weather permitting. Averages close to its capacity of 40 vendors.

Antiques and collectibles, books, new clothing, cookware, crafts, new and used furniture, jewelry and silver, new and used merchandise, porcelain, fresh produce, tools, and toys. Snacks are served on the premises.

VENDORS: $15 for two 10'x10' spaces per day; $125 monthly for two spaces for seven-day operation. Reserve four days in advance.

Contact Sharon or William Fuller, 145 Nicholason Way Road, Statesville, NC 28677. Tel: (704) 838-0940 or (704) 873-5352.

Thomasville
Eleven Acres Flea Market

At 825 Julian Avenue. Take Exit 103 off I-85 to Highway 109 north to Julian Avenue, and market will be on the right (one quarter mile from I-85).

Every Saturday and Sunday, 5 A.M. to lunchtime.

Free admission; free parking for up to 500 cars. In operation for over 12 years; indoors, outdoors, and under cover, rain or shine. Averages 125 to 250 vendors (capacity 300).

Antiques and collectibles, books, new and vintage clothing, coins and stamps, cookware, crafts, electronics (including car stereos and cellular phones), new and used furniture, jewelry and silver, livestock, new and used merchandise, porcelain, poultry and fresh produce, and toys. Snacks and hot meals are served on the premises.

VENDORS: $8 per table per day outdoors, or $20 per table indoors. Reservations are on a first-come, first-served basis for outdoor space; reserve a week ahead for indoor space.

Contact Andrew Pope, 825 Julian Avenue, Thomasville, NC 27360. Tel: (910) 472-0244 or (910) 476-9566.

Wilmington
Starway Flea Market

At 2346 Carolina Beach Road (Route 421), 12 miles from the beach at the old drive-in movie theater.

Every Friday, 7:30 A.M. to 4 P.M.; every Saturday, 6 A.M. to 4 P.M.; and every Sunday, 7:30 A.M. to 4 P.M.

Free admission; parking for up to 1,000 cars (50 cents per car on Saturday only). In operation for over 23 years; indoors year-round, and outdoors, weather permitting. Averages 175 to 200 vendors (capacity 109 vendors indoors plus at least 300 outdoors).

Antiques and collectibles, books, new and vintage clothing, coins and stamps, cookware, crafts and fine art, new and used furniture, jewelry and silver, new and used merchandise, porcelain, fresh produce, seafood, toys, and vehicles (boats, cars, etc.). Snacks and hot meals are served on the premises. Billed as the largest and oldest indoor/outdoor flea market in the Cape Fear region with 15 acres of selling space; lots of room for special events such as circuses and boat and car shows.

VENDORS: $5 per 10'x10' space on Friday or Sunday, $8 on Saturday. Reserve a week in advance (for inside building only).

Contact Doyle Penley, 2346 Carolina Beach Road, Wilmington, NC 28401. Tel: (910) 763-5520.

Wilmington
Tradewinds Swap-A-Rama

At 5919 Market Street, on Highway 17 North, three quarters of a mile off I-40.

Every Wednesday through Sunday, 10 A.M. to 5 P.M. (except 9 A.M. to 5 P.M. on Saturday).

Free admission; free parking for up to 100 cars. In operation for over five years; indoors and outdoors, rain or shine. Averages 30 to 50 vendors (capacity 150 indoors and outdoors).

Antiques and collectibles, vintage clothing, new and used furniture including patio furniture, jewelry and silver, and new merchandise. Snacks are available on the premises.

VENDORS: $10 per space per day, or $25 per week. Reservations are not required.

Contact Henry Kuprion, 5919 Market Street, Wilmington, NC 28405. Tel: (919) 395-6880.

Winston-Salem
Cook's Flea Market

At 5721 University Parkway. Take Highway 52 North to University Parkway, then left at stoplight, and go to Robinwood Lane (second stoplight), and go left to market (behind Shoney's).

Every weekend, 8 A.M. to 5 P.M.

Free admission; free parking. In operation for over five years; indoors, year-round. Averages up to 400 vendors year-round on 80,000 square feet of selling space.

Antiques and collectibles, books, new clothing, cookware, crafts and fine art, new and used furniture, jewelry and silver, new and used merchandise, fresh produce, and toys. Snacks and hot meals are served on the premises.

VENDORS: $34 per 10'x10' space per weekend; tables are available at $2 per day; electricity is available at $4 per weekend. Reserve up to a year in advance.

Contact Cathie or Jack Hooks, P.O. Box 459, Rural Hall, NC 27045. Tel: (910) 945-0540 or (910) 661-0610.

NORTH DAKOTA

Minot

Mandan

Mandan
Dakota Midwest Antique Show Flea Market

At 901 Division Street, just off the Sunset Interchange, at the Mandan Community Center (across the river from Bismarck, North Dakota). Take Exit 152 off I-94 and go south one mile.

First weekend of every month (except January): Saturday, 8 A.M. to 5 P.M., and Sunday, 8 A.M. to 4 P.M.

Admission $1 per person; free parking for up to 300 cars. In operation for over eight years; indoors, year-round. Averages close to 70 vendors year-round.

Antiques and collectibles, books, vintage clothing, cookware, used furniture, American Indian artifacts, jewelry and silver, new and used merchandise, porcelain, and toys. Snacks and hot meals are served on the premises.

VENDORS: $15 per 8-foot space per day or $20 per weekend. Reservations are recommended.

Contact Barb or Bruce Skogen, 107 Estevan Drive, Bismarck, ND 58501-0318. Tel: (701) 223-6185.

Minot
Magic City Flea Market

On Business Highway 2, on the North Dakota State Fairgrounds.

About 14 weekends a year in all months but January, 9 A.M. to 4 P.M.—call for dates; a couple of shows a year specially feature antiques, coins, and baseball cards; three shows are devoted to arts and crafts.

Admission 50 cents; ample free parking. In operation for over 16 years; indoors year-round, with outdoor spaces available June through September, rain or shine. Averages 120 to 150 vendors (capacity 180).

Mainly antiques and collectibles, such as baseball cards, books, coins and stamps, crafts, used furniture, jewelry, silver, and toys. Food is available on premises. One of the largest markets in the area, heavily advertised and in a prime location.

VENDORS: $9 per day for wall space or corner space, all other indoor spaces $7. Single-day space $10; $2 setup fee; tables are available at $3 per day. All outdoor spaces $10 (available June through September). Reservations accepted with advance payment.

Contact Richard W. Timboe, P.O. Box 1672, Minot, ND 58702. Tel: (701) 852-1289 or (701) 838-1150.

OHIO

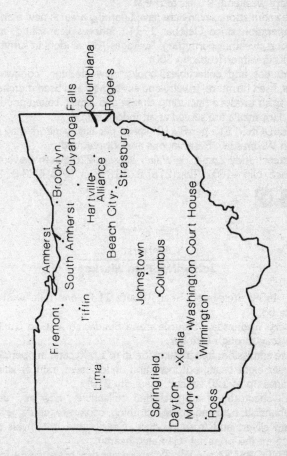

Alliance
Carnation Craft and Flea Market

At 2025 West State, just off State Route 62, directly across from Wally Armour Ford.

Every weekend, 9 A.M. to 5 P.M.

Free admission; seven-acre paved parking area. A new market (in operation since October 1994); indoors year-round, and outdoors, weather permitting. Averages 130 vendors in summer to 200 in winter (capacity 300).

Antiques and collectibles, books, new clothing, cookware, crafts, used furniture, jewelry and silver, new and used merchandise, fresh produce (including cheese and Amish baked goods), toys. Hot meals are served at an indoor café.

VENDORS: $15 per 8'x12' space per day; vendors may set up on Wednesday. Reservations are not required.

Contact Judy Zorger or Walter Nelson, 220 South Sawburg, Alliance, OH 44601. Tel: (216) 823-1898 or (216) 823-0744.

Amherst
Johnnie's Flea Market

At 46585 Telegraph Road (Route 113), one mile west of Route 58.

Every Wednesday, Saturday, and Sunday, 8 A.M. to 5 P.M., from May through October.

Free admission; free parking for up to 1,000 cars. In operation for over eight years; outdoors and under cover, rain or shine. Averages up to 120 vendors (capacity 210).

Full spectrum of antiques and collectibles, new and used merchandise, new and vintage clothing, cookware, crafts, jewelry and silver, and fresh produce. Snacks and hot meals are served on the premises. Camping nearby.

VENDORS: $7 per 12'x32' space per day; extra fee for food concessions. Reservations are not required.

Contact John Mayfield, 46585 Telegraph Road, Amherst, OH 44001. Tel: (216) 986-5681.

Beach City
Shady Rest Flea Market

On State Route 250.

Every Sunday, 5 A.M. to whenever.

Free admission; free parking. In operation for over 27 years; outdoors, weather permitting. Average number of vendors not reported.

Antiques and collectibles, books, new clothing, cookware, crafts, new and used furniture, porcelain, fresh produce, toys, and used merchandise. Snacks are served on the premises.

VENDORS: $6 per space per day. Reservations are not required.

Contact Mike Vukich, 1762 Johnstown Road, N.E., Dover, OH 44622. Tel: (216) 343-9508.

Brooklyn
Memphis Flea Market

At 10543 Memphis Avenue. Take Exit 13 (Tiedeman) off Route 480 and go north on Tiedeman to Memphis and turn left.

Every Wednesday, Saturday, and Sunday from April through October, 6 A.M. to 4 P.M.

Admission 50 cents per person; free parking for up to 1,300 cars. In operation for over 20 years; outdoors, rain or shine. Averages up to 400 vendors (capacity 450).

Antiques and collectibles, books, new clothing, coins and stamps, new and used furniture, jewelry and silver, porcelain, poultry, fresh produce, and toys. Snacks and hot meals are served on the premises.

VENDORS: $7 per space per day. Reservations are not required.

Contact William H. Applegarth, 10340 Memphis Avenue, Brooklyn, OH 44144. Tel: (216) 941-5995 or (216) 572-3725.

Columbiana
Theron's Country Flea Market

At 1641 State Route 164, one mile south of Columbiana county line. Take Ohio Turnpike to North Lima, then south on Route 164.

Every Sunday, 9 A.M. to 5 P.M.

Free admission; ample free parking. In operation for over 38 years; indoors and outdoors, rain or shine. Averages 45 to 55 vendors.

Antiques and collectibles, garage-sale items, glassware, jewelry, knives, and toys. Full family restaurant on the premises. Go-cart race every Sunday; auction for miscellany on Saturdays at 6:30 P.M.

VENDORS: $5 per space per day. Reservations are not required.

Contact Linda Wardy, 1641 Columbiana-Lisbon Road, Columbiana, OH 44408. Tel: (216) 482-4327.

Columbus
South Drive-In Theatre Flea Market

3050 South High Street.

Every Wednesday, Saturday, and Sunday from April through October, 7 A.M. to 2 P.M.

Admission 50 cents per carload; free parking. In operation for over 20 years; outdoors, weather permitting. Averages 250 to 300 vendors.

Antiques and collectibles, books, new and vintage clothing, cookware, crafts, new and used furniture, garage-sale items, jewelry, and used merchandise. Snacks are served on the premises.

VENDORS: $5 per space on Saturday or Sunday, $1 on Wednesday. Reservations are not required.

Contact Manager, Rainbow Theatres, 865 King Avenue, Columbus, OH 43212. Tel: (614) 275-4444.

Cuyahoga Falls
Oakwood Antiques and Collectibles

At 3265 Oakwood Drive at the corner of Fillmore, one block south of Graham Road, off Route 8 or 59 or 77 North.

Every Friday, Saturday, and Sunday, 10 A.M. to 5 P.M.

Free admission; free parking for up to 25 cars. In operation for over seven years; indoors and outdoors, rain or shine. Averages up to 10 vendors.

Antiques and collectibles, books, coins and stamps, fine art, used furniture, jewelry and silver, porcelain, tools, and toys. Snacks are available on the premises. A small operation.

VENDORS: $10 per 10'x20' space per day. Reserve a week in advance.

Contact Bill Kern, 3265 Oakwood Drive, Cuyahoga Falls, OH 44240. Tel: (216) 673-4762 or (216) 923-7745.

Dayton
Paris Flea Market

At 6201 North Dixie Drive, at the Dixie Drive-In Theater. Take I-75 to Needmore Road West to second stoplight and then go north three quarters of a mile on North Dixie Drive.

Every Sunday from April through October, 6 A.M. to 1:30 P.M.

OHIO /Fremont

Admission 75 cents per carload; free parking for up to 800 cars. In operation for over 30 years; outdoors, rain or shine. Averages up to 200 vendors (capacity 400).

Antiques and collectibles, books, new and vintage clothing, coins and stamps, cookware, crafts, jewelry, new and used merchandise, fresh produce, and toys. Snacks and hot meals are served on the premises.

VENDORS: $10 per space per day. Reservations are not required.

Contact Allen Levin, 111 West First Street, suite 848, Dayton, OH 45402. Tel: (513) 223-0222 or (513) 890-5513.

Fremont
Fremont Flea Market

At 821 Rawson Avenue, at the Fremont Fairgrounds, four miles south of the Ohio Turnpike (Exit 6).

Generally the second weekend of every month, Saturday, 10 a.m. to 5 P.M., and Sunday, 10 A.M. to 4 P.M.; several additional dates per year for crafts shows and extravaganzas, including the Fremont Racers' Flea Market and Swap Meet on or around the first weekend in April and November (billed as Ohio's largest high-performance car swap meet)—call for dates.

Free admission; free parking for up to 800 cars. In operation for over 14 years; indoors and outdoors, rain or shine. Averages 120 to 300 vendors (capacity 500).

Antiques and collectibles, cookware, crafts, jewelry and silver, fresh produce. Snack bar on premises, "home of the Fremont Famous Hungarian hot dog." Plenty of on-site camping at $5 per night with electrical hookup; auto racing every Saturday night in summer months.

VENDORS: Indoors: $13 per 10'x10' space for one day or $24 for weekend; outside: $12 for one day or $20 for weekend; tables are available at $2 each. Reserve two months in advance for indoor selling.

Contact Gary Kern or Dorothy Shilling, 821 Rawson Avenue,

Fremont, OH 43420. Tel: (419) 332-1200. Day of market, call (419) 332-6937.

Hartville
Hartville Flea Market

At 788 Edison Street. Take I-77 south of Akron to Route 619, then east about six miles to Hartville. Market is on Route 619.

Every Monday and Thursday, 7 A.M. to 6 P.M.

Free admission; ample parking at $1 per car. In operation for over 56 years; indoors year-round, and outdoors, weather permitting. Averages 125 to 800 vendors (capacity 1,000).

Antiques and collectibles, coins and stamps, toys, fresh produce, fish, new and vintage clothing, new and used furniture—"just about anything." Snacks and hot meals are served on the premises.

VENDORS: $6 per selling space. Reservations are preferred a week in advance.

Contact Marion Coblentz, 788 Edison Street, Hartville, OH 44632. Tel: (216) 877-9860.

Johnstown
Johnstown Lions Flea Market

On the Johnstown Public Square in the center of town, at the intersection of Routes 62 and 37.

Every Memorial Day, 7 A.M. to 5 P.M.

Free admission; free parking for up to 200 cars. In operation for over 25 years; outdoors, rain or shine. Averages up to 60 vendors (capacity 80).

Antiques and collectibles, books, cookware, crafts, used furniture, jewelry and silver, and toys. Snacks and hot meals are served on the premises.

VENDORS: $15 per 10'x24' space per day. Reservations are recommended.

Contact Dick Scovell, 6066 Johns Alex Road, Johnstown, OH 43031. Tel: (614) 967-1279.

Lima
Lima Antique Show and Flea Market

At the Allen County Fairgrounds. Take 309-E off I-75 to the fairgrounds, approximately one and a half miles.

First full weekend of January, March, April, May, October, November, and December, 9 A.M. to 5 P.M.

Admission 50 cents; free parking for over 5,000 cars. Duration of market not reported; indoors. Averages close to 50 vendors.

Antiques and collectibles such as baseball cards, books, bottles, coins, comics, and jewelry. Snacks and hot meals are served on the premises.

VENDORS: $35 per 13'x10½' space per day, or $55 per 20'x10½' space. Reserve two weeks in advance.

Contact Aubrey L. Martin, 716 South Main Street, Lima, OH 45804. Tel: (419) 228-1050 or (419) 339-7013.

Monroe
Turtle Creek Flea Market

At 320 North Garver Road. Take Exit 29 (Route 63) off I-75 and then go west one block on Route 63 to Garver Road (at McDonald's), then turn right and go one quarter mile to the market.

Every weekend, 9 A.M. to 5 P.M.

Free admission; ample free parking. In operation for over five years; indoors year-round, and outdoors, weather permitting. Averages 200 to 400 vendors (capacity 800).

Antiques and collectibles, books, new and vintage clothing, coins and stamps, cookware, crafts and fine art, new and used furniture, jewelry and silver, new and used merchandise, porcelain, fresh produce, and toys. Food is served on the premises.

VENDORS: Inquire for rates. Reservations are recommended.

Contact Louis Leven, 111 West First Street, Suite 848, Dayton, OH 45402. Tel: (513) 223-0222.

North Bloomfield
Bloomfield Flea Market

On Highway 87, a little less than a mile west of North Bloomfield.

Every Thursday, 8 A.M. to 3 P.M.

Free admission; free parking. In operation for over 52 years; indoors and outdoors, rain or shine. Averages 100 to 200 vendors.

Full spectrum of antiques, collectibles, new and used merchandise, fresh produce, and fresh and cured meats. Cheese deli, two sausage stands, elephant ears, cotton candy made on the premises. Livestock next door. Grounds available for concerts, auto shows, and other events.

VENDORS: $9 per booth per day indoors, $7 outdoors. Reservations are recommended.

Contact Jo or Bill Herman, P.O. Box 51, Kinsman, OH 44428. Tel: (216) 876-7233.

Rogers
Rogers Community Auction and Open Air Market

On State Route 154, eight miles.

Every Friday, 7 A.M. to whenever.

Free admission; ample free parking. In operation since 1955;

indoors and outdoors, year-round. Averages close to 1,300 vendors (capacity 300 under roof plus another 1,300 outdoors).

Antiques and collectibles, books, fresh produce, new and used merchandise, etc. Food is served on the premises; attracts up to 40,000 shoppers every Friday.

VENDORS: From $12 per 15'x30' space outdoors. Reservations are not required.

Contact Jim or Bill Baer or Pat McCoy, 5640 Raley Road, New Waterford, OH 44445. Tel: (216) 227-3233.

Ross
Stricker's Grove Flea Market

On Route 128, a mile from Ross in a western suburb of Cincinatti, ten miles from the Indiana border.

Every Thursday, 8 A.M. to 1 P.M.

Free admission; 26 acres of free parking. In operation since 1977; indoors year-round, and outdoors, weather permitting. Averages 32 to 100 vendors.

Antiques and collectibles, books, household items, new and used furniture. Snacks and hot meals are served on the premises.

VENDORS: $10 per space includes two tables. Reservations are not required.

Contact Gladys Jordan, 9468 Reading Road, Cincinnati, OH 45215. Tel: (513) 733-5885.

South Amherst
Jamie's Flea Market

On Route 113, half a mile west of Route 58.

Every Wednesday and Saturday, 8 A.M. to 4 P.M.

Free admission; free parking. In operation for over 23 years;

indoors and outdoors, rain or shine. Averages 200 to 600 vendors (200 indoors and 400 outdoors).

Antiques and collectibles, books, new and vintage clothing, cookware, crafts and fine art, dolls, new and used furniture, jewelry and silver, new and used merchandise, plants, porcelain, fresh produce, tools, toys, Avon and Tupperware products, "and much, much more!" Snacks and hot meals are served on the premises. Christmas special event the first Sunday in December.

VENDORS: Inquire for rates. Waiting list for indoor spaces; outdoor setups are on a first-come, first-served basis.

Contact Ralph or Lolita Mock, P.O. Box 183, Amherst, OH 44001. Tel: (216) 986-4402.

Springfield
Freedom Road Center Flea Market

At 1100 Sunset Avenue. Take Exit 54 off I-20, then right at bottom of exit ramp, then right at first stoplight, then left at second stoplight, then left again at first stoplight, and market will be on the right.

Every Friday, Saturday, and Sunday, 9 A.M. to 5 P.M.

Free admission; free parking for up to 1,000 cars. In operation for over nine years; indoors, year-round. Averages 25 to 40 vendors (capacity 80).

Antiques and collectibles, books, vintage clothing, crafts, used furniture, jewelry and silver, new and used merchandise. Hot meals are served on the premises. Auctions every Monday at 5:30 P.M.

VENDORS: $10 per 10'x10' space per weekend. Reservations are not required.

Contact Wilbur Pendegraft, 1100 Sunset Avenue, Springfield, OH 45505. Tel: (513) 322-5555.

Strasburg
Garver's Flea Market

On Wooster Avenue (State Routes 250 and 21) in downtown Strasburg, "between the stoplights." Take Exit 87 off I-77.

Every Sunday, 8 A.M. to 5 P.M.

Free admission; ample free parking. In operation since 1979; indoors year-round, and outdoors, weather permitting. Averages 190 to a capacity of 200 vendors.

Antiques and collectibles, books, new and vintage clothing, cookware, crafts, new and used furniture, jewelry and silver, new and used merchandise, porcelain, poultry, and toys—"plus anything you can imagine." Visit the lunch counter for good food and conversation. "Make a day of it."

VENDORS: Summer: $9 per booth downstairs, $7 upstairs; winter: $11 per space downstairs, $9 upstairs. Reserve a week in advance.

Contact Vic or Winnie Gessner, 2211 Second Street Northwest, Strasburg, OH 44680. Tel: (216) 878-5664.

Tiffin
Tiffin Flea Market

At the Seneca County Fairgrounds off State Routes 224 and 53, on Hopewell Avenue. Signs are posted.

Eight weekends annually from May through October. The 1996 dates: May 4–5, 18–19; June 1–2; July 6–7; August 17–18; September 7–8; October 5–6, 19–20; 9 A.M. to 5 P.M.

Free admission; free parking for up to 1,000 cars. In operation for over 18 years; indoors and outdoors, rain or shine. Averages up to 200 vendors (capacity 400).

Variety of offerings including antiques and collectibles, new and vintage clothing, crafts, glassware, new and used merchandise, fresh produce, tools, lawn mowers, and more. Snacks and hot meals are served on the premises; Sunday barbecues and dinners available. Camping, showers; market is advertised on radio, TV, and in 90 Ohio newspapers. One of the largest flea markets in northwestern Ohio, sponsored by the Seneca County Junior Fair Foundation, with proceeds going to Junior Fair youth—4-H, Scouts, Future Farmers of America, etc.

VENDORS: $8 per day for a 10'x10' space inside or a 15'x15' space outside; tables are $4. Reservations are required for indoor spaces; outdoor spaces are on a first-come, first-served basis.

Contact Don or June Ziegler, 6627 South Township Road 173, Bloomville, OH 44818. Tel: (419) 983-5084.

Washington Court House
Washington Court House Flea Market

On the Fayette County Fairgrounds, at 213 Fairview Avenue, on the southwest edge of town between Routes 22 and 62.

Monthly except July, 9 A.M. to 3 P.M.—call for dates.

Admission $1 per car during summer, otherwise free; free parking for up to 2,000 cars. In operation for over 45 years; indoors year-round, and outdoors, weather permitting. Averages 200 to 300 vendors on 62 acres of selling area.

Antiques and collectibles, books, crafts, jewelry and silver, knives, new and used merchandise, and toys. Snacks and hot meals are served on the premises.

VENDORS: Indoors: $20 per table per weekend; outdoors: $20 per 20-foot space per weekend. Reservations are not required.

Contact Janeann Bloomer, Fayette County Fair Board, P.O. Box 1017, Washington C.H., OH 43160. Tel: (614) 335-5856 during business hours or (614) 335-5345 evenings until 10 P.M.

Wilmington
Caesar Creek Flea Market

At 7763 State Route 73 West. From Dayton, south about 20 miles on I-75 to Route 73, then east on 73 to the market; from Cincinnati, north on I-71 to Exit 45, then left on Route 73 and go about one half mile to the market.

Every weekend plus Memorial Day and Labor Day, 9 A.M. to 5 P.M.

Admission 35 cents per person; free parking for up to 2,000 cars. In operation for over 15 years; indoors year-round, and outdoors, weather permitting. Averages 400 to 700 vendors (capacity 1,100).

Antiques and collectibles, books, new and vintage clothing, coins and stamps, cookware, crafts and fine art, new and used furniture, jewelry and silver, new and used merchandise, fresh produce, and toys. Food is available from seven food stands on the premises (specialty is "broasted" chicken). Up to 12,000 shoppers in attendance weekly.

VENDORS: From $34 to $42 per 10'x12' space per weekend, or $115 per 20'x25' space, or $130 per 20'x33' space. Reserve a week or two in advance for indoor spaces.

Contact Louis Levin, 111 West First Street, Suite 848, Dayton, OH 45402. Tel: (513) 223-0222. Day of market, call (513) 382-1669.

Xenia
Heartland Flea Market

At 457 Dayton Avenue (Route 35) in Xenia, 10 miles east of Dayton. Take Route 71 from Columbus or Cincinnati.

Every weekend, 10 A.M. to 5 P.M.

Free admission; free parking for up to 680 cars. A new market (in operation since 1994); indoors, year-round. Averages 45 to 50 vendors (capacity 200).

Antiques and collectibles, books, new and used clothing,

crafts, new and used furniture, jewelry, sporting goods, toys, and used merchandise. Snacks and hot meals are served on the premises; 24-hour security on the premises; heavy local advertising.

VENDORS: $10 per space per day, or $50 per month. Reservations are not required.

Contact Cindy Sanford, 457 Dayton Avenue, Xenia, OH 45385. Tel: (513) 372-6699; fax: (513) 372-5181.

OKLAHOMA

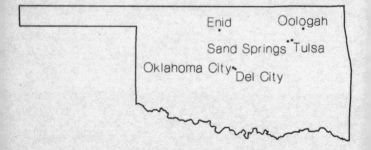

Del City
Cherokee Flea Market and Snack Bar

At 3101 Southeast 15th Street. Take Sunny Lane exit off I-40, then go right to Southeast 15th Street, then right to Bryant, and market is on the corner.

Daily, 7 A.M. to dark.

Free admission; free parking for up to 30 cars. In operation for over 23 years; indoors and outdoors, weather permitting. Averages near capacity of 40 vendors.

Antiques and collectibles, new and vintage clothing, new merchandise, fresh produce, and cookware. Snacks and hot meals are served on the premises. A small but friendly market—to "buy, sell, and trade."

VENDORS: From $40 per 4'x6' indoor space per month; outdoors: $3 per table per day. Reservations are not required.

Contact K. O. Jose, 3101 Southeast 15th Street, Del City, OK 73115. Tel: (405) 677-4056.

Enid
Enid Flea Market

At 1821 South Van Buren (Highway 81). From the intersection of routes 412/60 and Highway 81, go south nine blocks and market will be on the left.

Every Friday, Saturday, and Sunday, 9 A.M. to 6 P.M.

Free admission; free parking for up to 1,000 cars. In operation for over nine years; indoors year-round, and outdoors, weather permitting. Averages 30 to a capacity of 45 vendors.

Antiques and collectibles, books, new and vintage clothing, cookware, crafts and fine art, new and used furniture, jewelry and silver, new and used merchandise, porcelain, poultry, fresh produce, and toys. Snacks are served on the premises.

VENDORS: $5 per 12'x13' space per day or $50 per month; $80 per 13'x24' space per month. (Vendors may also set up for

$2 per space per day in parking lot). Reservations are not required.

Contact Peter Porter, Owner, or Bud Fowler, Manager, 1821 South Van Buren, Enid, OK 73701. Tel: (405) 237-5352 or (405) 237-4879.

Oklahoma City
AMC Flea Market

At 1001 North Pennsylvania Avenue. From westbound I-40, take Virginia exit, then one block north, then one block west, then north 10 blocks to the corner of Northwest Tenth and Pennsylvania. From eastbound I-40, take Pennsylvania exit to Northwest Tenth and Pennsylvania.

Every weekend, 9 A.M. to 6 P.M.

Free admission; free parking for up to 800 cars. In operation for over seven years; indoors and outdoors, rain or shine. Averages 520 to 570 vendors (capacity 600).

Variety of offerings including antiques and collectibles, new and used furniture, new and vintage clothing, jewelry and silver, books, grocery items, boots and shoes, cookware, and crafts. Four restaurants serving American, German, and Chinese food. A clean and safe shopping environment with 135,000 square feet of selling space.

VENDORS: Indoors: $40 per 8½'x12½' space per weekend or $144 per month; outdoors: $10 per 10'x24' space per day or $80 per month. Market is open to vendors on Monday and Friday, 9 A.M. to 5 P.M. Reservations are not required.

Contact Nick Adams, P.O. Box 76179, Oklahoma City, OK 73107. Tel: (405) 232-5061.

Oklahoma City
Mary's Ole Time Swap Meet

At 7905 Northeast 23rd Street, off I-35 or I-40.

Every weekend, from daylight to dark.

Free admission; 30 acres of free parking. In operation for over 30 years; indoors and outdoors, rain or shine. Averages 200 to 500 vendors.

Antiques and collectibles, books, vintage clothing, coins and stamps, cookware, crafts and fine art, new and used furniture, jewelry and silver, livestock, new merchandise, pottery and porcelain, poultry, fresh produce, and toys. Snacks and hot meals are served on the premises. Camping nearby.

VENDORS: $5 per stall per day; electricity is available at $2 per day. Reservations are not required.

Contact Dennis Sisemore, 7905 Northeast 23rd Street, Oklahoma City, OK 73141. Tel: (405) 427-0051.

Oologah
Oologah Flea Market

A quarter mile north of the intersection of State Highway 88 and Route 169.

Every Thursday through Sunday, 9 A.M. to 5 P.M.

Free admission; free parking for up to 80 cars. In operation for over eight years; indoors and outdoors, rain or shine. Averages 10 to a capacity of 20 vendors.

Antiques and collectibles, books, and used furniture. Food is not served on the premises.

VENDORS: $2 per space per day outdoors. Reservations are not required.

Contact Richard W. Plute, R.R. #1, Box 43, Oologah, OK 74053. Tel: (918) 443-2568.

Sand Springs
Expressway Flea Market

At 7626 Charles Page Boulevard.

Every Friday, Saturday, and Sunday, 8 A.M. to 6 P.M.

Free admission; free parking for up to 50 cars. In operation for over five years; indoors year-round, and outdoors, weather permitting. Averages close to 50 vendors year-round (capacity 100).

Antiques and collectibles, books, coins and stamps, cookware, crafts and fine art, used furniture, jewelry and silver, porcelain, fresh produce, new and used merchandise, and toys. Snacks are served on the premises.

VENDORS: $5 per space per day outdoors; from $20 to $40 per weekend indoors, depending on size. Reservations are not required.

Contact Jim or Rita Hammond, 7626 Charles Page Boulevard, Sand Springs, OK 74127. Tel: (918) 241-9809.

Tulsa
Great American Flea Market and Antique Mall

At 9216-9236 East Admiral.

Every Friday through Sunday, 10 A.M. to 6 P.M.(mall is open daily except Sunday).

Free admission; free parking for up to 800 cars. In operation for over six years; indoors and outdoors, rain or shine. Averages close to 225 vendors (capacity 300).

Antiques and collectibles, vintage clothing, coins and stamps, cookware, crafts, new and used furniture, jewelry and silver, and fresh produce. Hot and cold meals are served on the premises.

VENDORS: $30 per 8'x10' space for three days. Reservations are not required.

Contact Ty Hogan, 6019 South 66th East Avenue, Tulsa, OK 74145. Tel: (918) 492-3476.

Tulsa
Tulsa Flea Market

On the State fairgrounds. Take Yale exit off freeway, to 21st Street.

Every Saturday (except for four Saturdays in late September and early October), 8 A.M. to 5 P.M.

Free admission; ample free parking. In operation for over 23 years; indoors, year-round. Averages close to 235 vendors year-round.

Antiques and collectibles, books, new and vintage clothing, coins and stamps, cookware, crafts and fine art, used furniture, jewelry and silver, new merchandise, pottery and porcelain, plants, primitives, fresh produce, quilts, records, and toys. Snacks are available on the premises. Specializes in antiques, collectibles, and primitives.

VENDORS: $20 per 10'x12' space per day; tables are available at $3 each. Reserve four or five weeks in advance.

Contact Patsy Larry, P.O. Box 4511, Tulsa, OK 74159. Tel: (918) 744-1386 (call Wednesday through Friday, 8 A.M. to noon).

OREGON

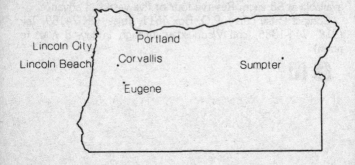

Lincoln City
Lincoln Beach
Portland
Corvallis
Sumpter
Eugene

Corvallis

Heart of the Valley Market and Bazaar

On the Benton County Fairgrounds, at 110 Southwest 53rd Street. Take Corvallis Exit (Highway 34) off I-5 and then Highway 99 to Highway 20 to Corvallis.

One day every month (usually first or second Saturday) from September through May—call for dates, 10 A.M. to 4 P.M.

Admission 25 cents per person; free parking for more than 200 cars. In operation for over 26 years; indoors, rain or shine. Averages up to 65 vendors (capacity 76 tables).

Antiques and collectibles, books, new and vintage clothing, coins and stamps, cookware, crafts and fine art, new and used furniture, garage-sale items, jewelry and silver, new and used merchandise, porcelain, tools, and toys. Snacks are served on the premises. Claims to be the oldest running flea market in the Willamette Valley.

VENDORS: $10 per table per day. Reserve one to three weeks in advance.

Contact Ileene or Spike Smith, 1010 Northwest 9th, Corvallis, OR 97330. Tel: (514) 758-3019.

Eugene

Picc-a-dilly Flea Market

At the Lane County Fairgrounds (all the way in the back). From northwest (99 North): 99 becomes Seventh Street, right on Garfield, left on 13th. From west (on West 11th): Go right on Garfield, left on 13th. From south: Take University of Oregon exit off I-5, becomes Franklin Boulevard, left on 11th, left on Monroe. From north: Take University of Oregon exit off I-5 to Jefferson, right on 11th, left on Monroe. From east: I-105 becomes Jefferson, then right on West 11th, left on Monroe.

Sundays, year-round, but not every Sunday (20 shows in 1996, in all months but July and August)—10 A.M. to 4 P.M., call for dates.

Admission $1; free parking for 2,500 cars. In operation for over 22 years; indoors. Averages up to 400 vendors (capacity 550).

Antiques and collectibles including baseball cards, bottles, new and vintage clothing, cookware, crafts, porcelain, and fresh produce. Snacks and hot meals are served on the premises. Smoking discouraged inside market area. Said to be the oldest and largest market in the area.

VENDORS: $13 per 8'x2½' table per day. Reservations are required as far as possible in advance.

Contact Rosemary Major, P.O. Box 2364, Eugene, OR 97402. Tel: (503) 683-5589, Monday through Saturday, 9 A.M. to 4 P.M. during week prior to each market day (answering machine is on all other days).

Lincoln Beach
Aunt Rosie's Flea Market

On the east side of Highway 101, six miles south of Lincoln City.

Daily, 10 A.M. to 5 P.M.

Free admission; free parking. In operation for over seven years; indoors and outdoors, rain or shine. Averages 5 to 20 vendors.

Antiques and collectibles, books, cookware, crafts, used furniture, jewelry and silver, new merchandise, fresh produce, and toys. Hot meals are available on the premises.

VENDORS: Outdoors: $5 per space per day; inquire for indoor rates. Reserve a day in advance.

Contact Robert or Stephanie Fischer, P.O. Box 1357, Depoe Bay, OR 97341. Tel: (503) 764-3782.

Lincoln City
Stuffy's Flea Market

At 1309 Northwest 12th Street.

Every weekend, 9 A.M. to 5 P.M.

Admission 25 cents; free parking for up to 40 cars. In operation for over 14 years; indoors, year-round. Averages 30 to 40 vendors (capacity 78 tables).

Antiques and collectibles, books, cookware, used furniture, jewelry, and new merchandise. Snacks and hot meals are served on the premises.

VENDORS: $7.50 per 3'x8' table per day. Reservations are recommended a week in advance.

Contact Stuffy Stone, 1320 Northwest 13th Street, Lincoln City, OR 97367. Tel: (503) 994-7711.

Portland
#1 Flea Market

At 17420 Southeast Division Street. Take 181st Street exit off I-85 East, then go south two miles and turn right onto Division Street.

Every weekend, 9 A.M. to 5 P.M.

Admission 50 cents per person, except 25 cents for senior citizens, and free admission for children under 12; free parking for up to 200 cars. In operation for over five years; indoors and outdoors, rain or shine. Averages 150 to 200 vendors (capacity 240).

Antiques and collectibles, books, new clothing, cookware, crafts, new and used furniture, vintage jewelry, new and used merchandise, and toys. Snacks and hot meals are served at a complete deli on the premises.

VENDORS: $10 per table per day. Reservations are recommended in winter (tables are rented on a first-come, first-served basis in summer).

Contact Lee Richardson, 17420 Southeast Division Street, Portland, OR 97236. Tel: (503) 761-4646.

Sumpter
Sumpter Valley Country Fair

Off Highway 7—follow the canary-yellow signs in town (in northeast Oregon).

Every Memorial Day, Fourth of July, Labor Day (usually the weekend plus Monday), 8 A.M. to 5 P.M.

Free admission; free parking for more than 300. In operation for over nine years; outdoors, rain or shine. Averages up to 150 vendors (capacity 160).

Antiques and collectibles, books, new clothing, cookware, crafts, new and used furniture, jewelry, new and used merchandise, toys, and lots more. Snacks and hot meals are served on the premises.

VENDORS: $1.50 per foot of frontage per day. Reservations are recommended.

Contact Nancy or Leland Myers, Sumpter Valley Days Association, P.O. Box 513, Sumpter, OR 97877. Tel: (503) 894-2264.

PENNSYLVANIA

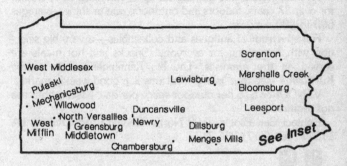

West Middlesex

Pulaski

Mechanicsburg

Wildwood

West Mifflin

North Versailles Newry

Greensburg

Middletown

Chambersburg

Duncansville

Dillsburg

Menges Mills

Lewisburg

Scranton

Marshalls Creek

Bloomsburg

Leesport

See Inset

SOUTHEASTERN PENNSYLVANIA

Quakertown

Kutztown

Gilbertsville

Adamstown

Ephrata

Morgantown

Leola

Downingtown

Cedars

Collegeville

Kulpsville

Elroy

New Hope

Hulmeville

Philadelphia

Chadds Ford

Adamstown
Renninger's #1 Antique Market

On Route 272, a half mile north of Exit 21 off the Pennsylvania Turnpike.

Every Sunday, 7:30 A.M. to 5 P.M.

Free admission; free parking for up to 800 cars. In operation for over 33 years; indoors and outdoors, rain or shine. Averages 500 to 800 vendors.

Full spectrum of antiques and collectibles—a very big selection with something for everyone. Snacks and hot meals are served on the premises. The big Renninger's is in nearby Kutztown—see that listing—but this is a good weekly market.

VENDORS: $15 per outdoor space per day. Reservations are not required.

Contact Carl Block, 2500 North Reading Road, Denver, PA 17517. Tel: (717) 336-2177.

Adamstown
Shupp's Grove

At 1686 Dry Tavern Road. Take Exit 21 off Pennsylvania Turnpike, then right on Route 272 North, then right on Route 897 South, and market will be three quarters of a mile ahead on the left.

Every weekend from April through October, 7 A.M. to 5 P.M. Three "extravaganza" weekends annually in April, June, and September (the Friday, Saturday, and Sunday after the fourth Thursday of the month).

Free admission; several acres of free parking. In operation since 1962; outdoors, weather permitting. Averages close to 250 vendors (capacity 500).

Antiques, art, and collectibles. Snacks and hot meals are served on the premises. (Hint: While in the area, stop at Friar Tuck's Deli in the thick of the woods for delicious homemade soups, sandwiches, pies, and cakes.) The first outdoor antiques market in beautiful Lancaster County, a favorite with antiquers nationwide.

VENDORS: $12 per space per day; $65 for three days during "extravaganza" weekends. Reservations are not required except during "extravaganza" weekends.

Contact Marilyn or Carl Gehman, P.O. Box 892, Adamstown, PA 19501. Tel: (717) 484-4115.

Bloomsburg
Pioneer Village Sales Market

On Route 11 North.

Every weekend from April through October, 9 A.M. to 5 P.M.

Free admission; ample free parking. In operation since 1980; indoors and outdoors, rain or shine. Averages close to 50 vendors.

Antiques and collectibles, books, new and used furniture, household items, new and used merchandise, and more. Snacks and hot meals are served on the premises.

VENDORS: Outdoors: from $6 per day for two tables, $2 each additional table; indoors from $8 per day. Reservations are not required.

Contact Harry W. Myers, P.O. Box 32, Bloomsburg, PA 17815. Tel: (717) 784-0734.

Cedars
Cedars Country Antique and Collectible Market

At the Cedars Country Store at Skippack Pike (Route 73) and Bustard Road.

Third Saturday of each month from May through October, 8 A.M. to 2 P.M.; Christmas bazaar in early November on Saturday—call for dates.

Free admission; free parking for up to 2,000 cars. In operation for over 31 years; outdoors, weather permitting (rain date is the following Saturday). Averages up to 115 vendors.

Antiques and collectibles, books, vintage clothing, coins and stamps, cookware, crafts and fine art, jewelry and silver, and toys. Snacks and full meals are available at the Cedars Country Store, billed as Pennsylvania's oldest country store.

VENDORS: $28 per space per event, with car in space; $260 for all six events with car ($230 without). Reservations are required.

Contact Denise at Ding's Den, P.O. Box 153, Cedars, PA 19423. Tel: (610) 584-8740 or (610) 584-4238.

Chadds Ford

Pennsbury-Chadds Ford Antique Mall

At 640 Baltimore Pike (Route 1), between Longwood Gardens and the Brandywine River Museum.

Lower level open Saturday and Sunday, and upper level open daily except Tuesday and Wednesday, 10 A.M. to 5 P.M.

Free admission; free parking for up to 250 cars. In operation for over 25 years; indoors, year-round. Averages close to 150 vendors year-round.

Antiques and collectibles, books, coins and stamps, ephemera, fine art, used and Victorian furniture, jewelry and silver, military items, oriental rugs, antique tools, and toys. Snacks are available on the premises. Upscale items.

VENDORS: Monthly rentals only, from $135 for an 8'x10' space. Reserve two months in advance.

Contact Alfred Delduco, 640 East Baltimore Pike, West Chester, PA 19317. Tel: (215) 388-6546.

Chambersburg

Chambersburg Antique and Flea Market

At 868 Lincoln Way West (Route 30 West), on the outskirts of town. Take Exit 6 off I-81.

Daily, 9 A.M. to 5 P.M.

Free admission; ample free parking. In operation for over seven years; indoors, year-round. Averages 40 to 50 vendors (capacity 70).

Antiques and collectibles, books, cookware, crafts, new furniture, jewelry, toys, and used merchandise. Snacks are served on the premises. In a new building with modern amenities.

VENDORS: $50 per 6'x8' space or $100 per 10'x12' space per month, plus 10 percent commission on sales. Reservations are not required.

Contact James Laye, 868 Lincoln Way West, Chambersburg, PA 17201. Tel: (717) 267-0886.

Collegeville

Power House Antique and Flea Market

At 45 First Avenue, on Route 29, three miles from Business Route 422 Bypass near Valley Forge.

Every Sunday, 9 A.M. to 5 P.M.

Free admission; free parking. In operation for over 24 years; indoors, year-round. Averages close to 40 vendors year-round.

Antiques and collectibles, books, vintage clothing, coins and stamps, used furniture, glassware, jewelry and silver, and toys. Snacks are available on the premises.

VENDORS: Inquire for rates. Filled to capacity; check far in advance for possible openings.

Contact Janet McDonnell, 45 First Avenue, Collegeville, PA 19426. Tel: (610) 489-7388.

Dillsburg
Haar's Flea Market

At 185 Logan Road, right off Route 15 a mile north of town. Twelve miles south of Harrisburg along Route 15 (to Ore Bank Road, then turn left to market).

Every Sunday, 7 A.M. to 4 P.M., and Tuesday and Friday evenings, 5:30 P.M. to 9 P.M.

Free admission; free parking for up to 300 cars. In operation for over eight years; indoors year-round, and outdoors, weather permitting. Average number of vendors not reported.

Antiques and collectibles, books, cookware, crafts, new and used furniture, jewelry, new and used merchandise, fresh produce, and toys—"something for everyone." Snacks and hot meals are served on the premises.

VENDORS: $10 per day indoors, $5 outdoors (Sunday only). Reserve a week in advance.

Contact Elwood Haar, 185 Logan Road, Dillsburg, PA 17019. Tel: (717) 432-3011 or (717) 432-4381.

Downingtown
Downingtown Marketplace

On Business Route 30/Lancaster Pike just east of Downingtown (next to Mickey Rooney's Tables Hotel). Take Exit 23 off the Pennsylvania Turnpike, then take Route 100 south for four miles to Route 30, then west for three miles, and market will be on the right.

Every Friday, Saturday, 10 A.M. to 10 P.M.; and every Sunday, 10 A.M. to 6 P.M.

Free admission; free parking. In operation for over 40 years; indoors all three days, and outdoors on Saturday and Sunday only, rain or shine. Averages 210 to 350 vendors (capacity 400).

Antiques and collectibles, books, new and vintage clothing, cookware, crafts and fine art, dolls, new and used furniture, jewelry and silver, new merchandise, pottery and porcelain. Snacks, meals, and grocery items are available on the premises. Home of Robin Hood's, a "salvage department store."

VENDORS: $15 per 12'x12' space per day; bring your own table or rent one for an additional $6 per table per day; some spaces have electrical hookup. Reserve one to two weeks in advance.

Contact Alexandre Schaefer, Business Route 30/Lancaster Pike, Downingtown, PA 19335. Tel: (215) 269-4511 or (215) 269-4050. Day of market, see Joe Piatkowski.

Duncansville
Duncansville Antique Depot Flea Market

At the intersection of Routes 22 and 764, 30 minutes north of Bedford and the Pennsylvania Turnpike (use Highway 220); from Pittsburgh, take Route 22 East.

Every weekend, 9 A.M. to 5 P.M., plus Thursdays outdoors from spring through early fall.

Free admission; free parking for up to 800 cars. A new market (in operation since 1994); indoors year-round, and outdoors, weather permitting. Averages 135 to 185 vendors on 60,000 square feet of selling space.

Antiques and collectibles, books, new clothing, coins and stamps, cookware, crafts, new and used furniture, jewelry and silver, new and used merchandise, porcelain, fresh produce, and toys. Coffee shop on the premises. Auction, craft show, and Antique Gallery—call for further information. Draws upwards of 5,000 shoppers each weekend.

VENDORS: $25 per space per weekend indoors, $12 outdoors; $8 per space outdoors on Thursday; tables are provided for indoor spaces; electricity is available at no additional charge.

Contact Tom Sasser, P.O. Box 111, Duncansville, PA 16635. Tel: (814) 696-4000. Day of market, ask for Clare Wascovich.

Elroy
Drafty Barn Antiques

At 117 Allentown Road, between Routes 63 and 113, three miles from the Lansdale exit off the Pennsylvania Turnpike.

First Saturday of every month from April through October (rain date is second Saturday of month), 8 A.M. to 4 P.M.

Free admission; free parking for up to 60 cars. A new market; outdoors, weather permitting. Averages 20 to a capacity of 35 vendors.

Antiques and collectibles, cookware, used furniture, jewelry, porcelain, and used merchandise. Snacks are served on the premises.

VENDORS: $10 per 15'x20' space. Reservations are required; available spaces on market day are rented on a first-come, first-served basis.

Contact Ken Cressman, 117 Allentown Road, Elroy, PA 18964. Tel: (215) 721-1677.

Ephrata
Green Dragon Farmer's Market and Auction

At 955 North State Street (spur of Route 272), between Route 322 and the Pennsylvania Turnpike (use Exit 21, Lancaster-Reading Interchange exit); look for the dragon and sign.

Every Friday, 9 A.M. to 10 P.M.

Free admission; 35 acres of free parking. In operation for over 63 years; indoors and outdoors, rain or shine. Averages 250 to a capacity of 400 vendors.

Antiques and collectibles, books, new and vintage clothing, coins and stamps, cookware, crafts and fine art, fish, meats and poultry, new and used furniture, jewelry and silver, livestock, new merchandise, pottery and porcelain, fresh produce and baked goods, and toys. Snacks and hot meals are served on the premises. "The dragon comes alive every Friday as the rooster crows early morn." Auction sales every Friday, with livestock, hay and straw, dry goods, etc.

VENDORS: $13 per 10'x20' space per day or $25 per 20'x20' space. Reserve a week in advance.

Contact Larry L. Loose, 955 North State Street, Ephrata, PA 17522. Tel: (717) 738-1117.

Gilbertsville
Zern's Farmers' Market and Auction

On Route 73, one mile east of Boyertown. From New York, take the New Jersey Turnpike to the Pennsylvania Turnpike; then take Exit 23 to Route 100 north for 19 miles to Route 73 (Boyertown exit), then turn right and go one half mile. From Washington, D.C., Take I-95 to Wilmington, Delaware, then follow Route 202 toward West Chester, then get on Route 100 North and go eight miles north of Pottstown to Route 73 (Gilbertsville exit), then turn right and go one half mile, and the market will be on the right.

Every Friday, 2 P.M. to 10 P.M.; every Saturday, 11 A.M. to 10 P.M.; and every Sunday, 9 A.M. to 5 P.M.

Free admission; free parking for up to 3,300 cars. In operation since 1922; indoors and outdoors, rain or shine. Averages 280 to a capacity of 472 vendors.

Antiques and collectibles, new and used books, new and vintage clothing, coins and stamps, cookware and crafts, fish, livestock, poultry and fresh produce, new and used furniture, household items, new merchandise, pottery and porcelain, and toys. Snacks, grocery and deli items, and hot meals are available on the premises. Vision center, camera shop, smoke shop, and barbershop on the premises. "The world's largest dutch treat . . . miles of aisles . . . nowhere else so many unusual departments!" Auctions of livestock and nursery items (Saturday at 6:30 P.M.), automobiles (Friday at 6:30 P.M.), and general merchandise (Friday at 5 P.M. and Saturday at 1 P.M.) every weekend.

VENDORS: $25 for two tables for Friday and Saturday; $10 per 15'x30' space on Sunday (bring your own tables). Reserve a week in advance for Friday and Saturday (reservations are not required on Sunday).

Contact John Speca or John Williams, Route 73, Gilbertsville, PA 19525. Tel: (610) 367-2461.

Greensburg
Greengate Flea Market

At the Green Gate Mall on Route 30, approximately seven miles from Exit 7 off the Pennsylvania Turnpike.

Every Sunday from April through October, 7 A.M. to 3 P.M.

Free admission; free parking for up to 5,000 cars. In operation for over five years; outdoors, rain or shine. Averages close to 105 vendors (capacity 130).

Antiques and collectibles, books, new clothing, cookware, crafts, new and used furniture, jewelry, new and used merchandise, porcelain, fresh produce, and toys. Two food concessions serve hot meals on the premises.

VENDORS: $9 per 11-foot space per day, $15 per 21-foot space. Reservations are recommended.

Contact Carol Craig, 214 Kenneth Street, Greensburg, PA 15601. Tel: (412) 837-6881.

Hulmeville
Old Mill Flea Market

At the intersection of Bellevue Avenue, Trenton and Hulmeville Roads, at Fricke's Mill. Near Exit 28 off the Pennsylvania Turnpike and Business Route 1; take Route 1 exit off I-95.

Every Thursday and Friday, 6 P.M. to 9 P.M.; every Saturday, noon to 9 P.M.; and every Sunday, noon to 5 P.M.

Free admission; free parking. In operation since 1971; indoors, year-round. Average number of vendors not reported.

Antiques and collectibles, books, ephemera, vintage clothing, coins and stamps, crafts, new and used furniture, glassware, jewelry, pottery, prints, and toys. Food is not available on the premises. Estate liquidations. Housed in an authentic Bucks County gristmill (built in 1881 and in operation as a mill until 1970). Billed as Lower Bucks County's oldest indoor flea market.

VENDORS: Inquire for rates. Transient vendors are not accommodated. Waiting list.

Contact Kathy Loeffler, P.O. Box 7069, Penndel, PA 19047. Tel: (215) 757-1777.

Kulpsville
Kulpsville Antique and Flea Market

At 1375 Forty Foot Road (Route 63). Take first two left turns from Exit 31 (Lansdale) off the northeast extension of the Pennsylvania Turnpike.

Every weekend plus holidays, 10 A.M. to 5 P.M.

Free admission; free parking for up to 150 cars. A new market (in operation since 1995); indoors, year-round. Averages 40 to 60 vendors.

Antiques and collectibles, books, new and vintage clothing, coins and stamps, cookware, new and used furniture, jewelry and silver, new and used merchandise, porcelain, tools, and toys. Snacks are served on the premises.

VENDORS: $15 per 10'x10' space per day (includes one table); monthly rate is $130 per space. Reserve a week in advance.

Contact Dawn Myers or Carl Schnabel, P.O. Box 189, Harleysville, PA 19438. Tel: (215) 361-7910 or (215) 256-9600.

Kutztown
Renninger's #2 Antique Market

At 740 Noble Street, off Route 222, a mile south of the middle of Kutztown, between Reading and Allentown.

Every Saturday, 8:30 A.M. to 5 P.M., except during "extravaganzas," three two-day events per year, usually in late April, late June, and late September—call for dates.

Free admission (except $5 per person for two-day extravaganza); ample free parking. In operation for over 20 years; indoors, year-round. Averages close to 250 vendors (but swells to over 1,200 vendors from 42 states for the extravaganzas).

Antiques and collectibles, books, new and vintage clothing, cookware, crafts and fine art, used furniture, jewelry and silver—you name it. Pennsylvania Dutch market on the premises. Extravaganza is a true antiques and collectibles blowout.

VENDORS: $8 per 10'x25' space per day in the pavilion, or $10 per 18'x25' space per day outdoors (extravaganza booths are from $95 to $115 per space per event). Reservations are recommended for extravaganza events.

Contact Renninger's Promotions, 27 Bensinger Drive, Schuykill Haven, PA 19501. Tel: (717) 385-0104 (Monday through Thursday) or (215) 683-6848 (Friday and Saturday); for extravaganzas: (717) 336-2177 (Monday through Friday) or (610) 683-6848 (Saturday).

Leesport
Leesport Farmers' Market

One block east of Route 161 at the north end of Leesport, 10 miles north of Reading and 8 miles south of Hamburg.

Every Wednesday year-round, plus the first Sunday of every month from April through December, 7 A.M. to 3 P.M.; farmers' market open every Wednesday year-round, 9 A.M. to 8 P.M.

Free admission; acres of free parking. In operation since 1947;

indoors and outdoors, rain or shine. Averages 200 to 500 vendors (capacity 700).

Antiques and collectibles, books, new and vintage clothing, coins and stamps, cookware and crafts, fabrics, new and used furniture, garden supplies, health and beauty aids, household items, jewelry and silver, new merchandise, pottery and porcelain, and toys. Fish, livestock, meats and cheeses, poultry, fresh produce, and Pennsylvania Dutch items at the farmers' market. Snacks and hot meals are served on the premises. Banquet hall with seating capacity of 800 available for private functions. Livestock auction every Wednesday at 1 P.M.; craft fairs on selected weekends throughout the year including Easter, springtime, midsummer, harvesttime, and Christmas—call for specific dates.

VENDORS: $10 per 12'x35' unsheltered space per day; $10 per 8-foot table in a 10-foot-wide unsheltered space; from $20 per space for all indoor and sheltered spaces. Reservations are not required.

Contact Daniel "Woody" or Bill Weist, P.O. Box B, Leesport, PA 19533. Tel: (215) 926-1307.

Leola
Meadowbrook Farmer's Market

On Route 23 five miles northeast of Lancaster. Take Exit 6 off Jersey Turnpike onto the Pennsylvania Turnpike, then go to Exit 22 (Morgantown), get off, and then after paying toll, go right (west) onto Route 23 for 20 miles and market will be on the right.

Every Friday and Saturday, 7 A.M. to 5 P.M.

Free admission; ample free parking. In operation for over 23 years; indoors and outdoors, rain or shine. Averages up to 200 vendors.

Antiques and collectibles, books, used furniture, new, used, and discount merchanise—a good variety. Snacks and hot meals are served on the premises. Fall is the big season.

VENDORS: In summer, $5 per car-size space on Friday and $10 on Saturday—rates double during fall season. Reservations are recommended.

Contact Frank Suraci, 339 West Main Street, Leola, PA 17540. Tel: (717) 656-2226.

Lewisburg
Route 15 Flea Market Center

On Route 15, two miles north of Lewisburg. Take Exit 30-A off I-80 and drive four miles south (if you see the McDonald's, then you've gone too far).

Every Sunday, 8 A.M. to 5 P.M.

Free admission; free parking for up to a thousand cars. In operation since 1989; indoors and outdoors, year round, rain or shine. Averages 600 to a capacity of 800 vendors.

Antiques and collectibles, books and magazines, new and bargain-priced clothing and furniture, coins and stamps, cookware, crafts, electronics, jewelry, new and used merchandise, all kinds of fresh produce, flowers, tools, and toys. Snacks and hot meals are served on the premises. Bingo every Wednesday night; special shows and auctions (call for dates). A family-owned and operated facility in a rural valley near the Susquehanna River, with "something for everyone, and always a warm welcome." As many as a million shoppers annually.

VENDORS: $26 per space per Sunday. Reservations are required in winter months.

Contact Sandy Keister, Manager, P.O. Box 73, West Milton, PA 17837. Tel: (717) 568-8080 or (717) 523-9952; fax: (717) 568-0452.

Marshalls Creek
Pocono Bazaar Flea Market

On Route 209, five miles north of I-80 (use Exit 52) and the Delaware Water Gap, near the New Jersey border.

Every weekend plus major holidays, 9 A.M. to 5 P.M.

Free admission; free parking for up to 2,000 cars. In operation for over eight years; indoors and outdoors, rain or shine. Averages 200 to 600 vendors.

Antiques and collectibles, books, new clothing, cookware, crafts and fine art, new and used furniture, jewelry and silver, new merchandise, and toys. Snacks and hot meals are served on the premises.

VENDORS: $25 per 12'x20' space per day. Reservations are not required.

Contact Kevin Hoffman, P.O. Box 248, Marshalls Creek, PA 18335. Tel: (717) 223-8640.

Mechanicsburg
Silver Springs Flea Market

At 6416 Carlisle Pike, on Route 11 midway between Harrisburg and Carlisle.

Every Sunday, 7 A.M. to 3 P.M.

Free admission; ample free parking. In operation since 1968; indoors and outdoors, rain or shine. Averages 500 to 1,000 vendors (virtually unlimited capacity).

Full spectrum of antiques, collectibles, new and used goods, fresh produce, postcards. Snacks and hot meals are served on the premises. Claims to be the biggest in Pennsylvania.

VENDORS: $10 per 12'x20' space per day outside; inside spaces are rented by the month: from $40 for a 3'x8' table. Reservations are not required for outdoor spaces.

Contact Manager, 6414 Carlisle Pike, Mechanicsburg, PA

17055. Tel: (717) 766-7215. Day of market, call Anna Smith at
(717) 766-9027.

Menges Mills
Colonial Valley Flea Market

On Colonial Valley Road, off Route 116 between York and
Hanover.

Every Sunday, 8:30 A.M. to 4:30 P.M.

Free admission; free parking. In operation for over 33 years;
indoors and outdoors, rain or shine. Averages up to 30 or so
vendors.

Antiques and collectibles, books, vintage clothing, coins and
stamps, crafts, used furniture, jewelry and silver, new merchandise, and toys. Snacks and hot meals are served on the premises.
Consignment sales. Petting zoo, antique and classic car shows,
etc.

VENDORS: $10 per space per day indoors, $8 outdoors.
Reservations are not required for outdoor spaces.

Contact Betty Staines, 621 East Rocky Hill Road, Sparks, MD
21152. Tel: (410) 472-2701.

Middletown
Saturday's Market

At 3751 East Harrisburg Pike (Route 230), between Middletown and Elizabethtown. Just off Route 283, exit Toll House
Road, left on 230, then one mile.

Every Saturday, 8 A.M. to 6 P.M.

Free admission; acres of free parking. In operation for over
eight years; indoors and outdoors, rain or shine. Averages 300 to
500 vendors (capacity 1,000).

The "total" farmers' and flea market, with antiques and

collectibles, new and vintage clothing, fine art, fish, poultry, fresh produce, and new merchandise. More than 15 different food concessions on the premises. Billed as "Pennsylvania's largest indoor market."

VENDORS: Indoors: $43 and up per month depending on size; outdoors: $10 per day for one space, $17 for two spaces, $24 for three spaces. Reservations are not required.

Contact Rod Rose, 3751 East Harrrisburg Pike, Middletown, PA 17057. Tel: (717) 944-2555.

Morgantown
The Market Place

At the intersection of Routes 10 and 23. Take Exit 22 off the Pennsylvania Turnpike.

Every Friday, 9 A.M. to 7 P.M.; every Saturday, 9 A.M. to 6 P.M.; and every Sunday, 10 A.M. to 4 P.M.

Free admission; free parking for up to 400 cars. In operation for over 23 years; indoors year-round, and outdoors, weather permitting. Average number of vendors not reported.

Antiques and collectibles, books, vintage clothing, coins and stamps, crafts and fine art, new and used furniture, jewelry and silver, toys, and used merchandise. Snacks and hot meals are served on the premises. In the heart of scenic Pennsylvania Dutch country.

VENDORS: $8 per space outdoors; tables are available at $2 each. Monthly rentals only on indoor spaces. Reservations are not required.

Contact Gae, Manager, Route 23, Morgantown, PA 19543. Tel: (610) 286-0611.

New Hope
Country Host Flea Market

On Route 202, one half mile from town and the intersection of Route 179.

Every Tuesday through Sunday, 7 A.M. to 5 P.M.

Free admission; free parking for up to 250 cars. In operation for over 23 years; outdoors, rain or shine. Averages 30 to 70 vendors (capacity 100).

Antiques and collectibles, books, new and vintage clothing, coins and stamps, crafts and fine art, new and used furniture, jewelry and silver, new and used merchandise, porcelain, and toys. Snacks and hot meals are served at an adjoining diner. Intimate market in the center of a good antiques area with shoppers from all around (many come from Philadelphia and New York areas).

VENDORS: $10 per space per weekday, includes two tables; $20 on Saturday, and $25 on Sunday. Reservations are recommended.

Contact Manager, Route 202, New Hope, PA 18938. Tel: (215) 862-3111.

New Hope
Rice's Market

At 6326 Greenhill Road.

Every Tuesday morning, 6 A.M. to 1 P.M.

Free admission; more than 10 acres of parking at $1 per car. In operation for over 100 years; indoors year-round, and outdoors, weather permitting. Averages up to 1,000 vendors; mostly outdoors.

Antiques and collectibles, books, coins and stamps, cookware, crafts and fine art, new and used furniture, jewelry, new and used merchandise, porcelain, fresh produce, seafood, and toys. Snacks and hot meals are served on the premises.

VENDORS: $20 per space per day or $80 per month. Reservations are recommended.

Contact Chuck Kane or John Blanche, 6326 Greenhill Road, New Hope, PA 18938. Tel: (215) 297-5993.

Newry
Leighty's 29-Acre Flea Market

On Old Route 220, near Altoona.

Every weekend, 7 A.M. to 5 P.M.

Free admission; ample free parking. In operation for over 20 years; indoors and outdoors, year-round. Averages 300 to 400 vendors.

Antiques and collectibles, books, new and vintage clothing, cookware, crafts, new and used furniture, garage-sale items, new and used merchandise—"all sorts of stuff." Snacks and hot meals are served on the premises.

VENDORS: From $9 per 11'x28' space per day. Reservations are not required.

Contact Roger Azzarello, Manager, P.O. Box 310, Newry, PA 16665. Tel: (814) 695-5052 or (814) 695-9120.

North Versailles
Super Flea Market

At the New Eastland Mall and Marketplace, 833 East Pittsburgh-McKeesport Boulevard, just off Lincoln Highway (Route 30) less than five miles east of Pittsburgh (between Forest Hills and McKeesport).

Every weekend, 9 A.M. to 5 P.M.

Free admission; free parking for over 5,000 cars and buses. In operation for over six years; indoors and outdoors, rain or shine. Averages close to 300 vendors year-round with virtually unlimited outdoor capacity.

Antiques and collectibles, books, new and vintage clothing, coins and stamps, cookware, crafts and fine art, new and used furniture, jewelry and silver, new and used merchandise, porcelain, poultry and fresh produce, seafood, and toys. Snacks and hot meals are served on the premises. Camping nearby; 24-hour security; on-site banking, beauty salons, bookstore, movie theater, and other services (complex offers over a million square feet of total retail space). "Everything from A to Z."

VENDORS: Indoors: $10 per day or $15 per weekend for a 2'x8' table with one chair in the back; middle aisle locations are $15 per day or $100 per month per 12-foot table with one chair. Outdoors: $15 per 18'x24' space per day; booths are $30 per weekend when available; monthly rates available for special areas and booths; vendors may set up on Friday from noon to 3 P.M. Reservations are not required.

Contact Ed Williams, Super Flea Manager, 833 East Pittsburgh-McKeesport Boulevard, North Versailles, PA 15137. Tel: (412) 678-8050; fax: (412) 678-5340; office hours are Monday through Friday, 9 A.M. to 5 P.M.

Philadelphia
Quaker City Flea Market

At Tacony and Comly Streets. Take the Bridge Street exit (to Northeast Philadelphia) off I-95.

Every weekend, 8 A.M. to 4 P.M.

Free admission; free parking for up to 200 cars. In operation for over 21 years; indoors year-round, and outdoors, weather permitting. Averages 140 to a capacity of 200 vendors.

Antiques and collectibles, books, new and vintage clothing, coins and stamps, cookware, crafts and fine art, used furniture, jewelry and silver, new merchandise, and toys. Snacks are available on the premises. Billed as the oldest flea market in Philadelphia.

VENDORS: Indoors: $35 to $60 per week; outdoors: $15 per day for used items, $20 per day for new items. Reservations are not required.

Contact Kay Williams, Tacony and Comly Streets, Philadelphia, PA 19135. Tel: (215) 744-2022.

Pulaski
Pulaski Flea Market

On Route 551. Take Route 60 to Route 208 to Pulaski, then right onto Route 551 for one mile.

Every Thursday, dawn to midafternoon.

Free admission; free parking for up to 300 cars. In operation for over 48 years; indoors and outdoors, rain or shine. Averages 60 to 175 vendors.

Antiques and collectibles, books, new clothing, coins and stamps, cookware, crafts, new and used furniture, jewelry, new merchandise, fresh produce, and toys—"most everything." Snack bar on the premises. Local Amish buy and sell at this market; country auction on the last Tuesday of each month at 6 P.M. (antiques, etc.).

VENDORS: $5 for a 16-foot space outdoors or $5 per table provided. Reservations are not required.

Contact Manager, 2210 Pulaski Road, New Castle, PA 16105. Tel: (412) 654-4012.

Quakertown
Quakertown Flea and Farmers' Market

At 201 Stations Road.

Every Friday and Saturday, 10 A.M. to 10 P.M., and every Sunday, 10 A.M. to 6 P.M.

Free admission; ample free parking. In operation for over 20 years; indoors and outdoors, rain or shine. Averages up to several hundred vendors.

Antiques and collectibles, cookware, crafts, new and used

merchandise, and fresh produce. Snacks and hot meals are served on the premises.

VENDORS: From $10 per outdoor space per day. Reservations are on a first-come, first-served basis.

Contact Joseph Kaye, 201 Stations Road, Quakertown, PA 18951. Tel: (215) 536-415.

Scranton
Circle Drive-in Theatre Flea Fair

At 12 Salem Avenue, on the Scranton-Carbondale Highway (Route 6).

Every Sunday from March through December, 7 A.M. to 4 P.M.

Free admission; limited parking at 50 cents per car. In operation for over 23 years; outdoors, rain or shine. Averages up to hundreds of vendors, thousands of buyers.

Antiques and collectibles, books, new and vintage clothing, coins and stamps, cookware, crafts and fine art, fish and fresh produce, new and used furniture, jewelry and silver, new merchandise, and toys. Modern refreshment stand. All paved. Billed as the largest flea market in northeast Pennsylvania.

VENDORS: $15 per 18'x18' space per day, plus a $5 Dickson City Boro selling permit. Reservations are on a first-come, first-served basis.

Contact Michael J. Delfino, 12 Salem Avenue, Carbondale, PA 18407. Tel: (717) 876-1400 or (717) 489-5731.

West Middlesex
Mentzer's Antique Market

At 101 North Sharon Road, 200 yards south of the interchange of I-80 (use Exit 1-N) and Route 18.

Every Wednesday through Sunday, 9 A.M. to 5 P.M.

Free admission; free parking. In operation for over 21 years; indoors and outdoors, rain or shine. Averages close to 50 indoor vendors year-round.

Antiques and collectibles, books, coins and stamps, fine art, used furniture, jewelry and silver, pottery and porcelain, and toys. Snacks and hot meals are served on the premises. Billed as the "largest and finest in western Pennsylvania," located in Pennsylvania Dutch country.

VENDORS: $15 per space per day indoors, $5 outdoors. Reserve two weeks in advance (for indoor spaces only).

Contact Fred Mentzer, 101 North Sharon Road, West Middlesex, PA 16159. Tel: (412) 654-7082 or (412) 528-2300.

West Mifflin
Woodland Flea Market

At 526 Thomson Run Road, two miles from Kennywood Park and two miles from the Allegheny County Airport—in the Woodland Drive-In Theatre.

Every weekend, plus Memorial Day, July Fourth, and Labor Day, 7 A.M. to 3 P.M.

Free admission; ample parking at $1 per car on Sunday and holidays, free on Saturday. In operation for over 33 years; indoors year-round, and outdoors, weather permitting. Averages 150 to 500 vendors.

Variety of offerings including antiques and collectibles, new and used goods, and fresh produce. Snacks and hot meals are served on the premises. The original shop-and-swap market.

VENDORS: $6 for one space or $10 for two spaces per day; garage rentals are available at $100 per month. Reserve a week in advance.

Contact Robert Kranack, 526 Thompson Run Road, West Mifflin, PA 15122. Tel: (412) 462-4334 or (412) 462-4370; fax: (412) 462-4334.

Wildwood

Wildwood Peddler's Fair

At 2330 Wildwood Road. From Pittsburgh, take Route 8 south to Wildwood Road (Yellow Belt); market is next to North Park.

Every Sunday, 6 A.M. to 4 P.M.

Free admission; parking available at $1 per car. In operation for over 26 years; indoors year-round, and outdoors, weather permitting. Averages 350 to 500 vendors (capacity 600).

Antiques and collectibles, books, new and vintage clothing, coins and stamps, cookware, crafts, new and used furniture, jewelry and silver, new merchandise, fish, poultry, fresh produce, and toys. Snacks and hot meals are served on the premises.

VENDORS: Outdoors: $12 per 14'x22' space per day; indoors: $72 per space per month. Reservations are not required.

Contact Vince Rutledge, 2330 Wildwood Road, Wildwood, PA 15091. Tel: (412) 487-2200.

RHODE ISLAND

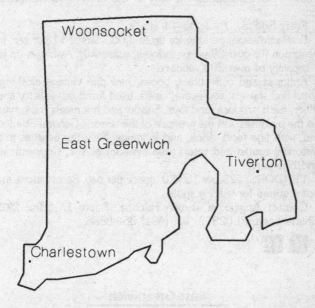

Woonsocket

East Greenwich

Tiverton

Charlestown

Charlestown ·
General Stanton Flea Market

At 4115 A and B Old Post Road (entrance off Route 1), a mile north of the junction with Route 2. From Connecticut, take Exit 92 off I-95, then go 3 miles to Route 78, to Route 1, then left (northbound) 12 miles (from Hartford, take Route 2 east to 78); from Massachusetts, take Exit 9 off I-95 to Route 4 to Route 2 to Route 1 southbound all the way to the Charlestown Beaches exit.

Every Sunday, 7 A.M. to 4 P.M.

Free admission; parking for up to 3,000 cars at $1 per car. In operation for over 29 years; indoors, seasonally. Averages up to a capacity of over 200 vendors.

Antiques and collectibles, books, new and vintage clothing, coins and stamps, cookware, crafts, used furniture, jewelry and silver, fresh produce, and toys. Snacks and hot meals are served on the premises. On the grounds of the historic General Stanton Inn, with fine food, drink, and lodgings. Near the beaches in a historical tourist and resort area between Mystic, Connecticut, and Newport.

VENDORS: $23 per 15'x20' space per day. Reservations are not required for weekly spots.

Contact Angelo or Janice Falcone, Route 1A, Box 222, Charlestown, RI 02813. Tel: (401) 364-8888.

East Greenwich
Rocky Hill Flea Market

On the Rocky Hill Fairgrounds, 1408 Division Road. Take Exit 8A (North or South) off I-95, then right at the stoplight.

Every Sunday, from the first Sunday in April through the last Sunday in November, 5 A.M. to 4 P.M.

Free admission; acres of parking at $1 per car. In operation for over 35 years; outdoors, rain or shine. Averages up to 380 vendors (capacity 400).

Antiques and collectibles, new and vintage clothing, cookware, crafts, jewelry and silver, pottery and porcelain, new merchandise, and fresh produce in season. Snacks and hot meals are served on the premises.

VENDORS: $17 per 20'x25' space. Reservations are recommended.

Contact Gary Hamilton, 12 Lockwood Street, West Warwick, RI 02893. Tel: (401) 884-4114.

Tiverton
Route 177 Flea Market

At 1650 Bulgar Marsh Road. From Boston, take Route 24 to Route 81 south, then left at only traffic light.

Every weekend plus holiday Mondays, 8 A.M. to 5 P.M.

Free admission; free parking for up to 300 cars. In operation for over 27 years; indoors year-round, and outdoors, weather permitting. Averages 35 to 70 vendors (capacity 100).

Antiques and collectibles, books, new and vintage clothing, coins and stamps, cookware, crafts and fine art, new and used furniture, jewelry and silver, new and used merchandise, porcelain, fresh produce, seafood, and toys. Hot meals are served on the premises. One of the oldest flea markets in the area.

VENDORS: $5 per space on Saturdays and holidays, $15 on Sundays. Reservations are not required.

Contact Tom Ouellette, 8 Campion Avenue, Tiverton, RI 02878. Tel: (401) 625-5954 or (401) 624-9354.

Woonsocket
Blackstone Valley Flea Market

At 401 Clinton Street.

Every weekend, 9 A.M. to 5 P.M. (marketplace open daily).

Free admission; ample free parking. In operation for over three years; indoors, year-round. Averages 40 to 50 vendors.

Antiques and collectibles, books, fresh produce, new and used merchandise. Food is available on the premises.

VENDORS: $25 per 8'x10' space per week. Reservations are recommended.

Contact Edward or Timothy Perkins, CAP Promotions, Inc., P.O. Box 1361, Westport, MA 02790. Tel: (508) 677-2244. Day of market, call Timothy Perkins at (401) 762-9101.

SOUTH CAROLINA

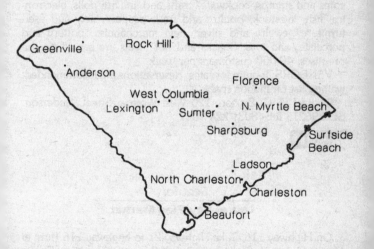

Greenville

Rock Hill

Anderson

Florence

West Columbia

Lexington   Sumter   N. Myrtle Beach

Sharpsburg

Surfside
Beach

Ladson

North Charleston

Charleston

Beaufort

Anderson

Anderson Jockey Lot and Farmers' Market

On Highway 29 between Greenville and Anderson. Take Exit 32 off I-85 North onto Highway 8 to Highway 29, or Exit 34 off I-85 South to Highway 29.

Every weekend: Saturday, 7 A.M. to 6 P.M., and Sunday, 9 A.M. to 6 P.M.

Free admission; acres of free parking. In operation since 1974; indoors, outdoors, and under cover, rain or shine. Averages 1,500 to 2,000 vendors on more than 65 acres of selling space.

Antiques and collectibles, books, new and vintage clothing, coins and stamps, cookware, crafts and fine art, dolls, electronics, fish, livestock, poultry and fresh produce, new and used furniture, jewelry and silver, new merchandise, pottery and porcelain, and toys. Snacks and hot meals are served on the premises; 40,000 customers per week.

VENDORS: Inquire for rates. Reservations are recommended; waiting list on indoor spaces.

Contact D. C. Bryson, 120 West Whitner Street, Anderson, SC 29621. Tel: (803) 224-2027.

Beaufort

Laurel Bay Flea Market

On Highway 116. Take Highway 21 to Highway 116 (turn at Marine Corps Air Station stoplight), then go three miles. Follow signs from Route 170 to "Laurel Bay." Twenty miles from Hilton Head.

Every Friday, Saturday, and Sunday, dawn to dusk.

Free admission; free parking for up to 250 cars. A new market (in operation since 1994); indoors year-round, and outdoors, weather permitting. Averages 50 to 125 vendors (capacity 50 indoors and 100 outdoors).

Antiques and collectibles, books, new and vintage clothing,

coins and stamps, cookware, crafts, used furniture, jewelry and silver, new and used merchandise, porcelain, fresh produce, and toys. Snacks and hot meals are served on the premises ("best chili dog in town!").

VENDORS: $5 per 8'x3' table per day outdoors; indoor space is available at 50 cents per square foot per month. Reservations are not required.

Contact Kathleen or Thomas McTeer, P.O. Box 1653, Beaufort, SC 29902. Tel: (803) 521-9794.

Charleston

Low Country Flea Market and Collectibles Shows

At the Gaillard Auditorium, 77 Calhoun Street (between Bay Street and Meeting Street).

Third full weekend of each month, 9 A.M. to 6 P.M., plus a big Christmas festival in late November.

Admission $1.50 per person; free admission for children; ample parking at $1 to $2 per car. In operation for over 17 years; indoors, year-round. Averages up to a capacity of 107 vendors.

Antiques and collectibles, books and prints, crafts and jewelry; mainly antique items such as furniture, silver, toys, quilts, and primitives. Snacks and hot meals are served on the premises. Caters to antiques dealers, decorators, and the like, as well as general collectors. "A fun place to be!"

VENDORS: $55 per 10'x10' space for the weekend, includes one table and two chairs. Reserve a month in advance.

Contact the Nelson Garretts, 513 Pelzer Drive, Mount Pleasant, SC 29464. Tel: (803) 884-7204. Day of market, call the auditorium at (803) 577-7400 or (803) 722-9286.

Florence
Florence Flea Market

At the corner of Highways 301N and 327.

Every weekend, all day.

Free admission; free parking. In operation for over 15 years; indoors year-round, and outdoors, weather permitting. Averages close to 400 vendors year-round.

Antiques and collectibles, new clothing, cookware, crafts, new and used furniture, jewelry, new and used merchandise, fresh produce, and toys. Hot meals are served on the premises. Presently strong on crafts.

VENDORS: $12 per 10'x10' space in the main shed (with cement floors and roll-up doors); $10 per space in the open shed; $8 per space in the yard. Reservations are recommended a week in advance for Saturday; walk-ins welcome on Sunday.

Contact Chuck Davis, 4001 East Palmetto, Florence, SC 29506. Tel: (803) 667-9895.

Greenville
Fairground Flea Market

On the old County Fairgrounds, 1300 White Horse Road. Take Exit 44 off I-85 and go north on White Horse Road for approximately one mile, and market will be on the right.

Every weekend, 5 A.M. to 5 P.M.

Free admission; free parking for over 2,000 cars. In operation for over five years; indoors and outdoors, rain or shine. Averages 600 to 850 vendors (capacity 900).

Full spectrum of antiques, collectibles, new and used goods, and fresh produce. Snacks and hot meals are served on the premises. Billed as one of the cleanest markets in the Southeast—"very accommodating."

VENDORS: $5 per space per day outdoors; $7 for a space under a new shed; $8 per space indoors. Reserve a week in advance.

Contact Paul F. Baker, 1300 White Horse Road, Greenville, SC 29611. Tel: (803) 295-1183.

Ladson
Coastal Carolina Flea Market

On Highway 78 (another entrance on College Park Road). Take Exit 203 off I-26, and there is an entrance about a block from the interstate.

Every weekend, 8 A.M. to 6 P.M.

Free admission; 15 acres of free parking. In operation for over 14 years; indoors year-round, and outdoors, weather permitting. Averages up to a capacity of 500 vendors indoors plus over 300 more outdoors.

Antiques and collectibles (including sports cards), books, new and vintage clothing, coins and stamps, cookware, wood crafts and fine art, new and used furniture, jewelry and silver, new and used merchandise, pets, porcelain, poultry and fresh produce, seafood (seasonal), and toys. Restaurant and three food concessions on the premises. Billed as the "Low Country's largest."

VENDORS: Indoors: $10 per 10'x10' space with one 8-foot table per day; outdoors: $6 per day. Reserve two weeks in advance for indoor spaces (there is sometimes a waiting list); outdoor spaces are on a first-come, first-served basis.

Contact Michael W. Masterson, P.O. Box 510, Highway 78, Ladson, SC 29456. Tel: (803) 797-0540. Office is open Wednesday through Sunday.

Limited

Lexington
Barnyard Flea Market

On Route 1 between Lexington and Columbia.
Every Friday, Saturday, and Sunday, all day.
Free admission; ample free parking. In operation since 1988;

indoors, outdoors, and under cover, year-round. Averages up to several hundred vendors.

Antiques and collectibles, books, new and vintage clothing, crafts, jewelry, new and used merchandise, and fresh produce. Food is available on the premises.

VENDORS: From $5 per 4'x8' table outdoors or from $8 per 10'x10' space indoors. Reservations are required.

Contact Richard Stewart, 4414 August Road, Lexington, SC 29072. Tel: (803) 957-6570 or (800) 628-7496.

North Charleston
Palmetto State Flea Market

At 7225 Rivers Avenue, just south of Ashley Phosphate Road. Take Exit 209 (Ashley Phosphate Road) off I-26.

Every weekend, 9 A.M. to 5 P.M. Outdoor market is open every day.

Free admission; plenty of free parking. In operation for over eight years; indoors and outdoors, rain or shine. Averages up to several hundred vendors.

Antiques and collectibles, books, new and vintage clothing, coins and stamps, cookware, crafts and fine art, fish, new and used furniture, jewelry and silver, leather goods, new merchandise, pottery and porcelain, fresh produce, and toys. Snacks and hot meals are served on the premises. Campers welcome.

VENDORS: $10 per space per day indoors; $5.50 outdoors. Reserve a week in advance.

Contact Ken Childress, 7225 Rivers Avenue, North Charleston, SC 29418. Tel: (803) 764-FLEA.

North Myrtle Beach
North Myrtle Beach Flea Market

At the intersection of Highways 17 and 9.

Every Friday, Saturday, and Sunday, 9 A.M. to 5 P.M.

Free admission; free parking for up to 500 cars. In operation for over 12 years; indoors, year-round. Averages close to its capacity of 300 vendors year-round.

Antiques and collectibles, books, new and vintage clothing, coins and stamps, cookware, crafts and fine art, new and used furniture, jewelry and silver, new merchandise, porcelain, fresh produce, shoes, old and new tools, toys, "hubcaps, etc., etc." Hot meals are served on the premises. Located one mile from the Atlantic Ocean in a tourist area that has as many as 450,000 visitors per week.

VENDORS: $10 per space per day. Reserve a week in advance.

Contact Jesse Medlock, P.O. Box 3467, North Myrtle Beach, SC 29582. Tel: (803) 249-4701.

Rock Hill
Vendors Gallery Flea Market

At 2188 Cherry Road (at the Rock Hill Mall). Take Exit 82-B off I-77 South, then follow Cherry Road one mile and the mall will be on the left.

Every Friday, 10 A.M. to 8 P.M.; every Saturday, 9 A.M. to 6 P.M.; and every Sunday, 1 P.M. to 6 P.M. (extended hours during holiday season).

Free admission; free parking for up to 1,000 cars. A new market (in operation since March 1992); indoors and outdoors, rain or shine. Averages 80 to 100 vendors (capacity 150).

Antiques and collectibles, Avon products, baseball and all sports cards, books, new and vintage clothing (including team sportswear), cookware and crafts, electronics, flowers, new and used furniture, gold jewelry, leather goods, new and used merchandise, pets, porcelain, fresh produce, toys, and wood-working; locksmith on premises. Snacks and hot meals are served on the premises. A 5,000-square-foot game room with pool tables, video games, pinball, and air hockey.

VENDORS: $15 per space per day, $35 for three-day weekend, or $115 per month. Reservations are on a first-come, first-served basis.

Contact William Bailey or Gene Hilton, 2188 Cherry Road, Rock Hill, SC 29730. Tel: (803) 366-6160 or (803) 366-3992 or (800) 671-8780.

Sharpsburg

Sharpsburg Flea Market

On Highway 301 between Wilson and Rocky Mount.
Every weekend, 9 A.M. to 5 P.M.

Free admission; free parking for up to 300 cars. In operation for over two years; indoors year-round, and outdoors, weather permitting. Averages 10 to 50 vendors on 10,000 square feet of selling area.

More old merchandise than new: antiques and collectibles, books, new and vintage clothing, cookware, crafts, used furniture, glassware, jewelry, new and used merchandise, porcelain, and toys. Snacks are served on the premises.

VENDORS: $10 per 15'x15' space per day. Reservations are not required.

Contact Ms. Moore, P.O. Box 2, Kenly, NC 27542. Tel: (919) 284-4718 or (919) 446-8007.

Sumter
The Market at Shaw

On Highway 378 East, across from Shaw AFB (approximately 30 miles east of Columbia). Take Exit 135 West off I-95 and then go approximately 23 miles on Highway 378.

Every Friday, 9 A.M. to 6 P.M.; every Saturday, 7 A.M. to 7 P.M.; and every Sunday, 1:30 P.M. to 6 P.M.

Free admission; 18 acres of free parking, mostly paved. In operation since 1990; outdoors and under cover, rain or shine. Averages 80 to 135 vendors on 22 acres of potential selling area.

Antiques and collectibles, books, new and vintage clothing, coins and stamps, cookware, crafts and fine art, new and used furniture, jewelry and silver, new and used merchandise, porcelain, fresh produce, and toys. Snacks and hot meals are served on the premises. All-steel building.

VENDORS: $5 per table on Friday, Saturday, or Sunday. Reserve a week to two weeks in advance.

Contact Mr. Weir or Mr. Firmbach, 4666 Broad Street Extension, Sumter, SC 29154. Tel: (803) 494-5500 or (803) 494-2635. Day of market, contact Jim Magee at (803) 494-5500.

Surfside Beach
Hudson's Surfside Flea Market

At 1040 South Kings Highway (Business Highway 17 South) at Tenth Avenue South.

Daily during tourist season, specific hours not reported.

Free admission; seven acres of free parking. In operation for over 21 years; indoors and outdoors, rain or shine. Averages 250 to a capacity of 450 vendors.

Full spectrum of antiques and collectibles, new and used goods such as clothing, furniture, silver and jewelry, and fresh produce. Hot meals are available on the premises. RVs and buses are welcome; located next to a 12-acre amusement park and arcade for children; three major campgrounds within two miles. Over 60,000 square feet of selling space. Formerly known as the Log Cabin Flea Market.

VENDORS: $10 per day for weekend and holiday rentals; $9 per day on weekdays; monthly rentals are available; space size is 10'x10'. Reserve two weeks in advance.

Contact Joe W. Hudson, 1040 South Kings Highway, Surfside Beach, SC 29575. Tel: (803) 238-0372.

West Columbia
U.S. #1 Metro Flea Market

At 3500 Augusta Road. Take Exit 111-A off I-26, then go one and a half miles, or take Exit 58 off I-20 and then go three and a half miles.

Every Friday, 8 A.M. to 5 P.M.; every Saturday, 6 A.M. to 6 P.M.; and every Sunday, 9 A.M. to 6 P.M.; wholesale market every Wednesday, 7 A.M. to noon.

Free admission; four acres of free parking. In operation for over 15 years; indoors and outdoors, rain or shine. Averages 500 to a capacity of 600 vendors.

Collectibles (including such items as baseball cards, bottles, coins, comics, jewelry, and toys), books, new and vintage clothing, cookware, used furniture, new merchandise, porcelain, and fresh produce. Snacks and hot meals are served on the premises. Just a few miles from the state capitol.

VENDORS: $12 per space per day indoors, $8 outdoors. Reservations are recommended.

Contact Richard J. Hook, P.O. Box 1457, Lexington, SC 29071. Tel: (803) 796-9294.

SOUTH DAKOTA

Rapid City

Sioux Falls

Rapid City
Black Hills Flea Market

At 5500 Mount Rushmore Road, at the city limits of Rapid City. Take Exit 57 off I-90 onto the I-90 Loop, then to Mount Rushmore Road (Route 16 West, the main highway to Mount Rushmore National Memorial).

Every weekend from May through September, 7 A.M. to dusk.

Free admission; ample free parking. In operation for over 21 years; indoors and outdoors, rain or shine. Averages up to 150 vendors (capacity 250).

Variety of offerings including antiques and collectibles, crafts, new and used merchandise, fresh produce in season, saddles and tack, and home-baked goodies—"something for everyone . . . anything from plants to collectible bits of Americana gleaned from cereal boxes of years ago." Snacks and hot meals are served on the premises. Several campgrounds nearby. Reputed to be a well-kept market with many regular dealers plus others passing through from various parts of the country on the flea market circuit. "The faces of Presidents Washington, Jefferson, Lincoln, and Roosevelt are an inspiration to us all."

VENDORS: $10 per day "tailgate" including one table; indoor booths $13 to $15 per day including tables. Arts and crafts indoor section $10 per day including one table; additional tables available at $2 each per day. Reservations are required a week in advance.

Contact Maybelle or Paul R. Ashland, 5500 Mount Rushmore Road, Rapid City, SD 57701. Tel: (605) 343-6477 or (605) 348-1981.

Sioux Falls

Benson's Flea Market
(aka Sioux Falls Flea Market)

On the Lyons Fairgrounds in Expo Building WH.

One weekend a month (except July and August), generally first weekend of the month—call for dates: Saturday, 9 A.M. to 5 P.M., and Sunday, 11 A.M. to 4 P.M.

Admission $1 per person; free parking. In operation for over 28 years; indoors. Averages up to 250 vendors.

Antiques and collectibles such as baseball cards, books, bottles, coins, comics, crafts, new and used furniture, household items, jewelry, and more. Snacks and hot meals are served on the premises.

VENDORS: $22 per 8-foot table per weekend, or $70 per booth with four tables. Reserve a month in advance.

Contact Ed or Bonnie Benson, Head Fleas, P.O. Box 236, Sioux Falls, SD 57101. Tel: (605) 361-1717 or (712) 277-4017.

Sioux Falls

Cliff Avenue Flea Vendors

At 3515 North Cliff Avenue, about a mile and a half south of the Cliff Avenue exit off I-90.

Every day except Wednesday, 10 A.M. to 5 P.M.

Free admission; ample free parking. In operation for over 10 years; indoors year-round, and outdoors, weather permitting. Averages close to 30 vendors year-round.

Antiques and collectibles, books, bottles, comics, fine art, used furniture, jewelry, porcelain, and used merchandise. Food is not served on the premises.

VENDORS: Inquire for rates. Reservations are recommended.

Contact Naomi Carman, 3515 North Cliff Avenue, Sioux Falls, SD 57104. Tel: (605) 338-8975.

TENNESSEE

Knoxville
Sevierville
Sweetwater
Crossville
Lebanon
Springfield
Mount Juliet
Nashville
Dickson
Trenton
Memphis

Crossville
Crossville Flea Market

On Highway 70 North. Take Exit 317 off I-40 going toward Crossville (midway between Knoxville and Nashville) and travel on Highway 127, then right onto Highway 70 North, and the market will be a mile and a half farther on the right.

Every weekend plus holiday Mondays, 6 A.M. to 4 P.M.

Free admission; free parking for up to 12,000 cars. In operation since 1970; indoors, outdoors, and under cover, rain or shine. Averages 300 to a capacity of 400 vendors.

Antiques and collectibles, books, new and vintage clothing, coins and stamps, cookware, crafts and fine art, new and used furniture, jewelry and silver, livestock, new and used merchandise, porcelain, poultry and fresh produce, seafood, and toys. Snacks and hot meals are served on the premises. Also known as Dixon's. Billed as the largest weekly open-air market in the state—"where a flea market is still a flea market." Member of the Tennessee Flea Market Association.

VENDORS: Saturday: $6 per 12'x14' space ($8 under shed), includes two tables; Sunday: $4 per space ($5 under shed) with free tables. Reservations are not required (but most reserve at least a day in advance).

Contact Cordell Dixon or Lois Wilbanks, P.O. Box 30264, Knoxville, TN 37930. Tel: (615) 484-9970 or (615) 691-4126.

Dickson
Log Cabin Antiques and Flea Market

At 1635 Highway 46 South. Take Exit 172 off I-40, then right onto Highway 46, and go approximately two and a half miles; market will be on the right beside the Log House.

Every Thursday through Sunday of the first Saturday of every month (except January, July, and August), plus Monday of Labor Day weekend, 8 A.M. to whenever.

TENNESSEE / Knoxville

Free admission; free parking for more than 150 cars. In operation for over 10 years; outdoors, weather permitting. Averages half a dozen to 60 vendors (capacity 72).

Antiques and collectibles, books, new clothing, glassware, crafts, used furniture, household items, jewelry, new and used merchandise, and toys. Snacks are served on the premises, and several restaurants are nearby.

VENDORS: $5 per 20'x20' space per day; electricity is available at $2 per day; state tax permits are required and available for $5 per month or $15 per quarter or $45 per year. Reservations are recommended, especially for Saturday.

Contact Wayne or Reba Harris, 1635 Highway 46 South, Dickson, TN 37055. Tel: (615) 446-4438.

Knoxville
Esau's Antique and Collectible Market

At the Knoxville Fairgrounds. Take Exit 392 (Rutledge Park exit) off I-40 East through Knoxville.

Third weekend of every month, 9 A.M. to 5 P.M.

Admission $3 per person, good for both days; 20 acres of free parking. In operation for over 20 years; indoors and outdoors, rain or shine. Averages 300 to a capacity of 350 vendors.

Antiques and collectibles, books, new and vintage clothing, coins and stamps, crafts and fine art, jewelry and silver, new merchandise, pottery and porcelain. Snacks and hot meals are served on the premises. A member of the Tennessee Flea Market Association. "Bring your truck."

VENDORS: $60 per space per weekend indoors, $33 outdoors; Tennessee sales tax number required (or a sales tax certificate may be purchased from the market). Reserve a month in advance.

Contact Cindy Crabtree, P.O. Box 50096, Knoxville, TN 37950. Tel: (615) 588-1233.

388

Lebanon
Gracie T.'s Flea Market

At 1022 Murfreesboro Road. Take Exit 238 off I-40, then go south one half mile on Highway 231 and market will be on the right.

Every weekend plus holidays, 8 A.M. to 5 P.M.

Free admission; free parking for up to 200 cars. In operation for over five years; indoors year-round, and outdoors, weather permitting. Averages 35 to 55 vendors (capacity 65).

Antiques and collectibles, books, new and vintage clothing, coins and stamps, cookware, crafts and fine art, new and used furniture, jewelry and silver, livestock, new and used merchandise, porcelain, poultry and fresh produce, and toys. Snacks are served on the premises. Game room.

VENDORS: From $10 to $35 per space per day depending on size and location. Reservations are not required.

Contact Twenty Five, Inc., 479 Dick Buchanan Street, Lavergne, TN 37086. Tel: (615) 444-5177 or (615) 330-3653.

Lebanon
Parkland Flea Market

On Highway 231, six miles south of Exit 238 off I-40 (across from Cedars of Lebanon State Park), between Lebanon and Murfreesboro; 30 miles from Nashville.

Every weekend from March through Christmas, 7 A.M. to 5 P.M.

Free admission; free parking for up to 400 cars. In operation since 1977; indoors and outdoors, rain or shine. Averages close to 300 vendors year-round.

Antiques and collectibles, books, new clothing, crafts, new furniture, jewelry, livestock, new merchandise, poultry and fresh produce, and toys. Snacks and hot meals are served on the premises. Close to state park and campgrounds. Attracts some 8,000 customers each week.

TENNESSEE /Memphis

VENDORS: $10 per 12'x12' space per day, with two tables included. Reserve two weeks in advance.

Contact E. Gwynn Lanius, President, 403 Cambridge Road, Lebanon, TN 37087-4207. Tel: (615) 444-1279. Day of market, call (615) 449-6050.

Memphis
Memphis Fairgrounds Flea Market

On the Mid-South Fairgrounds, at Central Avenue and East Parkway in midtown Memphis.

The third weekend of each month except September, 9 A.M. to 6 P.M.

Free admission; free parking for up to 5,000 cars. In operation since 1971; indoors year-round, and outdoors, weather permitting. Averages 600 to 700 vendors.

Antiques and collectibles, new and vintage clothing, coins and stamps, crafts and fine art, pottery and porcelain, new and used furniture, jewelry and silver. Snack bar on premises.

VENDORS: $60 for the weekend; tables are $5 each. Reservations are recommended.

Contact Sam J. Simmons, Coleman-Simmons Promotions, P.O. Box 40776, Memphis, TN 38174-0776. Tel: (901) 725-0052.

Mount Juliet
P.J.'s Flea Market

At 11520 Lebanon Road. Take Exit 226B off I-40 and go five miles to dead end, turn left and go a block and market will be on the left.

Daily, 10 A.M. to 6 P.M.

Free admission; ample free parking. In operation since 1994;

indoors, year-round. Averages close to its capacity of 50 vendors year-round.

Antiques and collectibles, books, new and vintage clothing, cookware, new and used furniture, jewelry and silver, porcelain, toys, and used merchandise. Food is not served on the premises. Twenty minutes from Opryland and downtown Nashville.

VENDORS: Inquire for rates. Reservations are recommended.

Contact Ruth or Paul Johnson, 5445 Vanderbilt Road, Old Hickory, TN 37138. Tel: (615) 754-6232 or (615) 754-9291.

Mount Juliet
Rawlings Flea Market

At 13338 Lebanon Road (Highway 70). Take Exit 226 off I-40 to Highway North to Highway 70 and then head west about a mile and market will be on the right.

Daily except Sunday, 9:30 A.M. to 5:30 P.M.

Free admission; free parking. In operation for over four years; indoors, year-round. Averages close to its capacity of 30 vendors.

Antiques and collectibles, books, vintage clothing, crafts, used furniture, costume jewelry, toys, and used merchandise. Food is not served on the premises.

VENDORS: $35 to $50 per month plus 10 percent commission on sales. Reservations are required.

Contact Betty Ann and Joe Henderson, Managers, 13338 Lebanon Road, Mount Juliet, TN 37122. Tel: (615) 754-7457.

Nashville
Nashville Flea Mart and Auction Center

At 1364 Murfreesboro Pike near the airport, one half mile east of Briley Parkway, between Highways I-24 and I-40.

Every Friday, 4 P.M. to 9 P.M.; every Saturday and Sunday, 10 A.M. to 6 P.M.

Free admission; free parking for up to 700 cars. A new market; indoors, rain or shine. Averages 200 to 240 vendors (capacity 240).

Baseball cards, coins and stamps, cookware, crafts, new and used furniture, Mexican crafts, semiprecious stones, and live animals and aquariums; the "Nashville T-shirts and socks headquarters." Snacks and hot meals are served on the premises. Located in an old Zayre's store near the airport. "The best prices in town."

VENDORS: From about $65 per booth weekly, or from $200 monthly. Reservations are recommended for transient vendors.

Contact the de Jaeger Family, Managers, 1364 Murfreesboro Pike, Nashville, TN 37217. Tel: (615) 360-7613 or (615) 360-7627.

Nashville
Tennessee State Fairgrounds Flea Market

On the State Fairgrounds at Wedgewood Avenue and Nolensville Road. Take Exit 81 (Wedgewood) off I-65.

Fourth weekend of every month: Saturday, 6 A.M. to 6 P.M., and Sunday, 7 A.M. to 5 P.M.

Free admission; free parking for up to 800 cars. In operation for over 27 years; indoors, outdoors, and under cover, rain or shine. Averages 1,000 to 1,200 vendors (capacity more than 2,000).

Antiques and collectibles, books, new and vintage clothing, coins and stamps, cookware, crafts and fine art, new and used

furniture, jewelry and silver, new and used merchandise, porcelain, and toys. Snacks and hot meals are served on the premises.

VENDORS: Average $70 per space per weekend indoors, $55 under sheds, and $55 outdoors. Reserve a month in advance.

Contact Mary Snider, Tennessee State Fairgrounds Flea Market, P.O. Box 40208, Nashville, TN 37204. Tel: (615) 262-5016.

Sevierville
Great Smokies Flea Market

At 220 Dumplin Valley Road West. Take Exit 407 off I-40 and go right on Dumplin Valley Road.

Every Friday, 10 A.M. to 6 P.M., and every Saturday and Sunday, 9 A.M. to 6 P.M.

Free admission; free parking. In operation since 1990; indoors, outdoors, and under cover, rain or shine. Averages 230 to 300 vendors (capacity 230 vendors indoors plus over 100 outdoors).

Antiques and collectibles, clothing, crafts, factory-direct items of all kinds, furniture, tools, and toys. Food court on premises. Tour buses welcome.

VENDORS: $55 per weekend indoors, or $10 per day outdoors. Reserve a week in advance for outdoor spaces; waiting list for indoor spaces.

Contact Evelyn Ogle, 220 Dumplin Valley Road, Kodak, TN 37764. Tel: (615) 932-FLEA.

Springfield
Highway 41 Flea Market

At 2862 Highway 41 South. Take Exit 98 (Millersville/Springfield exit) off I-65, then go eight miles north on Highway 41; or take the Ashland City/Springfield exit off I-24 and go east on Highway 49 to Springfield.

Every weekend from March through Christmas, 7 A.M. to 5 P.M.

Free admission; free parking for up to 400 cars. In operation for over seven years; indoors and outdoors, rain or shine. Averages 140 to 175 vendors in up to 200 booths plus shaded outdoor spaces.

Antiques and collectibles, books, new clothing, cookware, crafts, farm equipment (lawn mowers, garden tools, etc.), new and used furniture, jewelry and silver, new and used merchandise including various yard-sale items, porcelain, fresh produce, and toys. Snacks and hot meals are served on the premises. Camping and RV accommodations within seven miles of the market. On five acres with lots of shade.

VENDORS: $10 per space per day; electricity is available in all booths. Reservations are not required; call anytime.

Contact Manager, 2862 Highway 41 South, Springfield, TN 37172. Tel: (615) 643-4763.

Sweetwater
Fleas Unlimited

Highway 68 West near Exit 60 off I-75.

Every weekend, 8 A.M. to 5 P.M.

Free admission; free parking. In operation for over six years; indoors and outdoors, weather permitting. Averages 300 to 350 vendors.

Antiques and collectibles, books, new and vintage clothing, coins and stamps, cookware, crafts and fine art, new and used furniture, jewelry and silver, new and used merchandise, porce-

lain, fresh produce, and toys. Snacks and hot meals are served on the premises. "A trader's paradise."

VENDORS: From $16 per space per day. Reservations are recommended.

Contact Rhonda Busby, 121 Country Road 308, Sweetwater, TN 37874. Tel: (615) 337-FLEA.

Trenton
First Monday Flea Market

On the Gibson County Fairgrounds, just off Business Route 45 West, on "Manufacturers Row."

First Monday of every month and the preceding Saturday and Sunday (special dates in May, October, and November), from daybreak to dark.

Free admission; ample free parking. In operation for over 100 years; indoors, outdoors, and under cover, year-round. Averages 150 to 400 vendors.

Antiques and collectibles, books, new clothing, cookware, crafts, new and used furniture, jewelry, livestock, new and used merchandise, poultry and fresh produce, and toys. Snacks and hot meals are served from concessions on the fairgrounds.

VENDORS: $7 per 20'x20' space per day outdoors; electricity is available at $4 per day/overnight. Reservations are not required.

Contact Sonny Shanklin, Apartment #5, Box 5, Belew Drive, Bradford, TN 38316. Tel: (901) 855-2981 or (901) 742-3496.

TEXAS

- Amarillo
- Lubbock
- Wichita Falls
- See Inset
- Canton
- Seven Points
- Gun Barrel City
- Midland
- El Paso
- Odessa
- Waco
- Nacogdoches
- Coldspring
- Austin
- Cleveland
- Schertz
- Houston
- San Antonio
- Pearland
- Corpus Christi
- Alamo

DALLAS-FORT WORTH AREA

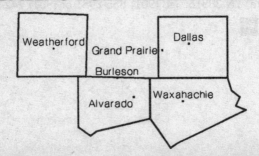

- Weatherford
- Grand Prairie
- Dallas
- Burleson
- Alvarado
- Waxahachie

Alamo
All-Valley Flea Market

On Morningside Road at the intersection of Expressway 83, between Alamo and San Juan.

Every weekend, from daybreak to dark.

Admission 50 cents per carload; parking for more than 500 cars (free with admission). In operation for over 27 years; indoors year-round, and outdoors, weather permitting. Averages 600 to a capacity of more than 1,000 vendors.

Antiques and collectibles, books, new and vintage clothing, coins and stamps, cookware, crafts and fine art, new and used furniture, jewelry and silver, livestock, new and used merchandise, porcelain, poultry and fresh produce, and toys. Food is available on the premises. Forty trailer hookups, showers. Billed as the largest flea market south of Dallas/Fort Worth, with as many as 30,000 shoppers on winter weekends or 15,000 on summer weekends.

VENDORS: $35 per space (as big as required) on Saturday, includes tables; $70 per 11'x18' space on Sunday, includes one table. Reserve a week in advance for covered spaces.

Contact Harvey Bruns, P.O. Drawer 1099, Alamo, TX 78516. Tel: (210) 781-1911.

Alvarado
I-35 West Flea Market and Auto Swap Meets

Near Exit 30 (F.M. 917) off I-35 West, four miles north of Alvarado, between Cleburne and Dallas.

Every Friday, Saturday, and Sunday, 6 A.M. to 6 P.M.

Free admission; free parking for over 500 cars. In operation for over seven years; indoors and outdoors, rain or shine. Averages 75 to 300 vendors (capacity 1,000).

Antiques and collectibles, books, new and vintage clothing, coins and stamps, cookware, crafts and fine art, new and used furniture, jewelry and silver, new and used merchandise, porce-

lain, poultry and fresh produce, and toys. Snacks and hot meals are served on the premises.

VENDORS: From $5 per space per day; $90 per month for two spaces with electricity and free showers; overnight camping at $5 per night or $30 per week with electricity. Reservations are not required.

Contact Fred, A.A.T.F.M. Shows, 3004 South I-35W, Burleson, TX 76028. Tel: (817) 783-5468.

Amarillo
Old ICX Flea Market

At 513 South Ross Street. Take Ross Street exit off I-40 and go north on Ross past two sets of stoplights, and market will be on the right.

Every Friday, Saturday, and Sunday, 9 A.M. to 6 P.M.

Free admission; free parking for up to 200 cars. In operation for over six years; indoors and outdoors, rain or shine. Averages 70 to a capacity of 100 vendors.

Full spectrum of antiques and collectibles, jewelry, new and used goods, and fresh produce. Snacks and hot meals are served on the premises. Strong on collectibles such as baseball cards, coins, and toys, including a Star Trek booth.

VENDORS: $25 per 10'x10' space for three days; $35 per 10'x15' space, or 20 cents per square foot per month. Reservations are recommended—sometimes there's a waiting list.

Contact Shirley Roberts, 513 South Ross Street, Amarillo, TX 79104. Tel: (806) 373-3215 Monday through Thursday, 9 A.M. to 3 P.M.

Amarillo
T-Anchor Flea Market

At 1401 Ross Street (off I-40), across from Burger King.
Every weekend, 9 A.M. to 5 P.M.

Free admission; free parking. In operation since 1978; indoors year-round, and outdoors in summertime. Averages close to 165 vendors year-round (capacity 347 spaces indoors and 40 outdoors).

Antiques and collectibles, books, new and vintage clothing, coins and stamps, cookware, crafts and fine art, new and used furniture, jewelry and silver, new and used merchandise, fresh produce, and toys. Food is available on the premises.

VENDORS: Indoors: from $21.50 per 10'x10' space per weekend; outdoors: $8.25 per 10'x25' space per weekend. Reservations are on a first-come, first-served basis.

Contact Claudia Blythe, P.O. Box 31182, Amarillo, TX 79120. Tel: (806) 373-0430 (every day except Tuesday and Wednesday).

Austin
Austin Country Flea Mart

At 9500 Highway 290 East. Take Highway 290 East toward Houston for five miles from I-35.
Every Saturday and Sunday, 10 A.M. to 6 P.M.

Free admission; free parking. In operation over 12 years; indoors and outdoors, rain or shine. Averages up to a capacity of 550 vendors.

A bit of everything, including antiques and collectibles, new and used merchandise, gold, shoes, and fine foods. Variety of food concessions on the premises.

VENDORS: $35 per weekend. Reservations are recommended.

Contact Buz Cook, 9500 Highway 290 East, Austin, TX 78724. Tel: (512) 928-2795.

Burleson
All American Texas Flea Market

On I-35 West, five miles south of Burleson.

Daily, 9 A.M. to 4 P.M. (weekends from 7 A.M. to dark).

Free admission; unlimited free parking. In operation for over six years; indoors and outdoors, rain or shine. Averages up to 300 vendors (capacity 500).

Antiques and collectibles, books, new and vintage clothing, cookware, crafts and fine art, used furniture, jewelry and silver, porcelain, toys, and used merchandise. Snacks and hot meals are served on the premises.

VENDORS: From $5 per space per day. Reservations are not required.

Contact Paul, Manager, 3004 SI35W, Burleson, TX 76028. Tel: (817) 783-5468.

Canton
First Monday Trade Days

Entrances on Highway 19 and F.M. 859 in Canton, just off I-20 (55 miles east of Dallas); 35 miles west of Tyler (use Highway 64).

Friday, Saturday, and Sunday preceding the first Monday of every month, dawn to dusk.

Free admission; parking for up to half a million visitors at $3 per car. In operation since before 1873; indoors, outdoors, and under cover, rain or shine. Averages 1,500 to 3,000 vendors (capacity over 3,000).

A virtually unlimited range of items, including all types of antiques and collectibles, baskets, books, new and vintage clothing (including Western wear), coins and stamps, cookware, crafts and fine art, dolls, electronics, antique firearms, new and used furniture, glassware, household items, jewelry and silver, new merchandise, pottery and porcelain, livestock, poultry and pets (in "Dog Alley"), fresh produce, tools, and toys. A wide range of snacks, deli items, and hot meals are served on the premises. First aid facilities, information centers, shower facilities, local lodging (book well in advance!), and RV facilities available (promoters call the town a "haven for RV owners"); fishing, golf, tennis, and other recreational facilities. The market publishes its own free newspaper and promotional guide. This is a world-famous flea market and one of the biggest in the country; there are many special events such as East Texas Native American Pow Wow (May), RV rallies, gun shows (January, April, August, and October), classic motorcycle rally (June), bluegrass festival (April and June), and classic car swap (May and October)—call for information.

VENDORS: $40 for the first two adjoining 12'x20' spaces, $35 thereafter. Reservations are required for some areas.

Contact City of Canton, P.O. Box 245, Canton, TX 75103. Tel: (903) 567-6556.

Cleveland
Olde Security Square

On Highway 105, between Cleveland and Conroe.

Every weekend, 10 A.M. to 6 P.M.

Free admission; five acres of free parking. In operation for over 10 years; indoors and outdoors, rain or shine. Averages up to a capacity of 85 indoor spaces plus over 165 tables for outdoor vendors.

Antiques and collectibles, books, new and vintage clothing, coins and stamps, cookware, crafts, antique firearms, new and used furniture, jewelry and silver, new merchandise, pottery and porcelain, fresh produce, and toys. Snacks and hot meals are served on the premises. RV hookups. Family-oriented market with "some of everything," growing fast with plenty of room for expansion.

VENDORS: Outdoors (under awning): $8 per 4'x8' table per day. Reservations are required; long waiting list on indoor spaces.

Contact Manager, 20024 Highway 105, Cleveland, TX 77327. Tel: (713) 592-6017.

Coldspring
Courthouse Square Trade Days

At the square; out of Shepherd, take F.M. 150 off Highway 59; or take F.M. 190 off Highway 45, then go right onto 156.

Fourth Saturday of each month from March through November, 10 A.M. to 4 P.M.

Free admission; parking for over 200 cars. In operation for over 10 years; outdoors, weather permitting. Averages 36 to 45 vendors (capacity 75).

Antiques and collectibles, books, new and vintage clothing, cookware and crafts, new and used furniture, jewelry and silver, and toys. Snacks and hot meals are served nearby. This market is run by the San Jacinto County Heritage Society in the historical Old Town.

VENDORS: $20 per space per day. Reservations are not required.

Contact Jane Guissinger, P.O. Box 505, Coldspring, TX 77331. Tel: (409) 653-2009 or (409) 653-6118.

Coldspring
Old School House Co-op

On the grounds of the Old Jail Museum (open Thursday through Friday) in the historic Old Town of Coldspring. From Shepherd, take F.M. 150 off Highway 59, then turn left on Slade

Street in Coldspring; or take F.M. 190 eastbound off Highway 45, then right onto Route 156, then left on Slade Street in Coldspring.

Every Friday and Saturday, 10 A.M. to 4 P.M.

Free admission; ample free parking. In operation since 1991; indoors, year-round. Averages close to 13 vendors year-round.

Antiques and collectibles, new and vintage clothing, crafts, furniture, jewelry, pottery and porcelain, quilts, and old toys. Food is available in town. This is a small market operated by the San Jacinto County Heritage Society.

VENDORS: Semiannual leases only; no transients. Waiting list.

Contact Jane Guissinger, P.O. Box 505, Coldspring, TX 77331. Tel: (409) 653-2009 or (409) 628-6118.

Corpus Christi
Corpus Christi Trade Center

At 2833 South Padre Island Drive, on the south end of that street (between Kostoryz and Ayers).

Every Friday, Saturday, and Sunday, 9 A.M. to 7 P.M.

Free admission; free parking for up to 500 cars. In operation since 1983; indoors, year-round. Averages close to 150 vendors year-round (capacity 200) on 75,000 square feet of selling space.

Antiques and collectibles, books, new and vintage clothing, coins and stamps, cookware, crafts and fine art, new and used furniture, jewelry and silver, new merchandise, plants, pottery and porcelain, fresh produce, and toys. Snack bar on the premises. Veterinarian; sewing machine and television repair; custom-made boots; door prizes.

VENDORS: From $45 per space per weekend. Reservations are recommended.

Contact Manager, 2833 South Padre Island Drive, Corpus Christi, TX 78415. Tel: (512) 854-4943.

Dallas
Bargain City Bazaar

At 735 North Westmoreland, one mile south of I-30.

Every Friday, Saturday, and Sunday, 10 A.M. to 7 P.M.

Free admission; free parking for up to 700 cars. In operation for over 14 years; indoors, year-round. Averages up to a capacity of 150 vendors.

Variety of offerings including new and used furniture, collectibles such as baseball cards, silver and jewelry, toys, new clothing, pottery and porcelain, and fresh produce. Snacks and hot meals are served on the premises. Offers 100,000 square feet of selling space.

VENDORS: $15 to $20 per space per day; call for availability. Booths are rented monthly except for a few temporary spaces when available.

Contact Rod Lehr and Brady Bryant, 735 North Westmoreland, Dallas, TX 75211. Tel: (214) 330-8111.

Dallas
Lone Star Bazaar

At 10724 Garland Road, two miles southeast of Route 635 (LBJ Freeway), on the Dallas side, next to the K Mart.

Every Friday, noon to 6 P.M., and every Saturday and Sunday, 10 A.M. to 6 P.M.

Free admission; free parking for up to 144 cars. In operation for over six years; indoors, rain or shine. Averages close to 60 vendors year-round (capacity 70).

Antiques and collectibles, crafts and fine art, electronics including computers, used furniture, jewelry and silver, military items, new and used merchandise, porcelain, records, sports equipment, toys, and video games. Hot meals are served on the premises.

VENDORS: Inquire for rates, which vary (minimum lease is 90 days). Reserve a week in advance.

Contact Lloyd Wingfield, 10724 Garland Road, Dallas, TX 75218. Tel: (214) 324-1484.

El Paso
Ascarate Flea Market

AT 6701 Delta Drive, at the Ascarate Drive-In Theater.
Every weekend, 5 A.M. to 6 P.M.

Free admission; free parking for up to 600 cars. In operation for over 23 years; outdoors, weather permitting. Averages 300 to 350 vendors (capacity 400).

Antiques and collectibles, new and vintage clothing, coins and stamps, cookware, crafts and fine art, new and used furniture, jewelry and silver, new and used merchandise, porcelain, poultry and fresh produce, and toys. Snacks and hot meals are served on the premises.

VENDORS: $13 per 18'x24' space on Saturday, $8 on Sunday. Reservations are not required.

Contact Jose Luis Saucedo, 6701 Delta Drive, El Paso, TX 79905. Tel: (915) 779-2303.

Grand Prairie
Traders Village

At 2602 Mayfield Road, just off Highway 360, a mile north of I-20, or five miles south of Six Flags Over Texas theme park.
Every weekend, 8 A.M. to dusk.

Free admission; parking at $2 per car (lot capacity 7,000 cars). In operation for over 21 years; indoors, outdoors, and under cover, rain or shine. Averages 1,400 to 1,600 vendors (capacity 1,700).

Antiques and collectibles, crafts, electronics, auto accessories (and automobiles, sometimes!), Western riding tack and saddles, sporting goods, haircuts, plants, new and vintage clothing, fish,

TEXAS /Gun Barrel City

fresh produce, poultry, livestock, imports, and office equipment. Pizza by the slice, German sausages, Texas-size baked potatoes, southern fried chicken and catfish, Mexican food, funnel cakes, and hot dogs available. Large RV park nearby with extensive facilities; 4,000-plus-seat outdoor rodeo arena. "Traders Village Texas" Antique Auto Swap Meet, second weekend in June; National Championship Indian Pow-Wow, weekend after Labor Day; Oktoberfest; Prairie Dog Chili Cook-off and World Championship of Pickled Quail Eating, early April. In the heart of the Dallas-Fort Worth area. They publicize that over 27 million people have visited the market.

VENDORS: $20 per day for an open lot or a kiosk; $25 per day for a covered lot; monthly rental only in enclosed buildings. Reserve a week in advance if possible.

Contact Ron Simmons, 2602 Mayfield Road, Grand Prairie, TX 75051. Tel: (214) 647-2331.

Gun Barrel City
Gun Barrel Flea Market

At 1307 West Main in Gun Barrel City (near Cedar Creek Lake). From Dallas, take I-175 to Mabank, then right at stoplight, then three miles, then right again, then two miles to light; Wal-Mart will be on right, market on left.

Every weekend, 8 A.M. to 5 P.M.

Free admission; free parking for more than 150 cars. In operation for over 25 years; indoors year-round, and outdoors, weather permitting. Averages 50 to 75 vendors (capacity 175).

Antiques and collectibles, books, new and vintage clothing, coins and stamps, cookware, crafts and fine art, new and used furniture, jewelry and silver, livestock, new and used merchandise, odds and ends, porcelain, poultry and fresh produce, and toys. Snacks and hot meals are served on the premises. RV hookups.

VENDORS: From $8 to $15 per space per weekend. Reservations are not required.

Contact Lorene Cheshier, 1307 West Main Street, Gun Barrel City, TX 75147-8021. Tel: (903) 887-1000 or (903) 887-1972.

Houston
The Houston Flea Market
(aka The Original Common Market)

6116 Southwest Freeway (Route 59). Take the Fountainview exit off 59 South, or the Chimney Rock exit off 59 North, then U-turn under the freeway.

Every weekend, 8 A.M. to 6 P.M.

Free admission; seven acres of parking at $1 per car. In operation since 1968; indoors and outdoors, rain or shine. Averages 275 to 350 vendors (capacity 375).

Antiques and collectibles, appliances, books, new and vintage clothing, cookware, crafts and fine art, electronics, new and used furniture, jewelry, new and used merchandise, pets, porcelain, fresh produce, toys, and Western wear. Snacks and hot meals are served on the premises. Special events pavilion. Billed as Houston's original flea market with large weekend crowds.

VENDORS: $18 per space on Saturday and $29 on Sunday. Reservations are recommended no later than the Friday preceding market day.

Contact Mary Wright or Bebe or Joseph Cooper, P.O. Box 573007, Houston, TX 77257-3007. Tel: (713) 782-0391.

Houston
Traders Village

At 7979 North Eldridge Road, three tenths of a mile south of Highway 290 (Northwest Freeway) or eight miles north of I-10 (Katy Freeway).

Every weekend, 7 A.M. to 6 P.M.

Free admission; ample parking at $2 per car. In operation for over six years; indoors, outdoors, and under cover, rain or shine. Averages 500 to 700 vendors (capacity 800).

Antiques, collectibles, new and used goods, fresh produce, poultry, plants, office equipment, auto accessories, sporting goods. Snacks and hot meals are served on the premises, including concessions run by Traders Village. First aid facilities, ATM machine, kiddie rides, and large full-service RV park nearby. This is a fast-growing offshoot of the original location in Grand Prairie. "Free enterprise at its best."

VENDORS: $20 per day for an open lot, or $41 per weekend for a reserved space. Reserve two days in advance.

Contact Charles Portales, 7979 North Eldridge Parkway, Houston, TX 77041. Tel: (713) 890-5500; fax: (713) 890-6568.

Houston
Trading Fair II

At 5512 South Loop East. From Astrodome, use 610 Loop east (toward the Galveston Freeway) for four miles, exit at Crestmont, at which point the market is highly visible.

Every Friday, Saturday, and Sunday, 10 A.M. to 6 P.M.

Free admission; ample fee parking. In operation since 1974; indoors, year-round. Averages up to 450 vendors.

All types of antiques and collectibles, jewelry, fine art, new merchandise, and toys. Snacks and hot meals are served on the premises. "On a par with major department stores" for selection and value.

VENDORS: $50 per 10'x10' space per weekend. Reserve in advance if possible.

Contact W. S. Henkle, 5515 South Loop East, Houston, TX 77033. Tel: (713) 731-1111.

Lubbock
Flea Market

At 2323 Avenue K at 23rd Street in downtown Lubbock.
Every weekend, 7 A.M. to 5 P.M.

Free admission; free parking for up to 500 cars. In operation for over 19 years; indoors and outdoors, rain or shine. Averages 200 to a capacity of 300 vendors year-round.

Antiques and collectibles, new and vintage clothing, crafts, new and used furniture, jewelry, new and used merchandise, poultry, fresh produce, and toys. Snacks and hot meals are served on the premises.

VENDORS: From $8 per 10'x30' space per day. Reserve a week in advance.

Contact Nan Young, Manager, 1717 Avenue K, Lubbock, TX 79401. Tel: (806) 747-8281. Day of market contact Bert Thrush at 747-8281.

Midland
Rankin Highway Flea Market

At 2840 Rankin Highway.
Every weekend, 7:30 A.M. to 6 P.M.

Free admission; limited free parking. In operation for over eight years; indoors year-round, and outdoors, weather permitting (some outdoor vendors will stay open in inclement weather). Averages 60 to 70 vendors (capacity 110).

Antiques and collectibles, new and vintage clothing, cookware and crafts, new and used furniture, jewelry, new merchandise, and poultry and fresh produce. Snack bar on the premises.

VENDORS: Indoors: 100 mini storage spaces are rented on a monthly basis; outdoors: inquire for daily rates. Reservations are not required.

Contact Joseph or Joyce Romine, 2840 Rankin Highway, Midland, TX 79701. Tel: (915) 684-5060.

Nacogdoches
Piney Woods Trade Day

At 5001 Northwest Stallings Drive (Route 59).

Fourth Saturday of every month, plus the Friday and Sunday surrounding it, all day.

Free admission; free parking for over 900 cars. In operation for over five years; outdoors, rain or shine. Averages up to a capacity of several hundred vendors.

Full spectrum of antiques and collectibles, new and used merchandise, and fresh produce. Snacks and hot meals are served on the premises. Camping and 200 24-hour RV hookups nearby (call number below for information); laundry room; free dump station.

VENDORS: From $15 per 14'x30' space per weekend. Reserve 10 days in advance.

Contact Manager, P.O. Box 631523, Nacogdoches, TX 75963-1523. Tel: (409) 560-1287.

Odessa
Henry's Flea Market Mall

At 7715 Andrews Highway (Highway 385), across from County Airport north of Odessa.

Every weekend, 9 A.M. to 5 P.M.

Free admission; two and a half acres of free parking. In operation for over 12 years; indoors year-round, and outdoors, weather permitting. Averages close to 50 vendors year-round (capacity 65).

Antiques and collectibles, books, new and vintage clothing, coins and stamps, cookware, crafts and fine art, used furniture, jewelry and silver, new and used merchandise, porcelain, and toys. Grocery store, restaurant, and concessions on the premises. "Five acres of family fun."

VENDORS: $7 per space per day outdoors and $12 indoors. Reservations are not required (inside spaces are limited).

Contact Frances or Ray Henry, 7715 Andrews Highway, Odessa, TX 79765. Tel: (915) 366-8189.

Pearland
Cole's Antique Village and Flea Market

At 1014 North Main (Route 35/Telephone Road).
Every weekend, 6:30 A.M. to 6 P.M.
Admission $1 per person; parking is free with admission. In operation for over 25 years; indoors and outdoors, year-round. Averages 600 to 700 vendors.

Antiques and collectibles, books, new and vintage clothing, cookware, crafts, new and used furniture, garage-sale items, new and used merchandise, fresh produce, and toys. Snacks and hot meals are served on the premises.

VENDORS: $12 per 10'x20' space on Saturday and $17 on Sunday. Reservations are recommended.

Contact E. J. Cole, 1014 North Main Street, Pearland, TX 77581. Tel: (713) 485-2277.

San Antonio
Eisenhauer Road Flea Market

At 3903 Eisenhauer Road. Go west on Eisenhauer Road from 410 Loop or IH-35 down one mile on right.
Every day: Monday through Friday, noon to 7 P.M.; weekends, 9 A.M. to 7 P.M.
Free admission; 10 acres of free parking. In operation for over

16 years; indoors daily, outdoors on weekends only. Averages up to 200 or more vendors.

Wide range of new and used merchandise, collectibles, jewelry, and fresh produce. Snacks and hot meals (including barbecue) are served on the premises. Two and a half acres under roof, air-conditioned.

VENDORS: From $5 per space on Saturday or Sunday (outdoors only, to 130 square feet); $25 per week for indoor table. Reservations are not required.

Contact Pat Walker, 3903 Eisenhauer Road, San Antonio, TX 78218. Tel: (210) 653-7592.

San Antonio
Flea Mart San Antonio

At 12280 Highway 16 South, a mile and a half south of Loop 410.

Every weekend, 10 A.M. to 6 P.M.

Free admission; free parking for up to 2,200 cars. In operation for over eight years; outdoors and under cover, rain or shine. Averages up to a capacity of 750 vendors.

New and used merchandise and fresh produce. Snacks and hot meals are served on the premises. Not for antiquers.

VENDORS: $40 per space per weekend. Reservations are not required.

Contact Tom Browning, 12280 South Highway 16, P.O. Box 21595, San Antonio, TX 78221. Tel: (210) 624-2666.

San Antonio
Northwest Center Flea Market

At 3600 Fredericksburg Road.

Every weekend, 8 A.M. to 5 P.M.

Free admission; free parking for up to 1,000 cars. In operation for over 22 years; indoors year-round, and outdoors, weather permitting. Averages close to 180 vendors year-round.

Antiques and collectibles, books, new and vintage clothing, cookware, crafts, new and used furniture, jewelry and silver, new and used merchandise, porcelain, fresh produce, and toys. Snacks and hot meals are served on the premises. "For the unusual."

VENDORS: Indoors: $11 per space on Saturday, $22 on Sunday; outdoors: $18 on Saturday or Sunday or $32 for both days. Reservations are not required.

Contact Jim Markwell, 3600 Fredericksburg Road, Suite 126, San Antonio, TX 78201. Tel: (210) 736-6655 or (210) 736-6677.

Schertz
Bussey's Flea Market

At 18738 IH-35 North. Take Exit 175 or 177 off I-35 north of San Antonio.

Every weekend, 7 A.M. to 6 P.M.

Free admission; parking for up to 1,500 cars at $1 per car. In operation for over 16 years; outdoors, rain or shine. Averages close to 500 vendors per weekend year-round (capacity 500).

Antiques and collectibles, books, new and vintage clothing, coins and stamps, cookware, crafts and fine art, new and used furniture, jewelry and silver, new and used merchandise, Mexican imports, fresh produce, and toys. Hot meals are available on the premises. Attracts up to 5,000 shoppers on Saturdays and more than 13,000 on Sundays.

VENDORS: $7 per space on Saturday, from $15 to $20 on Sunday. Reservations are recommended.

Contact Harold J. Smith, 18738 IH-35 North, Schertz, TX 78154. Tel: (210) 651-6830.

Seven Points
Abner's Flea Market

On Highway 334, two miles east of the stoplight in Seven Points.

Every weekend, 8 A.M. to 5 P.M.

Free admission; free parking for up to 600 cars. In operation for over eight years; indoors and outdoors, rain or shine. Averages close to 100 vendors year-round.

Antiques and collectibles, books, vintage clothing, cookware and crafts, used furniture, jewelry, new and used merchandise, fresh produce, toys. Hot meals are available on the premises.

VENDORS: $8 per 20'x20' space per day in the barn. Reservations are not required.

Contact Earlene Abner, P.O. Box 43295, Seven Points, TX 75143. Tel: (903) 432-4067.

Seven Points
Big Daddy's Flea Market

On Highway 274, a mile south of town (60 miles east of Dallas and 20 miles south of Canton), near Cedar Creek Lake. Take Route 175 from Dallas east to Route 274 south at Kemp.

Every weekend, 8 A.M. to 6 P.M.

Free admission; four acres of free parking. In operation for over four years; indoors, outdoors, and under cover, rain or shine. Averages 75 to 100 vendors (capacity 100 indoors).

Antiques and collectibles, books, new clothing, crafts, jewelry, new and used merchandise, fresh produce, and toys. Snacks and hot meals are served on the premises. Shower facilities. A heavily advertised market with about 50 percent new merchandise.

VENDORS: Indoors: $105 per 10'x20' space per month; under roof: $22 per weekend; outdoors: $7 per weekend. Reservations are not required.

Contact Manager, Route 9, Box 584-1, Grand Prairie, TX 75143. Tel: (903) 432-4911.

[handwritten annotations] Antique Mall 335A Ⓛ 4th Ⓛ ~~ Waco 335C 300

Price's Unlimited Flea Market

At 2728 La Salle Street, at the corner of I-35 on the Circle. Every weekend, from dawn to dark.

Free admission; free parking for up to 1,500 cars. In operation for over 23 years; indoors and outdoors, rain or shine. Averages 300 to 450 vendors (capacity 500).

Full spectrum of antiques, collectibles, new and used goods, and fresh produce. Snacks and hot meals are served on the premises.

VENDORS: $10 per space per day; $8 for overnight. Reservations are required.

Contact Darrell or Lorene Goetsch, 2728 La Salle Street, Waco, TX 76706. Tel: (817) 662-6616 or (817) 662-6720.

Waxahachie
Waxahachie Flea Market

On Howard Road (F.M. 877). Take Exit 399-A off I-35 South, then go across the freeway and take a right at the first stoplight, and the market will be exactly one mile ahead on the right.

Every weekend, 10 A.M. to 6 P.M.

Free admission; five acres of free parking. In operation for over 11 years; indoors and outdoors, rain or shine. Averages 40 to 60 vendors (capacity 90 vendors indoors alone).

Antiques and collectibles, books, new and vintage clothing, cookware, crafts, electronics, jewelry, new and used merchandise, fresh produce, and toys. Snack bar and steak house on the premises. Camping nearby.

VENDORS: $25 per 8'x10' space per day, or $1 per square foot per month. Reservations are not required.

Contact Shirley Peel, P.O. Box 1056, Waxahachie, TX 75165. Tel: (214) 937-4277.

Weatherford
Crowder's First Monday Trade Grounds

At 400 Santa Fe Drive in downtown Weatherford, 25 miles west of Fort Worth. Take Exit 409 off I-20 onto Clear Lake Road, which becomes Santa Fe Drive.

Every Friday, Saturday, and Sunday preceding the first Monday of every month, 7 A.M. to 7 P.M.

Free admission; street parking. In operation for over 103 years; outdoors, rain or shine. Average number of vendors not reported.

Antiques and collectibles, books, new and vintage clothing, coins and stamps, cookware, crafts, new and used furniture, jewelry and silver, new merchandise, and poultry and fresh produce. Snacks and hot meals are served on the premises. Racetrack nearby. An old-time, fun market with animals, antiques, and everything in between, located on five acres right next to the city's Trade Days operation (which charges $10 for vendors, plus $4 for electricity, according to Barbara Crowder).

VENDORS: $24 per 12'x25' space per weekend; different rates for food vendors. Reservations are recommended; drop-ins are welcome if market is not sold out.

Contact Barbara Crowder or Thelma Hull, P.O. Box 1504, Weatherford, TX 76086. Tel: (817) 594-8054 or (817) 924-8692.

Wichita Falls
Holliday Street Flea Market

At 2820 Holliday Street, about three blocks west of Highway 287, in the south-central part of town near the Bank of Holliday Creek.

Every weekend, 7 A.M. to whenever.

Free admission; free parking for up to 1,000 cars. In operation for over 29 years; indoors and outdoors, rain or shine. Averages 150 to 210 vendors (capacity more than 225).

Antiques and collectibles, army surplus, books, new and vintage clothing, cookware, crafts, new and used furniture, jewelry and silver, poultry and fresh produce, toys, and used merchandise. Snacks and hot meals are served on the premises.

VENDORS: Under sheds: $10 per 12'x12' space per day; outdoors: $7 per 12'x30' space; electricity is available at an extra charge (some spaces require long extension cables for electrical hookup). Shed spaces by reservation; outdoor spaces on a first-come, first-served basis; 75 lockable booths are rented on a monthly basis. Vendors may arrive on Friday morning after 8 A.M.

Contact Jim or Vivian Parish, 2820 Holliday Street, Wichita Falls, TX 76301. Tel: (817) 767-9038.

UTAH

Salt Lake City

Salt Lake City
Redwood Swap Meet

At 3600 South Redwood Road, at the Redwood Drive-In Theatre. Take the 33rd Street South exit off I-15, and go west to 1700 West (Redwood Road), then turn left to the market.

Every weekend, 8 A.M. to 4 P.M.

Admission 50 cents per person; free parking for up to 2,000 cars; overnights OK. In operation for over 18 years; indoors year-round, and outdoors, weather permitting. Averages 200 vendors in winter to a capacity of 600 during spring, summer, and fall.

Antiques and collectibles, books, new clothing, crafts, new and used furniture, jewelry, new and used merchandise, fresh produce, and toys. Snacks and hot meals are served on the premises. Showers are available for visitors.

VENDORS: $12 per space on Saturday and $15 on Sunday. Reservations are not required.

Contact Manager, 3688 South Redwood Road, West Valley City, UT 84119. Tel: (801) 973-6060.

VERMONT

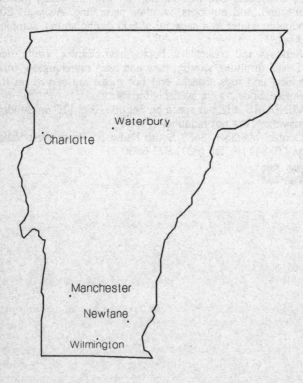

Waterbury

Charlotte

Manchester

Newfane

Wilmington

Charlotte
Charlotte Flea Market

On Route 7, 10 miles south of Burlington and 10 miles north of Vergennes.

Every weekend, from April through October, 6 A.M. to 6 P.M.

Free admission; five acres of free parking. In operation for over 26 years; outdoors, rain or shine. Averages up to 100 vendors (capacity 150).

Antiques and collectibles, books, new and vintage clothing, coins and stamps, cookware, crafts and fine art, new and used furniture, household items, jewelry and silver, new and used merchandise, pottery and porcelain, and toys. Snacks and hot meals are served on the premises. A pleasant country market located in the lovely Champlain Valley.

VENDORS: $10 per space per day, including three 8-foot tables. Reservations are not required.

Contact Larry Lavalette, P.O. Box 415, Shelburne, VT 05482. Tel: (802) 425-2844.

Manchester
Manchester Flea Market

On Routes 11 and 30, three miles from the traffic light in Manchester Center.

Every Saturday from the third week of May through October, 9 A.M. to 5 P.M.

Free admission; three acres of free parking. In operation for over 25 years; outdoors, rain or shine. Averages up to 35 vendors (capacity 40).

Antiques and collectibles (baseball cards, coins and stamps, comics, and toys); vintage clothing, antique furniture, crafts, fishing tackle, household items, hardware, new merchandise, and fresh produce. Snacks and hot meals are served on the premises. Primarily an antiques market that steers away from "plastic garbage and cheap clothes."

VENDORS: From $15 to $20 per space per day. Reservations are not required.

Contact Wessner's Auction Surplus and Flea Market, R.R. #1, Box 1960, Manchester Center, VT 05255. Tel: (802) 362-1631.

Newfane
The Original Newfane Flea Market

On Route 30, 12 miles north of Brattleboro, Vermont. Take Exit 2 off I-91 and pick up Route 30 North.

Every Sunday from May through November, 7 A.M. to whenever.

Free admission; five acres of free parking. In operation for over 28 years; outdoors, weather permitting. Averages up to 150 vendors (capacity 200).

Antiques and collectibles, books, new and vintage clothing, coins and stamps, cookware, crafts, new and used furniture, jewelry and silver, new and used merchandise, porcelain, fresh produce, and toys. Snacks and hot meals are served on the premises. Saturday night camping OK. Vendors from all over the East Coast come to sell here; visit the large general store, too.

VENDORS: $20 per van or car length space per day. Reservations are not required.

Contact Earle W. Morse, Owner, or Mark A. Morse, Manager, P.O. Box 5, Newfane, VT 05345. Tel: (802) 365-7771 or (802) 365-7685.

Waterbury
Waterbury Flea Market

On Route 2, right off I-89 on the field by the two silos.

Every weekend and holidays from May through October, all day.

Free admission; ample free parking. In operation for over 19 years; outdoors, weather permitting. Averages up to 75 vendors.

Antiques and collectibles, books, new and vintage clothing, crafts and fine art, new and used furniture, household items, jewelry and silver, new and used merchandise, fresh produce, and toys. Snacks are available on the premises. A good one, and it sure is pretty in that part of the world.

VENDORS: $10 per 25'x25' space per day. Reservations are not required.

Contact Jim McAlister, P.O. Box 850, Williamstown, VT 05679. Tel: (802) 433-6638.

Waterbury Center
Stowe Road Flea Market

On Stowe Road (Route 100), four miles east of the Waterbury/Stowe exit off I-89.

Every weekend from June through the foliage season, 8 A.M. to 5 P.M.

Free admission; two acres of free parking. In operation since 1992; outdoors and under cover, weather permitting. Averages up to 30 vendors (capacity 85 vendors on five acres).

Antiques and collectibles, books, crafts and fine art, used furniture, jewelry, new and used merchandise, fresh produce, and toys. High-quality professional caterer on the premises serving meals and "sinfully delicious" desserts. Along a heavily traveled tourist route amid the gorgeous peaks of Vermont's Green Mountains.

VENDORS: From $8 per 25'x20' space per day. Reservations are recommended.

VERMONT /Wilmington

Contact the Woodwards or the Flatows, R.R. #1, Box 2550, Waterbury Center, VT 05677. Tel: (802) 244-8879 (Barbara and Richard Woodward) or (802) 244-8817 (Walter and Marie Flatow).

Wilmington
Wilmington Antique and Flea Market

At the junction of Routes 100 and 9 East. Take Exit 2 West off I-91 and go 22 miles west on Route 9; from Albany, take Route 7 East 50 miles to Bennington, and then go east on Route 9.

Every weekend plus holiday Mondays from mid-May through mid-October, all day.

Free admission; free parking for up to 200 cars. In operation for over 13 years; outdoors, weather permitting. Averages up to 90 vendors (capacity 120).

Antiques and collectibles, books, new and vintage clothing, coins and stamps, cookware, crafts and fine art, new and used furniture, jewelry and silver, new merchandise, pottery and porcelain, fresh produce, and toys. Caterer on the premises. Bus groups welcome. Choice location with heavy east-west travel through southern Vermont.

VENDORS: $15 per space per day. Reservations are not required.

Contact the Gores, P.O. Box 22, Wilmington, VT 05363-0022. Tel: (802) 464-3345.

VIRGINIA

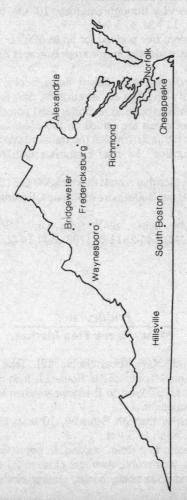

Alexandria
The Many Market

At 8750 Richmond Highway. Take Fort Belvior exit off I-95 to Route 1, then north two miles.

Every Wednesday through Saturday, 10 A.M. to 7 P.M., and every Sunday, 11 A.M. to 6 P.M.

Free admission; free parking for up to 500 cars. In operation for over six years; indoors, year-round. Averages 27 to a capacity of 35 vendors.

Antiques and collectibles, bakery items, books, new clothing, cookware, crafts and fine art, electronics, new and used furniture, jewelry, new merchandise, pottery and porcelain, and toys. Snacks and hot meals are served on the premises. More like a mini-mall than a true flea market (no transient vendors), but calls itself an "incubator" for new businesses with room for new product lines.

VENDORS: Monthly rentals only at $200 per 150-square-foot space, or $350 per 300-square-foot space. Reservations are not required.

Contact Lynn Glaser, 8903 Arley Drive, Springfield, VA 22153. Tel: (703) 644-2611 or (703) 644-1477.

Bridgewater
Mossy Creek Flea Market

At 205 South Main Street (Route 42). Take Exit 240 off Route 81 and go left onto 257 to Route 11, then right on Route 11, then left on 257 West to Bridgewater, then left onto Main Street at the stoplight.

Every Thursday through Saturday, 10 A.M. to 5 P.M., and every Sunday, noon to 5 P.M.

Free admission; free street parking. In operation for over six years; indoors, year-round. Averages close to 20 vendors.

Antiques and collectibles, books, vintage clothing, new and

used furniture, jewelry and silver, new and used merchandise, porcelain, and toys. Food is not served on the premises.

VENDORS: Inquire for rates. Reserve a week in advance.

Contact Bruce or Betty Knicely, Route 2, Box 488, Bridgewater, VA 22812. Tel: (703) 828-3924.

Chesapeake
Oak Grove Flea Market

At 910 Oak Grove Road. Off Route 64 South take Route 168 (Battlefield Boulevard) to stoplight at Wendy's, then left and go two blocks, and market will be on the right.

Every Thursday through Monday, 10 A.M. to 5 P.M.

Free admission; free parking for up to 100 cars. In operation for over 22 years; indoors year-round, and outdoors, weather permitting. Averages 20 to 30 vendors on 18,000 square feet of selling space.

Antiques and collectibles, books, carpets, cookware, crafts and fine art, new and used furniture, jewelry, new and used merchandise, and tools. Food is not served on the premises.

VENDORS: $50 per table outdoors; inquire for indoor rates. Reservations are not required.

Contact John Corbman, 910 Oak Grove Road, Chesapeake, VA 23320. Tel: (804) 547-1500.

Fredericksburg
Manor Mart Flea Market

On U.S. Highway 1, three miles south of Fredericksburg. Take the Massaponax exit off I-95 and go south two miles.

Every weekend, 7 A.M. to 4 P.M.

Free admission; free parking for up to 250 cars. In operation since 1983; indoors year-round, and outdoors, weather permitting. Averages up to 100 vendors (capacity 150).

VIRGINIA / Hillsville

Antiques and collectibles, books, new clothing, cookware and crafts, dolls, eyewear, new and used furniture, jewelry, NASCAR items, new and used merchandise, porcelain, fresh produce and grocery items, and toys. Snacks are available on the premises.

VENDORS: Indoors: $12 per space per day (includes table and shelf); outdoors: $10 for 16 feet of frontage; tables are available at $2 per day for outdoor vendors. Reservations are not required (space is always available).

Contact Nick Dommisse, 609 Breezewood Drive, Fredericksburg, VA 22407. Tel: (703) 898-4685.

Hillsville

VFW Flea Market

At the VFW Complex, 701 West Stuart Drive, one mile off I-77 Exit 3 (Hillsville exit) on Route 221.

Every Labor Day and the preceding Friday, Saturday, and Sunday, 8 A.M. to 6 P.M.

Admission $1 per person; free admission for children under 12; ample free parking. In operation for over 28 years; indoors and outdoors, rain or shine. Averages up to a capacity of 700 vendors.

Antiques and collectibles, new and vintage clothing, crafts and fine art, jewelry and silver, new merchandise, and firearms. Snacks and hot meals are served on the premises. Run by the VFW Grover King Post 1115. There is a large gun show held along with the flea market.

VENDORS: $50 per 9'x20' space, with town license. Reserve at least a year in advance; there may be a waiting list.

Contact Willie "Bo" Smith, Route 6, Box 60-B, Galax, VA 24333. Tel: (703) 728-7188. Day of market, call (703) 728-2911. For information about the gun show, call (703) 728-9810.

Norfolk
The Flea Market of Norfolk

At 3416 North Military Highway, near the airport.

Every weekend, from 7 A.M. until whenever.

Free admission; free parking for up to 250 cars. In operation for over seven years; indoors and outdoors, rain or shine. Averages 50 to 100 vendors (capacity 45 shops indoors plus three and a half acres of outdoor space).

Full spectrum of antiques and collectibles, new and used goods, new and vintage clothing, cookware, crafts, and fresh produce; specialties include dolls, electronics, records, CDs, videos, rugs, army suplus, auto parts and accessories, sporting goods, and T-shirts. Snacks and hot meals are served on the premises. Claims to be the largest indoor/outdoor flea market in the Norfolk-Virginia Beach area.

VENDORS: $10 per table per day, plus $5 per additional table; inquire for monthly rates. Reservations are on a first-come, first-served basis.

Contact Robert L. Ingram, 3416 North Military Highway, Norfolk, VA 23518. Tel: (804) 857-7824 or (804) 855-3331.

Richmond
Bellwood Flea Market

At 9201 Jefferson Davis Highway, at Willis Road, at the drive-in theater. Take Exit 64 off I-95 south of Richmond.

Every weekend, 5:30 A.M. to 4:30 P.M.

Admission $1 per person; free parking for up to 1,200 cars. In operation for over 25 years; outdoors, weather permitting. Averages 100 to 300 vendors (capacity 450).

Antiques and collectibles, books, new and vintage clothing, coins and stamps, cookware, crafts and fine art, new and used furniture, jewelry and silver, new and used merchandise, porcelain, poultry and fresh produce, and toys. Snacks and hot meals are served on the premises.

429

VIRGINIA /South Boston

VENDORS: $12 per 20'x20' space per day. Reservations are not required.

Contact Alvin Kline, 9201 Jefferson Davis Highway, Richmond, VA 23237. Tel: (804) 275-1187 or (800) 793-0707.

South Boston
Mini Market

On Halifax Road (Route 501) between South Boston and Centerville. Take Route 58 to South Boston, then go north on Route 501 to the Halifax Square Shopping Center.

Every Friday, noon to 6 P.M.; every Saturday, 8 A.M. to 6 P.M.; and every Sunday, noon to 5 P.M.; operates next to "Eve's Place" antiques mall, which is open every Tuesday through Friday, noon to 8 P.M., and every Saturday and Sunday, 8 A.M. to 6 P.M.

Free admission; free parking for up to 250 cars. In operation since 1995 (as Mini Market—formerly South Boston Mega Flea Market); indoors year-round, and outdoors, weather permitting. Averages close to 20 vendors and growing.

Mostly discount "junque," with antiques next door at Eve's Place. Eve's Kitchen serves snacks and light lunches.

VENDORS: $25 per 10'x10' space per weekend. Reservations are not required.

Contact Eve Vaughan, Halifax Square Shopping Center, Box 7, South Boston, VA 24592. Tel: (804) 575-6295.

Waynesboro
Skyline Flea Market

On Route 250 West in Waynesboro.

Every Sunday from March through November, 7 A.M. to 4 P.M.

Admission 25 cents per person; free parking for up to 400

cars. In operation for over 28 years; outdoors, weather permitting. Averages 40 to 50 vendors (capacity 75).

Antiques and collectibles, books, coins and stamps, cookware and crafts, used furniture, jewelry and silver, new and used merchandise, porcelain, fresh produce, and toys. Hot meals are served on the premises.

VENDORS: $10 per space per day. Reservations are not required.

Contact Melvin Twitchell, 966 Northgate Avenue, Waynesboro, VA 22980. Tel: (703) 942-1738.

WASHINGTON

Everett
Puget Park Swap

At 13026 Meridian Avenue South. Take Exit 128 (128th Street SW exit) off I-5; coming from the north, take a left off exit; coming from the south, take a right off exit; then onto Third Avenue S.E., then right.

Every weekend, April through October, 9 A.M. to 4 P.M. (vendors arrive at 7 A.M.).

Admission $1 per person; plenty of free parking. In operation for approximately 23 years; outdoors, rain or shine. Averages up to 230 vendors (capacity 255).

Antiques and collectibles, new and vintage clothing, cookware, crafts, new and used furniture, jewelry, and fresh produce. Snacks and hot meals are served on the premises.

VENDORS: $11 per 20'x20' space per day; $15 per 20'x25' space with electricity. Reservations are not required.

Contact Dan Sutton, 13026 Meridian Avenue South, Everett, WA 98204. Tel: (206) 337-1435.

Pasco
Pasco Flea Market

At the corner of Highway 12 and East Lewis Street.

Every weekend from March through November, 6 A.M. to 4 P.M.

Admission $1 per carload; free parking. In operation for over eight years; outdoors, rain or shine. Averages up to 300 vendors.

Antiques and collectibles, automotive supplies, books, new and vintage clothing, cookware, crafts and fine art, new and used furniture, jewelry and silver, livestock, new and used merchandise, porcelain, poultry and fresh produce, and toys. Snacks and hot meals are served on the premises. Billed as the largest open-air flea market in eastern Washington.

VENDORS: $7 per space per day; electricity is available at nominal charge. Reservations are not required.

WASHINGTON / Seattle

Contact Bill Robinson, Jr., 3713 West Nixon, Pasco, WA 99301. Tel: (509) 547-7057 or (509) 547-5035.

Seattle
Fremont Sunday Market

At the corner of Evanston Avenue and North 34th.

Every Sunday from May through October, 10 A.M. to 5 P.M.

Free admission; free parking. In operation since 1989; outdoors, rain or shine. Averages 120 to a capacity of 175 vendors.

Antiques and collectibles, books, new and vintage clothing, crafts and fine art, used furniture, jewelry, fresh produce, sporting goods, tools, toys, and used merchandise. Snacks and hot meals are served on the premises.

VENDORS: $15 per space per day for flea market items, $20 for crafts and imports. Reservations are not required.

Contact John Hegeman, Manager, 3416 Evanston, Seattle, WA 98103. Tel: (206) 634-2150 or (206) 282-5706.

WEST VIRGINIA

Bluefield
Bluefield City Flea Market

At the Parking Building (a large blue structure) on Princeton Avenue (Route 19) in downtown Bluefield.

Every Saturday, 6 A.M. to 3 P.M., from March through November.

Free admission; metered street parking; pay parking lot nearby. In operation for over 13 years; indoors. Averages up to 175 vendors (capacity 250).

Antiques and collectibles, new and used merchandise, bake sale items, cookware, crafts, and fresh produce. Snacks and hot meals are served on the premises. Managed by the City Parking Commission.

VENDORS: $5 per day for one and a half parking spaces; a few monthly spaces are available on the first floor. Reservations are not required.

Contact Manager, 514 Scott Street, Bluefield, WV 24701. Tel: (304) 327-8031.

Charleston
Capitol Flea Market

Near the Capitol High School. Take Exit 99 off I-64, or the Greenbrier (State Capitol and Airport) exit off I-77, then 3.6 miles on Route 114 South, or take Exit 5 (Big Chimney exit) off I-79, then go 3.6 miles on Route 114 South.

Every Friday, Saturday, and Sunday, 8 A.M. to 5 P.M.

Free admission; paved parking for up to 500 cars. A new market (in operation just over four years); indoors and outdoors, year-round. Averages up to 150 or so vendors on more than three football fields' area of selling space.

Wide range of new and used merchandise. Hot meals are available on the premises. Tour buses welcome.

VENDORS: $25 per 10'x14' space for three days. Reserve approximately three weeks in advance.

Contact Robert Fuentes, 24 Meadow Brook Plaza, Charleston, WV 25311. Tel: (304) 342-1626.

Harpers Ferry
Harpers Ferry Flea Market

At the Fort Drive-In, at 904 Oregon Trail (Route 340, Dual Highway), a mile past the entrance to Harpers Ferry National Park, on the left. One hour from Washington, D.C.; take Route 270 north to Frederick, then pick up Route 340 westbound.

Every weekend from mid-March through November, dawn to dusk.

Free admission; seven acres of free parking. In operation for over 12 years; outdoors, rain or shine. Averages 140 to 200 vendors (capacity 250) on three acres of selling area.

Antiques and collectibles, new and vintage clothing, coins and stamps, cookware, crafts and fine art, new and used furniture, jewelry and silver, and new merchandise. Snacks and hot meals are served on the premises. In a tourist area near a national park, horse and car racing, white-water rafting, fishing, antiques shops, etc. Billed as the largest flea market in the area.

VENDORS: $11 per space per day; electricity is available at $3 per day. Reservations are not required.

Contact Ron Nowell or Dan Barnett, 904 Oregon Trail, Harpers Ferry, WV 25425. Tel: (304) 725-0092 (Dan) or (304) 725-4141 (Ron). Day of market, call Ron or Dan at (304) 535-2575.

Martinsburg
I-81 Flea Market

On Route 11 at Spring Mills Road. Take Exit 20 off I-81, go east to Route 11, then go right approximately 2,000 feet and market will be on the right.

Every Friday, Saturday, and Sunday, plus selected holiday Mondays, 8 A.M. to 6 P.M.

Free admission; plenty of free parking. In operation for over five years; outdoors, weather permitting. (The market lost its indoor space to fire in 1995.) Averages 125 to 250 vendors.

Antiques and collectibles, books, new and vintage clothing, coins and stamps, cookware, crafts and fine art, fish, new and used furniture, jewelry and silver, new merchandise, pottery and porcelain, poultry, fresh produce, toys, and Pennsylvania Dutch products (meats, cheese, etc.). Hot meals including soups, sandwiches, and grocery items.

VENDORS: $5 per 8'x12' table (provided) on Friday, $11 on Saturday or Sunday. Reservations are recommended.

Contact Sam Pannuty or Betty Kline, Route 2, Box 230, Martinsburg, WV 25401. Tel: (304) 274-1313 or (304) 267-3131.

Milton
Milton Flea Market

At 1215 U.S. Route 60, a half mile east of Milton and one mile from the Milton exit off I-64.

Every Friday, Saturday, and Sunday, 8 A.M. to 5 P.M.

Free admission; free parking for up to 500 cars. In operation since 1989; indoors and outdoors, rain or shine. Averages up to a capacity of 300 vendors indoors plus 200 outdoors.

Antiques and collectibles, books, new clothing, crafts, new and used furniture, jewelry and silver, new merchandise, fresh produce, and toys. Snacks and sandwiches are available on the premises.

VENDORS: $7 per 10'x20' space outdoors under shed per weekend, or $5 per space in open air. Reservations are not required for outdoor spaces; waiting list for indoor spaces.

Contact Boyd L. Meadows, P.O. Box 549, Milton, WV 25541. Tel: (304) 743-1123 or (304) 743-9862.

Morgantown
Indoor Antique Flea Market

At 1389 University Avenue (Route 119). Take the University Avenue exit off I-68 onto University Avenue, then north about three miles, and market will be on the left.

Every Thursday through Sunday, 9 A.M. to 5 P.M.

Free admission, limited free parking. In operation for over 10 years; indoors, rain or shine. Averages 12 to 24 vendors (capacity 40—new vendors are welcome).

Antiques and collectibles, books, used and vintage clothing, coins and stamps, cookware and crafts, used furniture, glassware, jewelry and silver, porcelain, records, toys, used merchandise, no new merchandise. Food is not served on the premises. Under new management as of 1996.

VENDORS: $100 per 12'x12' space per month. Reservations are not required.

Contact Frank Wilkins, 1389 University Avenue, Morgantown, WV 26505. Tel: (304) 292–9230.

WISCONSIN

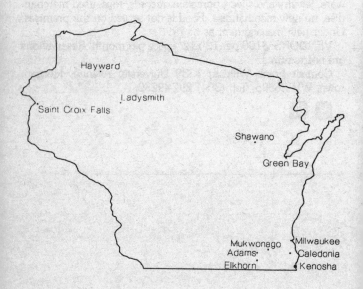

Hayward

Ladysmith

Saint Croix Falls

Shawano

Green Bay

Mukwonago   Milwaukee
Adams·   · Caledonia
Elkhorn   · Kenosha

Adams
Adams Flea Market

At 556 South Main, Highway 13, 25 miles north of Wisconsin Dells.

Weekends, May through October, plus Memorial Day, July Fourth, and Labor Day, 6 A.M. to 4 P.M.

Free admission; free parking for up to 400 cars. In operation for over 15 years; indoors and outdoors, rain or shine. Averages close to 75 vendors on 14 acres of selling area.

A good mixture of antiques and collectibles, new and vintage clothing, furniture, hardware, household items, jewelry, and produce. Hot and cold sandwiches, soda, coffee, and snacks on the premises. This is a growing market with a country look and a friendly atmosphere.

VENDORS: $7 per day, one table provided; $14 for two tables, but no limit on size of space; also yearly rentals of inside space. Reservations are not required.

Contact Irene Steffen, 556 South Main, Adams, WI 53910. Tel: (608) 339-3192. Day of market, call Irene Steffen at (608) 339-9223.

Caledonia
Seven-Mile Fair Flea Market

At 2720 West Seven Mile Road at intersection of I-94 (use Seven Mile Road exit), 15 miles south of Milwaukee and 25 miles north of the Illinois state line.

Every weekend, plus holidays. Summer hours (April through October): 7 A.M. to 5 P.M.; winter hours (November through March): 9 A.M. to 5 P.M.

Admission $1.25 per person; free parking. Duration of market not reported; indoors and outdoors, year-round. Averages up to several hundred vendors.

Antiques and collectibles, crafts, new and used merchandise, and fresh produce—"everything under the sun." Restaurant on

441

the premises. "The granddaddy of all indoor and outdoor flea markets."

VENDORS: Outdoors: Free on Friday, $10 on Saturday, and $15 on Sunday or holidays for a regular 12'x24' space (one vehicle or trailer allowed per space). Reservations are on a first-come, first-served basis.

Contact Manager, P.O. Box 7, Caledonia, WI 53108. Tel: (414) 835-2177; fax: (414) 835-2968.

Elkhorn
Antiques and Flea Market

At the Walworth County Fairgrounds on Highway 11 East.

Four times a year in May, June, August, and September, all day.

Admission $1 per person (kids free); ample free parking. In operation for over 14 years; indoors and outdoors, rain or shine. Averages close to 500 vendors.

Antiques and collectibles, new and used merchandise (and everything else). Food is available on the premises. Sellers come from all over for this one.

VENDORS: Inquire for rates. Reservations are recommended.

Contact Manager, P.O. Box 544, Elkhorn, WI 53121. Tel: (414) 723-5651.

Green Bay
Northeastern Wisconsin's Largest Flea Market and Craft Sale

At the Brown County Arena, 1901 South Oneida, in the southwest part of town on Lombardi Avenue, across from Parker Stadium.

Monthly from September through May, 8:30 A.M. to 3:30

P.M.—call for dates (which vary depending on availability of the space; generally held on a Saturday).

Admission $1.50 per person (or $1 with newspaper coupon); free parking for up to 750 cars. In operation for over 20 years; indoors. Averages up to a capacity of 250 vendors.

Antiques and collectibles, books, new clothing, coins and stamps, crafts, used furniture, jewelry, new merchandise, pottery and porcelain, general rummage items, and toys. Snacks and hot meals are served on the premises.

VENDORS: $19.50 per table per day (with one chair); electricity is available at $10 extra. Reserve a month in advance.

Contact John H. Van Stechelman, P.O. Box 10567, Green Bay, WI 54307. Tel: (414) 494-9507 (business) or (414) 494-7615 (residence). Day of market call Holly LeGros at (414) 494-9507.

Hayward
Hayward Fame Flea Market

At the junction of Highway 27 South and County Highway B, across from the National Fishing Hall of Fame.

Every Tuesday and Wednesday from late June through early September, 9 A.M. to 3 P.M.; added weekend dates in summer months—call for dates.

Free admission; free parking. In operation for over 17 years; indoors and outdoors, weather permitting. Averages 50 to 85 vendors (capacity 90).

Variety of offerings including antiques and collectibles, new and used goods, and fresh produce. Snacks and hot meals are served on the premises.

VENDORS: $8 per selling space per day. Reservations are required.

Contact Jan Thiry, Route 10, Box 195, Hayward, WI 54843. Tel: (715) 634-4794.

Kenosha
Kenosha Flea Market

At 5535 22nd Avenue, at the corner of 56th Street. Take Exit 342 (Highway 158) off I-94 and go east to 22nd Avenue, then right on 22nd Avenue, and go four blocks.

Every Friday, 10 A.M. to 5 P.M., and every Saturday and Sunday, 9 A.M. to 5 P.M.

Free admission; free parking for up to 80 cars. In operation for over 10 years; indoors, year-round. Averages 20 to a capacity of 40 vendors.

Antiques and collectibles, books, new clothing, cookware, crafts, electronics, new and used furniture, jewelry and silver, new and used merchandise, porcelain, tools, and toys. Snacks are served on the premises.

VENDORS: $25 per space for three days. Reserve a week in advance.

Contact Beth or Don Goll, 5535 22nd Avenue, Kenosha, WI 53140. Tel: (414) 658-FLEA.

Ladysmith
Van Wey's Community Auction and Flea Market

At W-10139 Van Wey Lane, on Highway 8, four miles west of Ladysmith (or four miles east of Bruce).

Generally the 5th and 20th of every month from April 20 through October, plus Memorial Day, July Fourth, and Labor Day weekends—call for dates, 6:30 A.M. to whenever.

Free admission; parking for over 1,000 cars at 50 cents per car. In operation since 1926; indoors and outdoors, rain or shine. Averages up to 100 vendors.

Antiques and collectibles, books, new and vintage clothing, cookware, crafts and fine art, fish, new and used furniture, jewelry and silver, new merchandise, pottery and porcelain, poultry and fresh produce, toys, and "many other items too numerous to mention." Snacks (French fries, hot sandwiches, etc.) are available at a coffee shop on the premises. The third generation of a family-owned business.

VENDORS: $8 per 12'x30' space per day. Rentals are on a first-come, first-served basis.

Contact Mark or Judy Van Wey, W-10139 Van Wey Lane, Ladysmith, WI 54848. Tel: (715) 532-6044.

Milwaukee
Rummage-O-Rama

At the State Fair Park, 84th Street and Greenfield Avenue, just south of I-94 at 84th Street exit (Exit 306).

Fourteen weekends per year, generally in all months except June and July, 10 A.M. to 5 P.M.—call for dates.

Admission $1.50 per person; discounts for seniors and children; acres of free parking (75,000-car capacity). In operation for over 23 years; indoors, year-round. Averages up to 500 vendors.

Antiques and collectibles, new clothing, books, coins and stamps, crafts and fine art, pottery and porcelain, fresh produce, spices, closeouts, vacuum cleaners and supplies, jewelry, school and office supplies, household items, toys for all ages, pet supplies, tools, water purifiers, vitamins, and holiday ideas. Snacks and hot meals are served on the premises. Motels and camping facilities nearby. Police protection of vendors' property left on grounds over Friday and Saturday nights. Claims to be Wisconsin's only (and the Midwest's largest) "high-class" indoor flea market. Average attendance is 14,000 to 19,000 per weekend. Well advertised.

VENDORS: From $63 to $75 per 10'x10' space per weekend; tables are extra. Reserve at least a month in advance; spaces are reserved on a first-paid basis.

Contact Walter Rasner, P.O. Box 51619, New Berlin, WI 53151. Tel: (414) 521-2111.

445

Mukwonago
Maxwell Street Days

At Field Park, with entrances on Highway 83 and Highway "NN." Take I-43 to Highway 83 North to the north end of the village, located in the southwest corner of Waukesha County.

The second weekend in June and September and the third weekend in July and August, 8 A.M. to 5 P.M.

Free admission; parking for more than 1,000 at up to $3 per car. In operation for over 39 years; outdoors, weather permitting. Averages close to its capacity of 685 vendors.

Antiques and collectibles, books, new clothing, cookware, crafts, used furniture, jewelry, fresh produce, toys, and used merchandise. Snacks and hot meals are served on the premises. Sponsored by the American Legion.

VENDORS: $30 per space per two-day event. Reserve two weeks in advance.

Contact Mukwonago Community American Legion Post #375, P.O. Box 97, Mukwonago, WI 53149-0097. Tel: (414) 363-2003.

Saint Croix Falls
Pea Pickin' Flea Market

On Highway 8 East, five miles east of Saint Croix Falls (50 miles northeast of Twin Cities, Minnesota). Take Highway 35W north to Highway 8 East.

Every weekend (plus holidays) from the third weekend in April through the third weekend in October, 6 A.M. to 5 P.M.

Free admission; free parking for up to 300 cars. In operation for over 25 years; indoors year-round, and outdoors, weather permitting. Averages up to 75 vendors (capacity 100, mostly located on grassy areas).

Antiques and collectibles, books, new and vintage clothing, cookware, crafts, used furniture, jewelry and silver, new merchandise, fresh produce, toys; frozen meats, sausage, cheese, and honey. Snacks and hot meals are served on the premises. Vendors are permitted to stay overnight on weekends.

VENDORS: $8 per 12-foot frontage for one day or $14 for the weekend (with room to park vehicle in space). Reservations are required one week in advance from June through August.

Contact Steve D. Hansen, 1938 Little Blake Lane, Luck, WI 54853. Tel: (715) 857-5479 or (715) 483-9460.

Shawano
Shawano Flea Market

At the Shawano County Fairgrounds on Highway 29/47, half an hour west of Green Bay.

Every Sunday, April through October, 6 A.M. to 5 P.M. Two added Saturdays in May and July; special three-day market on Memorial Day weekend.

Admission $1 per person; free parking for 1,500 cars. In operation for over 23 years; outdoors, rain or shine. Averages up to 200 vendors (capacity 300).

Antiques and collectibles, baseball cards, books, bottles, coins and stamps, comics, cookware, crafts, used furniture, jewelry, knives, pottery and porcelain, fresh produce, and old toys. About 80 percent antiques and collectibles. Snacks and hot meals are served on the premises. Northeast Wisconsin's largest weekly flea market.

VENDORS: $19.50 per day for 20-foot frontage; discount on sellers' space in April. Reservations are recommended.

Contact Bob Zurko, Zurko's Midwest Promotions, 211 West Green Bay Street, Shawano, WI 54166. Tel: (715) 526-9769.

WYOMING

Casper
■

Cheyenne
■

Casper

Casper Antique Show

At the Central Wyoming Fairgrounds on Route 220 in the southwest part of the city. Come in via Cy Avenue.

First full weekend in June and first full weekend in October, 10 A.M. to 5 P.M. There is also a "super flea market" in March, mid-August, and mid-November—call for dates.

Admission $1.25 per person; ample free parking. In operation for over 24 years; indoors, rain or shine. Averages up to about 40 vendors.

Antiques and collectibles of all kinds. Snacks and hot meals are served on the premises. Sponsored by Casper Antique and Collectors Club.

VENDORS: $25 per table per event. Reservations are required several months in advance, and there may be a waiting list.

Contact Bruce B. Smith, 1625 South Kenwood Street, Casper, WY 82601. Tel: (307) 234-6663.

Cheyenne

Avenues Flea Market and Auction

At 315½ East 7th Avenue, at Evans Avenue. From I-25 South, take Central Avenue South exit and go to 8th Avenue, then turn left past airport terminal (street bears right and becomes Evans Avenue); or take Central Avenue North exit off I-80.

Daily, 10 A.M. to 6 P.M. (open to 8 P.M. from July 15 through August 15).

Free admission; plenty of street parking. In operation since 1994; indoors, year-round. Averages close to its capacity of 35 vendors.

Antiques and collectibles, books, vintage clothing, used furniture, used merchandise and household goods, toys, and Western memorabilia. Snacks are served on the premises.

VENDORS: Monthly rates starting at $1.12 per square foot. No transient vendors.

Contact Edward L. Raner, 315½ East 7th Avenue, Cheyenne, WY 82001. Tel: (307) 635-5600.

Cheyenne
Bargain Barn Flea Market

At 2112 Snyder Avenue, on the west side of Cheyenne. Take I-80 to I-25, then north to the West Lincolnway exit, then east to Snyder Avenue, then north five blocks.

Daily: Monday through Saturday, 10 A.M. to 5 P.M., and Sunday, noon to 6 P.M.

Free admission; limited free parking. In operation for over eight years; indoors, year-round. Averages up to 25 vendors.

Variety of offerings including antiques and collectibles, books, new and used goods, cookware, crafts, carpet and tile products, and used furniture. Food is not available on the premises.

VENDORS: Monthly rentals only—no transient vendors. Inquire for rates. There is a waiting list.

Contact Bill M. Lucas, 2112 Snyder Avenue, Cheyenne, WY 82001. Tel: (307) 635-2844.

Cheyenne
Frontier Flea Market

At 1515 Carey Avenue.

Daily, 10 A.M. to 6 P.M. (except Sunday, noon to 5 P.M.).

Free admission; free parking. In operation for over nine years; indoors, year-round. Average number of vendors not reported.

Antiques and collectibles, books, cookware, crafts and fine art, new and used furniture, jewelry, new and used merchandise, porcelain, and toys. Snack food is available on the premises.

VENDORS: Inquire for rates. Reservations are not required.

Contact Erlinda Romero, 1515 Carey Avenue, Cheyenne, WY 82001. Tel: (307) 634-4004.

Cheyenne

Stanford and Son Flea Market and Consignment

At 715 South Greeley Highway (across from Town and Country).

Daily, 8 A.M. to 8 P.M.

Free admission; more than three acres of parking. A new market (in operation since spring 1995); indoors year-round, and outdoors, weather permitting. Averages 30 to a capacity of 50 vendors.

Antiques and collectibles, new and used merchandise including cookware, furniture, toys, and autos; fresh produce also available. Snacks are served on the premises.

VENDORS: $10 per space per day except $25 per day from July 15 through August 15. Reservations are not required.

Contact Terry W. Thompson, 715 South Greeley Highway, Cheyenne, WY 82007. Tel: (307) 635-6025.

APPENDIX: BRIEF LISTINGS

ALABAMA

Bessemer: Bessemer Flea Market. Every Friday, Saturday, and Sunday, 8 A.M. to 5 P.M. On Ninth Avenue North, behind McDonald's, one half mile off I-59 (take Exit 108 or Exit 112). Call Manager at (205) 425-8510.

Birmingham: Jefferson County Farmer's Market. Daily, all day. At 344 Finley Avenue West. Call Danny Jones, Manager, at (205) 251-8737.

Elmore: Elmore Flea Market. Every Thursday through Sunday, 8 A.M. to 5 P.M. On Route 143. Call Marty Greer at (334) 567-7731.

Florence: Uncle Charlie's Flea Market. Every weekend, 9 A.M. to 5 P.M. On Highway 72. Call Tom Mabry at (205) 757-1771.

Hammondville: I-59 Flea Market. Every weekend, 8 A.M. to 5 P.M. On I-59, at exit 231 (Hammondville/Valley Head), 10 miles north of Fort Pine and 40 miles south of Chattanooga. Call Manager at (205) 635-6899.

Harpersville: Dixieland Flea and Farmers' Market. Every Friday, Saturday, and Sunday, 6:30 A.M. to 5 P.M. On Route 25 between Wilsonville and Harpersville. Aggressively advertised and promoted. Call Mr. Jim Dalantis at (205) 672-2022; office hours are 9 A.M. to 5 P.M., Monday through Thursday.

Harpersville: Evans Flea Market. Every weekend, dawn to dusk. At 1447 Route 280 East. Call Margaret Evans at (205) 672-7462.

Huntsville: Flea Mall, The. At 7540-A South Memorial Parkway. Call Manager at (205) 881-1433.

Phenix City: Valley Flea and Farmers' Market. Every weekend, 8 A.M. to 4:30 P.M. At 3864 US Highway 80 West. "Acres and acres of bargains." Call Manager at (334) 298-3728.

Westover: Westover Flea Market. Call Manager at (205) 678-6729.

ARIZONA

Apache Junction: Apache Park 'N' Swap. Every Friday, Saturday, and Sunday, 5 P.M. to 10 P.M. At 2551 West Apache

Trail, at the Apache Greyhound Park. Call Mike Sleeseman at (602) 832-3270.

Flagstaff: Big Tree Campground and Swap Meet. Every weekend. Call Ruth, Owner, at (602) 526-2583.

Glendale: Glendale 9 Drive-In Swap Meet. Every weekend, 5 A.M. to 3 P.M. during summer and 5:30 A.M. to 3 P.M. during winter. At 5650 North 55th Avenue (western part of Phoenix) at Bethany Home Road. Call Charles Barone at (602) 939-9715; for the main office in San Francisco, call (415) 885-8400.

Phoenix: Indoor Swap Mart. Every Friday, Saturday, and Sunday, 10 A.M. to 6 P.M. At 5115 North 27th Avenue. Call Manager at (602) 246-9600.

Scottsdale: Scottsdale Swap Meet. Every weekend, 5 A.M. to 3 P.M. At 8101 East McKellips, on the corner of Hayden at the Scottsdale Drive-In Theatre. Call Ed Nezelek at (602) 994-3709.

Tucson: Marketplace U.S.A. Every Friday, noon to 9 P.M.; every Saturday, 10 A.M. to 9 P.M.; and every Sunday, 10 A.M. to 6 P.M. At 3750 East Irvington Road. Take Exit 264-B off I-10. "Southern Arizona's best business value." Call Manager at (602) 745-5000.

Tucson: Wilmot Bazaar and Swap Meet. Every Friday, 10 A.M. to 11 P.M., and every Saturday and Sunday, 7 A.M. to 11 P.M. At 6161 East Benson Highway, at the corner of I-10 (Exit 269) and Wilmot Road. Call Wayne Dennis at (602) 574-2772.

Yuma: Avenue 3-E Swap Meet. Every Thursday through Sunday, 6 A.M. to whenever. At 4151 South Avenue 3-E. Call Mike Ellis at (602) 344-2399.

Yuma: Yuma Park 'n Swap. Every Thursday through Sunday, 6 A.M. to 4 P.M. Call Manager at (520) 726-4655.

ARKANSAS

Eureka Springs: Old Town Flea Market. Daily, 10 A.M. to 6 P.M. At 78 Center Street. On the antiques mall side of the flea market category—long-term dealers only. Call Manager at (501) 253-6557.

Fort Smith: Fort Smith Flea Market. Every Friday, Saturday, and

Sunday, 9 A.M. to 5 P.M. At 3721 Towson Avenue. Call Manager at (501) 646-0410.

Fort Smith: Zero Street Flea Market. At 2425 South Zero Street. Call Manager at (501) 648-9909.

Judsonia: Exit 48 Flea Market. Every weekend. Call Manager at (501) 729-4769.

Rogers: Rose Hall Mall Flea Market. Daily, 9 A.M. to 6 P.M., except Sunday, noon to 5 P.M. At 2875 West Walnut (Highway 71). Call Manager at (501) 631-8940.

Springdale: Discount Corner Flea Market Mall. Daily, 9 A.M. to 6 P.M. Across from Layman's. Call Manager at (501) 756-0764.

CALIFORNIA

Anaheim: Anaheim Swap Meet. Every weekend, 6 A.M. to 3 P.M. At 1520 North Lemon Street. Call Luis Pintor, Manager, at (714) 525-3606.

Antioch: Antioch Flea Market. Every Friday, Saturday, and Sunday, 6 A.M. to 4 P.M. At 10th And L. Call Manager at (510) 778-6900.

Arcadia: Drive-in Swap Meet. Every weekend. At 4469 Live Oak Avenue. Call Salvador Sisneros, Manager, at (818) 447-8915.

Arlington: Van Buren Drive-In Swap Meet. Every weekend, 6:30 A.M. to 3 P.M. At 3035 Van Buren Blvd, just off 91 Freeway. Call Manager at (909) 688-2829 or (909) 688-2360 (drive-in).

Bakersfield: Pacific Theater Swap-O-Rama. Every weekend, 6 A.M. to 3 P.M. At 4501 Wible Road. Call Gary Rollins, Manager, at (805) 831-9346.

Berkeley: Berkeley Flea Market. Every weekend, 8 A.M. to 7:30 P.M. At the Ashby BART Station Parking Lot (Adeline and Ashby). Huge. Call Manager at (510) 644-0744.

Canoga Park: Valley Indoor Swap Meet. Every weekend, 10 A.M. to 6 P.M. At 6701 Variel Avenue. Call Debbie Gibson, Manager, at (818) 340-9120.

Casa de Fruta/Hollister: Casa de Fruta Antique and Collectors Nostalgic Peddler's Fair. Two weekends a year, generally at the end of May and in mid-August; Saturday, 3 P.M. to 9 P.M., and Sunday, 7 A.M. to 4 P.M.—call for dates. On Highway 152, between I-5 and State Highway 101, near Hollister and Gilroy. Parklike surroundings in a mountain setting. Barbecue and dance on Saturday night. Call Dick Clarke at (209) 683-2537.

City of Industry: Vineland Swap Meet. Daily, 6 A.M. to 3 P.M. At 443 North Vineland Avenue. Call Bob Simpson, Manager, at (818) 369-7224.

Clovis: Big Fresno Flea Market. Every weekend, 6 A.M. to 3 P.M. At the Fresno Fairgrounds. Call Manager at (209) 268-3646.

Clovis: Old Town Clovis Nostalgic Peddler's Fair. Three times a year, one day in spring and fall (around the end of March and the beginning of October), 8 A.M. to 4 P.M.—call for dates. In downtown Clovis (east of Fresno). Take Herndon exit off southbound Highway 99, then east to Clovis Avenue; northbound, use Clovis Avenue exit, then north to downtown Clovis. An antiques and collectibles street fair sponsored by the Business Organization of Old Town. "If you collect anything, you should be here." Call Dick Clarke at (209) 683-2537.

Concord: Solano Drive-In Flea Market. Every Saturday and Sunday, 7 A.M. to 4 P.M. At 1611 Solano Way, at the junction of Highway 4. Call Manager at (510) 687-6445 or (510) 825-1951.

Covina: Covina Indoor Swap Meet. Daily except Thursday. At 422 West Arrow Highway. Call Manager at (818) 967-1820.

Crescent City: Redwood Flea Market. Monthly—call for dates. At the fairgrounds. Call Amanda Plants, Manager, at (707) 839-3049.

Cupertino: De Anza College Flea Market. First Saturday of every month, 8 A.M. to 4 P.M. At 21250 Stevens Creek Boulevard on the college campus. Call Manager at (408) 864-8414.

Folsom: Annual Peddlers' Faire and Flea Market. Every September. On Sutter Street. Call Manager at (916) 985-7452.

Fresno: Sunnyside Swap Meet. Every Friday, Saturday, and Sunday, 6 A.M. to 3 P.M. At 5550 East Olive Street. Run by Pacific Theatres, 2500 East Carson, Lakewood, CA 90712—att: Tom Muller. Call Manager at (209) 255-7469.

Gardena: Vermont Swap Meet. Every weekend, 6 A.M. to 3 P.M.

At 17737 South Vermont Avenue. Call Manager at (310) 324-0923.

Lodi: Lodi District Chamber of Commerce Retail Merchants' Semi-Annual Flea Market. Twice annually—call for dates. In downtown Lodi. Call Lodi District Chamber of Commerce at (209) 367-7840.

Montclair/Pomona: Mission Drive-in Swap Meet. Every Wednesday, Friday, Saturday, and Sunday, 6 A.M. to 2 P.M. At 10798 Ramona, on the corner of Mission. Call Ronald Bacon or Manager at (909) 628-7943.

National City: National City Swap Meet. Every weekend, 7 A.M. to 4 P.M. At 3200 D Avenue. Call Elizabeth Gomez, Manager, at (619) 477-2203.

Niles: Niles Antique Flea Market. Annually, the last Sunday in August, all day. On the streets of Niles. Call Flea Market Committee at (510) 792-8023 from Tuesday through Friday, 11 A.M. to 1 P.M.

Orange: Orange Drive-in Swap Meet. Every weekend, 6 A.M. to 3:30 P.M. At 291 North State College Boulevard. Call Sandra Burnett, Manager, at (714) 634-4259.

Oroville: Chappell's Flea Market. Every weekend, 6:30 A.M. to 4 P.M. At 1141 Oro Dam Boulevard West. Call Manager at (916) 533-1324.

Pasadena: Pasadena Antique Market. Fourth Sunday of every month, 10 A.M. to 3 P.M. At 400 West Colorado Boulevard. Call Mr. Bill Coskey at (310) 455-2886.

Pico Rivera: Fiesta Swap Meet. Every weekend. At 8452 East Whittier Boulevard. Call Rick Millet, Chamber of Commerce, at (310) 949-5918.

Redding: Epperson Brothers Auction and Flea Market. Every weekend, 7 A.M. to 4 P.M. At 5091 Fig Tree Lane, off Airport Road, a mile south of the Redding Airport. Call Jack L. Epperson, Manager, at (916) 365-7242.

Reseda: Reseda Indoor Swap Meet. Daily except Monday, 6 A.M. to 10 P.M. At 18407 Sherman Way. Call Manager at (818) 344-6194.

Roseville: Denio's Roseville Farmer's Market and Auction (pronounced "Deny-oh"). Call Mr. Denio at (916) 782-2704 after 1 P.M.

Sacramento: Forty-niner Flea Market. Every Thursday through Sunday, 7 A.M. to 4 P.M. At 4450 Marysville Boulevard. Call Manager at (916) 923-9485 or (916) 920-3530 during swap meet hours.

San Fernando: San Fernando Swap Meet and Flea Market. Every Tuesday, Saturday, and Sunday, 7 A.M. to 4 P.M. At 585 Glenoaks Boulevard, at the corner of Arroyo; "100,000 bargains." Call Manager at (818) 361-1431.

San Francisco: America's Largest Antique and Collectible Sale. Three weekend events in February, May, and August: Saturday, 8 A.M. to 7 P.M., and Sunday, 8 A.M. to 5 P.M. At the Cow Palace. Take the Cow Palace exit off Route 280 or Route 101 and follow signposts. Upscale merchandise. Call Chris Palmer, Don Wirfs and Associates, at (503) 282-0877.

San Luis Obispo: Sunset Drive-in Theatre Swap Meet. Call Larry Rodkey, Manager, at (805) 544-4592.

San Ysidro: San Ysidro Swap Meet. Every Wednesday through Sunday, 8 A.M. to 5 P.M. At 2383 Via Segundo, on the west side of I-5, between Dairy Mart Road and the Via de San Ysidro. Call Manager at (619) 690-6756.

Santa Ana: Santa Ana Swap Meet. Daily, 10 A.M. to 8 P.M. At 3412 Westminster Avenue. No used or antique merchandise. Call Manager at (714) 554-8989.

Santa Cruz: Skyview Drive-in Flea Market. Every Thursday through Sunday. Call Manager at (408) 462-4442.

Slauson: Slauson Indoor Swap Meet. Daily. At 1600 West Slauson Avenue. Call Manager at (213) 778-6055.

South El Monte: Starlite Swap Meet. Every weekend, 6 A.M. to 3 P.M. At 2540 North Rosemead Boulevard. Call Shirley Chong at (818) 448-2810.

Spring Valley: Spring Valley Swap Meet. Every weekend. At 6377 Quarry Road. Call Rich or Mike, Managers, at (619) 463-1194.

Stockton: Stockton Flea Market. At 2542 South El Dorado. Call Tae W. Oh, Manager, at (209) 465-9933.

Thermalito: Oro Dam Flea Market. Every weekend. At 1141 Oro Dam Boulevard West. Call Manager at (916) 533-1324.

Torrance: Alpine Village Swap Meet. Every Tuesday through Sunday, 6 A.M. to 3:30 P.M. At 833 West Torrance Boulevard. Call Manager at (213) 770-1961.

APPENDIX / Colorado

Van Nuys: Mini Downtown Swap Meet. At 6357 Van Nuys Boulevard. Call Sam Hedjasi, Manager, at (818) 782-3161 or (818) 782-7185 or (818) 782-4470.
Venice: Fox Indoor Swap Meet. Daily. At 620 Lincoln Boulevard. Call Steven King, Manager, at (310) 392-3477.
Vernalis: Orchard Flea Market. Every weekend, 6 A.M. to 4 P.M. At Vernalis and Highway 132. Call Joe, Manager, at (209) 836-3148.
Whittier: Sundown Swap Meet. Every Thursday through Sunday. At 12322 East Washington Boulevard. Call Manager at (310) 696-7560.
Woodland Hills: Pierce College Swap Meet. Every Friday, Saturday, and Sunday, 5 A.M. to 4 P.M. On Winnetka Avenue. Call Manager at (818) 773-3661.
Yreka: Jim's Mill Street Flea Market. Every weekend, 7 A.M. to whenever. At 1420 Mill Road. Call Manager at (916) 842-6930.

COLORADO

Denver: Denver Collectors' Fair. At the National Western Complex. Call Manager at (303) 526-5494 or (800) 333-FLEA.
Denver: S-O-S Indoor Flea Market. Daily, 9 A.M. to 6 P.M., except Sunday, 10 A.M. to 5 P.M. At 3870 Tennyson Street. Call Adolph Greenmeyer, Manager, at (303) 458-8555.
Fort Collins: Foothills Indoor Flea Market. Daily, 10 A.M. to 6 P.M. At 6300 South College Street. Call Nan, Manager, at (303) 223-9069.
Longmont: Longmont Flea Market. Every weekend. At 473 Main Street. Call Cindy Grabrian at (303) 772-0968.

CONNECTICUT

Jewett City: College Mart Flea Market. Every Sunday, 9 A.M. to 4 P.M. On Wedgewood Drive, at Slater Mill Mall. Also auctioneers and appraisers. Call Bob Leone, Manager, at (203) 642-6248.
New Milford: Maplewood Indoor Flea Market. Every weekend 8 A.M. to 4 P.M. At 458 Danbury Road (Route 7), 4½ miles north of Exit 7 off I-84. Advertised as "Connecticut's largest indoor flea market." Call Manager at (203) 350-0454.

Woodbury: Woodbury Indoor Flea Market, The. Every weekend, 9 A.M. to 4 P.M. At 129 Main Street North, next to Books About Antiques. Take Exit 15 off I-84. Call Ron Varecka at (203) 263-5309.

DELAWARE

Dover: Spence's Auction and Flea Market. At 550 South New Street. Call Manager at (302) 734-3441.

Laurel: Route 13 Market. Every Friday, Saturday, and Sunday, 9 A.M. to 7 P.M. At the intersection of Routes 462 and 13. Call Manager at (302) 875-4800.

FLORIDA

Arcadia: Drive-in Auction and Flea Market. Every Saturday. At the old drive-in theater on Highway 17. Call Anthony DiLiberto, Manager, at (813) 494-2321.

Belleview: Antique Shop and Swap Meet. Every Tuesday, Wednesday, and Thursday, 10 A.M. to 4 P.M., and every Friday Saturday and Sunday, 7 A.M. to 4 P.M. At 12180 Highway 441, a mile south of Belleview. Also known as "Flea City U.S.A." Call Manager at (904) 245-FLEA.

Big Pine: Big Pine Flea Market. Every weekend, from October through May. On Route 1. Call Manager at (305) 872-4221.

Clearwater: Forty-niner Flea Market. Every weekend, 7 A.M. to 3 P.M. At 10525 49th Street North, near 105th Avenue North. Call Manager at (813) 573-3367.

Crystal River: Stokes Flea Market. Every Wednesday, Saturday, and Sunday (plus Thurdays, October through April), 7 A.M. to 5 P.M. Just off Route 44 East, four miles off Route 19 North. Call Dinah Williams, Manager, at (904) 746-7200.

Dade City: Joyland Drive-in Theatre Flea Market. Every weekend. At 2224 North Highway 301. Call Marvin Young at (904) 567-5085.

De Funiak Springs: De Funiak Flea Market. Every Friday, Saturday, and Sunday. On Route 90. Go north from I-10 on Route 331, then right at stoplight onto Route 90 to the market. Call Manager at (904) 892-3668.

Delray Beach: Delray Swap Shop and Flea Market. Every

Thursday and Friday, 8 A.M. to 2 P.M., and weekends, 8 A.M. to 3 P.M. At 2001 North Federal Highway. Call Loretta, Manager, at (407) 276-4012.

East Hillsboro: Funland Theatre and Swap Shop. Every Wednesday through Sunday, 6 A.M. to 2 P.M. At 2302 East Hillsboro Avenue, at the corner of 22nd Street. Call Manager at (813) 234-2311 (recording for theater) or (813) 237-0886.

Florida City: Florida City Swap Meet. Every weekend. At 450 Davis Parkway. Call Darrell Walrath, Manager, at (305) 247-2287.

Fort Myers: Ortiz Avenue Flea Market. Every Friday, 7 A.M. to 2 P.M.; every Saturday, 7 A.M. to 3 P.M.; and every Sunday, 6 A.M. to 3 P.M. At 1501 Ortiz Avenue. Take Exit 24 off I-75 onto Luckett Road, go to stoplight at the end of Luckett, then left to market. Call Mrs. Collins at (813) 694-5019.

Fruitland Park: North Lake Flea Market. Every Friday, Saturday, and Sunday, 7 A.M. to 3 P.M. Call Mr. Fudge or Manager at (904) 326-9335.

Homosassa: Howard's Flea Market. Every weekend, from 6 A.M. to whenever. At 6373 South Suncoast Boulevard (Route 19), approximately three miles south of Homosassa Springs. Call Tom and Alice Cushman, Managers, at (904) 628-3437.

Jacksonville: ABC Flea Market. Every Thursday through Sunday. At 10135 Beach Boulevard. Call Bill Lucas, Manager, at (904) 642-2717.

Jacksonville: Jacksonville Marketplace. Every Saturday and Sunday, 8 A.M. to 5 P.M. At 614 Pecan Park Road. Take Pecan Park exit off I-95. Big. Call Manager at (904) 751-6770.

Jacksonville: Playtime Twin Drive-in Flea Market. Every Wednesday, Friday, Saturday, and Sunday, 7 A.M. to 1 P.M. At 6300 Blanding Boulevard. Call Manager at (904) 771-9939 or (904) 771-2300.

Lake City: Lake City Flea Market. Every weekend, 7 A.M. to 4 P.M. At the fairgrounds. Call Ralph Tiner at (904) 752-1999.

Lake City: Webb's Antiques. On U.S. 41-441; take Exit 80 off I-75. Conveniently located between Lake City and High Springs. Formerly known as Grandpas's Barn Flea Market. Call Manager at (904) 758-5564.

Lake Worth: Trail Drive-in Swap Shop. Every Thursday, Saturday, and Sunday, dawn to 3 P.M. On Lake Worth Road between Congress Avenue and Military Trail, at the Trail Drive-In Theatre. Call Manager at (407) 965-4518.

Lauderdale Lakes: Bazaar Flea Market. Every Wednesday through Sunday, 10 A.M. to 6 P.M. (open to 9 P.M. Friday and Saturday). At 3200 West Oakland Park Boulevard. Call Manager at (305) 739-2805.

Miami: 183rd Street Flea Market Mini-Mall. Every Wednesday and Sunday, 10 A.M. to 7 P.M.; every Thursday, Friday, and Saturday, 10 A.M. to 9 P.M. At 18200 N.W. 27th Avenue, at 183rd Street, 16 blocks south of Joe Robbie Stadium (where the Dolphins play). Lots of shops but not for collectibles or used items; claims to have the largest selection of gold jewelry of any flea market in South Florida. Call Manager at (305) 624-1756.

Miami: Tropicaire Flea Market. Every weekend. At 9769 South Dixie Highway. Call Manager at (305) 663-6570.

New Port Richey: Indoor Fleas. Every Friday, Saturday, and Sunday. At 3621 U.S. Highway 19. Call Manager at (813) 842-3665 on Thursday, ask for Marie.

North Miami: North Miami Flea Market. At 14135 Northwest 7th Avenue. Call Kris Glaser at (305) 685-7721.

North Miami Beach: Oakland Park Flea Market. Call Shirley Pralins, Manager, at (305) 651-9530.

Oakland Park: Oakland Park Flea Market. Every Thursday through Sunday, 10 A.M. to whenever. At 3161 West Oakland Park Boulevard. Call Manager at (305) 949-7959 or (305) 733-4617.

Okeechobee: Market Place Flea Market. Every weekend, 8 A.M. to 3 P.M. At 3600 Highway 441 South. Call Manager at (813) 467-6803.

Orlando: Orlando Flea Market. Every weekend, 8 A.M. to 4 P.M. At 5022 South Orange Blossom Trail, south of Holden Avenue and north of Oak Ridge Road. Call Manager at (407) 857-0048.

Ormond Beach: Nova Swap Shop. Every Wednesday through Sunday, 6 A.M. to 2 P.M. On Nova Road at the junction with Route 40. Call Manager at (904) 672-3014 or (813) 646-2436 (main office).

Panama City: Springfield Flea Market. Every Friday and Saturday, 10 A.M. to 4 P.M. At 3425 East Business 98 at the junction of Route 22 (behind the discount tire store). Call Manager at (904) 769-4999.

Pensacola: B and B Flea Market. Daily, 9 A.M. to 5 P.M. At 3721-B Navy Boulevard. Call Jean Boucher, Manager, at (904) 455-3200.

Port Charlotte: Poor Jed's Flea Market. Every Friday, Saturday, and Sunday, 9 A.M. to 5 P.M. At 4628 Tamiami Trail (Route 41), at the corner of Kings Highway in Charlotte Harbor. Call Manager at (813) 629-1223 or (813) 629-2259. This is more of a "merchandise mart" than a true flea market, with mainly new/discount merchandise, but there are a few stalls with secondhand and collectible stuff too.

Port Charlotte: Sun Flea Market. Every Friday, Saturday, and Sunday, 9 A.M. to 4 P.M. At 18505 Paulson Drive, at the intersection of Route 776. Call Manager at (813) 255-3532.

Riviera Beach: Riviera Beach Swap Shop. Every Wednesday, Friday, Saturday, and Sunday, 6 A.M. to 3 P.M. At the Riviera Beach Drive-In. Call Manager at (407) 844-5836.

Saint Augustine: Saint John's Marketplace. Every weekend, 9 A.M. to 5 P.M. At 2495 S.R. 207. Call John Alexon or Bob Hunter at (904) 824-4210 or (904) 824-9840.

Seffner: Joe and Jackie's Flea Market. Every weekend, 8 A.M. to 4 P.M. At 311 Martin Luther King, Jr., Boulevard (Highway 574). Call Joe Miller, Manager, at (813) 689-6318.

Tallahassee: Flea Market Tallahassee. Every weekend, 9 A.M. to 5 P.M. At 200 Capital Circle Southwest. Up to 30,000 shoppers each weekend. Call Manager at (904) 877-3811; fax: (904) 656-3137 (office hours are market hours plus Friday, 9 A.M. to 4 P.M., and Monday, 9 A.M. to noon).

Tallahassee: Uncle Bob's Flea Market. Every weekend. At 1501 Capital Circle Northwest. Call Manager at (904) 576-2949.

Tampa: American Legion Market, The. At 929 East 139th Avenue. Call North Tampa Post 334 at (813) 971-3699.

Tampa: Golden Nugget Flea Market. Every weekend. At 8504 Adamo Drive East (Highway 60). Call at (813) 621-0045.

Thonotosassa: North 301 Flea Market. Every Thursday through Sunday, 7 A.M. to 5 P.M. Call Jim Shafer, Manager, at (813) 986-1023.

GEORGIA

Albany: Albany Flea Market. Every weekend, 9 A.M. to 5 P.M. (vendors may arrive as early as 7 A.M.). On U.S. Route 19 at Jefferson. Call Manager at (912) 435-0409.

Albany: Kitty's Flea Market. Every Friday, Saturday, and Sunday, 6 A.M. to 5 P.M. At 3229 Sylvester Road. Call Manager at (912) 432-0007.

Atlanta: Atlanta Flea Market and Antique Center. Every Friday, Saturday, and Sunday, 11 A.M. to 7 P.M. At 5360 Peachtree Industrial Boulevard. Call Manager at (404) 458-0456.

Atlanta: Great Five Points Flea Market. Every Monday through Saturday. At 82 Peachtree Street Southwest. Call Lt. Evans, Manager, at (404) 681-9439.

Chamblee: Buford Highway Flea Market. Every Friday and Saturday, 11 A.M. to 9:30 P.M., and every Sunday, noon to 7 P.M. At 5000 Buford Highway, one mile inside Perimeter (I-285) in the northern area of the city of Atlanta. Good for bargain hunters chasing discounts on new products. Call Manager at (404) 452-7140.

Cumming: Dixie 400 Flea Market. Every weekend, 9 A.M. to 6 P.M. On Highway 400, about eight miles north of town. Call Manager at (404) 889-5895.

Decatur: Flea Market Candler. Every·Wednesday through Sunday, noon to 7 P.M. On Candler Road. Call Manager at (404) 289-0804.

Decatur: Kudzu Flea Market. Every weekend. At 2874 East Ponce de Leon. Call Manager at (404) 373-6498.

Waycross: Chrystal's Flea Market. Every weekend: Saturday, 8 A.M. to 5 P.M., and Sunday, noon to 4 P.M. At 1631 Genoa Street. Call Jimmy Langford at (912) 283-9808.

West Point: Hood's Flea Market and Crafts. Daily except Wednesday and Sunday, 9 A.M. to 5:30 P.M. At 710 Third Avenue, in downtown West Point. Call Syble Hood or Angelia Anderson at (706) 643-4771.

IDAHO

Cascade: Cascade Farmer's and Flea Market. Every Friday, Saturday, and Sunday plus holiday Mondays from Labor Day through Memorial Day (length of season depends on weather), plus a two-week run starting July Fourth weekend. On Highway 55. Call Manager at (208) 382-3600 or (208) 382-4894.

Donnelly: Donnelly Flea Market. Every Friday, Saturday, and Sunday from May through September. On Highway 55. Call Manager at (208) 325-8604.

ILLINOIS

Amboy: Amboy Flea Market. Third Sunday of every month from February through November. At the Lee County Fairgrounds. Call Bill Edwards, Manager, at (815) 626-7601.

Bloomington: Third Sunday Market. Third Sunday of every month. Call Carol Raycraft, Manager, at (309) 452-7926.

Chicago: Buyers Market. Every weekend, 8 A.M. to 5 P.M. At 4545 West Division Street. Call Manager at (312) 342-4546 or (312) 227-1189.

Chicago: Loew's Double Outdoor Flea Market. Every weekend, 5:30 A.M. to 3 P.M. At 2800 West Columbus Avenue. Call Manager at (312) 925-9602.

Chicago: Morgan Market. Every weekend. At 375 North Morgan Street. Call Bonnie-Ann Ryser, Manager, at (312) 455-8900.

Peotone: Antique Show. Fourth Sunday of every month. At the fairgrounds. Call Robert W. Mitchell, Sr., at (815) 857-2253.

Princeton: Second Sunday Flea Market. Second Sunday of every month, all day. On the Bureau County Fairgrounds. Call Tony Martin, Manager, at (815) 872-1601 or (815) 875-1948 (fairgrounds).

Tinley Park: I-80 Flea Market. Every weekend. Call R. Bruno at (708) 532-8238.

Wheaton: Du Page Antique and Flea Market. Third Sunday of every month, all day. At the Du Page County Fairgrounds. Call Marilyn Sugarman, Manager, at (708) 455-6090.

INDIANA

Centerville: Centerville Flea Market. Every weekend, 7 A.M. to 6 P.M. At 2131 North Centerville Road. Call Ed Newman at (317) 855-3912.

Fort Wayne: Fort Wayne Flea Market. Every Friday, Saturday, and Sunday, 9 A.M. to 6 P.M. Call Manager at (219) 447-0081.

Indianapolis: Indiana Flea Market. Monthly on Friday and Saturday—call for dates. On the Indiana State Fairgrounds at 1202 East 38th Street. Call the fairgrounds at (317) 927-7500.

Kingman: Jipville Corner Flea Market. Every weekend in summer (plus a festival in mid-October—call for dates). At the junction of Routes 41 and 234. Call Penny, Manager, at (317) 397-8352.

Lake Station: Central Avenue Flea Market. Every weekend, 9 A.M. to 5 P.M. At 2750 Central Avenue. Take I-94 to Ripley Street. Call Verne, Manager, at (219) 962-5524.

Monticello: Twin Lakes Flea Market. Every Friday, Saturday, Sunday, and holidays from the first weekend in May through Labor Day, 9 A.M. to 5 P.M. At 3016 West Shafer Drive. Take Route 24 to Sixth Street, one mile. Located in a resort community visited by over a million vacationers each summer. Market is one mile from Indiana Beach Resort. Call Guy Harrison at (219) 583-4146.

North Vernon: Green Meadow Flea Market. Every weekend. On Route 5. Call Charles Couchman, Manager, at (812) 346-1990.

IOWA

Des Moines: Fairgrounds Flea Market. Every month from October through April—call for dates. In the 4-H Building at the State Fairgrounds. Run by the Simpson Methodist Church. Call Manager, c/o Simpson Methodist Church, at (515) 262-4267.

What Cheer: Collector's Paradise Flea Market. Irregular schedule—call for dates. At the County Fairgrounds. Call Larry Nicholson at (515) 634-2109.

KANSAS

Kansas City: Boulevard Swap and Shop. Every weekend, 6 A.M. to 3 P.M. At 10510 Merriam Lane. Call Wesley Lane, Manager, at (913) 262-2414.

Topeka: Rollaway Flea Market. Every weekend, 10 A.M. to 4 P.M. At 3505 Southeast 10th Street. Call Manager at (913) 234-4420.

KENTUCKY

Flemingsburg: Flemingsburg Monday Court Days. Second Monday of every October, plus the preceding Saturday and Sunday, all day. All over town. Call Fleming County Rescue Squad at (606) 845-8801.

Guthrie: Southern Kentucky Flea Market. Every Wednesday through Sunday. At 10741 Dixie Beeline Highway (Highway 41), about a half mile out of town. Take Exit 4 off I-24 onto Route 79 to Route 41. Call Manager at (502) 483-9771 or (502) 483-2166.

Leitchfield: Bratcher's Flea Market. Every Wednesday and Saturday. On Highway 62 East. Call Gladys Bratcher at (502) 259-3571.

Lexington: Lexington Flea Market. Every Friday, Saturday, and Sunday. At 1059 Industry Road. Call Cathy, Manager, at (606) 252-1076.

Lexington: Mid-State Flea Market. Every Wednesday through Sunday, 9 A.M. to 6 P.M. Call Charles Reeves, Manager, at (606) 255-7419.

London: Flea Land Flea Market. Every weekend, 9 A.M. to 5 P.M. On Barberville Road (Route 229) at 192 Bypass. Take Exit 38 (London) off I-75 North, then right and to sixth stoplight, then right and "you're looking right at it." Call Manager at (606) 864-FLEA.

Louisville: Kentucky Flea Market. Several shows every summer, all day—call for dates. At the Kentucky Fair and Exposition Center. Big. Call Stewart Promotions at (502) 456-2244.

Paducah: Great American Flea Market. Third weekend of every month. At the racetrack. Call Dottie Stout, Manager, at (502) 443-5800.

LOUISIANA

Baton Rouge: Deep South Flea Market. Every Friday, Saturday, and Sunday. At 5350 Florida Boulevard. Call Billy Vallery at (504) 923-0333; (504) 923-0142 for rental info.

Baton Rouge: Merchant's Landing Flea Market. Every weekend. At 9800 Florida Boulevard, three blocks east of Airline Boulevard, at the Broadmoor Shopping Mall. Call Manager at (504) 925-1664.

MARYLAND

Baltimore: Hilltop Indoor Flea Market. Every weekend, 10 A.M. to 4 P.M. At 5437-39 Reisterstown Road at Menlo Drive. Call Delores Moore at (410) 358-5870.

Baltimore: North Point Drive-in Flea Market. Every weekend, 7 A.M. to 2 P.M. At 4001 North Point Boulevard. Call Manager at (410) 477-1337.

Columbia: Columbia Antiques Market. Every Sunday, from late April through late October, 10 A.M. to 4 P.M. At the Columbia Mall, between Baltimore and Washington, D.C. Take Exit 175 (Columbia exit) off I-95. Flea market operates in the parking lot, near the Sears (and almost 200 other shops). Call Bellman Corporation at (410) 329-2188 or (410) 679-2288.

Towson: Towson High School Flea Market. Second Sunday in November. On Cedar Avenue, at the high school. Temporarily suspended for renovation—call ahead. Call Mary Hague at (410) 377-0704.

MASSACHUSETTS

Brimfield: Brimfield Acres North. Every Friday through Monday from October through April, plus three three-day events annually in May, July, and September (timed to coincide with the other major Brimfield events), 7:30 A.M. to 3 P.M. On Route 20 a mile or so west of center of town—look for signs. Call Colleen James at (508) 754-4185.

Brimfield: Crystal Brook Flea Market. Three three-day events annually in May, July, and September (timed to coincide with the other major Brimfield events), dawn to dusk—call for dates. On Route 20 just west of town. Call Richard and Maureen Ethier at (413) 245-7647.

Brimfield: May's Antique Market. Three three-day events annually in May, July, and September (timed to coincide with the other major Brimfield events), 9 A.M. to whenever—call for dates. On Route 20. "There's always a crowd at May's." Call Richard or Laura May at (413) 245-9271.

Brockton: Cary Hill Flea Market. Every weekend. At 220 East Ashland Street. Call Manager at (508) 583-3100.

Chilmark: Community Church Flea Market. Every Saturday, 9 A.M. to noon. At the Chilmark Community Church, at the Menemsha Crossroad. Call Manager at (508) 645-3100.

Kingston: Kingston 106 Antiques Market. Every Sunday, 9 A.M. to 4 P.M. At 20 Wapping Road. Take Route 3 south to Route 106 and follow signposts. Not for transient vendors. Call Barbara Stevens at (617) 934-6711 or (617) 934-5843.

Ludlow: Ludlow Flea Market. Every Sunday, 6:30 A.M. to 5 P.M. At 1099 Center Street (Route 21 North), three miles from Exit 7 off the Massachusetts Turnpike. Call Jack or Grace Machado at (413) 589-0419.

Lynn: Merchandise Mart. Every weekend, 7 A.M. to 5 P.M. At 159 Washington Street. Mostly modern stuff, but a small market outside. Call Manager at (617) 598-5450.

Newbury: Byfield Expo. Every weekend in winter, 7:30 A.M. to 2 P.M.; vendor setup from 7 A.M. In Newbury at Bufield. Take Exit 55 off I-95. Call Dave Casey at (508) 462-4711; fax: (508) 463-0653.

North Quincy: Naponset Flea Market. Every weekend, 9 A.M. to 5 P.M. At 2 Hancock Street. Call David Stanton, Manager, at (617) 472-3558.

Norton: Norton Flea Market. Every Sunday from mid-April through mid-November. At 8 Smith Street. Call Manager at (508) 285-6765 or (508) 285-6640.

Revere: Revere Swap 'N' Shop. Every weekend, 7 A.M. to 4 P.M. At 565 Squire Road, just off the Northeast Expressway (I-95). Call John Nerich, Manager, at (617) 289-7100.

Rowley: Ginny's Flea Market. Every Sunday during summer. At 31 Main Street, on the Grounds of the Rowley Antique Center. Call Manager at (518) 948-2591.

Rowley: Todd Farm Flea Market. Every Sunday. On Route 1A. From Boston, take Route 1 or I-95 to Route 133, then east to Route 1A and then north one mile. Call Starr Todd at (603) 926-8163.

Sturbridge: Country Peddler Show. Annually, three days in late July: Friday, 5 P.M. to 9 P.M.; Saturday, 9 A.M. to 5 P.M.; and Sunday, 11 A.M. to 4 P.M.—call for dates. At the Sturbridge Host Hotel, on Route 20 west of I-86, opposite Old Sturbridge Village. Take Exit 9 off the Massachusetts Turnpike. Features high-end collectibles and antiques; not for "junktiquers" or transient vendors. Call American Memories, Inc., at (616) 423-8367.

Westboro: Westboro Antique and Flea Market. Every Sunday, 8 A.M. to 5 P.M. At the junction of Routes 9 and 135-E, across from Westmeadow Plaza. Call Jeff Salatin, Manager, at (508) 836-3880.

Worcester: Worcester Flea Market. Open weekends except summertime. At 72 Pullman Street. Call Manager at (508) 852-6622.

MICHIGAN

Armada: Armada Flea Market. Every Sunday and Tuesday from April through October (season depends on weather), 6 A.M. to 3 P.M. On Ridge Road, a mile east of town. Call Manager at (810) 784-9194.

Detroit: Grand River Flea Market. Every Thursday through Saturday, 10 A.M. to 6 P.M. At 12555 Grand River, at Meyers. Call Manager at (313) 834-4580.

Kalamazoo: Fairgrounds Flea Market. At the Kalamazoo County Fairgrounds. Call Manager at (616) 383-8778.

Lansing: Flea Market, The. Daily except Sunday, noon to 6 P.M. At 2016 East Michigan. Call Manager at (517) 372-5356.

Lapeer: Elba Lion's Club Flea Market. Every Sunday in summer. At 425 County Center Street. Call Manager at (313) 232-4879.

Marshall: Cornwell's Flea Market. Every weekend from May through September, 9 A.M. to 5 P.M. On 15-Mile Road about six miles west of Marshall. Call Manager at (616) 781-4293.

Muskegon: Golden Token Flea Market. Every Saturday, 6 A.M. to 2 P.M. At 1300 East Laketon Avenue, a block from U.S. Route 31. Call Manager at (616) 773-1137.

Muskegon: Select Auditorium Flea Market. Every Saturday, early morning to 2 P.M. At 1445 East Laketon Avenue. Call Manager at (616) 726-5707.

Paw Paw: Busy Bea's Flea Market. Every weekend (plus holiday Mondays), 8 A.M. to 5 P.M. On Red Arrow Highway. Take Paw Paw exit off Route 94, then left at light. Call Manager at (616) 657-6467.

Plainwell: Plainwell Flea Market. Every Wednesday through Sunday. At 79 South Tenth Street, in the north end of town. Call Manager at (616) 685-5443.

Port Huron: Wurzel's Flea Market. Every weekend, 10 A.M. to 5 P.M. At 4189 Keewahdin Road. Call Manager at (810) 385-4283.

Portland: Portland Flea Market. Every Wednesday, 10 A.M. to 9 P.M., and every Saturday and Sunday, 10 A.M. to 5 P.M. At 143 Kent Street, at Grand River. Call Manager at (517) 647-4484.

Ravenna: Ravenna Flea Market. Every Monday. At 1685 19-Mile Road. Call James Lund, Manager, at (616) 696-1247.

Romulus: Greenlawn Grove Flea Market. At 1172 West Front. Call Manager at (313) 941-6930.

Royal Oak: Royal Oak Flea Market. Every Sunday, 10 A.M. to 5 P.M. At 316 East Eleven Mile Road, a block and a half east of Main Street, between Woodward and I-75. Call Manager at (313) 548-8822.

Saginaw: Saginaw Flea Market. Every Thursday from mid-April through mid-October. Call Manager at (517) 790-9537.

Warren: Michigan Flea Market. Every Friday and Saturday, noon to 9 P.M., and every Sunday, 10 A.M. to 6 P.M. At 24100 Groesback Highway. Call Manager at (810) 771-3535.

Warren: Riverland Amusement Park Flea Market. Every Wednesday. At 44000 Van Dyke Road. Call Manager at (313) 731-9590.

Ypsilanti: Huron Trade Center and Flea Market. Every Friday, 4 P.M. to 9 P.M., and Saturday and Sunday, 10 A.M. to 6 P.M. At 210 East Michigan Avenue. Call Manager at (313) 480-1539.

MINNESOTA

Hopkins: Traders Market Flea Market. Two three-day events (Saturday through Monday) per year, in July and September, 8 A.M. to 5 P.M., except Sunday, 9 A.M. to 5 P.M. Twenty minutes south of the Twin Cities. Take Route 35W south and Elko-New Market Road (County Road 2), Exit 76. Call Manager at (612) 461-2400 or (for vendor info) (612) 931-9748.

MISSISSIPPI

Amory: Big Bee Waterway Trade Days. On the first Monday of every month, plus the preceding Friday, Saturday, and Sunday. At 30211 Highway 371 North. Call Manager at (601) 256-1226.

Charleston: Flo-Mart. Daily. On Highway 35 South. Small. Call Floyd B. Brown at (601) 647-5995.

Pascagoula: Jackson County Flea Market. Daily. At 2519 Telephone Road. Call Manager at (601) 762-9994.

Vicksburg: Battlefield Trade Days. The Friday, Saturday, and Sunday preceding the second Monday of every month. Take Exit 15 off I-20 at Flowers. Call Amanda Fulton, Manager, at (601) 852-5433.

MISSOURI

Imperial: Barnhart Flea Market. Every weekend, 6 A.M. to 5 P.M. At 6850 Highway 61/67. Take I-55 to Barnhart Antonio Exit, then go east to Highway 61/67, approximately one quarter mile. Call Manager at (314) 464-5503.

Joplin: Joplin Flea Market. Every weekend, 8 A.M. to 5 P.M. At 12th and Virginia Avenue, one block east of Main Street. Over 40,000 square feet of indoor selling area. Call LaVerne Miller at (417) 623-3743.

Pevely: Big Pevely Flea Market. Every Saturday and Sunday (sellers set up Friday), 7 A.M. to 5 P.M. At 61 South Drive-In Theatre in Pevely (south of Saint Louis). Said to be one of the larger markets in Missouri. Call Ken Smith, Manager, at (314) 479-5400.

471

Poplar Bluffs: Country Junction Flea Market. Daily except Tuesday, 9 A.M. to 5 P.M. Call Manager at (686-2275).

Sedalia: Sho-me Flea Market. Monthly. At the State Fairgrounds. Call Pat Klatt at (816) 530-5600 (State Fairgrounds).

Seligman: Highway 37 Flea Market. Daily except Friday, 9 A.M. to 5 P.M. On Highway 37. Call Manager at (417) 662-3890.

Springfield: Olde Towne Antiques Mall and Flea Market. Daily except Tuesday. At 600 Booneville Avenue. Call Manager at (417) 831-6665.

Springfield: Viking Flea Market. Every Monday through Saturday, 9 A.M. to 5 P.M., and every Sunday, noon to 5 P.M. At 628 West Chase. Call Manager at (417) 869-7075.

Wentzville: Wentzville Flea Market. Every Sunday. Sponsored by the Wentzville Community Club. Call Fred House, Manager, at (314) 332-9027 (after 9 P.M.).

MONTANA

Billings: Heartland Marketplace. Daily: every Monday through Saturday, 10 A.M. to 6 P.M., and every Sunday, noon to 4 P.M. At 3405 Central Avenue. Outdoors in summer (while it lasts). Call Mary, Manager, at (406) 655-0747.

Great Falls: Great Falls Farmer's Market. Every Wednesday and Saturday. At the Civic Center on Irish Lane. Call Manager at (406) 453-5874.

NEBRASKA

Lincoln: Flea Market Emporium. Daily: every Monday through Saturday, 9 A.M. to 6 P.M., and every Sunday, noon to 5 P.M. At 3235 South 13th Street, between High and Arapahoe (Indian Village Shopping Center). Call Ruth Trobee at (402) 423-5380.

NEVADA

Las Vegas: Gemco Swap Meet. Every Friday, Saturday, and Sunday, 10 A.M. to 6 P.M. At 3455 Boulder Highway. Call Mr. Mike Levy at (702) 641-7927.

Sparks/Reno: El Rancho Swap Meet. Every weekend, 6:30 A.M. to 4 P.M. At the theater, 555 El Rancho Drive. Call Manager at (702) 358-6920 or (702) 331-3227.

NEW HAMPSHIRE

Davisville: Davisville Barn Sale and Flea Market. Every Sunday from May through October. Take Exit 7 off I-89 (12 miles north of Concord, New Hampshire), then east on Route 103 one half mile. Look for signs. Call Mr. Toby Nickerson at (603) 746-4000 or (800) 662-2612.
Newington: Newington Star Center Flea Market. Every Sunday. At 26 Fox Run Road. Take Spaulding Turnpike off I-95 (from Portsmouth Rotary) and look for signs. Call Mr. Robert J. Hajjar at (603) 431-9403 or (617) 683-3870.

NEW JERSEY

Clementon: Route 30 Mall. Thursday through Saturday, 10 A.M. to 9 P.M., and Sunday, 10 A.M. to 6 P.M. At 260 White Horse Pike. Call Manager at (609) 784-6544.
Clifton: Boy's and Girl's Club of Clifton Flea Market. Monthly, all day—call for dates. At 802 Clifton Avenue. Call Jar Promotions at (201) 977-8134.
Hackensack: Packard's Variety Market. Every Thursday evening, 5 P.M. to 8 P.M., every Saturday, 10 A.M. to 8 P.M., and every Sunday, 10 A.M. to 6 P.M. At 630 Main Street. Call Philip LaPorta at (201) 489-8809 or (201) 933-4388.
Lambertville: Golden Nugget Antique Flea Market. Every weekend. On Route 29. Call Manager at (609) 397-0811.
Rahway: Rahway Italian-American Club Flea Market. Every Wednesday. At 530 New Brunswick Avenue, at the Italian-American club. Call Manager at (908) 574-3840.
Rancocas Woods: William Spencer's Antique Show and Sale. Second Sunday of every month from March through December, 9 A.M. to 5 P.M. There are also crafts shows, usually the fourth Sunday of every month—call for dates. At 118 Creek Road, one mile from Rancocas Woods exit (Exit 43) off I-295. Upscale merchandise. Call Orin Houser at (609) 235-1830.
Wayne: Wayne Elk Lodge Flea Market. Monthly—call for dates,

all day. At 50 Hinchman Avenue (near the King George Diner), at the Elk Lodge. Call Jar Promotions at (201) 977-8134.

Woodstown: Cowtown. Every Tuesday and Saturday, 8 A.M. to 4 P.M. On Route 40. Call Bob Becker at (609) 769-3000.

NEW MEXICO

Albuquerque: Open-Air Flea Market at the Fairgrounds. Every weekend except in September, 6 A.M. to 4 P.M. On the New Mexico State Fairgrounds. Good on Native American crafts as well as antiques, collectibles, etc. Call Manager at (505) 265-1791.

Albuquerque: Star Flea Market. At 543 Coors Boulevard Southwest. Call Manager at (505) 831-3106.

Carlsbad: Bullring, The. Every weekend. At 4303 Nationals Parks Highway. Call W. H. Reynolds at (505) 887-9174.

Elephant Butte: Elephant Butte Flea Market. On Highway 195. Call Manager at (505) 744-5702.

Gallup: Gallup Flea Market. Every weekend. In the heart of "Indian Country." Call Manager at (505) 722-7328.

Las Cruces: Big Daddy's Flea Market. Every weekend, 6 A.M. to 4 P.M. At 7320 North Main Street, out by the high school. Call Frank Sortino at (505) 382-9404.

NEW YORK

Bronx: Saint John's School Flea Market. Every Saturday, September through June. At 3030 Godwin Terrace. Call Manager at (718) 543-3003.

Clarence: Antique World and Marketplace. Every Sunday, 8 A.M. to 4 P.M. At 10995 Main Street. Call Katy, Manager, at (716) 759-8483.

Commack: Long Island Arena Flea Market. Every weekend. At 88 Veterans Highway. Call Bernadette Cosgrove, Manager, at (516) 499-0800.

Long Island City: Busy Flea Market. Every Saturday, 9 A.M. to 4 P.M. At 46th Street and Northern Boulevard. Call at (718) 397-1898.

Lowman: Lowman Flea Market. Every weekend, 8 A.M. to 4 P.M. On Route 17. Call Mike LeRose at (607) 734-3670.

Madison: Country Walk Antiques Flea Market. Every Sunday, 8 A.M. to 4 P.M. On Route 20 between Madison and Bouckville. Call Manager at (315) 893-7621.

Maybrook: Maybrook Flea Market. Every Sunday, 8 A.M. to 4 P.M. (vendors begin setting up as early as 5:30 A.M.). On Route 208. Call Manager at (914) 427-2715.

New York City: Stonewall Festival and Village Reform Democratic Club Street Fair. Twice annually, on a Saturday in mid-June (Village Reform Democratic Club) and on a Saturday in late September (Stonewall), noon to 7 P.M. On Washington Place between Broadway and Washington Square East, and along sidewalk of Broadway between West Fourth and Waverly Place. Call Celebration Enterprises, Inc., at (212) 751-4932.

New York City: Third Avenue Midtown Festival. Annually on a Sunday in mid-October, 11 A.M. to 6 P.M. On Third Avenue between 46th and 56th Streets. Sponsored by the East 50s Association. Call Celebration Enterprises, Inc., at (212) 751-4932.

Plattsburgh: Bargaineer Flea Market. Daily. At 39 Bridge Street. Fewer than a dozen vendors, but mainly collectibles and antiques. Call John Silver, Manager, at (518) 561-3525.

Queens: Bingo Hall Flea Market. Every Sunday. At 117-09 Hillside Avenue (at Myrtle Avenue) in Richmond Hill, Queens. Call David Gross at (718) 847-1418.

Schenectady: White House Flea Market. Every Wednesday through Sunday, 9 A.M. to 5 P.M., except Thursday, 9 A.M. to 9 P.M. At 952 State Street (Route 5), close to Exit 25 off the New York State Thruway (I-87). Call Rudy or Jeanette Fecketter at (518) 346-7851.

Valley Cottage: Antique Garage Sale. First Sunday of every month. Take Exit 12 off I-87 South (New York State Thruway), then left at exit, two miles north of intersection, two tenths mile past Lake Ridge Plaza (look for sign on left). Call Dominick, Manager, at (914) 268-1730.

Weedsport: New Weedsport Flea Market. Every weekend. On Route 31. Call Paul Jackson, Manager, at (315) 834-6843.

NORTH CAROLINA

Asheville: Dreamland Flea Market. Every Wednesday, Friday, Saturday, and Sunday, 7 A.M. to 4:30 P.M. On South Tunnel Road. Call Manager at (704) 255-7777.

Cherokee: Gateway Flea Market. Every Friday, Saturday, and Sunday. On Highway 441. Call Manager at (704) 497-9664.

Durham: Starlite Drive-in Flea Market. Every weekend, 8 A.M. to 4 P.M. At 2523 East Club Boulevard, two blocks from Exit 179 off I-85. Call Manager at (919) 688-1037.

Eden: Eden Flea Market. Every weekend. At 122 North Van Buren Road. Small. Call Manager at (910) 627-9440.

Fayetteville: Great American Marketplace. At 4909 Raeford Road. Friendly atmosphere and courteous staff. Call Manager at (919) 423-4440.

Fayetteville: U.S. Flea Market Mall. Every Friday, Saturday, and Sunday, 10 A.M. to 7 P.M. At 504 North McPherson Church Road. Take I-95 to Business 95 (301) to Owen Drive to McPherson Church Road. 95 percent new merchandise. Call Manager at (910) 868-5011.

Franklin: Franklin Flea and Craft Market. Daily except Monday and Wednesday from April through November. On Highlands Road (Route 64). Call Manager at (704) 524-6658 (office hours are 8 A.M. to 5 P.M., Thursday through Sunday).

Gastonia: Interstate 85 Flea Market. On Bessemer City Road; take Exit 15 off I-85. Call Manager at (704) 867-2317.

Gastonia: State Line Flea Market. Every weekend. On Anne Neely Road. Call Bill Hall, Manager, at (704) 861-8874.

Goldsboro: Wayne County Flea Market. Every weekend, 8 A.M. to 5 P.M. At the fairgrounds, on Highway 70. Call Manager at (919) 731-2854.

Greensboro: Flea, The. Every Friday, 4 P.M. to 9 P.M.; Saturday, 8 A.M. to 6 P.M.; and Sunday, 8 A.M. to 5 P.M. At 3220 North O'Henry Boulevard. Thirty thousand square feet of selling area. Call Paul Cockman at (910) 621-9210.

Greensboro: Piedmont Triad Flea Market. Every weekend. At 7061 Albert Pick Road, near the airport. Take Exit 210 off I-40. Call Manager at (910) 668-7283.

Hickory: Hickory Flea and Farmers Market. Every Thursday. At

951 Cloninger Road Northeast (Route 1). Call Manager at (704) 324-7354.

Jacksonville: Market Place of Jacksonville, The. At 174 College Plaza (Western Boulevard). "Over 800,000 square feet of food, fun, and bargains." Family owned and operated. Call Gene Ballard at (910) 347-2747.

Kannapolis: Koco's Flea Mall. Every Friday, Saturday, and Sunday. At 485 South Cannon Boulevard. Over 50,000 square feet of selling space. Call Manager at (704) 938-9100.

Lexington: Farmer's Market and Flea Market. Every Tuesday, 6 A.M. to 3 P.M. Take I-85 to Business 85 to Old 64 West, then one mile; look for signs. On Monday evening from 3 P.M. to 9 P.M., and on Tuesday mornings from 5:30 A.M. to 1 P.M. There is also a wholesale market with up to 200 vendors (this part of the market is not open to the public). Call Manager at (704) 246-2157.

Lumberton: Trader's Station Flea and Farmer's Market. Every Friday, Saturday, and Sunday, 8 A.M. to 6 P.M. On Route 41 East. Take Exit 20 off I-95 and follow signs to Route 41 East, then three miles on the right. Call Manager at (910) 618-0004 or (910) 739-4268.

Monroe: Sweet Union Flea Market. Every weekend. On Highway 74. Call Manager at (704) 283-7985.

Mount Airy: Greyhound Flea Market. Every weekend; open every Friday for vendors from 10 A.M. to 5 P.M. At 2134 Pine Street/Highway 89. Twenty thousand square feet of selling area in a new building. Call Mr. Jim Davis at (910) 789-0417.

North Wilkesboro: C.J.'s Flea Market. On Highway 268 East. Call Clint Blevins at (910) 667-6877.

Oxford: Oxford Flea Mall. Every weekend, 9 A.M. to 5 P.M. At Oak Plaza, at the junction of Highway 15 and Industry Drive. Call Jay Street at (919) 603-1994 (Monday through Friday, 9 A.M. to 5 P.M.).

Raleigh: Watson's Flea Market. Every weekend. At 1436 Rock Quarry Road. Call Manager at (919) 832-6232.

Reidsville: Reidsville Flea Market. Every weekend. At 1624 Freeway Drive (Highway 14). Call Sharon Hall, Manager, at (910) 349-4811.

Smithfield: I-95 Antique Mall and Flea Market. Every weekend. Call Manager at (919) 934-1148.

OHIO

Akron: Akron Antique Market. Four weekends a year in May, August, October, and December, 9 A.M. to 4 P.M. At the Summit County Fairgrounds, State Route 91 at East Howe Road. Call Luck Pro, Inc., Manager, at (216) 867-6724.

Cleveland: Clark Avenue Flea Market. Every Wednesday through Saturday. At 5109 Clark Avenue. Call Velma, Manager, at (216) 398-5283.

Columbus: Amos Flea Market. Every Friday, Saturday, and Sunday, 10 A.M. to 7 P.M. At 3454 Cleveland Avenue. Call Paul Westland at (614) 262-0044.

Columbus: Scott Antique Market at the Ohio State Fairgrounds. Monthly from November through June, generally the second weekend of every month—call for dates: Saturday, 9 A.M. to 6 P.M., and Sunday, 9 A.M. to 5 P.M. At the State Fairgrounds. Take the 17th Avenue exit off I-71. Call Don or Betty Scott at (614) 569-4112 or (614) 569-4912.

Dayton: Olive Road Flea Market. At 2222 Olive Road. Call Mrs. Richard Jackson at (513) 836-2641.

Delaware: Kingman Drive-in Theatre. Every weekend in summer months. On Route 23. Call Manager at (614) 262-0044.

Monroe: Trader's World. Every weekend. At 601 Union Road. Call Mr. Jay Frick at (513) 424-5708.

Navarre: Navarre Indoor Flea Market. Every weekend. At 2 Main Street. Call Max Schweizer at (216) 879-0252.

Piqua: Piqua Flea Market. Every weekend, 9 A.M. to 5 P.M. At 8225 Looney Road. Call Manager at (513) 773-4131.

Reynoldsburg: 40 East Drive-in Theatre Flea Market. Every Sunday. On Route 40. Call Manager at (614) 262-0044.

Springfield: Springfield Antique Show and Flea Market. Generally on the third weekend of every month—call for dates. At the Fairgrounds. Call Bruce Knight at (513) 325-0053.

Tippecanoe: Tippecanoe Flea Market. Every Friday, Saturday, and Sunday. At the intersection of Milarcik Road and State Route 800. Call Manager at (614) 658-3949.

OKLAHOMA

Cromwell: Hillbilly Flea Market. Every weekend, 6 A.M. to 5 P.M. On Highway 56, three miles south of mile marker 212 on I-40. Call Manager at (405) 944-5777.

Fort Gibson: Green Country Flea Market. Every Friday, Saturday, and Sunday, 9 A.M. to 5 P.M. At 1801 Highway 62 East. Call Manager at (918) 478-3422.

Gore: Shady Deals Flea Market. Every Friday, Saturday, and Sunday. On Highway 100, next to the church. Call Bob, Manager, at (918) 489-5345.

Muskogee: Good Stuff Flea Market. Every weekend. At 2541 South 32nd Street. Call Manager at (918) 682-9226.

Oklahoma City: Old Paris Flea Market. Every weekend, 9 A.M. to 6 P.M. At 1111 Southeastern Avenue; take Eastern exit off I-40 and go south onto Southeastern Avenue. Family owned and run. Call Wise and Wise at (405) 670-2611.

Ponca City: Fran's Flea Market. Every weekend, 7 A.M. to 5 P.M. At 3501 North 14th Street. Call Manager at (405) 762-6501.

OREGON

Cloverdale: Red Barn Flea Market. Daily in summer, 9 A.M. to 5 P.M. At 33920 Highway 101. Call Marge Hitchman, Manager, at (503) 392-3973.

Hillsboro: Banner Flea Market. Every Friday, Saturday, and Sunday. At 4871 S.E. Tualatin Valley Highway. Call Manager at (503) 640-6755.

Klamath Falls: Linkville Flea Market. Monthly—call for dates. At the fairgrounds. Call Elizabeth Boorman at (503) 884-4352.

Medford: Giant Flea Market. Monthly on a Sunday, all day—call for dates. At 1701 South Pacific Highway, at the National Guard Armory. Lots of antiques and collectibles. Call Manager at (503) 772-8211.

Portland: America's Largest Antique and Collectible Sale. Three weekend events in March, July, and October: Saturday, 8 A.M. to 7 P.M., and Sunday, 9 A.M. to 5 P.M. At the Portland Expo Center. Take Expo Center exit (306-B) off I-5 and follow signposts. Upscale merchandise. Call Chris Palmer, Donald M. Wirfs and Associates, at (503) 282-0877.

Portland: Catlin Gabel Rummage Sale. Every Thursday through Sunday. At 8825 Southwest Barnes Road. Call Marilyn Cooper, c/o Catlin Gabel School, at (503) 297-1894.

Portland: Salvage Sally's Flea Market. Every weekend, 9 A.M. to 5 P.M. At 2330 Southeast 82nd Street, four buildings north of Division Street. Call Manager at (503) 761-0250.

Portland: Sandy Barr's Flea-Mart. Every weekend, 8 A.M. to 3 P.M. (vendors arrive at 7 A.M.). At 1225 North Marine Drive. (A second location at the Interstate Pavilion, 1225 Marine Drive, is open every Saturday and Sunday, 8 A.M. to 3 P.M. Vendor rates are $8 per table on Saturday and $10 on Sunday.). Call Sandy Barr at (503) 283-6993.

Portland: Saturday Market. Every Saturday "and Sunday too" from May through November, all day. At 108 West Burnside, on the west side of the Willamette River beneath the Burnside Bridge, in the Old Town section of Portland. Call Manager at (503) 222-6072. Mostly a crafts market with handmade goods by local artists, with little or no used or antique merchandise. "Everybody knows about it."

Salem: Salem Collectors Market. Generally the second and fourth Sundays of the month (but not every month), plus several two-day events—call for dates, 9:30 A.M. to 4 P.M. On the State Fairgrounds, at 17th Street and Silverton Road. Take the Market Street exit off I-5 and follow signposts. Call Karen or Greg Huston at (503) 393-1261.

PENNSYLVANIA

Claysville: Claysville Big Flea Market. Every weekend and holidays, 6 A.M. to 4 P.M. Call William Varner, Manager, at (412) 663-5337.

Fayetteville: Fayetteville Antique Mall and Flea Market. Daily except Thanksgiving, Christmas, and New Year's days, 9 A.M. to 5 P.M. At 3625-53 Lincoln Way East, 18 miles west of Gettysburg, or 4 miles east of Chambersburg, on Route 30. Take Exit 6 off I-81 and go east 4 miles on Route 30. Call L. L. Diamond, Jr., at (717) 352-8485.

Greensburg: Flea Market at the Green Gate Mall. Every Sunday from April through October, 7 A.M. to 3 P.M. Call Carol J. Craig at (412) 837-6881.

Hazen: Warsaw Township Volunteer Fire Company Flea Market. First weekend of every month from May through October, all day. Right in front of the Fire Hall. Call Clyde Lindemuth at (814) 328-2536 or the Fire Hall at (814) 328-2528.

Lancaster: Black Angus. Every Sunday, 7:30 A.M. to 5 P.M. A good one for antiques. Call Carl Barto, Manager, at (717) 569-3536.

Lancaster: Jockey Lot. Every Thursday through Monday, 9 A.M. to 5:30 P.M. On Route 272, 12 miles south of Lancaster. Call Rhoda Fisher at (717) 284-4984 or (717) 284-4965.

Perkiomenville: Perkiomenville Flea Market. Every Monday. On Route 29. Call Bob Landis, Manager, at (215) 234-4733.

Saylorsburg: Blue Ridge Flea Market. Every weekend from April through December, 7 A.M. to 5 P.M. At the Blue Ridge Drive-in. Call Manager at (717) 992-8044.

Waynesboro: Annual Antiques and Collectibles Market. Annually in June—call for dates, all day. On Main Street. Call Greater Waynesboro Chamber of Commerce at (717) 762-7123.

RHODE ISLAND

Ashaway: Ashaway Flea Market. Every weekend. At 1 Juniper Drive. Call Mr. John Marley at (401) 377-4947.

Warwick: Rocky Point Flea Market. Every weekend, noon to 11 P.M. At Rocky Point Amusement Park Complex. Corn cake window open daily. Call Manager at (401) 737-8000.

SOUTH CAROLINA

Chesterfield: Chesterfield Flea Market. Every weekend, 8 A.M. to 6 P.M. At the Highway 9 Bypass West, next to the Hardee's (in an old peach packing house). Call Darrell Horne at (803) 623-3999.

Greenville: Mary's Route 253 Flea Market. At 1710 West Bramlett Road. Call Manager at (803) 269-9929.

Myrtle Beach: Myrtle Beach Flea Market. Every Thursday through Sunday, 10 A.M. to 4 P.M. Highway 17. "Shopping and fun rolled into one." Call Theresa Garrison, Manager, at (803) 477-1550.

Rock Hill: I-77 Flea Market. Every Friday, Saturday, and Sunday, 9 A.M. to 5 P.M. (Saturday can start as early as 7 A.M.). At Celanese By-Pass and North Cherry Road (Exit 82-B off I-77). Call Kaye Settlemeyer at (803) 329-5114.

Spartanburg: Spartanburg Flea Market. Every weekend. At 8010 Asheville Highway. Call Terry O'Sullivan at (803) 578-9026.

Springfield: Springfield Flea Market. Every Saturday and Monday, 5 A.M. to 2 P.M., and every Sunday, noon to 4 P.M. At the intersection of Highways 3 and 4, one mile east of Springfield. This well-established, old-fashioned market attracts crowds in excess of 8,000 customers on nearly every Saturday (the biggest of the three market days). Call W. Henry Cooper at (803) 258-3192.

SOUTH DAKOTA

Sioux Falls: Koenig's Flea Market. Daily except Sunday, 9:30 A.M. to 5:30 P.M. At 1103 North Main Avenue. Call Manager at (605) 338-0297.

TENNESSEE

Baxter: Baxter Flea Market. Every weekend, 8 A.M. to 5 P.M. Take Exit 280 off I-40 and go north 100 yards, then turn right. Billed as "Tennessee's Friendliest Market." Call Mary Hall at (615) 868-5152.

Clarksville: Carol's Flea Market. At 1690 Guthrie Highway. Call Carol Atkins at (615) 552-1952.

Cleveland: Forest Flea Market. Every weekend. At 1054 King Street. Call Manager at (615) 472-0630.

Jonesborough/Telford: Jonesborough Flea Market. Every Sunday. On Highway 11 East toward Greeneville. "Support your local flea market." Call J and A Development at (615) 753-4241 or (615) 753-4999.

Lawrenceburg/Pulaski: Green Valley Flea Market. Every weekend plus holidays (Memorial and Labor Day Mondays), 7 A.M.

to 5 P.M. On Route 64, halfway between Lawrenceburg and Pulaski. Call Marth Williams at (615) 363-6562.

Memphis: Friendly Frank's Flea Market. Third weekend of most months—9 A.M. to 6 P.M., call for dates. On the Memphis Fairgrounds (home of the Liberty Bowl every December). Follow signs (well posted). Call Betty Mullikin at (901) 755-6561.

Memphis: Midtown Flea Market. Every Friday, Saturday, and Sunday, 9 A.M. to 5 P.M. Call Mr. Art Yeager, Manager, at (901) 726-9059.

Waverly: Dot's Country Flea Market. On Highway 13 South, six and a half miles from Waverly. Call Manager at (615) 296-9022.

TEXAS

Abilene: Old Abilene Town Flea Market. Every Friday, Saturday, and Sunday, 10 A.M. to 5 P.M. At 3300 E IH 20 (Exit 390), just east of Loop 322. Call Manager at (915) 675-6588.

Amarillo: Historic Route 66 Flea Market. On Route 66. Call Manager, c/o Amarillo Chamber of Commerce, at (800) 692-1338.

Aransas Pass: Shrimp Capital Flea Market. Every weekend. On Route 35, next to the lumber company. Call Mary Manning, Manager, at (512) 758-5812.

Austin: Oakhill Flea Market. Every weekend. At 5526 Highway 290 West. Call M. L. Cook, Jr., at (512) 892-0492.

Beasley: Charlie's Flea Market. Every Friday, Saturday, and Sunday. Call Charlie Cameron, Manager, at (409) 849-8763.

Beaumont: Larry's Old Time Trade Days. Weekend following first Monday of every month, 9 A.M. to 6 P.M. At 70150 East Tex Freeway. Take exit off Route 69 at the intersection with Route 105. Call Larry Tinkel at (409) 892-4000.

Buffalo Gap: Buffalo Gap Flea Market. Weekend of the third Saturday of each month. On Highway 89. Call Manager at (915) 572-3327.

Channelview: White Elephant Flea Market. Every weekend. At 15662 East Freeway. Call Manager's Office at (713) 452-9022 (office hours are Monday through Friday, 8 A.M. to 4:30 P.M.).

Cleveland: Frontier Flea Market. Every weekend. At 18431 Highway 105. Call Randy Maffett, Manager, at (713) 592-2101.

Dallas: Big T Bazaar. Daily: every Sunday through Wednesday, noon to 8 P.M., and every Thursday through Saturday, 10 A.M. to 9 P.M. At Ledbetter and I-35. Call Kenneth Lee, Manager, at (214) 372-9173.

Dallas: Frances's Flea Market. At 310 South Carroll Avenue, off Route 30. Call Frances, Manager, at (214) 821-8757.

Denton: 380 Flea Market. Every Friday, Saturday, and Sunday. On Route 380, about three miles east of Denton. Call John Lillard, Owner, at (817) 382-2490 or (817) 566-5060.

Dibol: Olde Frontier Town Traders. Daily. On Highway 59. Call Melba, Manager, at (409) 632-8696.

El Paso: Bronco Swap Meet. Every weekend. At 8408 Alameda Avenue. Call Mr. Sandoval, Manager, at (915) 858-5555.

Fort Worth: Big Country Flea Market. Every weekend, 7 A.M. to whenever. At 930 University Drive, at Jacksboro Highway (Route 199), 16 blocks from downtown. Mostly used and old merchandise. Call Manager at (817) 626-4731.

Garland: Vikon Village Flea Market. Every weekend, 10 A.M. to 6 P.M. Call C. J. Piercy at (214) 271-0565.

Harlingen: Harlingen Flea Market. At 4300 South 83 Expressway. Call Fred Schurba, Manager, at (210) 423-4535.

Houston: Sunny Flea Market. Every weekend, 7:30 A.M. to 7:30 P.M. At 8705 Airline Drive. Call Manager at (713) 447-8729; weekdays call (713) 923-2425.

Jewett: Flea Market of Jewett. Second Saturday of each month and the Friday preceding and Sunday following. On Highway 79. Call Jeanette Thomas, Manager, at (903) 626-4225 or (903) 623-5674 or (903) 536-7689.

Killeen: Oma's Flea Market. Every Monday through Saturday, 9 A.M. to 6 P.M. On Highway 195, just south of Killeen. Call Manager at (817) 634-3836.

Laredo: Border Town Flea Market. Every Thursday through Sunday. On Freeway 359. Call Javier Morales, Manager, at (512) 726-1186.

Lubbock: National Flea Market. Every Wednesday through Sunday. At 1808 Clovis Road at the corner of Avenue "Q." Call Mr. Paul Earnhart at (806) 744-4979.

Mathis: Bizarre Bazaar of Mathis. Every Friday, Saturday, and Sunday. At 221 North Front. From nearby Corpus Christi: take Exit 36 off I-37, go right at fork, then around and across railroad tracks, and market will be on the right. Call Manager at (512) 547-6031.

McKinney: Third Monday Trade Day. Every Thursday through Sunday. On Highway 380 West, two miles west of the Central Expressway 75. Call Manager at (214) 542-7174.

Mercedes: Mercedes Flea Market. Every weekend, 6 A.M. to 6 P.M. At the two-mile marker on Expressway 83 just west of town. Billed as one of the oldest markets in the Rio Grande Valley, with an average total of 10,000 customers per weekend. Call Felipe Reyes, Manager, at (210) 843-9306.

Mission: All Valley Flea Market. Every weekend, 6 A.M. to 3 P.M. Call Harvey Bruns, Owner, at (210) 781-1911.

San Angelo: Flea's Mart. Every Thursday through Monday, 10 A.M. to 6 P.M. At 8151 U.S. 87 North. Call Walter Hoes or Donna Driskill at (915) 658-4368 or (915) 659-1425.

San Angelo: San Angelo Flea Market. At 5589 South Route 306. Call Manager at (915) 651-7489.

San Antonio: Austin Highway Flea Market. At 1428 Austin Highway. Call Manager at (210) 828-1488 or (210) 828-9188.

Texarkana: Great American Flea Market. Every Tuesday through Sunday. At 2615 New Boston Road. Call Lloyd Price at (903) 793-7700.

VERMONT

Ely: Conval Antique Mall and Auction House. Daily except Tuesday (closed Christmas and New Year's Day), 10 A.M. to 5 P.M. On Route 5, two miles south of Exit 15 (Fairlee exit) off I-91. Mall is on the left as you approach. "A little bit of everything—some things old, some things new, some things funky and furniture too." Call Martin or Kitty Diggins at (802) 333-9971.

Fairlee: Railroad Station Flea Market. Every weekend from May through October. On Route 5. Take Exit 15 off I-91. Outside of LeBarron's Antiques, which is open daily. Call Manager at (802) 333-4574.

Salisbury: Flea Market Center. Daily, 10 A.M. to 5 P.M. On Route 7 in Salisbury, six miles south of Middlebury. More like an antiques mall, with long-term dealers only. Call Jo McGettrick at (802) 352-4426.

VIRGINIA

Altavista: First Saturday Trade Lot. First Saturday of every month plus preceding Friday, from noon on Friday to 4 P.M. on Saturday. On Seventh Street. Take Business Route 29 (Main Street) into the center of town and go one block west to Seventh Street. Profits support the bands in the Altavista schools. Contact Carl Davis (inquiries by mail only, c/o Altavista Band Boosters, P.O. Box 333, Altavista, VA 24517).

Bristol: Carrier's Flea Market. Every weekend, dawn to 3 P.M. At 191 White Top Road (Route 11E). From Route 81, take exit 59 and follow signs toward Bristol Raceway on 11 E, and market is about a quarter mile south of the raceway. Call J. W. Carrier at (615) 538-7177.

Cana: Mountain Man Market. Every Sunday, all afternoon. On Highway 52. Call Manager at (703) 755-3871.

Norfolk: Big Top Flea Market. Every Tuesday, Saturday, and Sunday. At 7600 Sewells Point Road. Call Mr. Song, Manager, at (804) 480-3122.

Roanoke: Happy's Flea Market. Every weekend. At 5411 Williamson Road Northwest. Call Manager at (703) 563-4473.

Roanoke: Melrose Flea Market and Mall. At 4215 Melrose Avenue. Call at (703) 362-2201.

Rustburg: Big B Flea Market. Every weekend, 7 A.M. to 4 P.M. On Route 1. Call Nellie Dalton at (804) 821-1326.

Verona: Verona Antique and Flea Market. Every Thursday through Sunday, 9 A.M. to 5 P.M. On Route 11, directly across the street from the firehouse. Call Manager at (540) 248-FLEA.

WASHINGTON

Kent: Midway Swap 'N' Shop. Every weekend, 8 A.M. to 4 P.M. At 24050 Pacific Highway South. Call Frank Wilson, Manager, at (206) 878-1802.

Prosser: Harvest Festival Flea Market. Annually in September. In downtown Prosser. In conjunction with the balloon festival. Call Chamber of Commerce at (509) 786-3177.

Tacoma: Star-lite Swap 'n' Shop. Every Tuesday through Friday (indoors), 10 A.M. to 6 P.M., and every Saturday and Sunday (indoors and outdoors), 8 A.M. to 4 P.M. At the Star-lite Drive-In Theatre, 8327 South Tacoma Way at 84th, one half mile west of I-5. Call Manager at (206) 588-8090 or fax at: (206) 588-8929.

WEST VIRGINIA

Morgantown: Walnut Street Indoor Flea Market. Every Wednesday through Sunday, 10 A.M. to 5 P.M. At 218 Walnut Street. Call Alma Mercer or Irene Twigg at (304) 292-9278 or (304) 296-5972.

Pipestem: Sun Valley Flea Market. Every Sunday. On Route 20, approximately seven miles north of Athens. Call Manager at (304) 384-7382.

Pockview: Pineville Drive-in Theatre Flea Market. Every Thursday. On Route 10. Call Manager at (304) 732-7492 after 7:30 P.M. Friday through Monday.

Wheeling: Wheeling Civic Center Antique Flea Market. First and third Sunday of every month—call for dates. At the Wheeling Civic Center, at 2 Fourteenth Street. Call Lee Karges at (304) 233-7000 (office hours are Monday through Friday, 9 A.M. to 5 P.M.).

Yawkey: Midge's Flea Market. Every weekend. On Route 3. Call Manager at (304) 524-7639.

WISCONSIN

Cedarburg: Maxwell Street Days. On Maxwell Street. Call Manager at (414) 375-7630.

Janesville: Janesville Flea Market. Every weekend, 8 A.M. to 5 P.M. At 3030 Prairie Avenue (intersection of Route 351 and Country Trunk G). Call Manager at (608) 755-9830.

Wautoma: Wautoma Flea Market. Every Sunday from April through November. On Route 21. Call Milt Sommer at (414) 787-2300.

WYOMING

Casper: Second Look Flea Market. Every weekend. On Poplar Street across from the Dairy Queen and Casper's Cafe, down by the old bus depot. Call Manager at (307) 234-0756.

Cheyenne: Bart's Flea Market. Every Sunday through Thursday, 10 A.M. to 6 P.M., and every Friday and Saturday, 9 A.M. to 6 P.M. At the corner of Lincolnway and Evans. Call Mike, Manager, at (307) 632-0063.

Cheyenne: Odds 'N Ends Flea Market. Daily. At 1408 South Greeley Highway. Call Brent Lamphair, Manager, at (307) 635-3136.

Cheyenne: Tee Pee Flea Market. Daily, 10 A.M. to 6 P.M. At 3208 South Greeley Highway, three miles south of Lincoln Highway. Call Brent Lamphair, Manager, at (307) 778-8312.

Jackson Hole: Mangy Moose Antique Show and Sale. Annually in July. Call Jan Perkins, Manager, at (208) 345-0755.

INDEX

INDEX

INDEX

COLORADO

INDEX

INDEX

INDIANA

INDEX

INDEX

MICHIGAN

INDEX

NORTH CAROLINA

OKLAHOMA

INDEX

INDEX

INDEX